A COURSE BOOK IN
•MODERN WORLD•
HISTORY

A COURSE BOOK IN
MODERN WORLD HISTORY

P. F. SPEED

ARNOLD-WHEATON

Arnold-Wheaton
A Division of E. J. Arnold & Son Limited
Parkside Lane, Leeds, LS11 5TD

A subsidiary of Pergamon Press Ltd.,
Headington Hill Hall, Oxford, OX3 0BW

Pergamon Press Inc.
Maxwell House, Fairview Park, Elmsford, New York 10523

Pergamon Press Canada Ltd
Suite 104, 150 Consumers Road, Willowdale, Ontario M2J 1P9

Pergamon Press (Australia) Pty Ltd
P.O. Box 544, Potts Point, N.S.W. 2011

Pergamon Press GmbH
Hammerweg 6, D-6242 Kronberg, Federal Republic of Germany

Copyright © 1982 P. F. Speed

First published 1982

Reprinted 1984, 1985

Typeset by Oxprint Ltd, Oxford

Printed in Great Britain by A. Wheaton & Co. Ltd, Exeter

ISBN 0-08-026419-0

Notes for the Teacher

The aims of this book are to introduce students to the history of the world in the twentieth century, and at the same time, help prepare them for their O Level and C.S.E. examinations.

Supporting the text there are work sections. It will be obvious why they contain problems and exercises in interpreting source material, but the questions on each of the chapters may need some explanation. In the first place, the student may answer them as he reads, so making sure that he understands his work. Naturally, this has to be followed by discussion in class. Later, the student can use the questions as catechisms. When he can answer them without looking at the text he has gone a fair way towards knowing his facts.

Learning by rote may still be out of favour in some places, but it is hard to see how we can fulfil the more liberal aims of the teaching of history unless our pupils have a fair amount of basic knowledge.

Contents

Chapter One

Introduction

PERHAPS the most significant feature of the twentieth century is the rapidly increasing pace of change. An enormous number of things have happened and all this book can attempt to do is to have a quick look at some of the more important events. They alone are confusing enough, but it will help us to pick our way through them if we have some understanding of the beliefs which have guided people in this century.

One has been the Divine Right of monarchs. According to this belief a monarch has authority from God so he has absolute power over his people. They must all obey him, because to go against him is to go against God. Since the execution of Charles I in 1649, no English king has believed seriously in Divine Right, so it seems quaint and old-fashioned to us. However, at the beginning of this century, absolute monarchs ruled three of the most powerful countries in Europe. They were Kaiser William II of Germany, the Emperor Francis Joseph of Austria–Hungary and Tsar Nicholas II of Russia.

These three States were all defeated in the First World War and their rulers were overthrown. Since then no important country has had an absolute monarch. Where monarchies survive, as in Britain, they are constitutional, which means they have no real power.

A more important idea than absolute monarchy is democracy, or the rule of the people. It was born, perhaps, in Ancient Greece, but the country that did most to develop it in modern times was Britain. Britain also introduced it to those parts of the world she colonized, such as Australia, New Zealand, Canada and, of course, the United States of America. She also did her best to persuade her subject States to adopt it before she gave them their freedom: it survived in some, notably India, but not in others, such as Pakistan. Today, democracy is strong, not only in Britain and her former possessions, but also in Western Europe.

People in a democracy have a good deal of freedom, religious, political and economic. There are, none the less, limits to this freedom. Everyone, of course, has to obey the law. There can be quite strong economic controls, for trade unions may dictate to the rest of the community, governments have monopolies, while anyone who earns himself a high income will lose much of it in taxes. There can be injustices in a democracy. Some people can be very poor, and racial minorities may be victimized.

1

Along with democracy there is always a certain amount of capitalism, for this is the result of allowing economic freedom. A capitalist is someone who owns, or has a share in, any institution that produces wealth. It may be a factory, a shop, a bank, a trading company or a farm. Usually, capitalists employ other people to work for them. Firms are run to make profits for their owners. Workers have no share of the profits, but simply draw their wages, which their employers will often try to keep as low as possible. The State has no obvious direct benefits either, except for the taxes it levies on the profits. There is a great deal of argument about whether capitalism is bad or good. Some people say it has been responsible for social evils like poverty and slum housing, and hold that all businesses should be nationalized so that they can be run for the good of their workers and the State. Others maintain that nationalized industries are rarely as efficient as those that are privately owned. Business men, they say, should be free to make themselves rich and they will then increase the wealth of the country, so that everyone benefits.

Democracy has been challenged by Fascism, and similar beliefs, like Nazism, which is the German brand. Their beliefs are best understood from the Roman emblem adopted by the Italian Fascists, the *Fascis*. It is an axe surrounded by a bundle of rods. The axe stands for authority. The rods show that unity is strength, for although they can be broken quite easily one at a time, this is impossible when they are bound together. Fascists, then, believe in strong government, and a united country. Fascist rule is totalitarian, which means that no political parties are allowed, except the one in power. There are strict limits on personal liberties, and people who are different, whether because of their religion, race or politics, are likely to suffer. Hitler's persecution of the Jews was a chilling example.

However, there is likely to be some economic freedom, with capitalism thriving as much as in a democracy. Fascist governments have usually come into power, and remained in power, with the support of big business. The Fascist government boasts about national unity and claims to be acting in the best interest of all its people, but it is significant that it will not allow workers to form trade unions. In fact, it is firmly on the side of the middle and upper classes.

Fascism thrived in countries where democracy failed. If politicians quarrelled too much among themselves, and if government was weak, so that there was danger of the country dissolving into chaos, or turning Communist, then people were glad to have a strong ruler, even if it was a man like Hitler.

Fascist governments usually followed aggressive foreign policies, because nothing unites a people as much as success abroad, particularly winning a war. It was the leading Fascist States, Germany, Japan and Italy, that caused the Second World War.

As the First World War overthrew the monarchies, so the Second World War overthrew most of the Fascist dictatorships. However, democracy was left facing its most serious challenge of all — Communism. This takes various forms, but all are founded on the teachings of Karl Marx, a German Jew who lived in England in the mid-nineteenth century.

Marx saw history as a class struggle. We can take England as an example: first of all, the nobles seized power from the monarch, when they made King John accept Magna Carta. Next, following the Wars of the Roses in the late fifteenth century, the landowners seized power from the nobles. In the eighteenth century came the Industrial Revolution, which created two new classes, the bourgeoisie, who were traders and manufacturers, and the proletariat, or town workers. The bourgeoisie took power from the landowners in the first half of the nineteenth century, as was shown by the Reform Act of 1832 and the repeal of the Corn Laws in 1846. Communists then waited confidently for a revolution by the proletariat. The rich, they thought, would become richer and fewer in numbers, while the poor became poorer, and greater in numbers. In the end the masses would rise, overthrow their masters, and set up a government which would take control of all factories and businesses. They would then be run for the benefit of everyone, not just the privileged few. Moreover, the revolution would be world-wide. Here we see one of the most important differences between Fascism and Communism, for while Fascism believes in the unity of the State, Communism believes in the unity of the working classes.

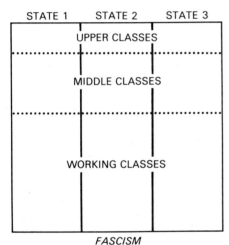

FASCISM
Fascists believe in national unity

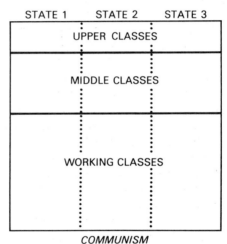

COMMUNISM
Communists believe in class unity

After the Revolution there would first of all be a socialist society, as the Russians believe they have today. Human nature cannot change overnight and many people would need incentives like overtime payments and bonus schemes, if they were to work hard. Soon, however, the Communist society would develop, which would operate on the principle of 'from each according to his means, to each according to his needs'. A feeble road-sweeper who could labour for only two hours a day, but who had a large family, would earn much more than a surgeon who could work full time and was a bachelor. The surgeon would be quite happy about this because in the ideal Communist society everyone thinks only of the common good, and not of himself.

3

Obviously, many things have gone wrong with the Communist theory. Communist States are a long way from being the heaven on earth that Marx predicted. There is still a good deal of inequality, the privileged few being the Communist Party bosses, instead of the bourgeoisie as in capitalist countries. George Orwell satirized the system in *Animal Farm*, where 'all animals are equal, but some animals are more equal than others'. It has also been said that while 'capitalism is the exploitation of man by man, Communism is just the reverse'.

In the second place, Communist governments do not have the support of all their people by any means. They cannot accept that their theories are wrong, so their answer to opposition is to crush it, using torture, the secret police and labour camps. Communist rule is totalitarian, as much as Fascist rule is, and it is often difficult for anyone in a democracy to decide which is the more evil. For example, in the 1930s Britain had to decide between Hitler and Stalin, and it was partly because of her hatred of Stalin that she allowed Hitler to go as far as he did.

Thirdly, since Communists believe they must spread their ideas by war and revolution, they have roused a lot of hatred. Many statesmen have acted more out of fear of Communism than anything else. People look askance at their own countrymen who are Communists, wondering if they are planning revolution. Non-Communist countries ask themselves if their Communist neighbours are going to invade them. Is there, indeed, a Communist plot to control the world?

Yet another idea that has been important in the twentieth century is imperialism. Industrial countries need raw materials for their factories and markets for their finished goods. Nearly always they meet foreign competition, rival traders bidding up the prices of things they want to buy, and forcing down the prices of those they want to sell. One answer is to have an empire from which foreigners can be excluded. The most imperialistic nation in modern times was Britain, her empire being at its peak when she took numbers of Germany's colonies at the end of the First World War. After that, she was struggling to hold what she had, but other countries were still hoping to expand as, for example, Japan in China and Germany in Eastern Europe.

Finally, we will consider nationalism, which has been, perhaps, the most important driving force of all. It has been particularly strong in Fascist countries, so much so that 'Fascism' and 'nationalism' are often given the same meaning. However, democracies have been nationalistic as well and have defended themselves against foreigners with great vigour. No government in a democracy would last long if its subjects thought it was not looking after their interests. Nor is it just a question of fighting off aggressors. The States of Western Europe badly need unity, but they are making only slow progress towards it because their people think of themselves as Englishmen, Frenchmen, Germans and so forth, rather than as Europeans.

Since Communism is an international movement, one might expect that its followers would be different, but they have not proved so. Stalin is an example. However good a Communist he might have been at home, abroad he was as much a Russian nationalist as any of the Tsars. It is significant that at the time of writing, the leading Communist powers, Russia and China, are far from working together for the overthrow of capitalism. Instead, they are bitter rivals, and China is angling for the friendship of the world's greatest capitalist country, the United States of America.

_____ *PART ONE* _____
The Great Powers since 1900

SECTION ONE

THE UNITED STATES OF
AMERICA

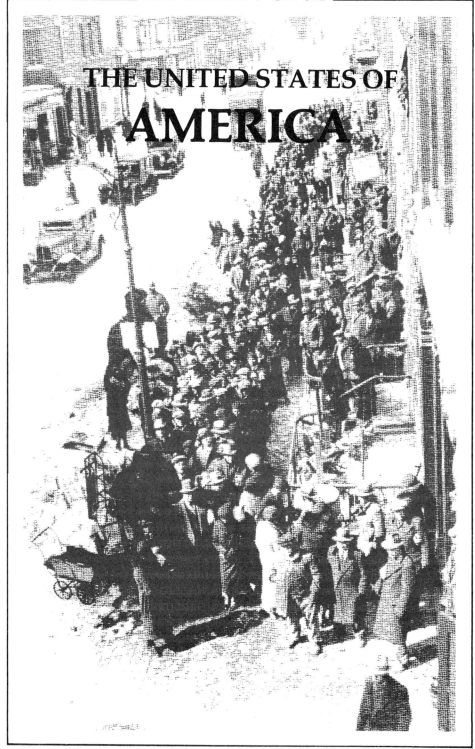

Chapter Two

The United States in the 1920s

UNTIL the late eighteenth century Great Britain owned thirteen colonies on the east coast of America. In 1783, the colonists rebelled, won their freedom, and founded the United States of America. Families from the original thirteen States, together with immigrants from Europe then moved west, so that in less than a hundred years they had occupied all the land between the Atlantic and the Pacific Oceans, and had created a rich, powerful new country. We must see what it was like in the 1920s.

The Government

The United States is a federation of fifty States. There is a Federal Government in Washington, which looks after things that concern the whole country, such as foreign policy and defence. Like all democratic governments, it has a legislature to make laws and an executive to carry them out.

The legislature is Congress and this has a lower House, the House of Representatives, and an upper House, the Senate. The House of Representatives is elected by the people every two years. There are elections for the Senate every two years as well, but only one-third of its members retire at a time, which means that it is not so much at the mercy of sudden changes in public opinion.

The head of the American executive is the President, who has as much authority as Congress, because he, too, is chosen directly by the people. There are presidential elections every leap year. Because there are separate elections it sometimes happens that the President belongs to one political party, while the majority in Congress belongs to the other. This causes disagreements, but the President cannot dissolve Congress, and Congress cannot dismiss the President.

As well as the Federal Government in Washington, each of the States has a government of its own. They make laws on many things, such as education, highways and capital punishment. It would seem extraordinary if, in England, you could be hanged for murder in Yorkshire, but not in Lancashire. However, America is vast, and some of the States are as large as the lesser European countries, so they want to go their own way as much as possible.

9

We can compare the American system to a three-sided game of football, played between Congress, the President and the States. Because it is like that, there have to be rules and a referee. The set of rules is the Constitution, which says how the country is to be governed. The referee is the Supreme Court and if it thinks anyone is acting against the Constitution, whether it be the President, Congress, or one of the States, then it can stop them.

In Britain we too have a legislature, which is Parliament; an executive, which is the government headed by the Prime Minister; county councils, and law courts. With us, though, Parliament is 'sovereign', or in simple language, is boss. Our system is like a three-sided game of football in which one team makes the rules, and everyone else has to obey, including the referee.

Politics

There were, and still are, two main political parties in the United States, the Republicans and the Democrats. In the 1920s they did not represent different social classes as the British Conservative and Labour Parties do. Some of the richest people voted Republican, but so also did the Negroes, who were among the poorest. What was even stranger was that there were no important differences between the policies of the two parties. Which one people supported depended not on their class or political ideas, but on where they lived, their race, and their religion. For example, Southerners, people whose families had recently arrived in America, Catholics, Lutherans and Jews were Democrats. On the other hand, Northerners, the descendants of British settlers, Negroes and Protestants were Republicans.

The Economy

America is large, and has many valuable minerals as well as much excellent farming land. Moreover, the American people had made good use of their resources. These figures will give some idea of what had happened in the late nineteenth century:

	1865	1900
Railways	56 000 km	320 000 km (more than all of Europe)
Steel production	74 000 tonnes	11 700 000 tonnes

National income increased, on average, 56 per cent every ten years between 1870 and 1910. By the 1920s America was the richest country in the world, for although she had only 6 per cent of its population, she produced 30 per cent of its wealth. From her factories came thousands of refrigerators, washing-machines, vacuum cleaners, radios and, above all, motor cars. Henry Ford was making a Model T every ten seconds. There were services, too. By 1929, 20 million homes and offices had a telephone, and every town had its cinema.

What was the reason for this prosperity? In the 1920s most Americans would have said it was because they were free. They admired 'rugged individualists' such as the pioneers of the West and the millionaires who had started life with nothing. These people struck out on their own and did great things, without bothering too much about their methods, which were called in polite language 'self-help'. Next, Americans believed in capitalism. Under this system all factories and businesses belong to individuals or private companies. The State owns nothing, except, perhaps, a few things that everyone needs, such as roads. Thirdly, Americans believed in *laissez-faire*, which is a set of ideas worked out by a Scotsman, Adam Smith, in the late eighteenth century. *Laissez-faire* means, literally, 'leave alone'. The theory is that no one, whether government, trade unions, or monopolies, should interfere with business men. Left to themselves they will produce all the goods and services their country needs, they will keep prices low, because of competition, and, for most of the time at least, they will give everyone a job.

However, though America was prosperous in the 1920s, the economy was not as sound as it appeared.

In the first place, some firms had become too big. They had done so by merging and driving competitors out of business. The large organizations were called 'corporations' and when they grew still more they were known as 'trusts'. A trust would enjoy a monopoly. For example, one of them, U.S. Steel, made all the steel in America. Trusts had their customers at their mercy because they could charge what they liked. The millionaire Cornelius Vanderbilt showed how they thought when someone told him railways should be run for the good of the public. 'The public be damned,' said Vanderbilt.

Obviously, trusts were against the whole spirit of *laissez-faire*. Governments realized this and made some half-hearted attempts to control them, but with little success.

A second problem was that the market for American goods was limited. It was difficult to sell abroad, because most countries put tariffs on imports, to protect their own industries. That left the domestic market, and seeing America had a population of 120 million, there should have been plenty of customers. However, 60 per cent of Americans earned barely enough to keep alive. Most farmers and farm labourers were poor, as well as many of the unskilled workers in the towns. These people could not afford radios and vacuum cleaners, still less motor cars. American industry, then, could go on prospering only as long as wealthy Americans went on buying. Unfortunately, the wealthy were a minority.

Society

In the 1920s America was, and indeed still is, a country of great contrasts. There were people of all religions, for immigrants did not change their beliefs when they changed their homes. There were members of Protestant sects, and Catholics, while many Jews arrived, especially in the late nineteenth and early twentieth centuries. America has also produced religious groups of her own, like the Mormons. It is true that many

11

Americans did not take religion seriously, but some were fanatics. In the 'Bible Belt', in the Deep South, many people were 'fundamentalists', which meant they believed every word in the Bible was true. To them, Darwin's theory of evolution was quite wrong, for how could man and the monkeys be descended from a common ancestor, when God had created man in His own image? They were so sure about this that they made it illegal to teach the theory of evolution in schools.

People also felt very strongly about the way they should lead their lives, depending on their religion, or lack of it.

As we have seen, many Americans were rich, and what is more, some of them were materialists who admired wealth for its own sake. President Coolidge said, 'The man who builds a factory, builds a temple. The man who works there, worships there.' These people enjoyed themselves to the full, and made a good deal of show. Young people caught the mood, girls in particular giving a lot of worry to their parents and grandparents. Modern young women were called 'flappers' and 'It-girls'. They smoked, they drank, they had their hair 'bobbed', they wore short skirts and they used make-up. Some wore trousers and rode motorbikes. There were dances which the older people thought disgusting, the Charleston and the tango, and there was a new, exciting music called jazz. The 1920s were indeed 'the roaring twenties'.

It is easy to imagine what the preachers in the Bible Belt said about all this behaviour and they were not alone. The puritans of rural America were determined to stop their country going to the dogs, so in 1919 they persuaded Congress and the States to make the famous 18th Amendment to the Constitution, introducing 'prohibition'. This forbade the 'manufacture, sale or importation of intoxicating liquors into the United States'. In theory America was 'dry', but few laws have been so widely ignored. Not only did people make their own 'moonshine', it was also easy to buy. Places that sold it were called 'speak-easies', and there were ten thousand of them in Chicago alone. All this had unfortunate results. Beer, which is harmless enough, is difficult to brew in a bath tub, so people made other drinks, many of which were not only stronger, but poisonous. Also, the trade in illegal liquor, called bootlegging, was in the hands of gangsters. It was profitable, the gangsters made a lot of money, and so they became powerful. For a time, Al Capone's private army virtually ruled Chicago.

As well as having different religions and different ways of living, the American people belonged to different races. Immigrants came from all over Europe and from China and Japan as well. Between 1880 and 1920, 23 million arrived, mainly Italians and Polish and Russians Jews. The flood dwindled to a trickle in the 1920s because the American government limited each foreign country to a quota, but the problem was already there. Most of the immigrants did not try to adapt but crowded together in the big cities, where they kept their own languages and, as far as possible, their own ways of living. These were the 'hyphenated' Americans, i.e. Irish–Americans, Italian–Americans, Polish–Americans, and so on. Quite different were the WASPs, or White Anglo-Saxon Protestant Americans. In the main, these were the descendants of immigrants from Britain and the longer their families had been in America, the more superior they felt. Anyone who could prove that his ancestors had sailed with the *Mayflower* was proud indeed.

Undoubtedly, though, the biggest problem was with the Negroes. After they had lost the Civil War in 1865, the Southerners had been compelled to set their slaves free, but they did everything in their power to stop the blacks gaining equal rights with themselves. They were particularly successful in keeping them poor.

The mixture of races led to race hatred. Here are two examples.

The first was the growth of the Ku-Klux-Klan, which had five million members by 1925. They hated Catholics and Jews, but most of all, they hated Negroes. Members of the Klan, in their sinister white hoods, terrorized the South for years, sometimes lynching their victims with horrible cruelty.

Ku Klux Klan meeting

The other example is the trial of Sacco and Vanzetti. They were arrested in Massachusetts in 1920, charged with murder. To this day we do not know whether they committed the crime: the trial is famous because it was obviously unfair. The two men were anarchists, and they were foreigners, which was enough to convince many Americans, including the judge, that they were guilty. Out of court, the judge called them 'anarchist bastards', 'dagos' and 'sons of bitches'. As Vanzetti said, 'I am suffering because I am a radical, and indeed I am a radical: I have suffered because I was an Italian, and indeed I am an Italian.' Including appeals, the case dragged on until 1927, when both men were executed. Fifty years later, the Governor of Massachusetts admitted there had been a mistrial and apologized to Sacco's grandson.

America, then, was divided by religion and race. However, differences in wealth were perhaps even more important. In 1919, 5 per cent of the population took one-third of the national income: 60 per cent had barely enough to keep alive. Among the wealthy was Andrew Carnegie, who in 1900 had an income that was 20 000 times the national average. Among the poor was a Negro, Richard Wright, who described his life as a boy:

> Hunger stole upon me so slowly that at first I was not aware of what hunger really meant. Hunger had always been more or less at my elbow when I played, but this new hunger baffled me, scared me, made me angry and insistent. Whenever I begged for food now, my mother would pour me a cup of tea which would still the clamour in my stomach for a moment or two; but a little later, I would feel hunger nudging my ribs, twisting my empty guts until they ached. I would grow dizzy and my vision would dim.

One reason why the poor suffered was that the trade unions were only interested in skilled men and would not negotiate higher wages for the unskilled. Also, the government did nothing to help. There were no old-age pensions, no dole for the unemployed, no sick pay, and no family allowances. These would have undermined 'rugged individualism', 'self-help' and *laissez-faire*. America's leaders thought it was better to let some of the people starve rather than give up those principles, which, so it seemed, had made America great.

Chapter Three

The Economic Depression

WE HAVE seen that in the 1920s, America was the richest country in the world and that many, if not all of her people were prosperous. In 1929 the dream was shattered by an economic depression which grew rapidly worse and worse until 1933. Even though the economy began to pick up after that, it did not recover completely until the Second World War.

The Cause of the Depression

As the last chapter explains, the market for American goods was limited. Foreigners could not buy them, because of tariffs, and neither could plenty of Americans because they were too poor. The customers, then, were the more wealthy Americans. They went on buying for a long time, but there was a limit to what they wanted. When a family had a new car and all the latest household gadgets it would stop spending for a while, until something wore out. America's factories had flooded the country with far more goods than were needed. Manufacturers tried to tempt people by cutting prices, even though it meant lower profits. However, cutting prices did not work, so manufacturers cut production. They then had to sack some of their workers, so fewer people could buy goods. A man who is out of work cannot replace his car, or give his wife a new washing-machine. Manufacturers had to cut production yet again, create even more unemployment, and make the market still smaller. Once it had begun to slide, the whole economy spiralled downwards, faster and faster. Industrial production fell by 77 per cent from August 1929 to March 1933. By 1933 there were 13 million unemployed, which was one-quarter of the country's workers.

The Wall Street Crash

This was one of the first results of the Depression. Wall Street is where the New York Stock Exchange is, and to understand what went wrong, we must see how the Stock Exchange works.

Few people are rich enough to start a large firm on their own. Anyone who wishes to do so must ask others to invest money. He will decide how much he wants, he will divide that amount into a number of convenient slices, called shares, and he will offer them for sale on the Stock Exchange. If you buy one-tenth of the shares in a new factory you will, in effect, own one-tenth of it, and at the end of each year you will have one-tenth of its profits. This is called your dividend. If, after a time, you want the money you first invested you can sell your shares where you bought them, on the Stock Exchange. If, in the meantime, the firm has done badly and paid few dividends, then your shares will have fallen in value. If, on the other hand, the firm has done well, and paid good dividends, then your shares will be worth more than you paid, and you will have a profit on the sale.

There are people who make a lot of money because shares increase in value in this way. They pick a company which they think is going to do well, they buy shares in it, and when they go up in value, they sell them. This is called 'playing the market'. Of course, it is quite possible for the company to do badly, so that its shares fall. In normal times it can be as difficult to pick a winning company as it is to pick a winning racehorse.

However, in America in the late 1920s, almost every company was doing well, so it hardly mattered which shares you bought. Playing the market was like betting in a race in which every horse wins. There was a rush for shares and many people were so frantic that they borrowed large sums of money in order to buy. However, shares are like any other articles, in that when a lot of people want them, their price shoots up, much higher than their real value. Radio shares, for example, went up 500 per cent in 1928. By the late 1920s people were paying far more for shares than the profits of the firms warranted. Then, in 1929, as we have seen, many firms began to cut prices and make lower profits which meant, of course, paying lower dividends. In the end, the value of the shares would be bound to drop. The wiser investors saw this, and at once sold their shares. Others realized what was happening, and dumped their shares on the market as well, so that, in a short time, there was panic selling instead of panic buying. The market crashed on 24 October 1929, with the sale of 13 million shares: 29 October was Black Tuesday, for on that day 16½ million shares were sold. Shares were now worth only a fraction of their previous value. People who had invested their own money lost it, which was bad enough, but those who had borrowed money to buy now had debts they could not repay. Some even committed suicide.

There was a crisis in banking as well as on Wall Street. Some banks had not only lent to investors, but had themselves 'played the market' with their customers' money. Such a bank was unable to pay its depositors when they came to collect their money and had to close its doors. People realized what was happening so they rushed to draw out their money and soon quite responsible banks were in difficulty.

Unemployment

The Wall Street Crash and the bank failures troubled the more wealthy and the average Americans. The unemployed had much worse problems. As we have seen, there was no social security, so people who were without jobs were without money. They could not buy food and they could not pay

Queues of unemployed, New York

their rents or their mortgages: consequently, they went hungry and lost their homes. How were they to live? One way was to go on 'the breadline'. This was what they called a queue at a kitchen where charitable folk gave away bowls of soup and hunks of bread. However, there were not enough breadlines for everyone. The most desperate picked through dustbins, looking for scraps of food. For houses, some built rough shelters from old rubbish, on the outskirts of the cities.

Many people who had relations in the countryside went to live with them, but here there were troubles too. Farmers had been poor, even in the 1920s, and in 1934 came a drought which turned much of the Middle West into a vast 'dust bowl'. People streamed out of the area, large numbers going to California where they hoped they might find work picking fruit. Most of them hoped in vain. John Steinbeck described how they suffered in his novel *The Grapes of Wrath*.

President Hoover and the Depression

At the time of the Depression, there was a Republican President, Herbert Hoover. The Americans were quick to blame him. They chanted, 'In Hoover we trusted, and now we are busted.' They called the shanty towns where the homeless lived 'Hoovervilles' and the newspapers they used for bedding, 'Hoover blankets'. Then in 1932, a group of ex-servicemen went to Washington and built a Hooverville there. They were called the 'Bonus Marchers' because they were demanding immediate payment of a war bonus they had been promised for 1945. Instead of sending the money, Hoover sent General Douglas MacArthur, with a force of soldiers, to drive them away.

It was wrong to blame President Hoover for the Depression, but perhaps he could have done more to check it once it had begun. In fact, he did very little, because he still believed in *laissez-faire*. The Depression had brought low prices, and he was sure this would tempt people to buy. The factories would then increase production and employ more workers, so that the economy would recover without any interference from the government. 'Prosperity,' he said, 'is just around the corner.' The people refused to believe him: 1932 was election year, and they gave his rival, Franklin Delano Roosevelt, the biggest majority in American history.

17

Chapter Four

Roosevelt and the New Deal

FRANKLIN D. Roosevelt was born in 1882, at a mansion called Hyde Park, near New York. His father was rich. Roosevelt trained to be a lawyer, but entered politics instead. He had his first important post in 1912 when he became Assistant Secretary to the Navy, in Woodrow Wilson's government. In 1921 he had a bad attack of polio. Thanks largely to his courage and determination he recovered, though he was partly crippled for the rest of his life. Possibly his suffering helped him to be sympathetic: certainly this son of a wealthy family was to do a great deal for the poor of his country. In 1929 he was elected Governor of New York State, taking office right at the start of the Depression. He did all he could to help. Then, in 1932, the Democrats chose him as their presidential candidate and, as we have seen, he defeated Hoover by a large majority. When he was sworn in as President in March 1933 he said, 'I pledge you, I pledge myself, to a New Deal for the American people.'

During his first weeks in office, a period that was to be known as the 'hundred days', Roosevelt worked himself and everyone else furiously hard. A flood of new laws and regulations poured out of Washington. Even after that, others followed, though rather more slowly. So that everyone would understand what he was trying to do, Roosevelt spoke regularly over the radio. He did not give fine speeches, but what he called 'fireside chats'. People were quite sentimental about them: a newspaper published a cartoon of him broadcasting, with the caption 'A man talking to his friends'.

In fact, no one knew how to cure the Depression, but, unlike Hoover, Roosevelt was determined to act. He simply tried anything that might work, hoping that some of his measures would succeed, even if others failed. However, though his methods were a little confused, as they were bound to be, Roosevelt had three clear aims. The first was relief, to stop people starving and losing their homes. The second was recovery, to pull America out of the Depression. The third was reform, to make the country a better place.

Relief

Roosevelt knew that people were starving and homeless, so at once the

Federal Government shared $500 million among the States. With it, they bought food for the hungry, and gave loans to people who were behind on their mortgage payments, so that they could keep their homes. However, Roosevelt wanted people to earn their keep, not live on State charity, so he set up a number of organizations to provide work. One was the Civilian Conservation Corps (C.C.C.) which helped young men. They were given healthy outdoor jobs, like clearing tracks through forests, planting trees and strengthening river banks. All they had was their food and a dollar a day, but at least they were not wandering round the country in vain, hoping to find work. Next, there was the Public Works Administration (P.W.A.) under Harold Ickes. This started a number of expensive schemes like the Grand Boulder Dam, Triborough Bridge in New York, and the Texas port of Brownsville. The P.W.A. gave work to a lot of people, but not nearly enough, so Roosevelt set up the Works Progress Administration (W.P.A.) under Harry Hopkins. This tackled smaller projects, such as building hospitals, schools, and roads, but there were so many of them, that they made work for eight million people. Hopkins even found employment for writers, artists and musicians.

Recovery

Creating jobs helped agriculture and industry to recover, because people spent their wages on food and goods. However, Roosevelt did other, more direct things as well.

One of his first steps was to ask Congress for an Emergency Banking Act. That closed all the banks, which stopped people draining them of money. Next, the government investigated the banks, and those that were badly run remained closed. The others reopened, with government loans to help where necessary. Roosevelt promised that money was more safe in a reopened bank than it was under the mattress, and people began, once more, to make deposits.

Then there was the National Recovery Administration (N.R.A.). This tried to make sure that factories produced a steady flow of goods at steady prices. It also tried to win decent wages and reasonable hours for the workers. Firms that drew up codes of conduct for themselves had the right to display a blue eagle with the proud motto 'We do our part'. However, there were plenty of employers who, like Henry Ford, wanted nothing to do with the scheme, and others who joined, but cheated. As the codes were voluntary, the government could not make firms obey them. This part of the New Deal was a failure.

To help farming there was the Agricultural Adjustment Administration (A.A.A.). Farmers were poor because they were growing so much food that prices were absurdly low. The A.A.A. persuaded them to grow less, and then gave them subsidies, as compensation. As there was no longer a surplus, the price of farm goods crept upwards and, at last, country people began to enjoy a little prosperity. All the same, it seemed odd to cut food production while there were people in the cities who were hungry.

19

Reform

Roosevelt made many reforms, but we will look at just three of the most important ones, the National Labour Relations Board, the Social Security Act, and the Tennessee Valley Authority.

The Labour Relations Board made sure all workers were free to join trade unions. It was a success, and at last unskilled workers began to have their own unions — as had happened in Britain fifty years earlier.

The Social Security Act provided State insurance for old age, unemployment and illness. There were pensions for the elderly, dole for those who had no jobs, and sick pay for those who were away from work because they were unwell. However, there was no national health service. To this day, Americans have to pay their own doctors' fees and hospital bills.

The duty of the Tennessee Valley Authority was to bring prosperity to that unfortunate region. The river often flooded: there was little industry: farmers had exhausted their land, and rain washed it away. To tame the river the T.V.A. built dams:

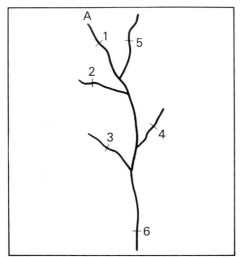

T.V.A. dams and (above) Boulder Dam

Let us suppose there is heavy rain in A. Dam 1 is closed to check the flood, at least until it is full. Dams 2, 3, 4 and 5 are closed so that the flood waters have the main river all to themselves. To make way for them, Dam 6 is drained.

The dams were useful in other ways. At each one there was a hydro-electricity station so that the whole valley had cheap electricity. Farmers used it in their homes and to run equipment like milking-machines. Other people started industries such as the manufacture of fertilizers, flour-milling, aluminium smelting and paper-making.

Formerly, the river had run dry in summer, but the T.V.A. stored water in its dams, which it turned on and off like taps. That kept the river level right, so it could be used for irrigation. It also became a waterway, 1000 km long, joining the rivers Ohio and Mississippi.

Finally, the lakes behind the dams were splendid places for people to go boating and fishing.

As well as building dams the T.V.A. helped farmers by selling them fertilizers cheaply, planting trees to check soil erosion and teaching them better farming methods. The farmers had exhausted their soil by growing cotton, tobacco and maize, which need regular ploughing. The best way to help it recover was to sow it with grass mixed with clover, and leave it for a few years. After that it could be ploughed again and would give far better crops than before. The T.V.A. had no powers to compel farmers to change their ways, so it started test demonstration farms, where they could come and see for themselves. That way, they were persuaded to adopt the new methods of their own free will.

The T.V.A. was a triumph for democracy. A backward part of the United States began to thrive because the government had given, not orders, but opportunities, help and advice. In Chapter 10 you will see how different things were in Russia.

Enemies of the New Deal

In spite of his success, Roosevelt had enemies. You will have noticed that the new organizations were known by initials, and there were many more that are not listed here. The former president, Herbert Hoover, jested sourly, 'There are only four letters of the alphabet not now in use by the administration. When we establish the Quick Loans Corporation for Xylophones, Yachts and Zithers, the alphabet of our fathers will be exhausted.' Many conservatives were too worried to jest. 'What is happening to rugged individualism?' they asked. The American voters dealt with these people when in 1936 they re-elected Roosevelt with an even bigger majority than in 1932, and re-elected him yet again in 1940.

However, there was opposition as well from the Supreme Court. As you saw in Chapter 2 the Court can stop any law which it thinks is unconstitutional. Judges are usually conservative and the nine members of the Supreme Court were no exception. They declared several of Roosevelt's measures unconstitutional even though it was often by no more than a five to four majority. Roosevelt thought that a few fussy old judges were going to ruin everything he was doing for the American people. He asked Congress for a law to reform the Supreme Court which would, in effect, have allowed him to 'pack' it with judges who agreed with him. Congress refused, and to his dismay the ordinary Americans turned against him. The Supreme Court looked after the Constitution, the Constitution guaranteed the freedom of the people, and not even Roosevelt was going to threaten that. The day was saved when one of the most conservative judges retired and the court no longer blocked Roosevelt's measures.

Results of the New Deal

In the first place, the New Deal helped pull America out of the Depression.

It began in 1929 when people stopped buying goods, because they had all they needed: in 1933 they were still not buying, but then it was because they were too poor. What was needed was to put money into their pockets, and this was what the New Deal did. People began spending, manufacturers began making goods again, they employed workers, who in turn spent their wages: manufacturers then produced even more goods, employed even more workers and so on. It was a slow business, though. In the end it was not the New Deal that found jobs for everybody in America, but the Second World War.

Secondly, the New Deal changed the American government. Before, the Federal Government had left as much as it could to the States. Under Roosevelt, it took far more power upon itself. We can get some idea of what happened from the increase in the number of people the Federal Government employed. There were about 600 000 in the 1920s and well over a million by 1940.

Thirdly, there were changes in American politics. We have seen that in the 1920s, neither the Republicans nor the Democrats appealed to any particular social class. Now, the poor saw what a Democratic President was doing for them, so they voted for him, whatever their race or religion might be.

Fourthly, there were changes in American society. Americans still believe in 'rugged individualism' and 'self-help', but not to the same extent. The great Depression and the New Deal showed that the government had a duty to help people in need. America is now a welfare state, though she has not gone as far as Britain.

Finally, there are some writers who think that the New Deal saved democracy in America. They point out that when the Depression reached Germany, it led to the rise of Hitler. They claim that something similar might have happened in America, for she too had a Fascist Party. We can never know if American democracy really was in danger. However, if it was, then although Roosevelt changed much, he preserved a great deal more.

Chapter Five

The United States since 1941

IN THIS chapter we will look first at the considerable progress, and many successes of the United States since 1941, and then at her problems.

Population

In 1940, the population was 130 million: by 1975 it was 214 million. Much of the increase was due to a 'baby boom' just after the Second World War: young couples who were unwilling to start families during the war were anxious to do so when it ended. However, the birth rate began to fall in the late 1950s, so the increase is now much slower.

Science

The war encouraged progress in science. There were medical discoveries, like the insecticide D.D.T., and the use of dried plasma: there were discoveries that helped industry, such as synthetic rubber: radar, though a British invention, was developed for navigation: above all, there was the Manhattan Project, which produced the atom bomb.

Since the war, space exploration has gone ahead quickly, partly because of Russian competition. In 1957 the Russians launched their first satellite, Sputnik 1. It shocked the Americans that their enemies were so far ahead, and in 1958, President Eisenhower set up the National Aeronautics and Space Administration (N.A.S.A.). In July 1969 Apollo II took three men to the moon. Neil Armstrong was the first man to set foot on it.

Economic Progress

The war did wonders for the American economy. In President Roosevelt's words, his country became the 'arsenal of democracy'. Between 1941 and 1945 she made 6500 warships, 90 000 tanks and 300 000 aircraft. Industry was also more efficient. For example, Henry Kaiser found ways of building a merchant ship in 22 days, a task that needed 280 days during the First World War. The war meant there was no unemployment, so it finished what President Roosevelt had begun with his New Deal.

Some people feared that there might be a depression when the war ended. All that happened was that factories had to switch to making peace-time goods and the economy was soon growing rapidly again. The gross national product rose from $214 billion in 1945 to $1692 billion in 1976. Important industries were plastics, man-made fibres, aircraft and motor cars. There were 40 million motor cars in the U.S.A. in 1950 and 110 million in 1975.

America became the 'affluent society'. Homes had central heating for winter and air-conditioning for summer: families owned not just washing-machines and radios, as before the war, but also dishwashers, colour televisions, stereophonic record-players and tape-recorders: many had several cars. The first supermarkets were American, and by 1970, a house-wife who went shopping had a choice of 6500 products.

For many people, work was pleasanter, since there were fewer 'blue collar' jobs and more 'white collar' ones. Factories had machines for the unpleasant tasks, and the service industries, such as advertising, insurance and hotels, all grew. An important new service was air trans-port. In 1930 passengers on domestic flights flew, between them 137 000 km: in 1970 the figure was 160 billion.

Also the luckier Americans were able to leave the noisy, crowded inner cities, and buy luxury homes in the new suburbs. The father drove to his work in town quickly enough, along an eight-lane highway. The mother with a car of her own could easily take the children to school, shop at the supermarket, or visit her friends.

Flyovers and underpasses on a New York freeway

24

In a way, this was the 1920s all over again, but with the important difference that the boom has now gone on for over thirty years and has not yet ended in another Depression. Why is this?

In the first place, America herself was a far better market for goods after the war than she had been in the 1920s. There were more customers: not only was the population larger, but the new wealth was shared more evenly, so a higher proportion had plenty of money to spend. Also, business men created a 'consumer economy'. That meant advertising with posters and neon signs which covered the cities, and with endless commercials on television: it meant hire-purchase, so that when people did not have the money to buy what they wanted, they could borrow: it also meant 'built-in obsolescence'. A manufacturer of washing-machines, for example, makes them so that they will not last, changes his models frequently, and ensures there are no spare parts for the older machines. Not only will the washing-machine break down quickly, but it will be impossible to repair, so the customer has to buy a new one.

Secondly, there was a good foreign market. During the war American traders won customers from other countries, especially Britain. After the war the government found as many outlets as possible for American goods. For example, in 1961 President Kennedy signed an 'Alliance for Progress' with a number of Latin American states. Its aim was to encourage United States investment in them. American firms like I.B.M., Ford and Safeway opened branches abroad. Also, there was economic aid, such as the Marshall Plan. When a country received aid of, say, a billion dollars it usually meant that it had American goods to that value. This pleased the business men who supplied the goods, though not the taxpayers who paid the bill. However, foreign aid usually helped the whole of America in the end, because countries used it to develop their industries. They were then good trading partners. Had America allowed the nations of Europe to stay poor after the war, she would have been like a shopkeeper whose shop is full of goods, but whose customers have no money.

The third reason why there has been no depression since the war is government spending. The Federal Government has employed more and more people — two million in 1946 and three million in 1970. Wars have been expensive, the one with Vietnam costing perhaps $17 000 billion. Even when there is no war, the government still spends hugely on defence. Their budget was $12 000 million a year before the Korean War, it went up to $60 000 million immediately afterwards, and reached $89 000 million by 1974. Also, there was the space programme, an expensive project indeed.

Economic Problems

Even though it has done so well, the American economy has its problems.

In the first place there is unemployment. Though never as bad as during the Depression there have been as many as five million people out of work at times.

Secondly, there is inflation. Prices have risen continuously since the

25

war, sometimes steadily, sometimes rapidly. This means hardship for the poor. It also means endless trouble with the trade unions. Congress tried to limit their power with the Taft-Hartley Act of 1947, but with little success.

Thirdly, there is the 'military–industrial complex', which is a partnership between armaments manufacturers, and the chiefs of the armed forces. They keep each other in business, the service chiefs supplying the manufacturers with orders, and the manufacturers supplying the services with weapons. The problem is that both gain from the Cold War and do not want America to be on good terms with Russia or China. As you will see in Chapter 10, it is quite possible they wrecked the Paris summit meeting between Eisenhower and Khrushchev in 1960. It was Eisenhower who invented the term 'military–industrial complex'. Someone else called America the 'welfare–warfare state'.

Finally, in the 1970s there was an oil crisis. Once, America had all the oil she needed, but her people used much of it, mainly in their huge motor cars. Now the United States has to import from the Middle East. However, since the Yom Kippur War, the OPEC countries have raised their oil prices steeply. This has forced America and, indeed, most of the industrial countries of the world, into recession. Though by no means as bad as the depression of the 1930s, it checks growth and causes inflation and unemployment. President Carter did his best to explain to his people that they must save fuel, but they blamed him for the high prices, which were still less than half those in Britain, and voted him 'the most unpopular President in American history'. There were ugly scenes at filling-stations, with two motorists shot for queue-jumping. In August 1979, a bemused judge heard a case brought by a trade union, that for Arab countries to raise their oil prices was against the Constitution of the United States.

Poverty

There was a good deal less poverty in America after the war than there had been before it. None the less, in 1966, 30 million people were below the poverty line, which was 16 per cent of the population. The miners of Pennsylvania were badly paid: farm incomes were one-fifth of the national average: there was distress in the inner cities, especially the black ghettos: as we have seen there were sometimes five million unemployed.

Unlike before the war, all governments were willing to help, but it was three Democratic Presidents who attempted the most — Truman, Kennedy and Johnson.

When Roosevelt died in 1945, his Vice-President, Harry S. Truman, automatically took his place. Truman was himself elected in 1948. To continue Roosevelt's 'New Deal', he announced a 'Fair Deal' which was an ambitious plan to help the poor. In 1946, Congress passed an Employment Act which set up a Council of Economic Affairs to advise the government how to cure unemployment. However, the Republicans won a majority in Congress in the mid-term elections, and refused to pass any more of Truman's bills.

President Harry S. Truman   *President Lyndon B. Johnson*

John. F. Kennedy became President in 1961. He was the first Catholic to hold the office and, at 44, the youngest man to do so. He was very aware of his country's problems, and to solve them he drew up a programme he called the 'New Frontier'. The Red Indians and bad men of the old frontier days had been tamed long ago, but in Kennedy's view, it was just as important to wage war on poverty, disease and ignorance. As we shall see he tried to help the blacks, and he also tried to cure unemployment. One way he chose was to plunge the Federal Government into debt, deliberately, by spending more than it collected in taxes. That, in effect, pumped money into the economy which people spent, so creating jobs. Another way was to cut taxes which, again, gave people money to spend. At first, Congress refused to do as Kennedy asked, then in 1963 he was assassinated. Throughout the country there was a surge of loyalty to him such as he had never enjoyed during his life, and Congress passed his bills willingly.

Lyndon B. Johnson was Kennedy's Vice-President, so he took over after the assassination. He was himself elected in 1964. Johnson's aim was to make America the 'Great Society', by declaring a 'War on Poverty'. The Economic Opportunity Act introduced training schemes for unemployed youths, grants for small business men and better education for ghetto children. The Appalachian Regional Development Act set up an authority very like the T.V.A. to help people living in the Appalachians, another of America's distressed areas. The Medical Care for the Aged Act helped old people pay their doctors' bills and hospital fees. It is the closest America has come to having a national health service. The Department of Housing and Urban Development built new houses for people living in slums.

Unfortunately, Johnson made the mistake of trying to win the war in Vietnam as quickly as possible. It took so much money that the country could not afford to become the 'Great Society'.

Poverty is still a problem in America, and partly this is because many people lack the will to deal with it. They think welfare benefits encourage people to be idle. 'Self-help', 'rugged individualism' and a firm belief that personal freedom is more important than anything else — these are the ideals of the nineteenth century which went on flourishing in the 1920s, survived the Depression and are still alive today.

The Negro Problem

In the early twentieth century, most blacks lived in the South, where their ancestors had been slaves on the cotton and tobacco plantations. Here they suffered in a number of ways.

In the first place there was discrimination. Negroes had to do unpleasant jobs, and even then they were the last to be employed and the first to be sacked. They could not serve on juries, so no black who was accused of a crime could expect a fair trial. Most Negroes could not vote. It would have been against the Constitution to stop them because of their colour, but the Southern States got round that by saying voters had to own a certain amount of property and know how to read and write. In the main, it was the blacks who were poor and illiterate.

Next there was segregation. A number of 'Jim Crow' laws created something very like apartheid in South Africa today. Blacks had to stay away from whites in such places as hotels, restaurants and buses, while their children went to separate schools. In 1896, in the case of Plessey v. Ferguson, the Supreme Court ruled that this was all quite legal, provided the facilities for white and black were equal. Of course they were not.

Finally, there was intimidation. For example, a black who had the vote would be afraid to use it, through fear of the Ku-Klux-Klan.

Before the Second World War, then, the blacks had every reason to complain, but they were so used to being poor and downtrodden that they did little about it. However, since 1945, their problems have become more urgent.

In the first place, the blacks had higher hopes. The young men who went to the war were told they were fighting for 'freedom and democracy'. Why, they asked, should there be no freedom and democracy for themselves, in America? Also, when the war was over, many African countries won their freedom. If black Africans could throw off white rule, why should black Americans not do the same?

Secondly, the blacks had a higher birth rate than the whites, so their numbers grew more rapidly:

	Number of Blacks (millions)	Percentage of Population
1910	11	10
1970	28	13

Thirdly, the problem of poverty was, to quite an extent, the same thing as the black problem. For example, in 1969 one-third of the blacks were below the poverty line, but only 13 per cent of the whites.

Fourthly, there was migration. Depression in farming and mechanization drove the blacks from the agricultural South in large numbers. They went into cities all over the United States, hoping to find work or, failing that, at least better welfare benefits. In 1910, 98 per cent of American blacks lived in the South, but by 1970 that had fallen to 54 per cent. It was no longer possible to dismiss the black problem as one that worried only a small number of States.

Finally, and closely linked to migration, was the problem of the ghettos. We have seen how the wealthier Americans left the inner cities, and it was here that the blacks went to live. During the 1960s, 3½ million blacks moved into them, while 2½ million whites moved out. The city centres became ghettos. Their problems are crime, especially crimes of violence, high unemployment, slum housing, poor schools, broken homes, bad health and drug addiction. Above all, there is poverty. The ghetto people are not only poor but they compare themselves with people around them. They see enough of the more fortunate whites to realize how much better off they are and every day they pass shops full of goods they are unable to buy.

A white may leave the ghetto if he makes enough money, but a black has the problem of his race. A black doctor or lawyer may indeed live in a white suburb. His white neighbours will accept him, because he will live as they do and because he does not threaten their jobs. The poor blacks have to face the 'blue collar' Americans, who cannot afford to live in the suburbs but who ring the ghetto area. They have escaped from it, but only just. They fear the blacks, because if they move into their street they may turn it into a slum area, and because they compete for the same jobs. That is why there is still so much discrimination against blacks in housing and employment.

To tackle these problems the blacks organized a Civil Rights Movement. As early as 1910, W. E. B. Dubois formed the National Association for the Advancement of Coloured People (N.A.A.C.P.). After the Second World War, one of its leaders was Martin Luther King. Everything the N.A.A.C.P. did was legal, or at least peaceful. They fought cases in the courts, they organized 'sit-ins' in cafés that refused to serve them: in 1955 they boycotted the buses of Montgomery, Alabama, until the company was nearly bankrupt and agreed to let black people sit where they wished: in 1963 Martin Luther King led a march to Washington to petition President Kennedy. Numbers of whites helped them, especially young people. In 1964, 1000 white students went on what they called their Mississippi Summer Project. They lived with black families in the Deep South, ran schools for the children and persuaded the adults to vote. In doing these things, they were risking their lives.

The problem with the N.A.A.C.P. was that its progress was very slow. Many blacks began to lose patience, and then, in 1964 there were race riots in a number of cities, including New York. The police were virtually at war with the ghettos, and were so vicious that the more extreme blacks decided to break from the N.A.A.C.P. and win their way with force. They organized a number of groups, the most important being Black Power, led by Stokely Carmichael. When asked how violent they were prepared to be they answered, 'The sky's the limit.' In 1968 Martin Luther King was assassinated, which made the extreme blacks even more sure that their way was right. There was a great deal of disorder in the 1960s. It has since died down, though it is difficult to see why.

The Federal Government has also helped. One reason the North fought the Civil War was to end slavery, and when it was over in 1865, an amendment to the Constitution made it illegal. In the twentieth century little was done until 1948 when there was an end to segregation in the armed forces. Black and white servicemen had to work together on equal terms. In 1954, in the case of Brown v. Topeka Board of Education, the Supreme Court reversed Plessey v. Ferguson. After that it was illegal to make blacks and whites use separate facilities, even though they were equal. In 1957, the Federal Government showed it was determined to see the law obeyed. It had been decided to admit seventeen black children to the Central High School, Little Rock, in the Southern State of Arkansas. Governor Faubus ordered a force of the National Guard to keep them out, saying he had to do this to stop a riot. President Eisenhower at once put the Arkansas National Guard under the command of the regular army, and sent in 1000 paratroops. They cleared away the demonstrators at bayonet point, escorted the Negro children to school and stayed in Little Rock until all was quiet.

Since then, blacks have been admitted to Southern universities, a certain number of places have been reserved for them in higher education and, in some States, children have been 'bussed' to school. If a town has white areas and black areas, then it will tend to have white and black schools. To prevent that happening, the authorities have sent children by bus to schools in different parts of the town. Black parents have protested about that, as well as white ones, because they do not want their children travelling long distances every day, when they may have a school just round the corner.

As we have seen, when John F. Kennedy was President, Martin Luther King led a march on Washington. Kennedy admitted that the Negro had little chance of a good education, and that he also had 'twice as much chance of becoming unemployed: about one-seventh as much chance of earning $10 000 a year: a life expectancy which is seven years less, and the prospect of earning only half as much as a white man'. He drew up a number of bills which were passed after his assassination. For example the Civil Rights Acts of 1964 and 1968 made race discrimination in housing and jobs illegal.

Today, blacks vote more readily than they did in the past, while some have become mayors of towns, or have won seats in State governments and in Congress. However, it is one thing to make people obey the letter of the law, and it is quite another to change how they think. Many still hate and fear the blacks, and will favour whites when giving jobs. The only difference is that to avoid breaking the law they hide their feelings and disguise their actions.

Political Problems — McCarthyism

America has had a number of political problems since the war, but we will look at just two, the 'Red Scare' raised by Senator Joseph McCarthy between 1950 and 1954 and the Watergate scandal of 1972.

The Americans have feared Communism since the Russian Revolution of 1917, but they did not lose their heads until McCarthy started his campaign in 1950. 'McCarthyism' came about for two main reasons. In the first place, the Communists did well after the war. The Russians took most of Eastern Europe and, in 1949, exploded their first atom bomb: in China Mao Tse-tung's forces defeated the Nationalists. Secondly, there seemed to be treason in high places. A British scientist, Klaus Fuchs, confessed that he had given atomic secrets to the Russians: in America, a former member of the State Department, Alger Hiss, was accused of having been a Communist back in the 1930s. The State Department is like the British Foreign Office, so if there were Communists there, it would indeed be worrying. People began to wonder what was wrong.

Joseph McCarthy seized on this feeling, hoping he could use it to become famous. He made many wild accusations. He said he had a list of 205 members of the State Department who were Communists: he said the Secretary of State, Dean Acheson, was a 'friend of Moscow': he accused the Secretary of Defense, General Marshall, of a wicked, treacherous plot, though he did not say what it was. Marshall was a war hero, and a close friend of General Eisenhower. In spite of everything, McCarthy won a lot of support. 'McCarthy Clubs' sprang up over the country and even Congress caught the mood and passed the McCarran Internal Security Act. This made the left-wing political parties send lists of their members to the Attorney General, so that the government would know who the likely traitors were. McCarthy's most valuable supporters, though, were the leaders of the Republican Party, who saw he was winning them votes. He was allowed to be chairman of a Senate sub-committee that questioned suspected Communists.

Because of McCarthyism, there was fear and suspicion all over the country. As well as the unlucky few who were dragged before McCarthy's Senate sub-committee to be humiliated and ruined, nine million Americans were investigated by the authorities or their employers, and many more had to take an oath of loyalty. It was a veritable witch-hunt. In fact, Communism (from within) has never been a threat to America. Most people knew that, but few had the courage to speak.

The end came for McCarthy when he attacked the army. The proceedings were shown on television and the whole of America saw McCarthy snarling, sneering and bullying his victims. People at last realized what manner of man he was and were ashamed that they had ever agreed with him. The Republican leaders were afraid that he was now more likely to lose them votes than to win them, so they no longer supported him. In 1954, the Senate condemned him, saying he had 'acted contrary to senatorial ethics, and tended to bring the Senate into dishonour and disrepute'. After that he was heard no more, and people joked that 'McCarthyism' had become 'McCarthywasm'. During his four years of triumph, though, he had done much harm. America was anxious to show the world she was the champion of freedom and democracy: McCarthy seemed to show she was just the opposite.

Political Problems — The Watergate Scandal

When Richard Nixon was elected President in 1968, he already had the nickname 'Tricky Dicky'. He was energetic, imaginative and able, but as long as he got what he wanted, he was not too worried about the methods he used. Some of his staff at the White House were the same kind of people and did all sorts of unpleasant things like tapping telephones and 'bugging' offices. Misdeeds, lies and 'cover-ups' became quite normal. One thing these people wanted badly was to see Nixon re-elected because that would mean they kept their jobs. Accordingly they started a 'Campaign to Re-elect the President', usually known as CREEP. In 1972, the leaders of CREEP sent some men to burgle the Watergate Building in Washington, the headquarters of the Democratic Party. They hoped to find secret papers which might be useful to them.

The burglars were amateurs, so they were caught quite easily. For a time, though, they gave nothing away, so the Republicans were able to dismiss the whole thing as 'a prank'. Certainly it made no difference to the election, for Nixon won with a handsome majority. However, when the Watergate burglars were tried, Judge Sirica felt he had not been told everything, and hinted that if any of the accused liked to give more information, then he might receive a lighter sentence. One of them accepted the offer and said that the burglary was the idea of some of Nixon's men in the White House. The Senate began an investigation, and all manner of unpleasant facts came to light. The chief problem, though, was whether Nixon had known about the burglary, and tried to cover it up. Unluckily for him, he had been in the habit of recording the conversations he held in his office, the famous Oval Room at the White House. Judge Sirica demanded the tapes. After a lot of persuasion, Nixon delivered most of them, but he still held back a few. The Senate lost patience and decided Nixon would have to go, so they started impeachment proceedings, which is the only way to dismiss a President. In 1974, rather than let the impeachment go ahead, Nixon resigned.

The Vice-President, Spiro Agnew, had already been convicted of some minor offences, and placed on probation like a naughty boy, so another Republican leader, Gerald Ford, became President. Ford did much to win back respect for the American government. His problem was that he was too much of a 'nice guy', and having decided Nixon had suffered enough, he pardoned him for any misdeeds he might have committed. The American people were furious. Why should the chief criminal escape, while the lesser ones were in jail? Ford's mistaken kindness cost him dear, for the voters turned against him, and in 1976, elected the Democratic candidate, Jimmy Carter, as President.

President Richard Nixon

Demonstration in New York 1959

Questions

1 What reforms are the people in this procession demanding?
2 What social reforms were made by Presidents Truman, Kennedy and Johnson?
3 What name did each President give his programme of reform?
4 What attitudes among the American people make it difficult for a President to introduce social reforms?

Prohibition

Document One

Prohibition went into effect throughout the United States on 16 January 1920, and the country settled back with an air of 'Well that's settled.' No prophet arose to foretell the awful things that were coming — the rum ships prowling off the coasts, the illicit breweries and distilleries, the bootleggers and the speakeasies, the corruption of police and judiciary, the hijackers and their machine guns, the gang wars, the multi-millionaire booze barons, the murders and assassinations, the national breakdown of morals and manners, and all the rest of the long train of evils that sprang from the Eighteenth Amendment.

(*The Noble Experiment of Izzie and Moe —*
Herbert Asbury)

Document Two

To enforce the law the government employed 'prohibition agents'. They would go shopping for drink, and then arrest whoever was selling it. This extract is about one of these prohibition agents:
Izzie made up a sort of schedule showing the time it took him to get a drink in various cities. New Orleans won first prize. When Izzie arrived there he climbed into an ancient taxicab, and as the machine got under way he asked the driver where he could get a drink. 'Right here, suh,' said the driver and pulled out a bottle. 'Fo' bits'. Time — thirty-five seconds.

In Chicago he bought a drink without leaving the railroad station, and duplicated this feat in St Louis. It took longer in Washington than anywhere else; Izzie roamed the city for a whole hour before he could locate a gin-mill. He finally had to ask a policeman, who provided him with the necessary directions.

(*The Noble Experiment of Izzie and Moe —*
Herbert Asbury)

34

Questions

Document One

1 What was 'prohibition'?
2 Which Americans wanted prohibition?
3 According to this writer, what unfortunate results did prohibition have? You must put his ideas into your own words.
4 What other unfortunate results did you read about in this book?
5 The author mentions the Eighteenth Amendment. What was amended? Find out from reference books how such an amendment is made.

Document Two

6 Judging by this extract:
  (a) How effective was prohibition?
  (b) How much respect did ordinary people have for the law?
7 When did prohibition end in the United States?

Parade of the Ku-Klux-Klan at Night

There were thirty bands: but as usual in Klan parades there was no music, only the sound of drums. They rolled the slow, heavy tempo of the march from the far north end of town to Foster Park, where the Klan had put up a twenty-five foot 'fiery cross'. There were 300 mounted Klansmen interspersed in companies among the 50 000 hooded men, women and children on foot. The marchers moved in good order, and the measured tread of their feet, timed to the rumbling of the drums and accented by the off-beat clatter of the horses' hoofs, filled the night with an overpowering sound. Many of the marchers carried flaming torches whose light threw grotesque shadows up and down Main Street.

(*Konklave in Kokomo* — Robert Coughlace)

Questions

1 How many Americans were members of the Ku-Klux-Klan in 1925?
2 What was their uniform?
3 Name three groups of people they hated.
4 In what part of America was the Klan particularly active?
5 What did it do to some of its victims?

6 Having read the extract say what the Klan had done to make their parade impressive and frightening.
7 From reference books, find out when and how the Ku-Klux-Klan began and read more about its history.

The Wall Street Crash

In 1929 it was strictly a gambling casino with loaded dice. The few sharks taking advantage of the multitide of suckers. There had been a recession in 1921. We came out of it about 1924. Then began the climb, the spurt, with no limit stakes. I saw shoeshine boys buying 50 000 dollars worth of stock with 500 dollars down. Everything was bought on hope.

Today, if you want to buy 100 dollars worth of stock, you have to put up 80 dollars, and the broker will put up 20 dollars. In those days you could put up 8 dollars or 10 dollars. That was really responsible for the collapse. The slightest shake-up caused calamity because people didn't have the money required to cover the other 90 dollars or so. There were not the controls you have today.

A cigar stock at the time was selling for 115 dollars a share. The market collapsed. The 115 dollars stock dropped to two dollars, and the company president jumped out of the window of his Wall Street office.

(Arthur A. Robertson in *Hard Times* by Studs Terkel)

Questions

1 Why were people anxious to buy shares, in the late 1920s?
2 How were they able to have far more shares than they could pay for?
3 According to this extract, what proportion of the price of the shares did the purchasers have to find?
4 Why did the price of shares begin to drop?
5 What happened on Black Tuesday?
6 What happenened to the cigar shares mentioned in this extract?
7 What did the company president do?
8 According to the author of this extract, what are the controls that would stop anything like the Wall Street Crash happening today?

The Bonus Marchers — 1932

When we got to Washington there was quite a few ex-servicemen there before us. There was no arrangements for housing. Most of the men that had wives and children were living in Hooverville.

They have come to petition Hoover to give them the bonus before it was due. He told them they couldn't get it because it would make the country go broke.

The question was now: How were they going to get them out of Washington? They were ordered out four or five times and they refused. Finally, the one they did get to shove these bedraggled ex-servicemen out of Washington was none other than the great MacArthur.

The picture I'll always remember . . . here is MacArthur coming down Pennyslvania Avenue. And, believe me, ladies and gentlemen, he came on a white horse. He was riding a white horse. Behind him were tanks, troops of the regular army.

They managed to get them out. A big colored guy, about six feet tall, had a big American flag he was carrying. He was one of the bonus marchers. He turned to one of the soldiers who was pushing him along, saying: 'Get along there, you big black bastard.' That was it. He turned and said, 'Don't try to push me. I fought for this flag. I fought for this flag in France and I'm gonna fight for it here on Pennyslvania Avenue.' The soldier hit him on the side of the legs with the bayonet.

The next day the newspapers deplored the fact and so forth, but they realized the necessity of getting these men off. Because they were causing a health hazard to the city. MacArthur was looked upon as a hero. He was aided by General George Patton and Major Dwight Eisenhower. 'Thank God', said President Hoover, 'we still have a government that knows how to deal with a mob.'

(Jim Sheridan in *Hard Times* by Studs Terkel)

Questions

1 Who were the bonus marchers?
2 When had they earned their bonus?
3 When were they due to have it?
4 Why, do you suppose, they wanted it in 1932?
5 What reason did President Hoover give for refusing it?
6 What was a Hooverville?

7 What made the coloured man in the extract angry? Explain the remarks he made to the soldier.
8 Why did the newspapers say the bonus marchers were a 'health hazard to the city'?
9 Who led the troops that dispersed the bonus marchers? Name the two officers who helped him. How did these three men later become famous? (Look them up in this book, using the index.)

The Civilian Conservation Corps

We had to go out and beg for coal, buy bread that's two, three days old. My dad died when I was an infant. I went to an orphan house for fellas. Stood there till I was seventeen years old. I came out into the big wide world, and my mother who was trying to raise my six younger brothers and sisters couldn't afford another mouth to feed. So I enlisted in the Civilian Conservation Corps.

These big trees you see along the highways — all these big forests were all built by the C.C.C. We went along plain, barren ground. There were no trees. We just dug trenches and kept planting trees. You could plant a hundred an hour.

I really enjoyed it. I had three wonderful square meals a day. No matter what they put on the table we ate and were glad to get it. Nobody ever turned down food. They sure made a man out of ya, because you learned that everyone here was equal. We never had any race riots. Couple of colored guys there, they minded their business: we minded ours.

(Black Gold in *Hard Times* by Studs Terkel)

Questions

1 Which of his three main aims did Roosevelt have in mind when he started the C.C.C.?
2 What work is described in this extract? What other work did the C.C.C. do?
3 What pay did members of the C.C.C. have?
4 Why did the youth in extract join the C.C.C.?
5 What did he think about the work and the food? What does he say the C.C.C. did for him?
6 What do you think of this young man's attitude to the two blacks?

Agriculture and the New Deal

Hog prices had gone to hell. What were they — four, five cents a pound? The farmers were starving to death. They were at the mercy of the packers. We decided to slaughter piggy sows. You know what a piggy sow is? A pregnant pig. We decided to pay the farmers to kill them and the little pigs. Lots of 'em went into fertilizer. That lowered the supply going to market and the prices immediately went up. Then a great cry went up from the press about Henry Wallace, The Secretary for Agriculture, slaughtering these little pigs. You'd think they were precious babies.

You had a similar situation on cotton. Prices were down to four cents a pound and the cost of producing was probably ten. So a program was initiated to plow up cotton. A third of the crop, if I remember. Cotton prices went up to ten cents, maybe eleven.

(C. B. Baldwin, Assistant to Henry Wallace, in *Hard Times* by Studs Terkel)

Questions

1 Which organization was responsible for agriculture?
2 Which of his three main aims did Roosevelt have in mind when he started it?
3 Why were farm prices low?
4 What was done to increase the price of pork and cotton?
5 What did the government do for farmers who agreed to cut production?
6 Why do you suppose the newspapers objected to the slaughter of pigs?

Civil Rights

Document One

It ought to be possible for American students of any color to attend any public institution without having to be backed up by troops. It ought to be possible for American consumers of any color to receive equal service in places of public accommodation, such as hotels and restaurants and theatres and retail stores, without being forced to resort to demonstrations in the streets, and it ought to be possible for American citizens of any color to vote in a free election without interference or fear of reprisal. In short, every American ought to have the right to be treated as he would wish to be treated, as one would wish his children to be treated. But this is not the case.

(Speech by President Kennedy, 1963)

Document Two

We were beginning to hear this summer (1963) about the phenomenon of the white blacklash. Politicans, especially those in touch with Polish–American and Irish–American communities, were pessimistic. They described widespread panic in traditional Democratic districts over the prospective inundation of their neighbourhoods and schools by Negroes: some thought that civil rights might very well lose the election for Kennedy in 1964. Samuel Lubell, sampling a working-class precinct in Birmingham which had given Kennedy a clear majority in 1960, found only one Kennedy supporter left. Others said 'He's cramming the nigger down our throats', or 'If he's elected it will be the end of America.'

(*A Thousand Days* — Arthur M. Schlesinger)

Questions

Document One

1 In what ways does Kennedy say the blacks are suffering?
2 When and where had troops been used to make sure blacks could attend a public institution?
3 What were 'Jim Crow' laws? Which States had them? Which court case upheld them? Which court case reversed this decision?
4 Why were blacks often frightened to vote?
5 What bills did President Kennedy draw up to help the blacks? When were they passed? How effective were they?

Document Two

6 What was the 'white backlash' against?
7 To which political party did President Kennedy belong?
8 What nicknames is given to Polish–Americans, Irish–Americans etc.? How had they voted in the past? How were they expected to vote in 1964? Why?
9 Of which State is Birmingham the capital? How had white people in this part of America voted in the past? How were they expected to vote in 1964? Why?
10 Why was it the working-class whites who especially disliked Kennedy's policy towards the blacks?
11 Why did Kennedy not stand for election in 1964?

37

The Great Depression in the U.S.A.

	Income (Dollars per head)	Expenditure (Dollars per head)	Percentage of Workforce Unemployed	Millions of Shares sold
1928	643	630	4.4	920
1929	682	648	3.2	1125
1930	621	592	8.7	810
1931	580	558	15.9	577
1932	490	496	23.6	425
1933	482	490	24.9	
1934	527	526	21.7	
1935	572	553	20.1	

Questions

1 Plot the figures above on graphs, the first two on the same sheet and the others separately.
2 Explain the changes which your curves show.
3 When was expenditure higher than income?
4 What made it necessary for people to spend more than they were earning?
5 How was it possible for them to do this, do you suppose?
6 When was the peak of the Depression (a) for the stock market and (b) for the labour market?
7 You will see that unemployment was still high in 1933. When was this problem cured?

The United States in the 1920s

Questions

1 What are the duties of the Federal Government of the United States of America?
2 What is its legislature? Name the two Houses and describe how each is elected.
3 Who is the head of the executive? How is he chosen?
4 What laws do the States make?
5 What document lays down how the United States is to be governed?
6 What is the duty of the Supreme Court?
7 How is the British system different from the American?

8 What are the two main political parties? What people supported each in the 1920s?
9 How much of the world's wealth was America producing in the 1920s? What goods and services were being provided?
10 What three reasons did Americans give to explain their prosperity?
11 How did firms grow in size? What were the large firms called? What advantage did they have?
12 Why was the market for goods limited (a) at home and (b) abroad?
13 What were the main religious denominations? What are 'fundamentalists'? Where were they strongest?
14 Why were the 1920s called the 'roaring twenties'?
15 What measure introduced prohibition? What problems did it create?
16 From which countries did immigrants come? How did they live? What are 'hyphenated Americans' and WASP Americans?
17 Which racial minority caused the biggest problem?
18 How strong was the Ku-Klux-Klan in 1925? What people did its members hate?
19 Who were Sacco and Vanzetti? Why did they become famous?
20 How many people were poor? Why did (a) trade unions and (b) the government not help the poor?

Give an account of the United States in the 1920s under the headings: The Government/Politics/The Economy/Society.

The Economic Depression

Questions

1 Which group of people bought most goods? Why did they stop buying?
2 Why did manufacturers cut production? How did unemployment lead to still more cuts?
3 How much did industrial production fall between 1929 and 1933? How many unemployed were there by 1933?
4 Why did the price of shares rise much higher than their real value in the late 1920s?
5 Why did the price of shares begin to drop? Why did they fall to a fraction of what they had been? When did the market crash?
6 Why did many banks go bankrupt?
7 Why did the unemployed suffer? What was done to help them? What did they do for themselves?
8 What problems were there in the countryside?
9 Who was the President during the Depression? How was he abused?
10 Who were the 'bonus marchers'? What happened to them?
11 Why did Hoover do little to relieve the Depression? How did he think it would be cured?
12 Who was elected President in 1932?

Give an account of the Depression under the headings:
Causes/The Wall Street Crash/Unemployment/President Hoover and the Depression.

Roosevelt and the New Deal

Questions

1 When was Roosevelt elected President? What promise did he make?
2 What happened during the 'hundred days'? How did Roosevelt explain his measures to the American people?
3 Why were Roosevelt's methods sometimes confused? What were his aims?
4 What was the purpose of the $500 million grant to the States?
5 Name three organizations that provided work. Say what each of them did.

6 What Act was passed to help banks? What measures were taken under the Act?
7 What do the letters N.R.A. mean? What were the aims of this organization? Why did it fail?
8 What organization helped farmers? What did it do? Why did its policy seem strange?
9 What was the work of the National Labour Relations Board?
10 What was the purpose of the Social Security Act? What social reform was *not* made?
11 Why did the Tennessee Valley Authority build dams? (Five reasons)
12 What farming methods did the T.V.A. encourage? What else was done for farmers?
13 Why did politicians like Hoover oppose the New Deal?
14 How was the Supreme Court able to block many of Roosevelt's measures?
15 How did Roosevelt propose to deal with the Court? Why did he fail? How was the problem solved in the end?
16 How did the New Deal help to end the Depression? What, finally, cured unemployment?
17 How did the New Deal change (a) government, (b) politics, (c) society?
18 What other result may the New Deal have had?

Give an account of Roosevelt and the New Deal under the headings:
Roosevelt's Election/Roosevelt's Methods and Aims/Relief Recovery Reform/Enemies of the New Deal/Results of the New Deal.

The United States since 1941

Questions

1 How much did population increase between 1940 and 1975? When was there a baby boom?
2 What scientific progress was made during the war? Name one field of science in which there has been spectacular progress. What happened in July 1960?
3 How did the war affect the economy?
4 How much did America's gross national product increase from 1945 to 1976? Which industries were especially important?

5 What is meant by saying America became 'the affluent society'?

6 In what ways was working life pleasanter?

7 Where did wealthier Americans live?

8 What was the difference between the post-war boom and the one of the 1920s?

9 In what ways is America a better market for her own goods?

10 How has the foreign market improved?

11 Give four ways in which the government has spent a lot of money.

12 How much unemployment has there been, at times, since the war?

13 What problems have been caused by inflation?

14 What is the 'military–industrial complex'? How does it influence foreign policy?

15 Why was there an oil crisis? How did this affect the economy?

16 How many Americans are below the poverty line? Which groups suffer most?

17 What was the name of Truman's programme? What Act did Congress pass? Why did it refuse to pass any more of Truman's bills?

18 What was the name of Kennedy's programme? Name two ways in which he tried to cure unemployment. What made Congress willing to pass his bills?

19 What was Johnson's aim? Name four of his measures. Why did Johnson not achieve his aim?

20 What ideas hinder attempts to cure poverty?

21 Where did most blacks live in the early twentieth century? Give three ways in which they were ill-treated.

22 How did the Second World War and events in Africa influence the thinking of the blacks?

23 How has the black population grown?

24 What proportion of blacks are below the poverty line, compared with whites?

25 Why did many blacks leave the South?

26 How have black ghettos been created? What are their problems? Why is it difficult for a black to leave a ghetto?

27 What movement did the blacks organize? What was the N.A.A.C.P.? Name one of its leaders after the Second World War. Describe its activities.

28 Why did some blacks form more extreme organizations? Name one of them and its leader. What was its aim?

29 What legal decision was made in 1896? When was it reversed? What happened at Little Rock in 1957?

30 What steps have been taken to end segregation in schools since then?

31 What did Kennedy say about the blacks? Name two of his Acts that were passed to help them.

32 What progress have the blacks made? What problems remain?

33 Give two reasons for McCarthyism.

34 Name some of the accusations McCarthy made.

35 What Act did Congress pass?

36 How many Americans were investigated?

37 Why did McCarthy lose his popularity? What harm had he done?

38 Who burgled the Watergate Building in 1972? Why?

39 What information did one of the burglars give Judge Sirica? What problem did this raise about Nixon? Why did he resign?

40 Who succeeded Nixon as President? Give one reason why he lost the election in 1976.

Give an account of the United States since 1941 under the headings:
Population/Science/Economic Progress/Economic Problems/Poverty/The Negro Problem/Political Problems/McCarthyism and Watergate.

Problems

1 What are the main differences between the American and the British systems of government?

2 Why had America become the richest country in the world by the 1920s?

3 What weaknesses were there in the American economy in the 1920s?

4 What divisions were there in American society in the 1920s and what problems did they create?

5 'The roaring twenties.' How far is this a good description of America in the 1920s?

6 Why was there an economic depression in America in 1929 and the early 1930s?

7 What measures did Roosevelt take to cure the Depression? How far was he successful?

8 Why has Roosevelt been called the 'best loved and best hated President in American history'?

9 What changes did the Second World War make to America?

10 What have been America's main achievements at home since 1945?

11 Why has there been no serious economic depression in America since the 1930s?

12 Is 'the welfare–warfare state' a good description of America?

13 What internal problems has America had to face since 1945? How far have they been overcome?

14 In what ways did the Negro problem become more serious after the Second World War? What attempts were made to solve it (a) by the government, (b) by the blacks themselves?

SECTION TWO

RUSSIA

Chapter Six

Russia in 1900

The Country and Its People

RUSSIA is the largest country in the world, covering as it does one-sixth of the land surface of the globe. It has important mountain ranges, like the Urals, but most of it is one vast monotonous plain, on which the main features are the rivers. However, vast though the country is, the Russian people do not find it easy to make contact with the outside world. Their northern coast is frozen for most of the year, as are their Baltic and Pacific coasts during the winter. To the south, mountains and deserts divide them from Asia. In the west, most of the countries have been hostile: for example, the Turks have long barred the way into the Mediterranean and, with NATO help, still do. It is partly because they are hemmed in that the Russians have tried to make their vast country even bigger: they have been conquering new lands since the days of Tsar Ivan the Terrible in the sixteenth century.

In 1900 the population was 130 million, and was growing rapidly, having doubled since 1850. Over half these people were subject races, belonging to lands which the Russians had conquered. In the south were Armenia, Georgia and the Ukraine. Around the Baltic Sea there were Finland, Estonia, Latvia and Lithuania. To the west was Poland: that country had been divided between Germany, Austria–Hungary and Russia, but the lion's share had gone to Russia. All of these subject people were unhappy under Russian rule, especially the Poles.

In the early twentieth century, Russia was the most backward of the great powers. Her villages were, in many ways, like those of medieval England. They had huge open fields, divided into hundreds of small strips, while the only pieces of equipment the peasants could afford were clumsy wooden ploughs and simple hand tools, like the scythe.

Even in the nineteenth century, the peasants had been serfs, which meant they were the property of the nobles. In 1861, Tsar Alexander II liberated the serfs, and compelled the nobles to give them some of their land. However, the peasants gained little, for they had to pay for the land over a period of 40 years. Moreover, they held it in common so no one could call the piece of land he was cultivating his own. There was a further problem that came from the increase in population. In most villages, the farms grew smaller and smaller, for almost every peasant had to divide his land among two or more sons. Soon, many men could not grow enough food for their families and were desperate for more land. As it happened, the nobles still owned a great deal of land which they were willing to let, but there was so much competition for it that they were able to charge high rents. This made the nobles highly unpopular.

Russia's industry, though still very backward, was at least beginning to make progress. There were extractive industries like oil drilling around Baku, and coal-mining in the Donets Basin. There were manufacturing industries; for example, steel making at Krivoy Rog, and textiles at Moscow and Petrograd. At Petrograd there was engineering as well, the Putilov works being especially important. The railway network was growing. The Trans-Siberian Railway, begun in 1891, promised to open trade with the Far East. There were other lines in the west which were also useful for trade, though the government built them mainly for military reasons.

A statesman who did a great deal to help industry was Count Sergey Witte, Minister of Finance from 1892 to 1903. Among other things, he encouraged foreign investment. Much of the capital that Russian industry needed came from abroad, especially from Britain, Germany and France.

As industry grew, so also did the number of factory workers. The most enterprising peasants came to the towns, because they could earn more money, but they were still discontented. They had to live in slums, or what was worse, communal barracks. The smaller factories were particularly unpleasant, being dirty and dangerous but in all of them people had to work long hours for low wages.

Another group that was growing was the middle class. There were factory owners, merchants, bankers, lawyers and doctors. Though still only a small proportion of the population, they were all well educated, and, for the most part, intelligent. They were to play an important part in the years to come.

The Government

The Russian government was as primitive as anything else in the country. The Tsar Nicholas II had much the same ideas as James I and Charles I of England, and they ruled in the early seventeenth century. Nicholas believed in Divine Right, which meant he had been chosen by God to rule his country. As a result, he was unwilling to share his power with anyone, for that would have meant going against God's will. Unfortunately, Nicholas did not have the personality an autocrat needs, for although he was obstinate, he was also weak. His wife, the Tsaritsa Alexandra, had much more character. Though she was devoted to Nicholas, her chief concern was for her son, the Tsarevich Alexis. She wanted the boy to inherit all his father's power and influence, so she, as much as Nicholas, was determined that the Russian people should have no say in the government of their country. Unhappily, Alexis had a rare blood disease, haemophilia, so he was often unwell, and unlikely to live for long.

To give advice, the Tsar had a Council of Ministers chosen by himself.

Tsar Nicholas II and his son Alexis

Below them came the Civil Service, which carried out the decisions made by the Tsar and his ministers. There were fourteen grades in the Civil Service, each with its salary, uniform and title. Men in the higher grades ranked with the nobility. Another branch of the Tsar's government was the Okhrana, or secret police. They arrested people suspected of plotting against the Tsar and often condemned them, without trial, to death, imprisonment, or exile in Siberia.

The only Russian institutions that were at all democratic were the zemstvos. They were rather like English county councils, being responsible

45

for such things as roads, hospitals, schools and poor relief. They did useful work, but the Tsar disliked them, partly because they were democratic, and partly because they were controlled by the middle classes, whom he felt were his enemies.

Social Groups and Their Political Parties

A number of social groups formed political parties which were hostile to the Tsar.

In the first place, there were the middle classes. They were liberals in that they wanted Russia to be a democracy, like Britain and France. They thought they would then have an important say in the government. In 1905 they formed the Constitutional Democratic Party, known from its Russian initials as the Cadet Party.

Others that looked to the West for their ideas were the intellectuals. They were people like artists, writers, teachers and, above all, university students. Many intellectuals, though, were not interested in a democracy run by respectable middle-class men, but had more extreme views. They formed revolutionary societies and one of these assassinated Alexander II, the grandfather of Nicholas II. However, though these little bands were determined they were too few to do much on their own. Accordingly, they tried to win support by spreading their ideas among the ordinary people of Russia.

One group went to the peasants. The peasants were under the influence of the Church, so many of them were loyal to the Tsar. Also, the height of their ambition was to rob the nobles of their land and share it among themselves. However, there were a few who were intelligent and willing enough to form a political party of their own, which they did in 1899. They called it the Social Revolutionary Party.

A second group of intellectuals went to the town workers, and in 1898 they formed the Social Democratic Party. They believed in Marxism (see Chapter 1), which to them was like a religion so they were willing to go to any lengths. They had secret printing presses for their propaganda, they had an underground organization to help political refugees escape, they hatched terrorist plots, and, to provide funds, they carried out daring robberies.

However, men of strong opinions usually find it hard to agree and when, in 1903, the Social Democrat leaders held a conference in London, the sessions were long and stormy. Soon, they divided into two groups. One of these wanted the party to be democratic, and to allow anyone to join, without being necessarily very active. The others wanted a smaller party of dedicated revolutionaries and, instead of democracy, close control by a central committee. These men found a leader in Vladimir Ilyich Ulyanov, a man better known as Lenin. In the end a number of delegates left the conference in disgust, so Lenin's party won the day. They called themselves 'Bolsheviks', which means 'majority'. Their defeated rivals were called 'Mensheviks', which means 'minority' though, in fact, they had far more followers in Russia itself.

Summary

We have seen that Russia was a backward country, governed by an autocratic Tsar, Nicholas II. However, her economy was just beginning to grow and so, too, was opposition to the government. There were three main groups of opponents:

1 The middle classes, who formed the Constitutional Democrats, or Cadet Party.
2 A minority of the peasants, led by a number of intellectuals, who formed the Social Revolutionary Party.
3 The town workers, led by another faction of intellectuals who were Marxists, and who formed the Social Democratic Party. In 1903 this party split into the Bolsheviks, led by Lenin, and the Mensheviks.

Other people who opposed the Tsar were the subject races. They wanted to break away from Russia, and form their own independent States.

Between them, these people could probably have overthrown the Tsar easily enough, but they were disunited. The middle classes feared the 'Dark People', as they called the lower classes: the peasants and town workers had little in common, while the town workers' party, small though it was, split into two: the subject races were not only against the Tsar, but wanted to throw off Russian government, whatever form that might take.

Chapter Seven

The Russian Revolutions

The Revolution of 1905

As WE SAW in the last chapter, there was a great deal of discontent in Russia. It was unlikely to come to a head, though, unless something happened to make the Tsar's enemies act together. That came in 1904 and 1905 when Russia went to war with Japan and was thoroughly beaten.

The troubles began on Sunday, 22 January 1905, which came to be known as 'Bloody Sunday'. A procession of 200 000 workers marched through Petrograd, to present a petition to the Tsar. They were worried about the war: they wanted better working conditions, including a minimum wage of a rouble (10p) a day: they wanted the government of Russia to be more democratic. The crowd did not intend to make a disturbance, still less a riot. Its leader was a priest, Father Gapon, who was loyal to the Tsar. As for the workers themselves, they felt that if only Nicholas knew about their plight he would be sure to give them what they wanted. They even sang *God Save the Tsar* as they marched. However, the soldiers guarding the Winter Palace lost their nerve and opened fire. They killed five hundred people and wounded thousands more. Nicholas was not even in Petrograd at the time, but nearly everyone blamed him for the massacre. There was violence all over Russia.

The Governor of Moscow was assassinated, and by the end of the year some 1500 government officials had been murdered. On the Black Sea the crew of the battleship *Potemkin* mutinied and bombarded Odessa. In the countryside peasants attacked their landlords. The Poles and the Lithuanians rose in rebellion. Peace was made with Japan in September, but then the defeated soldiers came home and made the troubles even worse. There was a general strike, so trade and industry came to a standstill.

It was at this point that the middle classes formed the Cadet Party. Its members supported the strike because they thought it would force the Tsar to give Russia a democratic government. At about the same time the workers in Petrograd elected their own council, or Soviet as they called it, to direct the strike. One of the leaders was a Menshevik, called Bronstein, better known as Trotsky.

The general strike left the Tsar no choice but to give in, so on the advice of Count Witte, he issued a document called the October Manifesto in which he promised that Russia should have an elected parliament. This satisfied the Cadets who at once withdrew their support for the strike. The socialist parties were less easily pleased, but they were not strong enough on their own so the Tsar put them down by force. All the members of the Petrograd Soviet were arrested, and even though many were soon released, Trotsky was sent to a very cold part of Siberia. In Moscow, government artillery crushed all resistance.

A Time of Progress 1906–14

The first Russian parliament, or duma as it was called, was elected in 1906. It had a majority of Cadets, which displeased Nicholas, so within a few weeks he dissolved it and ordered another election. The second duma was much the same as the first, and again Nicholas dissolved it. At the same time, he changed the electoral law. As a result most members of the third duma were landowners, who were loyal subjects of the Tsar, so it was allowed to remain. Such a duma was unlikely to be effective, but at least Russia had some kind of parliament and there was a chance that given time it might develop into something more like the one in Britain.

However, the Tsar realized he would have to do more than secure a well-behaved duma. There had to be vigorous measures as well, so he appointed as Prime Minister an outstanding statesman called Piotr Stolypin. Stolypin was determined to crush the revolutionary parties, so he arrested large numbers of them, perhaps as many as 100 000 and sent them to Siberia. At the same time he tried to win support for the Tsar by reforms. Education was improved, and there were sickness benefits and accident insurance for workers. The government encouraged industry so that, for example, iron and steel output increased by 50 per cent in four years. There were also changes in agriculture, which were even more important. As we have seen, most of the land which the peasants worked belonged, not to individuals, but to the whole village. Stolypin, however, made it possible for people to own their own farms by giving them State loans so that they could buy their land. The more ambitious peasants quickly took advantage, and became independent farmers with much better incomes than their neighbours. Those wealthier men were called kulaks. The socialist parties watched in dismay for they knew that if most of the peasants became contented there would be no chance of a revolution.

Stolypin was assassinated in his box at the Kiev Opera in 1911, but the reforms he had started went on. The period from 1906 to 1914 was one of hope, for although conditions in Russia were still dreadful, there were changes for the better. However, these promising developments stopped abruptly with the outbreak of war in 1914.

Russia during the War

As soon as the war began, the Russian people united against the Germans, and rallied to the Tsar. A vast crowd fell on its knees before him at Petrograd. However, this loyalty soon evaporated as one disaster followed another.

In the first place, the Russian armies suffered humiliating defeats and may have lost as many as eight million men, killed, wounded, or taken prisoner. Apart from a few able commanders, like Brusilov, few officers enjoyed the confidence of their own men. The Minister for War, General Vladimir Sukhomlinov, boasted he had not read a military manual in twenty-five years. Russia's industries were unable to equip her huge army with enough heavy artillery, machine-guns, or even rifles. In some sectors there was only one rifle to every ten men. Because of poor transport, soldiers were short of food and clothing.

Secondly, the war brought the economy near to collapse. One of the main problems was that the railways could not cope. They did not bring enough coal to the factories, so five hundred closed in Petrograd alone, as did several steel works in the south. Moreover, there was not enough food in the towns. The farmers in Siberia had grown plenty, but it was piled at the railway stations. Shortages meant an increase in prices, which went up 400 per cent from 1914 to 1917, while wages only doubled. The workers were more discontented than ever.

Thirdly, the Tsar's government lost what little respect it once had due to the influence of a so-called 'holy man' Grigori Rasputin. He had gained a hold over the Tsaritsa because he was able, by some strange power, to relieve the sufferings of her son Alexis, who had haemophilia. Rasputin used his influence to secure important posts for people who befriended him, and to see that others who disliked him were dismissed. Nicholas himself fell somewhat under the spell of Rasputin, but as long as he was at court, he was able to put a stop to the worst of the holy man's schemes. Then, in August 1915, the Tsar decided that, in order to encourage his soldiers, he must go to army headquarters. As a result, the government of Russia was in the hands of the Tsaritsa and Rasputin. In less than two years, there were over twenty changes of ministers, including four prime ministers, and, moreover, none of the men that Rasputin chose were at all suitable.

Many people were alarmed, especially as Russia was losing the war. The duma asked for a say in the appointment of ministers, but the Tsaritsa would not dream of allowing anyone to contradict Rasputin. At last, in December 1916, a group of nobles led by Prince Yusupov murdered him. They were trying to save the royal family from itself, but they were too late. The damage was already done.

The March Revolution 1917

There were many politicians, both inside and outside Russia, who were plotting revolution, but in the end it was the ordinary people who started it. During the long, cold winter of 1916 to 1917, there was more and more hunger and discontent until, in March, the workers of Petrograd came out on strike and rioted for food. Normally, the army would have restored order, but this time the soldiers not only refused to fire on the people, but joined them. At the same time, the sailors in the fleet mutinied. The mob then stormed every building in the city that represented the Tsar's authority — police stations, prisons, the Winter Palace, the Peter and Paul Fortress and the headquarters of the Okhrana.

After a while the mob came to its senses, and realized that Russia had to have a government of some kind. Accordingly, an excited crowd went to the Tauride Palace, where the duma met. Its members decided they must act quickly, so they sent Roczianko, the President of the duma, on to a balcony to announce the formation of a provisional government. The idea was that it should rule the country until it was possible to hold elections. Most of the men in the new government were Cadets, but there were some left-wingers too, including a Social Revolutionary, called Kerensky.

However, other people were busy as well. The soldiers, sailors and workers of Petrograd formed a Soviet, just as they had done in 1905. Most of its members were Mensheviks, and they did not trust the Provisional Government. They, too, decided to meet in the Tauride Palace, and they, too, claimed the right to give orders. Their Order No. 1 was especially important because it said that soldiers and sailors must not obey any political instructions from their officers, or the Provisional Government unless the Soviet approved them. In effect, Russia had two governments in the same building.

Meanwhile troops all over the country declared for the Revolution, and after a little persuasion, the Tsar abdicated on 15 March. He and his family were held prisoners at their country palace of Tsarskoe Selo, near Petrograd. Later they were moved to Ekaterinburg in Siberia, where the Bolsheviks murdered them.

The Provisional Government and the Revolution of November 1917

The man who dominated Russia from March to November 1917 was Alexander Kerensky. He was a Social Revolutionary, and a member of both the Petrograd Soviet and the Provisional Government. Kerensky was a man of great energy and he was a brilliant orator, so it was not long before he became Prime Minister.

The Provisional Government began well enough, for it abolished the secret police, released the political prisoners and granted Poland her independence, even though that country was occupied by the Germans. However, there were two serious mistakes. In the first place the government did not distribute land to the peasants. The wealthy members of the duma felt that, if the landlords were robbed, their turn would come next. The other mistake was to continue the war. The Provisional Government wanted Russia to be a democracy like Britain and France, so it felt it had to continue the struggle against Germany alongside those two powers. It so happened that General Brusilov had deserted the Tsar and offered his services to the Provisional Government. He had mounted a great offensive in 1916, the only one on the Russian front to have much success. Now he organized another, but by this time the Russian army had no heart for the fight, and was soon defeated. This was a serious blow to the Provisional Government.

Bolsheviks, Petrograd 1917

Meanwhile, the Bolsheviks had been busy. When war broke out, most of the leaders were in exile and in despair, but the revolution of March 1917 filled them with hope, so they wanted to return to Petrograd. Lenin and others were in Switzerland, and for them it looked as if the journey was impossible, since Britain and France would not help them, and Germany was at war with Russia. However, the Germans saw that the Bolsheviks were the one political party that was willing to make peace with them, so they gave Lenin and his friends a train which took them to the shores of the Baltic. From there they went through Sweden and Finland to Petrograd. Lenin was worried because he had come home through enemy territory but the crowd gave him a rapturous welcome and carried him in triumph to the Bolshevik party headquarters.

However, Lenin, was still a long way from being ruler of Russia. In June 1917 there was an All Russian Congress of Soviets at which a speaker said there was no party ready to rule Russia on its own. Lenin said, 'There is such a party', and everyone roared with laughter. The Bolsheviks were so few that nobody took them seriously. Why, then, did they succeed?

In the first place, Lenin would not allow the Bolsheviks to work with any other party, because they might confuse their aims. He knew exactly what he wanted, and would not turn from it. In the second place, the Bolsheviks won over many of the Russian people. They used slogans like 'Peace! Bread! Land!' which made a strong appeal to the soldiers, the townspeople and the peasants. Another slogan was 'All Power to the Soviets', which pleased the ordinary Russian worker, since he knew the Provisional Government was in the hands of the middle classes, whom he distrusted. Also, Bolshevik agitators spread their ideas among the factory workers, the sailors of the fleet and the soldiers. All of these were so discontented that they were willing to listen. The Bolsheviks were particularly successful with the soldiers which was the main reason that they won in the end. Thirdly, the Bolsheviks organized bands of armed workers called Red Guards.

There was one set-back. After Brusilov's defeat there were riots in Petrograd called the July Days Rising. The Bolsheviks denied they had any part in it, but they were blamed, and Lenin fled to Finland.

Then fate took another turn, for the Commander-in-Chief of the army, General Kornilov, decided to seize power. He marched on Petrograd, throwing the city into a panic. However, Bolshevik agitators had been busy among his men, and large numbers refused to follow him. Those who did attack Petrograd were defeated by a force many of whom were Red Guards. It certainly looked as if the Bolsheviks had saved the capital, so they suddenly became popular. Lenin returned from Finland: he had decided that this was the moment to strike.

On the night of 6 November 1917 the Bolsheviks seized all the key places in Petrograd — the railway stations, the power-station, the banks and the telephone exchange. Red Guards stood on the bridges of the River Neva. Moreover, Trotsky had won over the troops in the Peter and Paul Fortress, so the building and its arsenal were in rebel hands. Kerensky escaped from Petrograd, but several members of the Provisional Government remained in the Winter Palace. On the evening of 7 November, the Bolsheviks mounted their assault. First of all, there was a shot from the cruiser *Aurora* and then the Red Guards advanced. A painting by a Bolshevik artist shows a group of brave men, gallantly attacking, but in fact there was no need for heroism. The only defenders were a battalion of women and some officer cadets who were little more than boys. The Bolsheviks took the palace with the loss of six men, and arrested the members of the Provisional Government that were inside. Everything now depended on the army in the rest of Russia, but the Bolshevik agitators had done their work well, so regiment after regiment declared for the Revolution. Kerensky managed to gather a band of Cossacks, but the Bolsheviks defeated him easily and he fled from Russia.

Chapter Eight

From the Revolution to the Death of Lenin

DURING the period from 1917 to 1924 the Bolsheviks, or Communists as they soon called themselves, made sure of their hold on Russia. This was not easy, for only one Russian in six hundred was an active Communist.

Immediate Problems — Government, the Land Question and Peace with Germany

The first thing the Communists had to do was organize a government, so they set up a Council of People's Commissars with Lenin at its head. Each commissar was a government minister, with a department to run: Trotsky, for example, was Commissar for War.

Leon Trotsky

Revolutionary poster

At once the Communists faced a challenge. Ever since the March Revolution the people of Russia had been promised a Constituent Assembly; that is, an elected body which would draw up a constitution. The Communists felt bound to let the Assembly meet, so towards the end of 1917 the Russians voted in the only free election in the whole of their history. Had the Communists won a majority they would have been happy, but they took only a quarter of the seats. The members met one day in January 1918, but the following morning Red Guards turned them away. That was the end of the Constituent Assembly.

Seeing they had decided to rule alone, the Communists needed to terrorize their enemies. One of their leaders, Felix Dzerzhinsky, organized the Cheka, a secret police that was even more ruthless than the Okhrana. It was especially busy after an attempt on Lenin's life in August 1918. The wheel had come full circle. Formerly, the Tsar and a handful of nobles had ruled Russia with the aid of the Okhrana: now Lenin and a handful of Communists governed with the aid of the Cheka.

One thing the Communists had to do quickly was to pacify the peasants, since they were the majority of the Russian people. Accordingly the government issued a decree taking away all the land from the landlords, and giving it to the peasants. The peasants were very glad the Communists had come to power — for the time being, at any rate.

Another problem was the need to end the war. The Germans had Russia at their mercy so they demanded humiliating peace terms. The Communists did their best to bargain, but they knew their army would refuse to fight, so they had to give way. By the Treaty of Brest–Litovsk, signed in March 1918, Russia lost her Baltic Provinces, which became independent, while Germany took Poland. Also, the Germans and Hungarians were allowed to occupy much of Russia, including the Ukraine, during 1918. They took advantage of this to harvest the crops for themselves.

The Civil War

The Communists, or 'Reds', had enemies, known as 'Whites'. The Whites were simply everyone who was against the Communists, so they included Mensheviks, Social Revolutionaries, Cadets and Tsarists. They not only outnumbered the Reds, but they also had help from abroad. Other countries were afraid that a Communist victory would lead to world revolution, so America, Britain, France, Japan, Italy, and even Greece, sent weapons and soldiers. The Whites grew in strength.

In the south, General Denikin raised an army with French support. He captured Tsaritsyn and advanced to within 300 km of Moscow. In Siberia was Admiral Kolchak with an army based on Omsk. He had help from the Czech Legion, a force with a strange history. During the war, many Czechs fled from their Austrian masters to fight alongside the Russians. When Russia made peace with Germany, 40 000 Czechs asked to go to France in order to continue the struggle there, and Lenin agreed. The only way was to travel east along the Trans-Siberian Railway and continue right round the world. However, the Czechs had decided the Communists were worse enemies than the Germans so when they were strung out along the railway, they seized control of it. That gave Kolchak the chance to raise his army and he menaced Moscow from the south. In Latvia was an army led by General Yudenich and backed by Britain. It fought its way to the suburbs of Petrograd. In the north was a force of Social Revolutionaries helped, again, by the British. Finally, in the Far East, was yet another army supported by the Japanese.

Even though they had all these enemies the Red Armies won, and we must look at the reasons why.

In the first place the Communists had interior lines. They were able to switch men from one front to another quite easily, while the White armies found it nearly impossible to reinforce each other. Secondly, the Whites did not agree among themselves. All they had in common was a hatred of the Communists, and each group claimed to be the lawful rulers. At one time Russia had twenty rival governments. Thirdly, foreign support was lukewarm. Some statesmen like Winston Churchill were keen to crush the Communists, but the ordinary people had no wish to start a war in Russia as soon as the one against Germany was over. Fourthly, the Whites made enemies. Their soldiers were cruel, while following their armies came the landlords, who took back their estates from the peasants.

The Communists used these advantages to the full and defended themselves well. Trotsky made the Red Army a powerful force. When he did not have enough volunteers, he conscripted men: when he was he was short of officers he drafted some who had served the Tsar — and put a political commissar with each one to keep an eye on him. Troops going into battle fought bravely. They had to, because behind each army were units of the Cheka who had orders to machine-gun any men who ran away. To make sure the Red soldiers had weapons and food, Lenin introduced what he called 'war Communism'. All industries were nationalized, so they had to make whatever the government ordered. Many workers wanted to go back to their villages, hoping to find food, but they had to stay in the factories. The peasants were told to hand over any grain they did not need themselves and when they refused, armed bands went into the countryside, robbing the villages.

For these reasons, the Reds were able to defeat the White armies one by one, so that by the end of 1920, the civil war was over.

The War with Poland

At the Peace Conference of Versailles the Curzon Line was suggested as the frontier between Poland and Russia. The Poles, though, wanted their country to be much bigger, so they invaded the Ukraine and took Kiev. The Russians counter-attacked and carried the war into Poland, even taking Warsaw. However, the Polish leader, Marshal Pilsudski, refused to give in, while the French government sent one of its best soldiers, General Weygand, to advise him. By now, the Russians had outrun their communications. They were short of supplies, so when the Poles attacked, they had to retreat almost as far as they had come. Lenin agreed to make peace, and by the Treaty of Riga of 1921 gave Poland so much of White Russia and the Ukraine that she doubled her size.

Economic Ruin, Famine and the N.E.P.

Even now, Russia had to face still more disasters. By 1921 she had been through seven years of war, revolution and civil war. Her economy, which had never been very strong, now collapsed completely. Factories closed rapidly, one after another, for they had neither raw materials nor fuel. Agriculture was in a sorry state as well. The fighting had destroyed many farms, while under war Communism, as we have seen, the peasants had to give their surplus to the government. Their answer was to grow only enough for themselves. Then a drought hit much of the country, especially the Volga region. Food was already short, but now there was famine. Although foreign countries helped, especially America, five million people died.

Lenin and his government were wondering what to do, when the sailors at the Kronstadt naval base took action. Until 1921 they had been among the most loyal supporters of the Revolution, but they saw that power had fallen into the hands of a small minority, who were ruining their country. Accordingly, they rebelled. The sea was frozen, so the Red Army attacked over the ice and, at the third attempt, captured Kronstadt and its warships. However, even though the rebellion had failed, the Communists were worried since men they thought were their best friends had turned on them. Lenin decided he had better give up his more extreme ideas for the time being, and he introduced his New Economic Policy.

Under war Communism, all firms had been nationalized, but under the N.E.P. the State kept only the 'commanding heights' of the economy, like the large industries, and the banks. The smaller concerns were given back to their owners. As for the peasants, they had to hand over some of their produce as taxes, but they were allowed to sell the rest, for whatever price it might fetch. As there were serious shortages, prices were high, so many 'N.E.P. men' quickly became rich. All this must have distressed Lenin. He had wanted a Communist State in which everyone worked for the general good: instead, he had to accept a capitalist system, with people working for their own gain. Under the N.E.P., though, Russia gradually recovered so that by 1927 her factories and farms were producing as much as they had done in 1913.

Lenin died in 1924. He was greatly honoured. Petrograd was renamed Leningrad, and his body was laid in a magnificent mausoleum in Red Square in Moscow. Even today most Communists look on him, along with Karl Marx, as the greatest leader their movement has had.

Chapter Nine

Russia under Stalin 1924–39

Stalin's Rise to Power

STALIN'S real name was Joseph Djugashvili. He took the name 'Stalin', which means 'man of steel', when he grew up. He was born at Tiflis, in Georgia, in 1879. He trained to be a priest, until he was expelled from college for bad behaviour, and in 1903 he became a Bolshevik. He did a great deal for the party, including robbing banks to provide funds. After the March revolution of 1917 he was the editor of the official Bolshevik newspaper, *Pravda*, and after the October Revolution, Lenin made him Commissar for Nationalities in his new government. Stalin did well in the civil war, for it was he who saved Petrograd from General Yudenich.

However, at this stage no one took Stalin seriously. He was stocky and short; he did not seem at all clever; he was such a dull character that someone described him as a 'grey blur'. Certainly, he could not compare with Trotsky, who had created the Red Army which saved the Revolution, and whose brilliant, fiery personality made such an impression on everyone. Indeed, Lenin thought so little of Stalin that in 1922 he gave him one of the most humdrum posts he could find, which was General Secretary of the Communist Party.

When he took over his new position, Stalin saw he could use it for his own advantage. He was in touch with all the branches of the Communist Party throughout Russia, so he was able to put many of his supporters in key positions. Lenin at last realized what was happening so he warned the other Party leaders. 'Comrade Stalin', he wrote, 'has concentrated boundless power in his hands, and I am not certain he can always use this power with sufficient caution.' Lenin died soon afterwards, and this letter was read to the Central Committee of the Communist Party. It was too late. Stalin not only kept his position as General Secretary, but went on to gain more power.

By now there was a split in the party between the left wing, led by Trotsky, and the right wing, led by Bukharin and Rykov. Marx had said that the Revolution would be world-wide, and Trotsky held that the Russians should bring this about by encouraging Communist risings in other countries. Stalin, on the other hand, believed in 'Communism in one country'. He saw that Trotsky's policy would earn Russia many dangerous

Stalin

enemies at a time when she was still weak. It was more sensible, he urged, to concentrate on making Russia powerful. Thanks to the support he had gained from his post as General Secretary, and thanks to help from the right wing of the party, Stalin won. In 1927, Trotsky was driven into exile. He went to live in Mexico where he was assassinated, on Stalin's orders, in 1940.

Having used the right wing of the party to dispose of the left, Stalin now conspired with the centre to break the right. In 1927 Bukharin and Rykov lost their positions in the government and were even expelled from the Communist Party. Stalin was now ruler of Russia, with more absolute power than any of the Tsars had ever enjoyed. We must see how he used it.

Stalin's Industrial Policy

Stalin knew that one day there would be war with Germany, and he was determined to turn Russia into a great industrial power so that she would be strong enough to win. In his view, the New Economic Policy was wrong. Left to themselves, the manufacturers made things that ordinary people wanted to buy such as clothing and household goods. They would be no use in a war against Germany so instead, Stalin wanted to see steel-furnaces, engineering works and factories making armaments. He wanted them quickly, as well, hoping that Russia could make as much progress in ten years as Britain had done in a hundred. To do that, though, the government had to have complete control of industry.

59

Another problem with the N.E.P. was that it allowed people to make themselves rich, so encouraging capitalism, which was the one thing the Communists wanted to destroy.

Accordingly, Stalin ended the N.E.P. and began a series of Five Year Plans. The first ran from 1928 to 1932, the second from 1932 to 1937, while the third, beginning in 1937, ended with the German invasion of 1941.

The organization in charge was the State Planning Commission, known from its initials as Gosplan. It laid down targets, and these had the force of law. If a factory, for example, failed to produce what Gosplan said it should, then its manager was guilty of a crime. There were many worried managers in Russia, because the Five Year Plans were highly ambitious.

Since the aim was to make Russia powerful, the Plans concentrated on heavy industry, like iron and steel, hydroelectricity and coal-mining. The second Plan also developed transport. Thousands of dirt tracks were turned into metalled roads: there were new waterways, like the Baltic–White Sea Canal, which was over 225 km long: there were airports, so that it was possible to travel the length and breadth of the country in a matter of hours: the Moscow underground was built, a marvellous show-piece where just a few of the stations contained more marble than all the royal palaces in Russia put together.

There were many new industrial towns, like Magnitogorsk, which were built in the Urals and Western Siberia. These areas are rich in minerals, and, moreover, they are much further from Germany than the older industrial centres, Leningrad, Moscow and the Donets Basin.

It was important that everyone should work hard. From time to time there were trade-union meetings at which the members agreed enthusiastically to put in longer hours for less pay. This may seem unusual behaviour for trade unions, but they were controlled by the Communist Party, and anyone who disagreed was soon in trouble. Factory discipline was strict. A man would be punished if he stayed away, came late, or even if he went to the lavatory too often. For encouragement, people called 'Stakhanovites' were given honours and, what was more to the point, extra rations. They were workers who did outstandingly well. They took their name from Alexis Stakhanov, who dug 100 tonnes of coal in one six-hour shift. That was sixteen times the norm for his mine. The Cheka also played a part, for it arrested countless political prisoners who were then sent to labour camps. Thousands of them died digging the Baltic–White Sea Canal.

The ordinary folk suffered, too. Since the factories were making very few goods for sale in the shops, such things were expensive and had to be rationed. The only comfort the government could give the people was to tell them they were building the perfect Communist State. Some of the time they were prepared to joke about it. 'Why were Adam and Eve like the Russians?' was one riddle. Answer: 'Because they lived in Paradise and had no clothes.' Mostly, though, there was more and more discontent.

On the whole the Five Year Plans were a success. Output increased 400 per cent between 1928 and 1938, so Russia had indeed become a great industrial power in the space of ten years, just as Stalin had wanted. The German attack came in 1941, and though they had a bitter struggle, the Russian armies won in the end. Their weapons came from the new industries Stalin had created.

Stalin's Agricultural Policy

Stalin meant Russian agriculture to help industry in a number of ways.

In the first place he hoped for plenty of cheap food, so that it would be possible to pay factory workers low wages and keep down production costs. Secondly, farming was to be mechanized, so releasing men to come to the towns. Thirdly, the government intended to buy all the produce at rock-bottom prices, sell it at a profit, and use the money to develop industry. Finally, Stalin meant to export grain. It would earn foreign currency like dollars and pounds, which would pay for imports of such things as machine tools which the Russians were, as yet, unable to make for themselves.

As with industry, the N.E.P. stood in the way, for it encouraged the kulaks. They had, between them, 24 million little farms, most of them too small to be efficient. Also, the kulaks owned their land, which they worked to make profits for themselves, so they had no place in a Communist State. To Stalin it seemed both good economics and good politics to be rid of them.

The answer was to organize collective farms. Each was made of anything from fifty to a hundred small peasant farms whose owners had to give up not only their land, but their livestock and equipment as well. They then worked as a team on the collective. The main advantage seemed to be that a large farm is more efficient than fifty or so small ones, so the same land should have produced more food. To help, the government set up Machine Tractor Stations, where farmers on the collectives could hire heavy equipment. The M.T.S.s also gave out Communist propaganda.

Workers on a collective farm in Uzbekistan

The peasants, for their part, could see no advantages in collective farms. Some took up arms, while many more offered passive resistance. They refused to work, and, rather than give up their animals, they slaughtered them. By 1934 the number of livestock was half what it had been in 1928. The government's revenge was terrible. Some villages were surrounded by soldiers who machine-gunned the inhabitants, and everywhere the Cheka descended on the kulaks, deporting them to labour camps in their millions. Not surprisingly, the harvest of 1931 was a failure, and from 1932 to 1933 there was a famine. Even Stalin began to worry. He sensed that everyone was against him, though, at first, no one dared speak. Then, one day, his wife Nadya raved at him because of his cruelty to the Russian people. The following morning she was dead, though how it happened we do not know. In any event, Stalin was so shaken that he decided to change his ideas. He still refused to give up collective farms, but he did say that each man could have about half a hectare of land for himself and sell the produce for his own profit.

With most of the kulaks in labour camps, and with the rest of the peasants somewhat less discontented, agriculture recovered enough for food rationing to end in 1935. However, Stalin was later to admit to Churchill that collectivization had been a bigger disaster for Russia than the German invasion.

The Great Purge 1936–8

As we have seen, Stalin's policies for industry and agriculture caused a lot of discontent and this spread, even to the leaders of the Communist Party. Stalin was afraid, and frightened men are often dangerous. Moreover, Stalin was so ruthless that he was prepared to send an unlimited number of people to their deaths.

The excuse for starting the purge was the murder of Kirov, the leader of the Leningrad branch of the Communist Party. Probably Stalin ordered the assassination himself. At once the secret police, or O.G.P.U. as it was then called, began to round up suspects. They then went on to arrest many others on trumped-up charges of plotting with foreign powers or conspiring to murder Stalin. There was no evidence, but after torture, most of the victims went into the dock and confessed. For the most important of them, there were elaborate show trials that had a lot of publicity.

First of all, Stalin rid the Communist Party of everyone who had ever opposed him, criticized him, or even seemed at all uncertain in their loyalty to him. He was particularly savage towards members of the Old Bolsheviks' Association, men who had fought alongside him during the Revolution, but who were likely to have ideas of their own. In Lenin's first government, the Council of People's Commissars, there had been fifteen members. By 1938, only Stalin remained. Four had died natural deaths, but the other ten had been 'purged'. Next, Stalin rounded on the armed services, until in the end one-third of the officers had been arrested. Members of the civil service had their turn, and so did the ordinary people of Russia. Many were tortured to death, many more were executed, and perhaps 10 million went to labour camps.

By 1938 the strain had become too great. So many key people were under arrest that the country could not be run properly. Those who were still free lived under the dread of a knock on the door in the early hours of the morning and large numbers committed suicide, or had nervous break-downs. Even Stalin decided he had spilled enough blood and decided to call a halt. One last purge remained, that of the secret police. Numbers of them were executed, including their chief, an odious creature called Nikolai Yezhov. That way, Stalin put the blame for the purge on the men who had obeyed his orders.

After 1939, the midnight arrests, the tortures, the executions and the labour camps remained, but the victims were far fewer. The ordinary Russian, at least, could breathe more easily.

What had the purge achieved? Stalin's economic policy was so un-popular that he could not have forced it through without some terror. However, he went so far that he came close to destroying the country he was trying to build. To give just one example, the armed forces were in such a bad state that in 1939–40 Russia had the greatest difficulty in winning a war against the tiny State of Finland. That gave Hitler the encouragement he needed to invade Russia the following year.

Chapter Ten

Russia since 1940

DURING and after the war, Stalin continued to rule Russia, so the way the country was governed remained much the same. However, important social changes were taking place, which came to light after Stalin died and Nikita Khrushchev came to power.

Russian under Stalin 1941–53

The war brought terrible problems. Seven million houses, 31 000 factories and 1700 towns were destroyed. West of the Volga hardly a building, hardly even a telegraph-pole was left standing. Also, of the 20 million dead, most were men. In many villages there was not a single able-bodied male, so women, children and old people tilled the fields. Often, they harnessed themselves to the ploughs, because seven million horses had died in the war, and there were few tractors. Then, in 1940 there was a drought, and the harvest failed in many places. This time, though, there was no famine, for the government had the transport, and the power, to take food to the stricken areas.

Stalin made things worse. The peasants had broken up most of the collective farms, but he 'collectivized' them again, even though he knew they would grow less food. Stalin also started the Cold War, so, through fear of the West, he ordered his factories to go on making weapons, and his scientists to develop rockets and atom bombs. All this took money that was badly needed to help the country rebuild its shattered towns and villages.

In spite of their suffering, Stalin drove his people to work. In 1946, he announced a Five Year Plan, called the Plan of National Reconstruction. It concentrated, like the earlier ones, on heavy industry. The Russian people, who could not buy clothes, because the shops were empty, and who did not even have enough to eat, had to mine coal, drill for oil, make iron and steel and build power-stations. They were furious, and slacked as much as they dared. However, there were 10 million in the labour camps, who had no choice but work. Also, the Russians stripped the factories of East Germany and Manchuria of their machines, and took them for their own use. By 1953, Russian industry was producing as much as it had done before the war.

64

Stalin kept absolute control, making all the important decisions himself. To try and win support he portrayed himself as a genius and a hero. His portraits and his statues were everywhere, while several towns were named after him. In fact, many Russians did respect him. After all, he had saved them from the Germans, or so they thought. To stifle opposition, Stalin not only terrorized his enemies with the secret police, but even tried to control the way people thought. He gave this task to Andrey Zhdanov who, in 1946, ordered writers and artists to work as the Communist Party required. Novels, for example, had to have Communist heroes, while the villains were Tsarists or capitalists. Biologists even had to accept the strange theories of a scientist called Lysenko, because they fitted in with Communism. The only people who had any real freedom were the physicists who were working on important projects, such as making the atom bomb.

This was all bad enough, but in January 1953, nine doctors were arrested. Stalin said they had poisoned Zhdanov, who had died suddenly in 1949. The doctors were, moreover, accused of plotting to poison other Russian leaders. Stalin told his Minister of Security, 'If you do not obtain confessions from them, we will shorten you by a head.' It was unpleasantly like the beginning of the great purge in 1934, and men trembled for their lives. Then, in March 1953, Stalin had a stroke and died. His old colleagues put him beside Lenin, in the mausoleum in Red Square, but they showed little respect at the funeral. When it was over they were, as one writer has said, 'Like boys let out of school'.

Khrushchev's Rise to Power

When Stalin died, his henchmen clung together for a while. His going was like knocking the keystone out of an arch, and they felt if they were not careful, the whole government would collapse. There was, they claimed, 'collective leadership', and all of them were equally important. They would even go to the opera in the same car, and make sure they came out of it in alphabetical order. Sooner or later, though, someone was bound to take control, and four seemed possible, each one representing a powerful group in the Soviet Union. There was Beria, who was head of the secret police, there was Zhukov, who was Commander-in-Chief of the army, there was Malenkov, who was Prime Minister and who had the support of the technicians and managers who ran Russia's industries, and there was Khrushchev, who was General Secretary of the Communist Party. Everyone had had enough of the secret police, so Beria was executed. Moreover, it was soon clear that Zhukov did not have enough support from the army, so that left Malenkov and Khrushchev. Finally Khrushchev won. Malenkov resigned as Prime Minister in 1954, his place being taken by Bulganin. Khrushchev could rely on Bulganin to obey him, so, virtually, he was in command from that moment. However, in 1958 Bulganin resigned and Khrushchev became Prime Minister as well as First Secretary.

Khrushchev had to rule Russia through the Communist Party. but Stalin had purged it of anyone he thought dangerous which meant, in practice,

Nikita Khrushchev

anyone who had ability. The men in important posts were the ones that knew how to survive, but often, precious little else. Khrushchev replaced them with bright young Party members. However, there was no blood-bath. The majority were quietly retired and even Khrushchev's most dangerous rivals were simply given unimportant jobs in remote places.

Khrushchev's Reforms

Khrushchev realized he would have to govern Russia in quite a different way from Stalin. However, for many years, the Russian people had been taught that Stalin was a great man, a genius. Khrushchev himself had said so, a number of times. How, therefore, could Khrushchev give up Stalin's policies and do something quite different? He decided he must destroy Stalin's reputation. In 1956, at the 20th Congress of the Communist Party of the Soviet Union, he delivered a speech that was an attack on Stalin from beginning to end. He denounced the way he had pretended to be such a magnificent leader — the cult of personality Khrushchev called it: he denounced his tyranny and his cruelty: he denounced his mismanagement of industry and agriculture: he even exploded the myth that Stalin had won the war, saying that he planned campaigns on a library globe, gauging distances with a tape-measure.

Soon Stalin's statues were coming down, his body was taken from its place of honour beside Lenin's, and the inhabitants of Stalingrad found they were living in Volgagrad.

Khrushchev was now free to introduce his new policies, but why were they needed? Ironically, it was because of changes that had taken place, largely, under Stalin. This table shows how much industry had grown since the Revolution:

	Town Population	Percentage of Total	Rural Population	Percentage of Total
1917	26 million	20	104 million	80
1953	90 million	45	110 million	55

We also know that Stalin encouraged the basic, heavy industries such as coal, oil, electricity supply and steel. It was these developments and what flowed from them that moved Khrushchev to do the following things:

1. *Political Changes.* At the time of the Revolution, 80 per cent of Russians were illiterate. However, industry could not grow on its own: a new class of educated people had grown with it. They were the civil servants, the managers, the engineers and the technicians who ran the factories. They were not going to give the government unthinking obedience indefinitely: they were too intelligent for that, and also they were well paid. As Khrushchev himself said, 'We are getting richer, and when a person has more to eat, he gets more democratic.'

To please these people, Khrushchev ended the harshness of Stalin's days. He curbed the powers of the secret police, he freed most of the prisoners in the labour camps, and he told the law courts they must give fair trials. Artists and writers had more freedom, though that did not mean they could do entirely as they pleased. Boris Pasternak wrote the novel *Dr Zhivago*, which was a biting attack on Communism. However it won a Nobel Prize. The authorities would not allow it to be printed in Russia and they would not allow Pasternak to go to Stockholm to collect his prize. That was the only penalty he suffered, though. Under Stalin, he would certainly have been executed.

2. *Raising Living Standards.* Thanks to Stalin, Russia had plenty of coal, electricity, steel and so forth, but these are no good on their own: they must be used for something. They could have gone into even more armaments, and produced goods like furnaces, but Khrushchev wanted Russia to be more prosperous than America. He announced two seven-year plans, both concentrating on consumer goods, like clothing, furniture and household gadgets. Russia came nowhere near to overtaking America, but the plans did have some success. For example, between 1953 and 1958, the output of refrigerators went up from 49 000 a year to 360 000.

Inside G.U.M., Moscow's largest department store

3. *The Reorganization of Industry.* There are no private firms of any importance in Russia; instead all industries belong to the State. In Stalin's day
every industry had its own ministry in Moscow. If, for example, the
manager of a cement works needed electrical cable to install some new
machines, he had to write to Moscow. His own ministry would pass the
request to the one responsible for electrical engineering, which would then
instruct one of their factories to supply the cable. Usually, it took a long
time, and it was frustrating for the manager of the cement works to have
his machines standing idle for weeks, when a factory near by could have
sent him what he needed in a day or two.

To end a host of problems like this, Khrushchev disbanded the ministries
and divided Russia into 105 regions, each with its own Economic Council.
The Councils were responsible for all industries in their areas, 'from steel to
salt, from diesel locomotives to kitchen chairs'. They were able to organize
the exchange of goods much more quickly than the ministries had done.

The change was also a good political move, for the staffs of the Ministries
were loyal to Mikoyan, a Politburo member and supporter of Stalin.
Khrushchev was able to pack the Economic Councils with his own men.

Another change in industry was 'Libermannism', named after Professor
Libermann, who thought of it. Under Stalin each factory manager had to
produce a certain quantity of goods fixed by Gosplan, and provided he met
his target, no one looked at all closely at his methods or his costs. Libermann pointed out that a factory should be judged, not by the volume of
goods it churned out, but by its profits. Khrushchev seized on this idea,
and told his factory managers that in future their salaries, and the wages of
their workers, were going to depend on their profits. What is so remarkable about this is that it is quite against Communist thinking. To the true
Communist, 'profit' is a dirty word: a man should work for the good of the
State, not to put money in his own pocket.

4. *Agriculture*. When Stalin died, Soviet agriculture had not recovered from the two disasters of war and collectivization. In the whole of Russia there were only 600 000 tractors while the United States, with much less land to cultivate, had five times as many. Millions of cattle had died, and their numbers were still low. Yields were small, whether it was the amount of grain per hectare, the quantity of milk per cow, or the number of eggs per hen. Above all, there was the problem of the peasants. They still clung to their old farming methods, they were slovenly in their work, and they were superstitious. For example, they thought that the last drops of milk from a cow's udders had magical properties, so they tried to have as many last drops as possible, by milking up to six times a day.

All this distressed Khrushchev, for how could the Russians become as well off as the Americans if they did not have enough to eat? 'What kind of Communism is it,' he asked, 'that has no sausage?'

To improve agriculture Khrushchev provided money for tractors, machinery and buildings. To please the workers on the collective farms, he increased their wages and he closed the Mechanical and Tractor Stations. The peasants had hated these places, because they gave out propaganda more readily than equipment. It was not unusual to go to one of them for a tractor and come away with a handful of Communist leaflets instead. Khrushchev also encouraged better methods. He went to farm after farm himself, telling the workers what to do in minute detail. He spoke their own language, and made his lectures interesting with proverbs and funny stories. He had advice on how to grow corn, plant potatoes, fatten pigs and breed cows. Much that he said was sensible, though not all of it. For some reason he had great faith in maize as food for livestock and he always told farmers to grow it whether their soil and climate were suitable or not. In the end, they nicknamed him 'kukuzura', the Russian word for maize.

Khrushchev's most ambitious plan for farming was the Virgin Lands Scheme, started in 1954. The aim was to cultivate a vast, empty area of Kazakhstan and south-west Siberia, which is very like the American Prairies. Khrushchev sent half a million volunteers to do the work, in spite of warnings that ploughing the grasslands would turn them into a dust bowl.

> The scene of this huge gamble reminded one of nothing so much as the days of the covered wagon, as American settlers opened up the west, with hundreds of thousands of men and women, mostly young, torn up from their roots and scattered over the vast steppe in tents, in primitive huts, in dug-outs, freezing through the long, cruel darkness of the first winter, seared by the blazing summer sun, as they toiled at the first giant harvest over an area the size of France.
>
> (*Khrushchev's Russia* Edward Crankshaw — page 79)

All Khrushchev's work for farming achieved little. The peasants clung to their old ways and went on hating the collective farms. The Virgin Lands Scheme was a failure for, after a few good harvests, there was a drought, and the wind blew the dusty soil away, just as Khrushchev's critics had warned. The land is now back in grass, and the Russian government is trying to improve crop yields in the traditional arable areas like the Ukraine.

It is not having much success. Russia has more of the best wheat-growing land of the world than any other country, but from time to time her harvest is so poor that she has to import from the U.S.A. and Canada.

Anyone can see that the only way to make Russian farming prosper is to scrap the collective farms and divide the land among the more intelligent peasants. That, though, would mean the end of Communism in Russia. It is not a price the government will pay.

Khrushchev's Fall and After

In October 1964, Khrushchev went on holiday. His senior colleagues came to the station to wave him a friendly goodbye, and then, as soon as he had left, hatched a plot against him. Within a few days they had made their plans, so they ordered him back to Moscow and told him to resign. With everyone against him, he had no choice but to obey. Why he was overthrown is not clear. He had had failures at home, especially the Virgin Lands Scheme: abroad he had given way over the Cuban missile crisis, and quarrelled with China: he was often clowning and from time to time he had behaved in extraordinary ways, as when he took off his shoe and banged it on the desk in the United Nations. Probably, though, the main reason was that he was becoming too powerful and the other Russian leaders did not want to return to the rule of one man, even though Khrushchev was quite different from Stalin.

After Khrushchev's resignation Leonid Brezhnev became First Secretary of the Communist Party, and Alexei Kosygin Prime Minister. They have ruled more firmly than Khrushchev. Authors have had to be more careful what they write: Jews have been refused permission to emigrate: anyone the government thinks especially dangerous may still vanish, perhaps into one of the few labour camps that remain, or perhaps into a lunatic asylum. However, there has been no return to Stalinism, and it is hard to see how there could be. Russia has changed too much for that.

WORK SECTION — Russia

1 Give the dates of Stalin's Five Year Plans. Under which of them were these works most likely to have been built?
2 Why did Stalin wish to develop industries like this?
3 What other industries did he encourage?
4 Why were many works and factories established, like this one, in Siberia?
5 What organization set production targets for works like this?
6 Why did so much emphasis on heavy industry displease many Russians?
7 How successful were the new industries?

Steel works in Siberia

70

8 How would these works have contributed to the defeat of Germany in the Second World War?

The Russian Revolution

Document One

This is an extract from the diary of a Frenchman, Louis de Robien, employed in the French Embassy in Petrograd. It was written on 9 November 1917.

The Ministry has still not been constituted and it is generally thought that the Bolsheviks will not be able to remain in power under these conditions. I must admit that this is a disappointment to me, as I cannot deny having a certain sympathy for these men who at least have an ideal. Much as I hate the Revolution, the only result of which was to install a seedy-looking barnstormer in the Winter Palace instead of simply leaving the Emperor there, the more do I feel drawn towards the Bolsheviks, who dream of a future of peace and fraternity for all humanity. What seems to me the most hateful is the hybrid rule of bourgeois republics with imperial policies. If autocracy has had its day, if the aristocracy must disappear because it did not know how to fulfil its mission, then let it be in favour of a universal democracy in which all peoples are brothers and in which property will be fairly divided, and let the new state of things mark some progress in the happiness of men. But there is nothing more odious than a glorified riff-raff. Lenin at least, like Christ of old, brings something new and a different language to that of the governments of today. They are perhaps dreamers, but I prefer their dreams to the gross realism of the 'get-out-and-let-me-in' people of the first revolution.

(*Diary of a Diplomat in Russia* — Louis de Robien)

Document Two

This is what the same man wrote from Archangel in October 1918.

At the time of their rise to power the Bolsheviks were Utopians, humanitarians, and generous-minded visionaries: today they are raving madmen. Their criminal folly first manifested itself towards the beginning of July at the time of the execution of Admiral Chastny. It reached its full violence after the monstrous crime of Ekaterinburg. Alas, the epidemic shows no signs of weakening, and everything is to be feared for our unfortunate companions who have remained in Russia.

One hundred and fifty people have been shut up in Peter-and-Paul where they have been for four days without food and subjected to the worst treatment. Every night, below the windows of the dungeon into which they were crammed, the Bolsheviks shot some unfortunate officers who were accused of being counter-revolutionaries, and the sinister sounds of the shooting could be heard from the Embassy itself.

Things are even more atrocious at Kronstadt. They had deported about three thousand arrested officers to the island: the sailors immediately started shooting them down without any form of trial. Tovarich Posern, the Assistant to the War Commissariat, although a true Bolshevik, did at least go there and try and prevent the massacre. On his return he admitted that he could never have imagined any sight so ghastly as the one he had just seen.

Everywhere, mass arrests are taking place, and at a moment's notice the streets are blockaded at both ends by squads of Red Guards. All passers-by who happen to be between the blockades are apprehended, searched and interrogated, and immediately incarcerated if they can be suspected of being counter-revolutionaries, or if they are of French or English Nationality.

(*Diary of a Diplomat in Russia* — Louis de Robien)

Questions

1 Who seized power in Russia in March 1917?
2 When exactly did the Bolsheviks overthrow them?
3 Why did it seem unlikely the Bolsheviks would remain in power?
4 What steps did they take to keep power?

Document One

5 What type of government does de Robien seem to favour?
6 If it is overthrown, what type of government does he think should take its place?
7 Who was the 'seedy-looking barnstormer'?
8 What is de Robien's opinion of the government of Russia from March to November 1917? What does he mean by calling it a 'bourgeois republic with imperial policies'? Is this fair?
9 What is de Robien's opinion of Lenin?

71

Document Two

10 Why do you suppose de Robien moved from Petrograd to Archangel?
11 What change does he say has come over the Bolsheviks?
12 What was the 'monstrous crime of Ekaterinburg'?
13 What was 'Peter-and-Paul'? What was happening there?
14 What was there at Kronstadt? What atrocity was committed there?
15 Who were the Red Guards? What were they doing?
16 Why were the Bolsheviks behaving as de Robien describes?
17 Why did they hate the French and the English?
18 Here de Robien is describing the start of an unfortunate episode in Russian history. What was it? How did it end, and when?

Stalin's Purges

Document One

Khrushchev describes the fate of some of his acquaintances:

I was personally connected with many victims of the political terror. Take Ivan Kirilkin for instance. He was manager of the Ruchenkev mines in 1925 and later was made the director of the Makeyev metal works, which he ran very competently. Then there was Vasily Bazulin. He did a pretty good job supervising a factory near Yuzovka. Both men perished in 1937. They disappeared off the face of the earth without leaving so much as a trace. Nobody would tell me what had happened to either of them. I don't know how many factory directors and engineers perished in just the same way. In those days it was easy enough to get rid of someone you didn't like. All you had to do was submit a report denouncing him as an enemy of the people; the local Party organization would glance at your report, beat its breast in righteous indignation, and have the man taken care of.

I also knew Treivas. His name had been widely known in the twenties as a prominent figure in the Lenin League of Communist Youth. He was an intelligent, capable, decent man. Kaganovich once took me aside and warned me that Treivas's political record had a black mark on it. Apparently he had once signed a declaration in support of Trotsky. He didn't escape the meat mincer when the butchery began in 1937.

Sometimes you hear the name of Lomov mentioned on the radio. Where is this Lomov now? I knew him well. He was put in charge of coal output in the Ukraine, and I used to see him frequently in his office in Kharkov. He was much respected in the Party as a man with a Party record going back to the days of the pre-Revolutionary underground. But you still want to know, where is this Lomov now? The answer is — shot! No more Lomov.

(*Khrushchev Remembers*)

Document Two

Here Khrushchev describes what happened when Russia attacked Finland in 1939. The Finnish frontier was uncomfortably close to Leningrad and Stalin was afraid the Finns would allow the Germans to attack Russia through their country. He decided to occupy the Karelian Isthmus:

The war dragged on stubbornly. The Finns turned out to be good warriors. They had organized their defences brilliantly along the Mannerheim Line on the Karelian Isthmus, and they thwarted our attempts to break through. We soon realized we had bitten off more than we could chew. The Mannerheim Line was impregnable. Our casualties mounted alarmingly.

This was a terrible time — terrible because of our losses, and even more terrible in the wider perspective. The Germans were watching with undisguised glee as we took a drubbing from the Finns.

Our navy was engaged against the Finnish fleet. You wouldn't have thought that the Finns would have the advantage at sea, but our navy couldn't get anything right. I remember hearing that one of our submarines had been unable to sink a Swedish merchant vessel which it had mistaken for a Finnish ship. The Germans observed the incident and gave us a teasing pinch by offering their assistance: 'Are things that bad? You can't even sink an unarmed ship? Maybe you need some help from us?' You can imagine how painful this was to us. Hitler was letting us know that he recognized our helplessness and was gloating over it.

(*Khrushchev Remembers*)

Questions

1 When did Stalin begin the great purge? Why?
2 How many people may have suffered in the end?

3 What were the occupations of most of the men Khrushchev mentions in Document one?
4 What is his opinion of these men?
5 What happened to all of them?
6 What other groups of Russians were purged?
7 When did Russia attack Finland? Why?
8 What connection is there between Stalin's purge and the events Khrushchev describes in Document Two?
9 What did the Russian failure in Finland encourage Hitler to do?

Stalin and Khrushchev

Document One

This extract comes from a book written in 1959 by Edward Crankshaw. He is an English historian and an expert on Russia.
Every country has its Blimps and deadheads, its stuffed shirts, its squares: but in no country are they as thick on the ground as they are in the Soviet Union; and in no country do they contrast so sharply with the new entry, who might come from a different country and, in a certain sense, do. The confident and un-frightened men are springing up like grass.

The interesting question is, where will they go? It is fascinating to speculate if, at some formal interview, one sits round a table with the different generations. The head man, it may be an important newspaper editor, will be in his fifties, bleakly pompous and totally void, the orthodoxy, the slogans and catchwords, which saved his life during the terrible years, now the sum total of his being. His young assistants, easy and assured, with more brains in their little fingers than he has in his whole body, are doing their best not to show their chief up (or are they?): but they do show him up with every word they say, expressing with every intonation knowledge and understanding which he lacks. They are poker-faced and restrained, but they make him look like a clod and a dolt, and an impure clot at that. Yet he is a member of the Central Committee of the Communist Party, one of the select two hundred.

I think at this moment of one extremely well-known Soviet personage, another ornament of the Central Committee, whom I have watched bullying his own staff like a bad head-waiter bullying a bus boy: and I have seen that man white with fear and tense so that he trembled, positively grovelling, again like a bad head-waiter, in the presence of a senior member of his

Government. But his subordinates did not join him in this exhibition: and they were not struck dead.

(*Khrushchev's Russia* — Edward Crankshaw)

Document Two

This is an extract from Khrushchev's speech to the Twentieth Party Congress in 1956:
Stalin was very far from an understanding of the real situation which was developing at the front. This was natural because during the whole Patriotic War he never visited any section of the front or any liberated city except for one short ride during a stabilized situation. Simultaneously Stalin was interfering with operations and issuing orders which did not take into consideration the real situation at a given section of the front and which could not help but result in huge losses.

I will give you one example of how Stalin directed operations. When there had developed an exceptionally serious situation for our army in 1942 in the Kharkov region, we had correctly decided to drop an operation whose objective was to encircle Kharkov, because the real situation would have threatened our army with fatal consequences if this operation were continued. We communicated this to Stalin who rejected our suggestion and issued the order to continue the operation.

I telephoned Vasilevsky and begged him, 'Alexander Mikhaelovich, take a map and show Comrade Stalin the situation which has developed'. We should note that Stalin planned operations on a globe. Yes, comrades, he used to take the globe and trace the front line on it.

Vasilevsky replied saying that Stalin had already studied this problem, and that he would not see Stalin any further concerning the matter because the latter didn't want to hear any arguments on the subject of this operation.

After my talk with Vasilevsky I telephoned Stalin at his villa. But Stalin did not answer the telephone and Malenkov was at the receiver. I told Comrade Malenkov that I was calling from the front and that I wanted to speak personally to Stalin. Stalin informed me through Malenkov that I should speak with Malenkov. I stated for the second time that I wished to inform Stalin personally about the grave situation which had arisen at the front. But Stalin did not consider it convenient to raise the phone. He said, through Malenkov, 'Let everything remain as it is!'

And what was the result of this? The worst that we had expected. The Germans surrounded our army concentrations and consequently we lost hundreds of thousands of our soldiers. This is Stalin's military 'genius'; this is what it cost us.

Questions

Document One

1 What differences does Crankshaw say there are between the older Communist officials and the younger ones?
2 Why did many men of poor ability hold important positions under Stalin?
3 Why did Khrushchev wish to replace them?
4 How did he do so? How were his methods different from Stalin's?

Document Two

5 What criticism was Khrushchev making of Stalin in this extract from his speech?
6 Why did it come as a surprise to the Russian people?
7 What other criticisms did Khrushchev make of Stalin in the same speech?
8 What connection is there between the problems described in Document One and Khrushchev's denunciation of Stalin?
9 What changes took place in Russia after this speech by Khrushchev?
10 What changes were there in Russia's foreign policy after this speech? Consider the West, the satellite states and China (see pages 304–10).

Questions

1 What name is given to the kind of goods listed here?
2 Draw a diagram to show how their output increased in Russia between 1955 and 1966.

3 Draw a further diagram to show how Russia and America compared in 1966. (You will need a different scale from your previous diagram.)
4 What is the one item of which the Russians had more than the Americans? Why do you suppose this was?
5 Who was in power in Russia during most of the years from 1955 to 1966?
6 Why did he encourage the production of the goods listed above?
7 Why was it possible for him to do so?
8 How was his policy different from Stalin's?

Russia in 1900

Questions

1 What geographical problem has led Russia to conquer new lands?
2 What was the population in 1900? What subject races were there?
3 What was the condition of agriculture?
4 What reforms did Alexander II make in 1861? Why did the peasants gain little?
5 What problem did the increase in population cause the peasants? How did it result in them hating the nobles?
6 What industries were developing?
7 How were communications improving?
8 Who was Count Sergey Witte? What did he do for industry?
9 Why did the number of factory workers increase? In what ways was life unpleasant for them?
10 What other social group grew in importance?
11 What ideas did Nicholas II have on government?
12 What was the Tsaritsa's main ambition? What was wrong with her son?
13 Name three organizations in the Tsar's government.

	Goods per 1000 of Population		
	Russia 1955	Russia 1966	U.S.A. 1966
Cars	2	5	398
Radios	66	171	1300
TV Sets	4	82	376
Refrigerators	4	40	293
Washing-machines	1	77	259
Sewing-machines	31	151	136

14 What were zemstvos? What work did they do? Why did the Tsar dislike them?

15 What political party did the middle classes form? What were their aims?

16 Why were most peasants not interested in politics? Who tried to interest them? What party did they form?

17 Which workers supported the Social Democratic Party? In what did they believe? Describe some of their activities.

18 Why did the Social Democratic Party split in 1903? Name the two groups and the leader of one of them.

19 What did the subject races wish to do?

20 What was the main weakness of the Tsar's enemies?

Give an account of Russia in 1900 under the headings: The Country and Its People/Government/Social Groups and Their Political Parties

The Russian Revolutions

Questions

1 What united the Tsar's enemies against him in 1905?

2 What happened on 'Bloody Sunday'?

3 What other troubles were there in 1905?

4 What did the middle classes do? What did they hope would happen?

5 What did the Petrograd workers do? Name one of their leaders.

6 Why did the Tsar give in? What did he promise? What was the reaction of the middle classes? What happened to the socialist parties and their leaders?

7 Why were the first two dumas quickly dissolved? Why did the third one remain?

8 How did Stolypin treat the revolutionary parties?

9 What social reforms did Stolypin make?

10 What changes did Stolypin make in agriculture? What new social group appeared as a result?

11 Why did the reforms end?

12 What was the reaction of the Russian people when war began?

13 Why did the Russian armies do badly in the war?

14 What economic problems did the war cause?

15 How did Rasputin obtain his hold over the royal family? How did he damage the Russian government?

16 Who murdered Rasputin? Why?

17 Who started the March Revolution of 1917? What did the soldiers and sailors do?

18 Who decided to form the Provisional Government? To which party did most of its members belong?

19 Who formed the Petrograd Soviet? Where did it meet? What did its Order No. 1 say?

20 What forced the Tsar to abdicate? What happened to him finally?

21 Who led the Provisional Government?

22 What popular changes were made by the Provisional Government? Name two mistakes it made and why.

23 Where was Lenin when the Revolution began? How did he return to Russia?

24 Give three reasons why the Bolsheviks were successful.

25 What set-back did the Bolsheviks have in July 1917?

26 How did Kornilov's attempt to seize power help the Bolsheviks?

27 On what two days did the Bolsheviks seize power in Petrograd? How did they do this? Why did the Russian army support them?

Give an account of the Russian Revolution under the headings: The Revolution of 1905/A Time of Progress 1906–14/Russia during the War/The March Revolution 1917/The Provisional Government and the Revolution of November 1917

From the Revolution to the Death of Lenin

Questions

1 Why was it difficult for the Communists to keep their hold on Russia?

2 What government did the Communists organize? Who was at its head?

3 What was the purpose of the Constituent Assembly? When did it meet? What happened to it?

4 How did the Communists terrorize their enemies?

5 What was done to please the peasants?

6 What treaty was signed with Germany? When? What were its terms?

7 Who were the 'Whites'? What foreign countries supported them? Why?
8 Name five White armies. Give the area in which each one fought, and say what foreign power helped it.
9 Give four advantages the Red Army had.
10 Who created the Red Army? What methods did he use?
11 How did Lenin make sure the Red Army had weapons and food?
12 Why was there war between Poland and Russia? Why did the Poles win? What treaty ended the war? What were its terms?
13 Why did the Russian economy collapse? What happened in industry and agriculture? What natural disaster was there? What was the result?
14 Why was there a mutiny at Kronstadt? How was it put down? What did Lenin decide to do afterwards?
15 What happened to industry under the N.E.P.? What happened to agriculture? How did the N.E.P. affect the Russian economy?
16 When did Lenin die? What do Communists today think of him?

Give an account of Russia from the Revolution to the Death of Lenin under the headings: Immediate Problems/The Civil War/The War with Poland/Economic Ruin, Famine and the N.E.P.

Russia under Stalin 1924–39

Questions

1 What post did Lenin give Stalin in 1922? Why did he choose this particular position? What use did Stalin make of it?
2 In your own words, what warning did Lenin give before he died?
3 How did Trotsky think Communism should develop? What were Stalin's views?
4 Why was Stalin able to overthrow Trotsky? What happened to Trotsky in the end?
5 What was the final stage in Stalin's road to power?
6 Why did Stalin want Russia to be a great industrial power? Why did he

think the New Economic Policy was wrong? What did he want Russian industry to produce? What was necessary before it would do this?
7 In what way was the N.E.P. against Communism?
8 What were the dates of the Five Year Plans?
9 What organization was in charge of planning? What did it do?
10 On what kind of industry did the Plans concentrate? What did the second Plan also develop?
11 Where were new industrial towns built? Why were these areas chosen?
12 In what ways were people made, and encouraged to work hard? (Four methods)
13 How did ordinary people suffer?
14 How successful were the Five Year Plans?
15 Name four ways in which Stalin hoped agriculture would help industry.
16 What farmers did the N.E.P. encourage? Why did Stalin want to be rid of them?
17 Describe how a collective farm was organized. Why should it have been efficient? How did the government help the collective farms?
18 How did the peasants resist the creation of collective farms? How did the government take revenge? What disaster was there as a result? How did Stalin change his policy? Why?
19 How far had agriculture recovered by 1935?
20 Why did Stalin become frightened? What was he prepared to do to keep power?
21 What was Stalin's excuse for starting the purge? What happened to people who were arrested?
22 What groups were attacked? How many people may have been purged altogether?
23 Why did Stalin decide to end the purge? When? How did he try to escape the blame?
24 What may the purge have achieved? Name one disastrous result that it had.

Write an account of Russia under Stalin 1924–39 under the headings: Stalin's Rise to Power/Stalin's Industrial Policy/Stalin's Agricultural Policy/The Great Purge

Russia since 1940

Questions

1 Describe some of the damage caused by the war. What natural disaster was there?
2 How did Stalin add to the problems?
3 How did Stalin help Russian industry recover? Why did the Russian people dislike his methods?
4 How did Stalin try to win support? How did he deal with opposition?
5 What happened in 1953 which made it seem there might be another purge?
6 How was Russia governed immediately after Stalin's death? Who were Khrushchev's main rivals?
7 Why was the Communist Party important for Khrushchev? How did he reform it?
8 Why did Khrushchev denounce Stalin? When did he do this? What accusations did he make against him?
9 What changes took place in Russia's population under Stalin's rule? What industries had Stalin encouraged?
10 What new class of people had come into being as a result of the growth of industry? What did Khrushchev say about its members?
11 What were the aims of Khrushchev's Seven Year Plans?
12 What problems were there in the organization of industry in Stalin's day?
13 What system did Khrushchev introduce? Why was it better? What political advantage did it bring him?
14 What was 'Libermannism'? What was was remarkable about introducing it into a Communist country?
15 What problems were there in Russian agriculture? Why did they worry Khrushchev?
16 How did Khrushchev try to please the peasants? What did he encourage them to do?
17 What was the Virgin Lands Scheme?
18 How far were Khrushchev's plans for agriculture a success?
19 When did Khrushchev fall from power? What were the possible reasons for this?
20 Who succeeded Khrushchev? How was their rule different?

Give an account of Russia since 1940 under the headings: Russia under Stalin 1941–53/ Khruschev's Rise to Power/Khrushchev's Reforms/Political Changes, Living Standards, Industry, Agriculture/ Khruschev's Fall and After

Problems

1 Why were political parties slow to develop in Russia?
2 Why were several Russian political parties extreme?
3 How did the Tsar's economic policies help bring about his overthrow?
4 What links were there between economic, social and political developments in Tsarist Russia?
5 Why was the revolution of 1905 a success at first? Why was it a comparative failure in the end?
6 Why did revolutions break out in Russia in 1917?
7 How did foreign wars influence affairs in Russia from 1905 to 1917?
8 Why did Kerensky fail and Lenin succeed?
9 Explain why the Bolsheviks were able both to seize power and to keep it.
10 Why did the Red Army win the civil war?
11 Why was Stalin able to seize power?
12 Did Stalin's rule do Russia more harm than good?
13 What were the results of Stalin's policies (a) from 1924 to 1939, (b) from 1945 to 1953?
14 How did Stalin, unconsciously, prepare the way for Khrushchev's reforms?
15 How did Khrushchev make Russia a better place to live in?
16 Why were both Stalin and Khrushchev more successful in developing industry than agriculture?
17 How has the Russian peasant influenced the history of his country in the twentieth century?
18 Why has Russia, with more natural resources than the United States, failed to make as much economic progress?
19 Why has Russia not become a democracy?

GERMANY

Chapter Eleven

The Weimar Republic

The Second Empire

DURING the Middle Ages, Germany was part of the Holy Roman Empire. Its Emperor, or Kaiser, was the Archduke of Austria, but he had little authority outside Austria itself. The so-called Empire was divided into hundreds of independent States, some no larger than market towns. During the Reformation in the sixteenth century, there was yet another division, between the northern States, which became Protestant, and the southern States, which remained Catholic.

Eventually, however, the States began to join together, the larger ones absorbing the smaller. In the south, Bavaria became the leading power, while in the north it was Prussia: she, in fact, was much larger than Bavaria. Then, in 1862, Bismarck became Prime Minister of Prussia, and he decided the time had come to make Germany one nation. A good way to unite people is to fight a successful war, so, in 1870, Prussia formed an alliance with the south German States and attacked France. The Germans won a complete victory, and made France surrender the provinces of Alsace and Lorraine. What was even more important, though, was that all

The unification of Germany 1848 and 1871

the German States agreed to form one united country. It was to be called the Second Empire, the first having been the Holy Roman Empire. It was proclaimed on 18 January 1871 in the Hall of Mirrors at Versailles — the very heart of France, the defeated enemy.

King William of Prussia now became Kaiser William I of Germany, and he appointed Bismarck as Imperial Chancellor. William was virtually an absolute ruler for, although there was a parliament, or Reichstag, it had no real powers. The only important check on the Kaiser came from the States for they had not given up their freedom entirely, by any means. They kept their own rulers, raised their own taxes, looked after religion and education, and ran their own railways.

William I died in 1886, to be succeeded by his son, William II. The following year William II dismissed Bismarck, changed his policies, and finally led Germany into the First World War. During the war he allowed Generals Hindenburg and Ludendorff to rule the country in his name.

The Establishment of the Weimar Republic

In November 1918 the German army was still unbroken, but it was in full retreat and Hindenburg and Ludendorff knew they had lost the war. They were now eager for civilians to take power. For one thing, they hoped that a civilian government might win more generous peace terms from the

Demobilization of the German Army, 1918

allies. As the largest party in the Reichstag was the Social Democrats, it was their leader Philipp Scheidemann who, on 9 November 1918, proclaimed a republic. The Kaiser abdicated at once: the armistice was signed on 11 November. The new government was worried because the fleet had mutinied, and there were strikes and riots in many cities, including Berlin. However, the army leaders promised to give support, provided the government did its best to keep order, and put down Communists.

In January 1919, the German people elected a National Constituent Assembly whose task was to draw up a constitution. It should have met in Berlin, but because of the troubles there, it went instead to the little town of Weimar. The Assembly decided there should be a Reichstag, elected by proportional representation, and whose work would be to make laws. The government of the country was to be under a President, elected directly by the people. He had a lot of power. He appointed and dismissed the Chancellor, and all the ministers; he was Commander-in-Chief of the armed forces; he could rule by decree, without consulting the Reichstag, if ever there was an emergency.

Friedrich Ebert, a Social Democrat, became the first President and Philipp Scheidemann was Chancellor.

Problems and Weaknesses of the Weimar Republic

The Weimar Republic had problems from the beginning.

In the first place, because of proportional representation, no single party ever had an absolute majority in the Reichstag. Usually, the Social Democrats formed a coalition with the Democratic Party, which represented the middle classes, and the Centre Party, which represented the Catholics. Unfortunately, the coalition was so weak that when there was a crisis in 1933, the President had to take over and rule by decree. As we shall see, this helped prepare the way for Hitler.

A further handicap was that the politicians who had founded the Weimar Republic had also to sign the peace treaty. As we have seen, the German army was defeated, but not broken. It came home in such perfect order that people could not believe it had lost the war. The only explanation was that it had been 'stabbed in the back' by men like the Social Democrats. When those same men went on to accept the humiliating terms of the Treaty of Versailles, they were branded as the 'November criminals'.

Thirdly, there were political parties that were trying to overthrow the Republic.

One of these was the Communist Party. As the war ended Communists caused a lot of disorder, but the most serious trouble was in Berlin in 1919, when a group called the Spartacists started a rebellion. They took their name from a gladiator called Spartacus who led a slave revolt in ancient Rome. The Spartacists were soon put down, and their leaders Karl Liebnecht and Rosa Luxemburg were brutally murdered. That was not the end of the Communists, though. The party did increasingly well at elections, so that by 1932 it held 100 of the 600 seats in the Reichstag.

There was also a danger from the extreme right, the men who had held power under the Kaiser. They were the high-ranking army officers, the industrialists and the great landowners, or junkers. They formed the Nationalist Party, whose aims were to restore the Kaiser, put down the Communists and destroy the trade unions. To back their arguments, they formed armed bands called 'Free Corps', some of them as well organized as the regular army. Many soldiers who returned from the war had no jobs, and were craving for excitement, so they gladly joined the Free Corps. It was these men who crushed the Spartacists.

The right wing organized a putsch, or an attempt to take power by force, in 1920. It was called the Kapp Putsch, after its leader. Kapp managed to take Berlin, but the government at once ordered a general strike. The economy of the country ground to a halt, so Kapp found it impossible to govern and fled. However, the Nationalists were still a serious threat. For example, they threw out a short-lived Communist government in Bavaria, and seized power there.

A third group which wanted to overthrow the Weimar Republic were the National Socialists, or Nazi Party. In the end, they succeeded, as you will see in the next chapter.

A further problem for the Weimar Republic was how to pay the reparations required by the Treaty of Versailles. They were so heavy that Germany fell behind on her payments almost immediately. At this, the French and the Belgians sent troops into the Ruhr, Germany's most valuable mining area, intending to help themselves to the coal they needed. The German government ordered passive resistance which meant that the miners went on strike, so there was no coal for the French and the Belgians to take. At the same time the occupation of the Ruhr did so much damage to the economy of the whole country that Germany stopped paying reparations altogether. The French and Belgians lost heavily, but in Germany the mark collapsed with disastrous results. Fortunately, in 1923, a very able politician, Gustav Stresemann, became Chancellor.

Stresemann saw that passive resistance was doing his country serious damage, so he decided instead on a 'policy of fulfilment'. That meant Germany would do her best to carry out her obligations under the Treaty of Versailles and, at the same time, hope to win more lenient treatment from her former enemies. Accordingly, Stresemann sent the Ruhr miners back to work, and called for talks on reparations. The result of the talks was the Dawes Plan of 1924. Under it, there was to be a Transfer Committee which was to decide how much Germany was able to pay year by year, which was better for her than having to find the same amount every year, regardless of the state of her economy. Also, the American government agreed to lend Germany considerable sums of money, so that the new plan made a good start. The allied armies now withdrew from the Rhineland, where they had been since the war ended, and the French and Belgians withdrew from the Ruhr.

As further proof of her goodwill Germany signed the Locarno Treaty in 1925, and joined the League of Nations in 1926. There is more about this on page 212.

Finally, in 1929, the Young Plan reduced Germany's reparations, and spread their payment over a longer period.

Stresemann's 'policy of fulfilment', then, had won his country important advantages. Reparations were less, the Americans were lending money, and the allied armies left. All Germany had given in return was a show of friendship and, as time was to prove, even that was not sincere.

So far we have looked at four of the Weimar Republic's problems — its constitution, its humiliation at the peace conference, its political enemies and reparations. As we have seen, the last of these was practically solved, and the others might have been overcome. Unfortunately, though, the Weimar Republic had also to face two economic crises. The first weakened it, and the second destroyed it.

When the French occupied the Ruhr, Germany's industry came to a halt. Moreover, because her factories were producing nothing her money was soon worth nothing. For example, in 1918 a dollar was worth four marks, but by the end of 1923 the figure was 130 000 million marks. In Germany, a loaf had once cost little more than half a mark: by the end of 1923, it cost 201 000 million marks. A very few clever business men did well out of the inflation, but most Germans lost. Wages just could not keep up with prices. There are stories of teachers who gave their pay to friends at the school gates so that they could go shopping for them. Had they waited until school was over, prices might well have doubled. Those who suffered most were retired people, trying to live on their savings. They had worked hard and saved all their lives only to find in the end they did not have enough money to buy a slice of bread.

The crisis was solved in three ways. In the first place, the government scrapped all the worthless marks and introduced a new currency. This was the renten-mark, or rent mark. As its name suggests, its value was fixed according to the price of land, which gave people confidence in it. Secondly, Stresemann ended passive resistance in the Ruhr, so German industry began producing goods again. Thirdly, foreign countries invested heavily in Germany. We have seen that the American government made loans under the Dawes Plan, but that was only the beginning of a flood of foreign capital. As a result, Germany prospered from 1924 to 1929, and many of her people were content. However, those who had been ruined by the inflation were unwilling to forgive the Weimar Republic, which they blamed for their misfortune.

The second blow came in 1930. We saw in Chapter 3 that there was a severe depression in America, which began in 1929. From there it spread to the rest of the trading countries of the world, with serious results for all of them, and especially Germany. Here, as in America, there was little sale of goods, so factories worked short time or closed altogether. To make matters worse, Germany depended heavily on American loans, and now the Americans took back their money. This time there was no inflation and indeed prices tended to fall. What this crisis brought was unemployment. By 1933 six million people were out of work. Again, the Weimar Republic had to take the blame, so that more people than ever wanted to overthrow it. The end came in 1933 when Hitler seized power.

Chapter Twelve

Hitler's Rise to Power

Early Life

HITLER was born in 1889 in the Austrian village of Braunau. He did badly at school, and, when he left, he failed as an artist. He was quite determined he would not take a steady job so he went to Vienna, where he lived the life of a tramp. He had a hard time, and was often near to starvation, but he learnt a great deal. At that time, Vienna was the capital of the Austro–Hungarian Empire — a complete mixture of peoples, many of whom were dominated by the Germans of Austria. It was easy to believe, then, that the Germans were a master race, destined to rule others. Another tradition in Vienna was anti-Semitism, or hatred of the Jews. People accused them of all sorts of absurd things, from organizing an international conspiracy against the German people to the ritual murder of Christian babies. For a man like Hitler, who badly needed someone to hate, Jews were a perfect target.

As well as these crude racist ideas, Hitler also learnt how to survive. He was so poor that he had to struggle and found that it was best to pretend to act decently but to be, in fact, greedy, selfish, ruthless and dishonest. That was how Hitler behaved to the tramps in the doss houses in Vienna, it was how he behaved to the German politicians during his struggle for power, and it was how he behaved to the countries of Europe when he became dictator.

In 1913, Hitler left Vienna for Munich in south Germany. As soon as war broke out, he volunteered for the German army and was delighted when he was able to join the 16th Bavarian Reserve Infantry Regiment. He was a dedicated soldier for he was fighting for the one thing he held dear, the German race. He won the Iron Cross twice, but he was promoted only once and that was to the modest rank of lance-corporal. He was lonely, friendless, and given to black, sullen moods and violent outbursts of temper. His officers must have thought he was not fit to have charge of other men, particularly on the field of battle.

In 1918, Hitler was temporarily blinded by gas, so he was in hospital recovering when the war ended. He was overcome with rage and distress. His only comfort was that he was sure that the German army had been stabbed in the back by the 'November criminals'. No one hated the Weimar Republic more than he did.

The Early Years of the Nazi Party 1919–24

When the war was over, Hitler decided that the only way to lead an exciting life was to go into politics. He decided, too, that he would not join one of the important parties because in any of them he would be a nobody. However, in September 1919 he went to a meeting in Munich of the German Workers' Party. It was little more than a debating society with only forty members. None of them had such strong ideas as Hitler, or could speak as violently as he did, so he became their leader. Under Hitler, the meetings changed completely. Instead of small groups holding discussions, people gathered in their hundreds to listen to stormy speeches, and to shout and cheer. Hitler also gave the party a new name. It was now the National Socialist German Workers' Party, or Nazi Party for short.

For some time the Nazi Party was unimportant, but then it came under the protection of some high-ranking army officers, especially General Ernst Röhm. They were Nationalists, and they hoped the Nazis might win them some support from the ordinary people. A number of business men also became interested in the Nazis, and they gave them money. Hitler used it to start a newspaper, the *Volkischer Beobachter* or *People's Observer*, and to organize a private army of brown-shirted storm-troopers, known as the S.A.

Hitler and the S.A. at Kiel 1933

The Nazis went from strength to strength and then with the collapse of the mark and the inflation of 1923, Hitler thought his chance had come. He would organize a putsch in Munich, and march on Berlin, just as Mussolini had marched on Rome. To succeed, he needed the help of the Bavarian government and the local units of the German army, but their leaders could not decide whether to join the putsch or not. Hitler determined to make up their minds for them. He heard that on 8 November there was to be a meeting at a beer hall in Munich, and that von Kahr, the head of the Bavarian government, von Seisser, the chief of police, and von Lossow, the local army commander, would all be there. Hitler went to the meeting with some armed thugs and captured all three. He then proclaimed a new government that was to include the great General Ludendorff, and prepared to march on Berlin. This was the famous 'beer hall putsch'. However, von Kahr and von Lossow, far from being persuaded to join, escaped, so the Nazis had to march alone. Very soon they ran into a small body of police who opened fire, killing sixteen. Hitler and everyone else fled. Ludendorff alone went forward, brushing the policemen's rifles contemptuously aside as he strode through their ranks.

Shortly afterwards Hitler was captured and sentenced to five years imprisonment. While in jail he dictated *Mein Kampf* (My Struggle), one of the most famous books of all time, and also one of the most boring. The Bavarian authorities gave him as much comfort as he would have found in the best hotel and he served only nine months of his sentence anyway. However, when he left prison at the end of 1924, Hitler had learnt a lesson. He decided he would never organize another revolution, but would come to power legally.

Nazi Ideas and Tactics

As early as 1920 Hitler and his cronies had drawn up what they called their Twenty-five Points. These summarized the views of the National Socialist movement.

Some of the ideas were nationalist. All Nazis believed the Germans were a superior race, and they especially despised the Jews. They also hated Communists. Communism was an international movement aiming to unite the workers in every country against their rulers. That was quite contrary to what the Nazis wanted which was to unite Germans of all classes, rich and poor, to fight against enemy nations.

Other Nazi ideas were socialist, which is not surprising because the men who started the party were workers. They were against capitalists and the great landowners. They thought that the big firms should be nationalized, that the large stores should be broken up to give small shopkeepers a chance, and that the State should have power to confiscate any land it needed, without payment. However, such notions soon gave Hitler a problem. He needed money from industrialists and they were hardly likely to finance a party that planned to nationalize their factories. Accordingly, as time went on, Hitler did his best to drop the socialist ideas. However, that in turn created a difficulty, because if the Nazis favoured the rich, how

Germans! Stand up for yourselves! Don't buy from Jews!

could they persuade ordinary people to vote for them? All Hitler could do was be dishonest, and pretend to be on everyone's side. In the normal way he would never have succeeded, but in fact he was able to unite people of all walks of life behind him because of their common hatred of the Weimar Republic. This was particularly true during the economic crises. The collapse of the mark in 1923 encouraged the Nazis to carry out the beer hall putsch: the mass unemployment of the 1930s brought them to power.

Hitler's ideas, then, were crude and illogical. However, his methods were brilliant. He was one of the greatest demagogues that has ever lived. It is impossible to say quite what it was that enabled him to sway millions of Germans, but some of his tricks are clear enough.

In the first place, Hitler always expressed simple ideas, and repeated them constantly, so no one had the slightest difficulty in understanding him.

Secondly, though there was plenty of printed Nazi propaganda, Hitler relied mainly on the spoken word. It is much easier to move people with a rousing speech, than it is with a piece of writing.

Thirdly, Hitler played on powerful emotions. He had an uncanny feel for the mood of an audience, and once he had grasped it, he could induce his listeners almost to hysteria. Favourite topics were national pride, the evils of the Versailles Settlement, and hatred of the Jews. Fourthly, there were spectacular displays. Thousands of storm-troopers marched in perfect formation, great red and black flags with swastikas hung from the buildings, bands played stirring music, and when the time came for the speeches, a huge dome of searchlights shone over the packed square. At the end, the crowd burst into song, either the national anthem *Deutschland Uber Alles*, or the S.A.'s own anthem the *Horst Wessell* song. Finally, the Nazis used violence, tearing down posters, breaking up rival meetings and attacking speakers. There are some people who hate violence; there are, however, many others who are attracted to it, as anyone who has enjoyed a fight on television will know.

We can now begin to understand why Hitler came to power. The first reason was the weakness of the Weimar Republic. That is explained in the previous chapter. The second reason was the strength of the Nazis. No other party was as ruthless, as determined, or made such a strong appeal to the German people.

Hitler's Road to Power 1924–34

From 1924 to 1929 Germany prospered, so the Nazis, who thrived on discontent, made little progress. Hitler did not waste these years, for he organized branches of his party throughout Germany, so that he became well-known as a national politician and not just the leader of a movement in Bavaria. Apart from that, he could do little but wait. His chance came at last, with the economic depression of the 1930s.

In the first place, democratic government collapsed. The political parties should have worked together until the crisis was over, but, instead, they argued amongst themselves more fiercely than ever. No one party had a majority in the Reichstag, because of proportional representation, and now it was impossible to hold a coalition together. The President at that time was Hindenburg, who had been Commander-in-Chief during the war. Bruning, the Chancellor, told him he would have to use his emergency powers under the constitution, and rule by decree. Even when Hindenburg made his decrees, Bruning still could not govern the country so Hindenburg appointed Franz von Papen as Chancellor and then General Kurt von Schleicher. Neither did any better than Bruning because, like him, they did not have the support of the people. We can see then that it was not Hitler who destroyed democracy in Germany: the men who came before him did that.

Meanwhile the Nazi Party was growing in strength. Rich people feared the Communists, who were also becoming more powerful, so they gave the Nazis millions of marks in order to fight their election campaigns. The coal owners and the steel manufacturers of the Rhineland and Westphalia were particularly generous. The ordinary Germans could not give money, but many of them gave their votes, while 300 000 unemployed men joined the S.A.

In 1932 there were no less than five major elections. The Nazis had money, they had support from the people, and the S.A. was strong enough to terrorize its opponents. As a result they won more seats in the Reichstag than any other party, but they did not have the absolute majority Hitler needed. Towards the end of the year their strength began to wane, and Hitler was in despair.

At this point Franz von Papen intervened. He was the man who had been Chancellor for a short while, and during that time he had won over Hindenburg, who now had complete faith in him. Also, von Papen was friendly with the leaders of the Nationalist Party, which represented 'the old gang'. They were the industrialists, landowners and high-ranking army officers who had ruled Germany during the Kaiser's day. Von Papen's aim was to bring 'the old gang' back to power, but they had so few seats in the Reichstag that they could never do this alone. How could they possibly win support from the people? Von Papen's scheme was that they should join forces with the Nazis. Hitler would have to be Chancellor, because he represented the larger party, but von Papen was to be Vice-Chancellor and the Nazis were to have no more than three seats out of a total of eleven in the cabinet. In that way 'Foxy' von Papen hoped to use Hitler for his own ends. Hindenburg despised Hitler, but none the less he did as von Papen asked and appointed him Chancellor. This was on 30 January 1933. It was a fateful day in the history of Germany and the world.

Hitler, of course, had no intention of being used by von Papen, or anyone else, and was determined to have real power. His first move was to force yet another election hoping that the Nazis might at last win an absolute majority. It seemed that they had a good chance since, as Chancellor, Hitler could use the press and radio for propaganda, while the S.A. was now two million strong. Then on 27 February 1933, a week before election day, the Nazis had an incredible piece of good luck. The Reichstag was burnt down, and a half-witted Dutch Communist called van der Lubbe confessed to the crime. The Nazis screamed that there was a Communist plot to destroy Germany, so the very next day Hindenburg signed a decree 'for the protection of the People and the State'. In effect, it gave Hitler the power to arrest anyone he wished. Among the first were the Communist deputies in the Reichstag.

The election results were not all that the Nazis had hoped, as they still had less than half the seats in the Reichstag. However, putting the Communists in jail gave the Nazis a slight majority. Even that was not good enough for Hitler. He wanted an 'Enabling Law', which would allow him to rule for four years without the Reichstag, or the President, and so have absolute power. His excuse was that Germany needed strong government for a short time, until the economic crisis was over — though, of course, once he had gained power he had no intention of letting it go. However, the new law meant changing the Constitution, which needed a two-thirds majority and this the Nazis did not have.

Hitler worked hard to win over the Nationalists and the Catholic Centre Party. For the opening of the Reichstag he staged a magnificent ceremony in Potsdam Church. The S.A. paraded with the army: the Nazi deputies sat with the Nationalists: at the climax of the ceremony Hitler shook Hindenburg's hand, bowing low before him. When they saw the new Germany paying homage to the old in all these ways, the Nationalists were convinced Hitler was sincere in his wish to help his country. As for the Catholic Centre Party, Hitler was able to persuade them that he would always respect the rights of the Church. When the time came for the vote

89

on the Enabling Law, 441 deputies declared for it, and only 94 against. The Nazi deputies sprang to their feet, and with arms outstretched, roared the *Horst Wessel* song. They had every reason to be pleased.

Still Hitler was not satisfied, for he knew he would have a rival as long as Germany had a President. Hindenburg had lost most of his powers because of the Enabling Law, but he was still Commander-in-Chief of the armed forces. He was so old that Hitler was content to wait until he died. However, he was determined there should not be another President, but that he should have his power to himself. As this would make Hitler Commander-in-Chief, he had to persuade the army leaders to agree. They did indeed, but their price was a high one. Hitler must curb the S.A. As we have seen, the S.A. was two million strong, so it was twenty times the size of the regular army. Its commander was Ernst Röhm, the general who had helped Hitler in the early days of the Nazi Party. He wanted the S.A. to merge with the regular army and to take it over. The regular officers, though, were from wealthy and aristocratic families, and they objected strongly to their beloved Reichswehr being handed to the rabble. As we shall see, Hitler was by now finding the S.A. a nuisance so he was quite willing to destroy it, which he did in June 1934. What happened is described in the next chapter.

Hindenburg died two months later, aged 84. The offices of President and Chancellor were merged, Hitler taking the title of 'Führer and Reich Chancellor'.

Summary The story of Hitler's rise to power is complicated, so we will look at the main reasons for it.

In the first place, the Weimar Republic was weak, both politically and economically.

Secondly, powerful forces worked in the Nazis' favour, especially during the depression of the early 1930s. The Communists gained strength, which frightened the German industrialists into giving Hitler the money he needed to fight elections and pay his storm-troopers. Mass unemployment meant that some 40 per cent of the German people were willing to vote for the Nazis. The Nationalists thought they could use the Nazis to put themselves in power.

Thirdly, the Nazis were unscrupulous and determined. Hitler, their leader, was both these things, and, moreover, he had the cunning and the skill to make full use of every piece of good luck that came his way.

Chapter Thirteen

Germany under Hitler

HAVING become dictator Hitler tried to make sure he would never be overthrown. He developed new forms of government, he crushed his enemies, and he did a great deal to win the support of the German people.

The Nazi Government

We have already seen that the decree Hindenburg signed after the Reichstag fire meant Hitler could arrest his opponents, while the Enabling Law allowed him to make any law he pleased. Admittedly the Enabling Law was to last for only four years but Hitler simply renewed it as soon as the time was up. Further, when Hindenburg died, Hitler took over what was left of the President's authority, so that he had absolute power.

The Reichstag, Germany's parliament, was still there, but all the deputies were Nazis and when they held their rare meetings, there was only one speaker — Adolf Hitler.

Under the Second Empire and the Weimar Republic, the German States had enjoyed a good deal of freedom. Hitler would not tolerate that. Instead of State governments, elected by the people, there were State governors, appointed by Hitler.

The German law courts remained for all ordinary cases, but Hitler would not allow them to try his political opponents. There was always a chance they might return a fair verdict! Accordingly, there were special courts for treason and political offences.

The most sinister of Hitler's weapons, though, was the police. By 1936, all branches of the police were under the control of the S.S., headed by Heidrich Himmler. Originally, the S.S., or Protection Units, were Hitler's own bodyguard, but their numbers had grown, and so had their duties. Some of the S.S. belonged to the Gestapo, or State Security Police, and others were members of the S.D., or Security Service. Members of the Gestapo wore uniforms, but those in the S.D. were political detectives, sent to spy on the German people. No one knew where an S.D. agent might be lurking, so all sensible people were careful what they said, even when they were among those they imagined to be friends. One important duty the S.S. had was to run the concentration camps. These places held 25 000 prisoners by 1939, and ten times that number before the war ended.

The Removal of Opposition

The Nazis saw as their rivals the trade unions, the other political parties, and the Churches.

The trade unions were suppressed, their offices were closed and their leaders were arrested. Workmen now had to join an organization called the Labour Front. This negotiated wages for them but, on the whole, it did more to keep them under control than to help them. There were no more strikes.

All political parties were made illegal except, of course, the Nazis. Hitler hated Communists nearly as much as he did Jews, so it is not surprising that their party was smashed and its leaders sent to concentration camps. As was expected Hitler also broke up the Social Democratic Party, for that had always been against him. However, the members of the Nationalist Party, and the Catholic Centre Party, who had helped bring Hitler to power, expected that they at least would be left alone. To their indignation, the Nazis rounded on them as well, and destroyed their organizations.

As well as enemies outside the Nazi Party, Hitler saw others, possibly more dangerous, who were inside it. Some two million discontented Germans had joined the S.A. They had terrorized the opponents of the Nazis, they had fought many street battles and they felt that they, more than anyone, had brought Hitler to power. Now they expected him to find them easy, well-paid jobs as their reward. Also, many members of the S.A. were from working-class families, so they believed in the old socialist principles of the Nazi movement. For example, they wanted industry to be nationalized. Moreover, their leaders had ideas: we have already seen that Röhm hoped the S.A. would take over the army.

Hitler, on the other hand, wanted help from the industrialists. Only they could run the factories efficiently and make Germany rich and powerful. He also needed help from the army if he was to take over the power of the President. Even though many of the S.A. were Hitler's best friends and most loyal supporters, he did not hesitate. On the night of 30 June 1934, 'the night of the long knives', members of the S.S. murdered several hundred of the S.A. leaders. They included Ernst Röhm, the man who had given the Nazis invaluable help, especially during the early, difficult years in Bavaria. For that reason, the murders are known as the 'Röhm Purge'. It was not only S.A. men who died, for many other old scores were settled. 'Foxy' von Papen, who had hoped to make Hitler his puppet, felt he was lucky to escape with his life, and go to Vienna as ambassador.

So far then, we have seen how Hitler disposed of the trade unions and his political rivals. There remained the Churches, and they gave him more problems than the other two. He knew that many Germans were very religious, so he had to move carefully. His plan was to pretend to accept Christianity, but, at the same time, to work against it in as many under-hand ways as possible.

In the north of Germany most people were Protestants. Hitler tried to deal with them by uniting them all in a 'Reich Church' under Nazi control. Some pastors submitted to this, but others, led by Martin Niemöller, formed the 'Confessional Church', which opposed the Nazis. Niemöller was sent to a concentration camp, but the Confessional Church kept many followers until the end of the war.

The south of Germany was the stronghold of the Catholics. In 1933, to please them, Hitler made an agreement, or Concordat, with the Vatican. By this, he guaranteed the freedom of the Roman Catholic Religion. Almost at once, he broke his promise. Catholic schools became Nazi schools, the Catholic Youth League was destroyed and Catholic books and newspapers were banned. Some priests were murdered, while others were arrested on trumped-up charges. The Pope condemned Hitler's actions, and in Germany itself there were men brave enough to preach openly against Nazism. One of them was Cardinal Faulhaber of Munich, whose influence was so great that Hitler dared not order his arrest.

Generally, though, the churchmen who resisted Hitler, whether Protestant or Catholic, were only trying to defend their religion. They did not attempt to overthrow him. Nor were they all united against him, for there were some clergy who were willing to swear an oath of loyalty to him, and to say that good Christians should be Nazis. The Churches certainly irritated Hitler, but they were never a danger to him.

Measures to Win Support

Hitler was too clever to rely only on crushing his rivals. He had come to power with the backing of between a third and a half of the German people, and he meant to increase that support even more.

In the first place, the Nazis went on with their attacks on the Jews. A good many Germans hated the Jews, long before the Nazis appeared, and Hitler used this hatred to unite his people. Now that he was in power he was able to pass anti-Semitic laws. The most important were the Nuremberg Laws of 1935, which said the Jews were no longer German citizens and forbade them to marry Germans. There were other decrees which robbed the Jews of their freedom, especially the right to work. At first they were not allowed to be lawyers, doctors, civil servants, teachers or journalists. The list then grew longer, so that by 1939, half the Jews in Germany were unable to find jobs.

Many people followed Hitler's lead. Shops refused to serve Jews so that in some towns they could not buy medicines or milk for their children. There was a great deal of 'Jew-baiting' since anyone could annoy or attack a Jew without fear of the police. The most savage outburst before the war was on 9 November 1938. A young Polish Jew assassinated a German embassy official in Paris, and that led to an orgy of violence and destruction. Some 7000 shops were looted and so many windows were smashed that 9 November was known as 'Crystal Night'. The S.S. arrested 20 000 Jews while the government fined the Jewish people 1000 million marks.

Secondly, Hitler tried to win over the German people with propaganda. The man who organized it was Dr Goebbels. He had absolute control of the press and the radio, and he made them repeat the same lies so often that in the end even intelligent Germans were beginning to believe them. Also, to

93

Hitler addresses troops at Nuremberg, 1938

stop anyone reading anti-Nazi ideas there was a 'burning of the books'. Nazis went through the public and university libraries, seizing any books they disliked. They then threw them into bonfires, while crowds stood around and cheered. Displays and parades still went on, only now they were more spectacular than ever. There was a cycle of them through the year — rather like the Christian festivals — the climax being the Nuremberg Rally on 9 November. This was to commemorate the 'heroes' who died during the beer hall putsch of 1923. After a solemn procession, Hitler would pay homage before their iron coffins.

Thirdly, all young Germans were brought up to be good Nazis. Teachers had to belong to the National Socialist Teachers' League, so they were under the control of the Nazis. Many textbooks were rewritten, but especially history ones. However, the Hitler Youth was more important than the schools. Children had to join when they were six. They were taught Nazi beliefs, learning, for example, to hate Jews and admire Hitler. They also had plenty of fresh air and exercise, and after the age of fourteen, military training as well. The result was that when the war came, the young Germans made tough soldiers who were much fitter than their enemies, including the British.

Finally, Hitler won support because Germany began to prosper again. Unlike Stalin, who concentrated on heavy industry, Hitler allowed German factories to make consumer goods, so the shops filled with things the people wanted to buy. There was even a scheme to give every family the chance to own a Volkswagen, or 'people's car', though the war put a stop to that. Moreover, it was not long before everybody had a job. In 1933, there were six million unemployed, but by 1939 there were one million job vacancies. In fact, as we shall see, Hitler had very little to do with this apparent miracle, but of course he took all the credit. The average German had lost his trade union, he had lost his political freedom, he was afraid to speak as he felt, and the Nazis were even trying to stifle his right to think for himself. However all this seemed a small price to pay for a steady, secure job. Here then is the most important reason for Hitler's success. Mass unemployment brought him to power: full employment kept him there.

Economic Policy

Hitler was anxious that Germany should be wealthy, because he hoped there would be enough money to do two things. He wanted the ordinary people of Germany to be well off, so that they would be contented under Nazi rule. He also wanted to build up his armed forces until Germany was once again the most powerful country in Europe. Certainly, Germany recovered from the depression of the 1930s and was prosperous by 1939. We must look at the reasons why.

As soon as he came to power, Hitler started the 'Battle for Work', setting the unemployed to make the autobahn, and construct lavish public buildings. These were useful short-term measures, but it was more important to increase the output of manufactured goods. Here the government helped the factory owners by disciplining the workers. There were no more trade unions or strikes, workers could not leave their jobs without permission, and wages were held down. As a result firms made good profits. However, they were not allowed to pay dividends of more than 6 per cent to their shareholders, so there was plenty of money to build new factories, buy modern equipment and so forth.

A man who did excellent work was Dr Hjalmar Schacht, President of the Reichsbank and Minister of Economics. He was not a Nazi, but he was so able that Hitler was more than happy to use him. Schacht saw that one of Germany's main problems was a shortage of foreign currency. She was like a family with a low income, which must be careful how it spends, and do its best to earn more. Schacht's policy for Germany was much the same. He made traders spend the little foreign money they had on the goods Germany really needed. For example he encouraged them to buy iron ore, but put strict limits on imports of raw wool and cotton. So that Germany could earn more foreign money, Schacht encouraged exports. He rewarded firms who exported goods by paying them bounties, and he made trading agreements with countries all over the world.

However, the main reason for Germany's recovery was the revival of world trade that came with the easing of the depression after 1933. No one in Germany was responsible for that, but what Schacht did do was take full advantage of the good luck. Hitler had reason to be pleased, for as early as 1937 exports had increased 25 per cent and imports 32 per cent, while industrial output had doubled.

In time, it is likely that Hitler could have won both his aims of a wealthy people and a powerful country, but he grew impatient. In 1936, he ordered

95

Goering to draw up a Four Year Plan to prepare for war. Goering knew that as soon as the war began, Germany would be blockaded, so he tried to make her self-sufficient. By the treaty of Versailles she had lost Lorraine and with it, three-quarters of her iron ore. However, in many parts of the country there were deposits of ore which were so lean that no one had bothered with them. Now, special Hermann Goering Works were built to exploit them. German chemists were also busy: they discovered, for example, how to extract oil and petrol from coal, and how to make plastics and synthetic rubber.

Many of these new schemes were wasteful, as Schacht realized, but what really alarmed him was rearmament. Hitler introduced conscription, and raised the size of the regular army enormously. All these men who might have been producing wealth were instead doing military training, and what is more, they had to be clothed and fed. Hitler insisted, too, that the services should have the best of everything. Moreover, shipyards, aircraft factories and armaments works were busy producing weapons, and the money they took might have been used to make goods either for export, or for the German people to buy in the shops. Schacht saw the folly of it all and, after a stormy scene with Hitler, was allowed to resign. Goering now carried on alone, and even though he had none of Schacht's skill, Germany was ready for war in 1939. How was that possible?

The explanation is simple. As Hitler and Goering saw it, the country could either have guns or butter, and they decided it should be guns. That meant, in effect, that the ordinary workers had to pay for rearmament. This drove up prices for it created a shortage of goods of all kinds. However, wages stayed the same, so they bought less and less as time went on. Hitler had wanted his people to be prosperous and his country to be strong. When he found he could not have both, he chose the latter. Why, then, did he not have trouble? One reason, as we have already seen, was full employment. After all, the armaments works created jobs if they did not create wealth. Also, Hitler made the workers' sacrifice seem worthwhile, for he was brilliantly successful in his foreign policy. This is described in Chapter 30.

WORK SECTION — Germany

Questions

1 Where is the Ruhr Valley?
2 Why was it especially important for the German economy?
3 When did the French occupy it? Why?
4 Why were the Germans unable to prevent them?
5 What resistance did the Germans make?
6 What economic problems did the occupation of the Ruhr cause for Germany?
7 Who solved these problems and how?

French occupation of the Ruhr

8 What links are there between the French occupation of the Ruhr and Hitler's rise to power?

Hitler's Ideas

The following are extracts from Hitler's book *Mein Kampf* and from some of his speeches.

Document One

I do not remember ever having heard the word 'Jew' at home during my father's lifetime. Then, one day when passing through the Inner City of Vienna, I suddenly encountered a phenomenon in a long caftan and wearing black sidelocks. My first thought was: is this a Jew? I watched the man stealthily and cautiously, but the longer I gazed at this strange countenance and examined it section by section, the more the question shaped itself in my brain: is this a German? I turned to books for help in removing my doubts. For the first time in my life I bought myself some anti-Semitic pamphlets for a few pence.

(Mein Kampf)

Document Two

Was there any shady undertaking, any form of foulness, especially in cultural life, in which at least one Jew did not participate? On putting the probing knife carefully to that kind of abcess one immediately discovered, like a maggot in a putrescent body, a little Jew who was often blinded by the sudden light.

(Mein Kampf)

Document Three

My inner aversion to the Hapsburg State was increasing daily. This motley of Czechs, Poles, Hungarians, Ruthenians, Serbs and Croats, and always the bacillus which is the solvent of human society, the Jew, were here and there and everywhere. The longer I lived in that city the stronger became my hatred for the promiscuous swarm of foreign peoples which had begun to batten on that old nursery ground of German culture. All these considerations intensified my yearning to depart for that country for which my heart had been secretly longing since the days of my youth. I hoped to be among those who lived and worked in that land from which the movement should be launched, the object of which would be the fulfilment of what my heart had always longed for, the reunion of the country in which I was born with our common fatherland, the German Empire. *(Mein Kampf)*

Document Four

We want to call to account the November Criminals of 1918. It cannot be that two million Germans should have fallen in vain and that afterwards one should sit down as friends at the same table with traitors. No, we do not pardon, we demand — vengeance! The dishonouring of the nation must cease. For betrayers of the Fatherland and informers, the gallows is the proper place.

(Hitler at Munich, 18 September 1922)

Document Five

The Marxists taught — if you will not be my brother, I will bash your skull in. Our motto shall be — if you will not be a German, I will bash your skull in. For we are convinced that we cannot succeed without a struggle. We have to fight with ideas, but, if necessary, also with our fists.

(Hitler at Munich, 22 November, 1922)

Document Six

This is an extract from a speech to some German industrialists:
And when people cast in our teeth our intolerance, we proudly acknowledge it — yes we have formed the inexorable decision to destroy Marxism in Germany down to its very last root. Either we shall succeed in working out a body-politic hard as iron from this conglomeration of parties, associations and unions, and from this pride and madness of class, or else, lacking this internal consolidation, Germany will fall in final ruin.

Remember that it means sacrifice when today many hundreds of S.A. and S.S. men every day have to mount on their lorries, protect meetings, undertake marches, sacrifice themselves night after night and then come back in the grey dawn to workshop and factory, or as unemployed to take the pittance of the dole: it means sacrifice when from the little they possess they have to buy their uniforms, their shirts, their badges, yes, and even pay their own fares. But there is already in all this the force of an ideal — a great ideal! And if the whole German nation today had the same faith in its vocation as these hundred thousands, if the whole nation possessed this idealism, Germany would stand in the eyes of the world otherwise than she stands now!

(Hitler to the Industry Club at Dusseldorf, 27 January 1932)

Questions

1 What do the words *Mein Kampf* mean? When did Hitler write this book?

Document One

2 Why did the events Hitler describes here mark a turning-point in his life?

Document Two

3 What accusation does Hitler make against the Jews?

Document Three

4 What was the 'Hapsburg State'?
5 What did Hitler dislike about it?
6 Where did he long to go? When did he, in fact, go there?
7 What did he hope would one day happen?
8 When and how did this dream come true? (See page 214.)

Document Four

9 Who were the 'November Criminals'?
10 What does Hitler feel about them?

Document Five

11 Which of his ideas does Hitler express here?
12 What methods does he say he is willing to use?
13 When did he, in fact, use these methods? How effective were they?

Document Six

14 What is the 'inexorable decision' that Hitler says the Nazis have made?
15 Why would this please his audience?
16 Why was it especially important for him to please such people?
17 What does he say had gone wrong with Germany?
18 What does he say must be done to put things right?
19 According to Hitler what sacrifices are the S.A. and S.S. making?
20 What do you suppose is the 'ideal' which Hitler says they have?
21 Name some of the things done by the S.A. and S.S. at this time, which Hitler does not mention.
22 Make a list of Hitler's ideas which are shown in these extracts
23 Name some of the things which happened when Hitler put those ideas into practice.

The Persecution of the Jews

This is an extract from a book by Albert Speer who was first Hitler's architect and later his Minister of Armaments. He was sentenced to 20 years imprisonment at the Nuremberg trials.

On 10 November 1938, driving to the office, I passed the still smouldering ruins of the Berlin synagogues. Today, this memory is one of the most doleful of my life, chiefly because what really disturbed me at the time was the aspect of disorder that I saw on Fasanenstrasse: charred beams, collapsed facades, burned-out walls — anticipations of a scene that during the war would dominate much of Europe. Most of all I was troubled by the political revival of the 'gutter'. The smashed panes of shop windows offended my sense of middle-class order.

I did not see that more was being smashed than glass, that on that night Hitler had taken a step that irrevocably sealed the fate of his country. Did I sense, at least for a moment, that something was beginning which would end with the annihilation of one whole group of our nation? I do not know.

I accepted what had happened rather indifferently. I felt myself to be Hitler's architect. Political events did not concern me, I was expected to confine myself to the job of building.

During the years after my release from Spandau I have been repeatedly asked what thoughts I had on this subject during my two decades alone in the cell with myself: what I actually knew of the persecution, the deportation and the annihilation of the Jews: what I should have known and what conclusions I ought to have drawn.

I no longer give the answers with which I tried for so long to soothe the questioners, but chiefly myself: that in Hitler's system, as in every totalitarian regime, when a man's position rises, his isolation increases and he is therefore more sheltered from harsh reality; that with the application of technology to the process of murder, the number of murderers is reduced and therefore the possibility of ignorance grows; that the craze for secrecy built into the system makes it easy to escape observing inhuman cruelties.

I now longer give any of these answers. It is true that as a favourite and later as one of Hitler's most influential ministers I was isolated. It is also true that the habit of thinking within my own field provided me, both as architect and as Armaments Minister, with many opportunities for evasion. It is true that I did not know what was really beginning on 9

November 1938, and what ended in Auschwitz
and Maidanek. But in the final analysis I
myself determined the degree of my isolation,
the extremity of my evasions, and the extent of
my ignorance.

(*Inside the Third Reich* — Albert Speer)

Questions

1 What was the main reason for the persecution of the Jews?
2 What name was given to the night of 9
November 1938?
3 What happened on that night? What
had provoked the outburst?
4 What were Speer's feelings when he
saw the ruined synagogues?
5 What does he think should have
bothered him?
6 Why was he more or less indifferent in
1938?
7 What questions was he asked after his
release from Spandau prison?
8 What answers did he once give to those
questions?
9 Why does he no longer think those
answers are satisfactory?
10 As this extract suggests, Speer had
nothing directly to do with the persecution of the Jews. Do you agree that
he should have feelings of guilt?

The German Economy under Hitler

Questions

1 Draw graphs from the two tables
shown below.
2 Account for the growth of the German
economy between 1933 and 1939.

3 Who was the minister who did a great
deal to help this? Why did he resign?
4 Account for the rise in military expenditure.
5 What was the percentage increase
between 1933 and 1939 in (a) Gross
National Product and (b) Military Expenditure?
6 What did the difference in these two
growth rates mean for (a) the German
economy and (b) the German workers?

The Weimar Republic

Questions

1 Which statesman united Germany?
How did he do it? When? What did
Germany take from France at that
time?
2 How much power did the German
emperor have? What was his title? Who
was emperor at the time of the First
World War?
3 Why did Hindenburg and Ludendorff
want there to be a civilian government
when the war ended? Who proclaimed
the republic? On what condition did
the army give support to the new
government?
4 Where did the National Constituent
Assembly meet? Describe the work of
the Reichstag and the powers of the
President under the new constitution.
5 What problem did proportional representation create? What had to happen
in 1933?
6 What reason did the enemies of the
Weimar Republic give for Germany
losing the war?

	Gross National Product (1933 = 100)	Military Expenditure (Millions of marks)
1933	100	1900
1934	111	1900
1935	120	4000
1936	131	5800
1937	143	8200
1938	157	18 400
1939	173	32 300

A country's Gross National Product is its output of goods and services.
Here it is compared year by year with 1933.

7 What Communist group tried to seize power in 1919? What happened? How well did the Communist Party do after that?

8 What people belonged to the extreme right? What party did they form? What were the 'Free Corps'?

9 What right-wing leader tried to seize power in 1920? Why did he fail?

10 What other political party also wanted to overthrow the Weimar Republic?

11 Why did the French and Belgians occupy the Ruhr? What action did the German government take? What happened in Germany, as a result?

12 When did Stresemann become Chancellor? What did he mean by his 'policy of fulfilment'? What action did he take?

13 What was to happen under the Dawes Plan? What two areas of Germany were evacuated?

14 How else did Germany try to show goodwill?

15 What was to happen under the Young Plan?

16 What had Stresemann achieved by his 'policy of fulfilment'?

17 Why did the value of the mark collapse? How did wage-earners suffer? Who suffered even more?

18 Name three ways in which the crisis was solved.

19 When and where did the economic depression begin? How did it affect Germany?

20 What did the German people blame for the depression?

Give an account of the Weimar Republic under the headings:
The Second Empire/The Establishment of the Weimar Republic/Problems and Weaknesses of the Weimar Republic

Hitler's Rise to Power

Questions

1 When he was in Vienna, how did Hitler learn to think about (a) Germans, (b) Jews? How did he learn to behave?

2 What did Hitler do during the First World War? How did he feel when peace came?

3 Which political party did Hitler join? What new name did he give it?

4 Who gave the Nazis help? How did Hitler use this help?

5 Why did Hitler decide to seize power in 1923? What were his plans? What name is given to this plot? What famous German joined it? Why did it fail?

6 How did Hitler spend his time in prison? What did he decide when he came out?

7 What were the nationalist ideas of the Nazi Party?

8 What were the socialist ideas of the Nazi party? Why was Hitler dishonest about these? Why was he able to unite people behind him?

9 Name five things Hitler did to win support.

10 Why did the Nazis make little progress between 1924 and 1929? How did Hitler use the time? When did his chance come?

11 Why did democratic government collapse? What did Hindenburg have to do? Why were none of Hindenburg's Chancellors able to govern the country?

12 Why did the Nazi Party grow in strength?

13 How successful were the Nazis in the elections of 1932? Why was Hitler worried by the end of the year?

14 Who were the members of the Nationalist Party? How did von Papen and the Nationalist Party hope to use the Nazis? When was Hitler appointed Chancellor?

15 Why did Hitler force another election?

16 What powers did Hindenburg give Hitler after the Reichstag fire?

17 Why did Hitler want an 'Enabling Law'? What excuse did he give?

18 From which political parties did the Nazis win support for the Enabling Law?

19 Why did Hitler need the support of the army? What did he do to win it?

20 What title did Hitler take when Hindenburg died?

Give an account of Hitler's Rise to Power under the headings:
Early Life/The Early Years of the Nazi Party/Nazi Ideas and Tactics/Hitler's Road to Power 1924–34.

Germany under Hitler

Questions

1 What changes were made to the Reichstag?
2 What happened to the German States?
3 What new courts were created?
4 Who headed the S.S.? How did the S.S. begin? Name two of its branches. Name one important duty of the S.S.
5 What happened to trade unions? What replaced them?
6 What happened to the political parties?
7 How many Germans had joined the S.A.? What did the ordinary members want when Hitler came to power? What did the leaders want?
8 Give two reasons why Hitler wished to destroy the S.A. When and how was this done? What name is given to the murders?
9 How did Hitler deal with the Protestant Churches?
10 What promise did Hitler make to the Pope? How, in fact, did he treat the Catholics?
11 Why were German churchmen not a serious threat to Hitler?
12 What laws were passed against the Jews? How did they suffer as a result?
13 In what ways did ordinary Germans persecute Jews? What event led to the violence of Crystal Night? What happened during and after Crystal Night?
14 Who organized the Nazi propaganda? Name three methods that he used.
15 What changes did Hitler make in the schools?
16 What were the aims of the Hitler Youth?
17 What economic changes brought Hitler support?
18 Give two reasons why Hitler wanted Germany to be prosperous.
19 What was the 'Battle for Work'?
20 Why did many firms make good profits? Why did they have plenty of money for investment?
21 Who was Dr Schacht? How did he deal with Germany's shortage of foreign currency?
22 What was the main reason for Germany's economic recovery?
23 What was Goering's aim in his Four Year Plan? What was done under the Plan?
24 Why did Schacht object to rearmament?
25 Why was Germany ready for war in 1939?
26 How did rearmament affect the ordinary workers? Give two reasons why they did not cause trouble

Give an account of Germany under Hitler under the headings:
The Nazi Government/The Removal of Opposition/Measures to Win Support/Economic Policy.

Problems

1 Account for Hitler's rise to power.
2 What were the weaknesses of the Weimar Republic?
3 How far was the failure of democracy in Germany the fault of foreign governments?
4 Explain the appeal which the Nazi Party had for the German people.
5 What problems did Hitler encounter during his rise to power? How did he overcome them?
6 What pieces of good luck did Hitler have during his rise to power? How did he make use of them?
7 What were the main differences between Nazism and Communism?
8 Compare and contrast Hitler's role in Germany with Stalin's in Russia.
9 Why was Hitler able to keep power in Germany?
10 In what ways did Hitler pander to German public opinion?
11 Account for Germany's economic recovery after 1933. Say how far it was due to the policies of the government.
12 Why was Germany's economic recovery essential for Hitler?
13 What problems did rearmament create for Hitler?

SECTION FOUR

ITALY

Chapter Fourteen

The Rise of Fascism in Italy

Italy in 1919

At the end of the First World War, the Italians were disillusioned and discontented. There were several reasons for this.

In the first place, unlike Britain and France, Italy failed to win a colonial empire that was worth having. During the nineteenth century, her troops overran Eritrea and Somaliland, and then went on to invade Abyssinia. However, in 1896, the Abyssinians defeated the Italians at the Battle of Adowa, and drove them away. This was a terrible blow to Italian pride. Then, in 1911, the Italians took advantage of Turkey's weakness to capture some of the Dodecanese Islands and Libya. No one knew there was oil in Libya, and it seemed a useless place. People complained that while other countries had the best colonies, all Italy did was collect deserts.

Secondly, Italy was displeased at the peace settlement. When she entered the war, Britain and France had agreed to the Treaty of London, which promised Italy the Trentino, Istria, much of Dalmatia, and a share of Germany's colonial empire. However, the United States had not signed the Treaty and at Versailles President Wilson refused point-blank to allow Italy to take any of Dalmatia. That would have been contrary to the principle of self-determination, since its inhabitants were all Slavs. Nor did Italy have any of Germany's colonies. She did indeed gain the Trentino, and Istria, with the port of Trieste, but they seemed poor compensation for all the sufferings of the war.

Feeling ran so high that in 1919, a group of adventurers, led by the poet D'Annunzio, took the port of Fiume from Yugoslavia. It was a full year before the Italian navy chased them out and, eventually, Fiume became part of Italy. D'Annunzio showed what strong, determined action could achieve, and many people took note, including a certain Benito Mussolini.

Thirdly, Italy had economic problems. The south was especially poor, for there was no industry and the soil is infertile. The people suffered from malnutrition and disease. The north was not as unfortunate for it has industrial towns like Genoa, Turin and Milan, and the valley of the Po is good farming land. Even so, there was a good deal of poverty in the north, especially in the slums of the big cities. The war made these problems worse. Its cost was enormous, being twice as much as the government had spent in the fifty years down to 1914: there was unemployment since most demobilized soldiers did not find jobs: Italy was unable to earn foreign currency to pay for her imports. She relied on tourists and on exports of luxuries, like wine, and leather goods, but after the war the people of Europe could not afford holidays abroad or expensive luxuries.

Italians were discontented because they had no colonial empire, because they had not gained what they expected from the peace settlement, and because of their economic problems. As a result there was a good deal of disorder. In 1920 alone there were 2000 strikes. Also, workers took over numbers of factories and draped them with red flags. Many people became Communists including the agricultural labourers of the Po Valley. In 1920 they organized a bitter strike which lasted until the government made the landowners give way.

Italian politics were chaotic. There always had been too many political parties and after the war proportional representation was introduced, so there were even more, all bickering with each other. The two major parties, the Socialists and the Catholics, were deadly rivals, so there was no hope of forming a coalition containing both of them. As a result, there could be no stable government: there were twenty Prime Ministers between 1920 and 1922. Often, there was disorder in Parliament, with deputies throwing paper darts, like unruly schoolboys.

Yet another political problem was the relationship between Church and State. The Pope had once ruled much of central Italy, but he lost almost all his lands when the country was united in 1861. No Pope forgave the Italian government and, for a long time, all Catholics were forbidden to take part in politics, or even vote at elections. This ban was lifted in 1912, so the Church was then able to form its own political party. However, there were still problems. Most Italians were devout Catholics, so if the Pope quarrelled with the government, they were likely to side with the Pope.

Mussolini's Rise to Power

Mussolini was born in 1883, in the Romagna, a province in north-east Italy. His father was a blacksmith, and a dedicated Socialist. Mussolini became a Socialist, too. He was badly behaved, both as a boy and a young man, but he did pass his examinations, and became a teacher. After only one year he gave up his post and went to Switzerland, where he lived in poverty doing any odd jobs he could find. As always, he was unruly and outspoken so the Swiss government expelled him. He then went to Austria, where the same thing happened. He then returned to Italy, and became editor of *Avanti*, a Socialist newspaper. However, when the war began, he quarrelled with the Socialists, because they were pacifists and he favoured war. Accordingly, the Socialists expelled him from their party. This was a turning point in Mussolini's life for he now founded his own newspaper, *Popolo d'Italia*, and his own political party, the Fascists. Soon, however, he had to join the army. He was a good soldier, so he was promoted to the rank of lance-sergeant, but his war ended abruptly in 1917 when a trench mortar exploded, badly wounding him.

When peace came, Mussolini built up his political party in earnest. He had plenty of volunteers because, as we have seen, many disbanded soldiers were unemployed. They, and indeed other young Italians who were looking for excitement formed combat groups or *fasci di combattimento*. It was the word *fasci* which gave the Fascist Party its name. As a uniform the members had the same black shirts that many of them had worn as *arditi* or shock troops, during the war. One of their mottoes was *me ne frego* (I don't give a damn), which shows they did not think very deeply. However, they did have at least two firm ideas. In the first place they were nationalists. They all admired D'Annunzio and indeed, many had followed him to Fiume. Secondly, they were against Communists and Socialists. These were the traitors who had opposed the war, and had spat on officers when they came back from the fighting. Burning for revenge, the *fasci* broke up left-wing political parties and trades unions, and smashed strikes. They were so successful that they gained powerful friends. Industrialists and landowners lent them lorries when they went on their raids, and gave them money.

All this, however, was only a beginning. Mussolini wanted power, so he and his friends had to stand for Parliament. First of all they met disaster. In 1919, the Fascists polled only 2 per cent of the votes in Milan, which made them look ridiculous. However, in 1921, the Liberal Prime Minister, Giolitti, felt he could use the Fascists against the Socialists. In the general election of that year he gave them government support, and they won thirty-five seats. Once elected, they turned against Giolitti, so the confusion in Parliament was as bad as ever.

The crisis came in 1922. The *fasci* frightened their enemies with mass rallies, and still more attacks. Italo Balbo even occupied Ferrara with an army of 60 000 blackshirts until the government agreed to help the town by starting expensive public works. The Communists and Socialists were desperate so they tried to organize a general strike. It was a feeble effort which the Fascists crushed in a day. The government seemed powerless, for the Prime Minister, Facta, did not known what to do. Mussolini, on the other hand, had very clear ideas. He demanded to be made Prime Minister, and threatened to march on Rome with an army of Fascists.

Everything now depended on Victor Emmanuel III, King of Italy. He was a member of the House of Savoy, which was one of the oldest royal families in Europe. He was, moreover, the grandson of Victor Emmanuel I, who, together with Garibaldi, had united Italy in 1861. However, he was unsure of himself. Perhaps his size had something to do with this, for he was a tiny little man. His one concern was to remain king. To stop the march on Rome, all he had to do was declare a state of emergency. The 'marchers' were coming by train, so they could be delayed simply by pulling up a few tracks. Moreover, Rome was defended by 12 000 well-equipped loyal troops who were quite able to defeat Mussolini's rabble.

Victor Emmanuel saw, though, that there were bigger problems than the march on Rome. Reports were coming in that the Fascists had seized power in places all over Italy. They were arresting town councillors, and occupying key buildings like railway stations, police stations and

105

telephone exchanges. Next, whatever the Rome garrison might do, it was impossible to rely on the rest of the army. Some units were even giving arms to the Fascists. When the King asked one of his generals for advice, the man replied, 'Your Majesty, the army will do its duty, but it would be better not to put it to the test.' Thirdly, the King feared that if there were a civil war his tall, handsome cousin, the Duke of Aosta, would take advantage of it, to seize the throne for himself. Victor Emmanuel refused to declare a state of emergency. Instead, he sent for Mussolini and asked him to be Prime Minister.

The march on Rome was no longer needed, but Mussolini insisted that the Fascists should have a triumphal parade through the city. They held this on 31 October 1922.

The Fascist Dictatorship

At first, Mussolini was far from safe. There were only four Fascists in the government and, as we have seen, only thirty-five Fascist deputies in Parliament. The problem was to win a good majority. Mussolini first changed the law to say that the party which had the largest number of votes at a general election should have two-thirds of the seats in Parliament. He then dissolved Parliament and turned the *fasci* loose on the Italian electors. They attacked their opponents, broke up their meetings and, on election day, the polling stations were full of blackshirts. Not surprisingly, the Fascists polled 65 per cent of the votes, so they would have had their majority in Parliament even without the new electoral law.

Mussolini was now quite content to govern through Parliament, but he had reckoned without the Socialist leader, Giacomo Matteotti. Matteotti was indeed brave for when Parliament met, he made a speech exposing all the crimes the Fascists had committed during the election campaign. Almost at once a gang of thugs kidnapped and murdered him. It is most unlikely that Mussolini ordered the murder, but almost everyone blamed him for it. As the Fascists had a majority in Parliament, the opposition parties could not win a vote condemning Mussolini, so they simply walked out in protest. This was called the 'Aventine withdrawal' after an event in the history of ancient Rome. Mussolini now had no hope of governing through Parliament: he had either to resign, or make himself dictator. While he was wondering what to do a group of his more determined followers made up his mind for him. They invaded his office, told him he would be in serious trouble if he resigned, and then left, slamming the door. Mussolini decided to become a dictator.

Chapter Fifteen

Italy under Mussolini

Government

When Mussolini became dictator, Victor Emmanuel was still king, but he had little power. The man who mattered was the Prime Minister who was, of course, Mussolini himself. Under him there was a central government, in Rome, with a cabinet of ministers and a parliament, while local government was based on provincial councils and town councils. This pattern of government was much the same as in any normal country: what made Italy so different was that each one of these bodies had a Fascist organization alongside it to keep an eye on it. The equivalent of the cabinet was the Fascist Grand Council, which made sure that the cabinet minsters obeyed the party's orders. There were also Fascist Assemblies that corresponded to Parliament and the local councils. As for Mussolini, he was not only Prime Minister, but Duce, or leader of the Fascist Party. Thus, the Fascist Party controlled the government of Italy at every level, and Mussolini controlled the party. That was why he had absolute power.

```
                        King
                          |
Prime Minister —Mussolini—Duce
        Cabinet←                 —Fascist Grand Council
      Parliament←                — Fascist National Assembly
  Local Councils←                — Fascist Local Assemblies
        ————————→ = Lines of command.
```

We can see the same idea in quite small things. For example, they kept the National anthem, but there was also the Fascist anthem, *Giovinezza*. Soldiers still gave the ordinary military salute, but there was the Fascist one as well: it was the outstretched arm, the salute used in the armies of ancient Rome.

Mussolini described this system of government as one of 'twin beds', but that was hardly correct as the Fascist 'bed' was more important than the other.

In order to have even more power, Mussolini ended elections for Parliament and local councils: instead either he, or other leading Fascists nominated the members.

The Fascists also took control of the civil service. Not only did they see that it carried out their orders, but they made it more efficient. Foreigners who had known Italy in the old days were amazed at the changes they found when they returned. Before, trains had run more or less when their drivers pleased and it is said that one express was 400 hours late leaving the station. Mussolini, however, made the trains run on time.

Attempts to Keep Power

It was not enough for Mussolini to win power, he had to keep it. One way was to crush opposition. The Fascists disbanded all other political parties, driving many of their leaders abroad. They closed hostile newspapers and actually burnt down the office of *Avanti,* the Socialist newspaper which had given Mussolini the sack. They kept the *fasci di combattimento* who had done so much to bring Mussolini to power, but they were given a new name, the 'Voluntary Militia for National Security'. As such, they were a regular State force, with pay and uniforms. However, what did not change was their methods, for they went on terrorizing their enemies. They attacked and beat some, and made others drink large amounts of castor oil, or eat live toads. Mussolini also had his secret police. He called them the O.V.R.A. to make them sound sinister, but no one knew what the initials meant. The O.V.R.A. was not nearly as efficient as the Gestapo, nor was it as terrifying. Finally, there were special courts to try political offenders. In all, they sentenced 4000 people to prison and banished many others to barren islands in the Mediterranean. However, Mussolini had no concentration camps. What is more, until 1940, only ten people were executed for political offences and five of these were Slav terrorists.

As well as crushing his enemies, Mussolini tried to stay in power by winning support from the Italian people. There was much propaganda, the most important part of it being Mussolini's speeches. The Duce was a great demagogue, able to play on the emotions of a crowd and persuade it to believe whatever he wanted. He also made full use of the newspapers. As he had once been an editor he could tell them in detail how they were to report items; for example, how many columns to print, and what size the headlines had to be. From time to time there were impressive parades and rallies to show how powerful Fascism was. All the while, Mussolini tried to give the Italians pride in their country by reminding them of the glory of Ancient Rome. For example, the Roman symbol of authority, the *fasces,* was everywhere, and as we have seen the Roman salute was revived.

It was important that children should grow up to be good Fascists. All teachers had to belong to the Fascist Party, and teach Fascist beliefs. Many school texts had to be rewritten, especially history books. There were also Fascist youth movements, which children joined at the age of four.

One serious weakness Italian governments had had since 1860 was the quarrel with the Church. Most Italians were devout Catholics, so they found it difficult to be loyal to their country as long as its rulers disagreed with the Pope. Mussolini was determined to solve this problem, so in 1929 he negotiated the Lateran Treaty with the papacy. By this, the Pope recognized the Kingdom of Italy, and abandoned all claims to the lands his predecessors had held. In return, Mussolini gave the Pope complete control over the Vatican City, which became a separate State, with its own police and army. He also recognized the Roman Catholic religion as the official religion of Italy. The Lateran Treaty did as much as anything to make Mussolini popular. Catholics were now willing to support him, because he had reached an understanding with the Pope.

The Economy

One of Mussolini's chief ambitions was to make Italy strong: that meant he had to develop her economy.

When Mussolini came to power, there was a lot of unemployment, so to find people jobs, he started public works. There were many kilometres of roads, there were impressive public buildings adorned with Fascist symbols, and slum areas in Rome were cleared. The most important task, though, was to drain the Pontine Marshes, a malarial swamp, not far from the capital. For centuries, Italian rulers had wanted to do this, and Mussolini could boast that he succeeded where Caesar had failed.

Even though most of her people were farmers, Italy imported a lot of wheat. Mussolini wanted the country to grow all her own food, so he started the 'battle for grain'. He gave prizes to successful farmers, and often had his photograph taken in the harvest fields, helping with the threshing, or dancing with peasant girls. In the end, imports were cut by 75 per cent. However, it was not all gain, since, in order to grow wheat, farmers gave up other more valuable crops such as olives.

Mussolini threshing wheat

Mussolini felt that if Italy was to be powerful she had to have men, yet her population was small compared with the other important countries of Western Europe, especially Germany. Accordingly, he started the 'battle for births'. He gave rewards to mothers of large families, while bachelors had to pay a special tax. It was all in vain. In 1932 the birth rate was lower than it had ever been since the 1870s.

One of Mussolini's more original ideas was to set up what he called the 'Corporative State'. The aim was to make employers and workers act together, instead of quarrelling, as they had usually done in the past. All members of the same occupation, whatever their position, had to join a corporation. Strikes were illegal, and there were officials whose job it was to decide rates of pay, regulate working conditions and settle disputes. It looked such a good system that several foreign governments thought about copying it. However, the corporations were run by Fascists who used them to control the workers, while favouring the employers. Mussolini still needed the support of the same industrialists that had helped bring him to power. In addition, though some were not as bad as others, all the corporations were inefficient to a certain extent.

How far was Mussolini succesful? He crushed his political rivals and he came to terms with the Pope. Apart from these two things, however, he achieved little. The country remained poor and divided: though her economy grew slightly in the late 1930s, it was mainly because world trade revived. When war came in 1940, she was quite unprepared for it. One can almost say there were two Italys — the real one and the Fascist dream. Mussolini was full of show and boasting, but he was little better than the editor of a third-rate newspaper who believes his own lies. Churchill called him 'the swollen bullfrog of the Pontine Marshes'.

WORK SECTION— Italy

Members of the Young Fascist movement

The Balilla was a movement for children aged eight to fourteen.
There were other movements for those of different ages.

Questions

1 Why did the Fascists organize youth movements?
2 What kind of training were these boys given?
3 What salute are these boys giving?
4 Why was this one chosen for them?
5 Which other country copied it for its own army and youth movements?

Fascist Proclamation 1922

The Quadriumvirate mentioned here was four generals — De Bono, De Vecchi, Italo Balbo and Michele Bianchi:
Fascisti! Italians!
    The time for determined battle has come! Four years ago the National Army loosed at this season the final offensive that brought it to

Victory. Today the army of the Black Shirts takes again possession of that Victory, which has been mutilated, and going directly to Rome brings Victory again to the glory of that Capital. The martial law of Fascism now becomes a fact. By order of the Duce all the military, political and administrative functions of the Party management are taken over by a secret Quadriumvirate of Action with dictatorial powers.

The Army, the reserve and safeguard of the Nation, must not take part in this struggle. Fascism renews its highest homage given to the Army of Vittorio Veneto. Fascism, furthermore, does not march against the police, but against a political class both cowardly and imbecile, which in four long years has not been able to give a Government to the Nation. Those who form the productive class must know that Fascism wants to impose nothing more than order and discipline upon the Nation and to help to raise the strength which will renew progress and prosperity. The people who work in the fields and the factories, those who work on the railroads or in offices, have nothing to fear from the Fascist Government. Their just rights will be protected. We will even be generous with unarmed adversaries.

Fascism draws its sword to cut the multiple Gordian knots which tie and burden Italian life. We call God and the witness of our five hundred thousand dead to witness that only one impulse sends us on, that only one passion burns within us — the impulse and the passion to contribute to the safety and greatness of our Country.

Fascisti of all Italy!

Stretch forth like Romans your spirits and your fibres! We must win! We will!

Long live Italy! Long live Fascism!

Questions

1 Who, do you suppose, wrote this proclamation, or at least ordered it to be written?
2 What was the victory that had been won four years before?
3 Why is the victory described as mutilated?
4 Who are the Black Shirts?
5 What are they planning to do?
6 Did the Fascists have any right to proclaim martial law?
7 Who is given charge of the Fascist Party? Why do you suppose this was done?
8 What, according to the proclamation, should the army do?
9 Why did the Fascists want to be on good terms with it?
10 What, in fact, were many of its units doing at this time?
11 What was Vittorio Veneto?
12 Why do you suppose the Fascists wanted to be on good terms with the police?
13 Whom do the Fascists claim to be fighting?
14 What were the 'productive classes'?
15 What does the proclamation say to try and please them?
16 What had been the relations between the Fascists and many of the 'productive classes'?
17 Explain the reference to 'five hundred thousand dead'.
18 What, according to the proclamation, is the aim of the Fascist movement?
19 Whom are the Fascists urged to copy?
20 Describe, briefly, the events which followed the issue of this proclamation.

The Corporative State

This extract is from Mussolini's autobiography:

Amid the innovations and experiments of the new Fascist civilization, one interests the whole world: it is the corporative organization of the State.

It was necessary to emerge from a base, selfish habit of the competition of class, and to put aside hate and anger. After the war, especially with the subversive propaganda of Lenin, ill will had reached perilous proportions. Usually agitations and strikes were accompanied by fights, and there were dead and wounded men. The people went back to work with souls full of hate against their masters, and after every incident of disorder a new situation promised another and more difficult problem of conflict.

However, five years of harmonious work have transformed in its essential lines the economic life, and in consequence the political and moral life of Italy. Let me add that the discipline that I imposed is not a forced discipline and does not obey the selfish interests of categories and classes. Our discipline has one vision and one end, the welfare and the good name of the Italian nation.

Instead of the old trade unions we substituted Fascist corporations. In a meeting of 19 December 1923, I had occasion to affirm that:

111

'Peace within is primarily a task of Government. The Government has a clear outline of conduct. Public order must never be troubled for any reason whatsoever. That is the political side. But there is also the economic side: it is one of collaboration. I remind Italian industry of these principles. Until now it has been too individualistic. The old system and old ways must be abandoned.'

They were abandoned, little by little, the old Labour structure and associations. We were directed more and more towards the corporative conception of the State.

We have solved a series of problems of no little importance: we have abolished all the perennial troubles and disorder and doubt that poisoned our national soul. We have given a rhythm, a law and a protection to work: we have found in the collaboration of classes the reason for our possibilities, for our future power. We do not lose time in troubles, in strikes, which, while they vex the spirit, imperil also our own strength and the solidity of our economy. We consider conflict as a luxury for the rich. We must save strength.

(*My Autobiography* — Benito Mussolini.
Trs: Richard Washburn Child)

Questions

1 What is the Fascist experiment which has interested the whole world?
2 Which of the problems that Italy faced after the war does Mussolini describe here?
3 What kind of discipline does Mussolini say he has imposed? What is its aim?
4 What has replaced the trade unions?
5 What are the political and economic aims of the government?
6 What problems does Mussolini claim the corporations have solved?
7 How does this book disagree with Mussolini's description of corporations?
8 Compare this statement by Mussolini with Hitler's speech of 27 January 1932 (Document Six page 97). In what ways are the aims of the two dictators alike?

The Rise of Fascism in Italy

Questions

1 What countries were there in the Italian empire? Why were Italians dissatisfied with their empire?

2 What had Italy been promised when she entered the war? Why was she disappointed? What gains did she make?
3 What happened to Fiume?
4 What economic problems were there in the south of Italy and the north? What problems had the war created?
5 In what ways did the workers show their discontent?
6 Why was it impossible to form a stable government?
7 Why was there disagreement between the Pope and the government of Italy? What problem did this create for many Italians?
8 Which political party did Mussolini first join? Why was he expelled from it?
9 Why did the Fascist Party have many recruits after the war? What were *fasci*? What ideas did they have? Describe some of the things they did.
10 Why did the Fascists have some success in the elections in 1921?
11 Describe the activities of the Fascists in 1922. What did Mussolini demand? What did he threaten to do?
12 What was Victor Emmanuel's main concern? Give three reasons why he did not declare a state of emergency. What did he do instead?
13 What happened in Rome on 31 October 1922?
14 How did Mussolini change the electoral law? How successful were the Fascists in the elections of 1922? Why?
15 Who was Matteotti? Why was he murdered? Who was blamed? What was the Aventine withdrawal? What choice did that leave Mussolini? What did he decide to do? Why?

Give an account of the Rise of Fascism in Italy under the headings: Italy in 1919/Mussolini's Rise to Power/The Fascist Dictatorship

Italy under Mussolini

Questions

1 Draw a diagram to show the system of government in Italy.
2 How did Mussolini describe it?
3 What changes were made in Parliament and to the local councils?
4 What changes were made in the civil service?

5 What happened to the political parties? What did the *fasci* become? Describe some of their methods. Name two other methods Mussolini used to crush opposition.
6 What propaganda methods did Mussolini employ?
7 What was done to make sure children grew up to be good Fascists?
8 What treaty did Mussolini make with the Pope? When? What were its terms? What advantage did the treaty give Mussolini?
9 Why did Mussolini start public works? Name some of them and say which was the most important.
10 What change did Mussolini encourage in agriculture? How did he do this? What were the results?
11 What was the aim of the 'Corporative State'? How were the corporations organized? Why did they favour the employers? What other weakness did they have?
12 What successes and failures did Mussolini have? How did Churchill describe him?

Describe Italy under Mussolini under the headings: Government Attempts to Keep Power/The Economy

Problems

1 Why was Mussolini able to seize power in Italy?
2 Compare Mussolini's rise to power with Hitler's.
3 Compare and contrast Mussolini's rule with Hitler's.
4 Explain the Fascist system of government and show how it ensured that Mussolini had absolute power.
5 Which do you think was the more successful down to 1939, Mussolini or Hitler? Give reasons for your answers.
6 Explain why Mussolini was able to keep power.
7 How far do you think Mussolini's rule was of benefit to Italy?

JAPAN

Chapter Sixteen

The Modernization of Japan 1868–1918

The Meiji Restoration

IN THE early seventeenth century, two important things happened in Japan. The first was that the Commander-in-Chief of the army, the Shogun, seized power from the Emperor. The Emperor still went on living in his capital at Kyoto, but it was the Shogun who ruled from his own capital of Edo, which is now Tokyo. The office of Shogun was hereditary, so when one died his son took over. The second important event was that Japan shut herself off from the rest of the world. The first European explorers, some Portuguese, had arrived in 1542, and others followed. They wanted to trade and convert the people to Christianity, but the government distrusted them. In 1638 the Shogun issued the Seclusion Decrees which forbade any foreigners to enter Japan, or any of her own subjects to leave.

During the nineteenth century it became difficult for Japan to remain a 'closed society'. More and more ships sailed past her shores and their owners wanted to trade. The Americans were particularly interested, and, in 1853, Commodore Matthew Perry appeared off Edo with four warships. He brought a letter from the President of the United States asking that American merchants should be allowed to trade. Fearing there might be a war, the Shogun reluctantly agreed. Other countries now demanded the same rights, and Japan had to sign trading treaties with Britain, France, Holland and Russia. People from all these countries now arrived in Japan, but some Japanese disliked them so much that they attacked them. The foreign governments then hit back, for example, by sending warships to bombard coastal forts.

All of this made the Shogun unpopular, so in 1868 a group of nobles overthrew him and proclaimed the Emperor as the sole ruler of Japan. Their slogan was 'Revere the Emperor and expel the barbarians'. This rebellion is called the 'Meiji Restoration', Meiji being the Emperor's family name. However, he had no more power than before. Japan was now ruled by an oligarchy — the nobles who had overthrown the Shogun.

Japan's new masters were determined to keep out the Western Powers, and save their country from the same fate as India and China. They realized, though, that if they were to be powerful enough to do that, they would have to learn from the West. For a start, in 1871, Prince Iwacuru led

Rice fields

a mission on a tour of Europe and the United States. He came back with many good ideas and the government began the task of turning Japan into a modern State.

Society and Government

In the old Japan there had been five classes: samurai, peasants, artisans, traders and outcasts. Samurai were warriors. The Emperor and the nobles were samurai, but so also were many lesser men, some no better than brigands. In the new Japan there were three classes: nobles, gentry and commoners. Most of the nobles and gentry had been samurai, but they lost their special privileges, for example, the right to carry swords and to cut down any member of the lower classes in revenge for an insult.

There were changes in the government, apart from overthrowing the Shogun. In 1889 the Emperor granted a constitution so that Japan had an Imperial Diet. It was something like the British Parliament, for it had a House of Peers and an elected House of Representatives. However, the new system was not democratic, because only landowners had the right to vote, and the Diet had few powers.

Agriculture

Modernizing Japan meant, more than anything, modernizing her economy and in this agriculture led the way.

There were many improvements in farming, but the two most important were irrigation and the use of fertilizers. As a result, rice yields went up 50 per cent between 1880 and 1914. Farmers also produced more silk, which their wives spun and wove. The country's output of silk increased by 400 per cent between 1868 and 1914, by which time it accounted for one-third of exports.

Agriculture helped the rest of the economy in the following ways:

1 Farmers had more money, so they bought goods made in factories. That encouraged manufacturers to increase their output.
2 Landlords were able to charge higher rents, and they invested much of their new wealth in industry.
3 The extra food fed the growing population, so that many more people were able to live in towns, and work in industry.
4 Exports of silk earned Japan foreign currency, which meant she could buy raw materials and machinery for her factories.

Industry

Japanese industry grew rapidly, partly because of the boost from agriculture, but there were other reasons as well. The most important were government aid, help from the West and the First World War.

The government wanted Japan to have modern industries because it knew that she could not be powerful without them. The slogan was 'Rich country, strong army'. Accordingly, it started some industries itself, and gave subsidies to private companies that were doing important work. It also built many of the railways: indeed, all the lines were nationalized in 1966.

The Japanese found Western help invaluable. When Britain went through her own Industrial Revolution, her people had to discover everything for themselves: the Japanese had only to copy. However, they were quick to learn and, what is more, they did not allow foreigners to control their industries as, for example, the Chinese had done. An English visitor wrote in 1880, 'The Japanese look on foreigners as schoolmasters. As long as they cannot help themselves, they make use of them: and then they send them about their business.'

Though Japan made a lot of progress down to 1914, it was the First World War which turned her into a great industrial power. Japan did little fighting herself, so she was able to use the war for her own advantage. European countries had to make weapons, instead of goods for export, so Japan was able to steal their markets in America and Asia. Also, the U-boats sank so many vessels that Japan expanded her shipbuilding industry and increased her merchant navy considerably.

Among the first industries to develop were textiles, especially silk and cotton. The United States took a great deal of the silk while the cotton went to poorer countries, like China and India. Heavy industry grew as well — coal-mining, iron and steel, engineering, shipbuilding and armaments. It was heavy industry that the government did its best to help because it would make Japan powerful. Light industry produced goods for the

117

ordinary people — household equipment, clothing, bicycles and rick-shaws.

Broadly speaking, Japanese businesses were of two kinds. On the one hand there was a multitude of small firms each employing five people or less. These were the light industries. Weavers wove narrow cloth on handlooms: cobblers made shoes: little engineering workshops specialized in making different parts for bicycles. On the other hand, heavy industry was in the hands of a few gigantic concerns, like the Mitsui and Mitsubishi companies. They were called 'Zaibatsu'. Mitsubishi started by owning ships. It then expanded 'forwards' by going into trade and banking, and 'backwards' by developing shipbuilding, engineering and iron and steel. The Zaibatsu worked with the government. The government gave them subsidies, while they developed the industries which Japan most needed. The families that owned the Zaibatsu enjoyed great wealth and power.

Soon, the Japanese economy had grown enough for the country to have a powerful army and navy. By the early twentieth century Japan could make all her own weapons, even the largest warships. The army was reorganized on German lines and had modern rifles and artillery. In 1872 the navy had only 17 ships, totalling 14 000 tonnes. In 1903 it had 76 major warships, that is destroyers and larger, totalling 254 000 tonnes. There were also 600 smaller craft, including many motor torpedo boats.

Ideas

Though they were eager to learn all they could from Western people, the one thing most Japanese were not prepared to do was to think like them. After all, the main reason for modernizing their country was to make it strong enough to resist foreigners. If we are to understand the history of Japan we must know something of the way her people thought.

For one thing, the Japanese did not bother too much about personal freedom, as we do in the West. We want to say what we like, read what we like, think what we like, and join whichever political party we like. A Japanese, however, always put the group before himself, whether it was his family, his school, his firm or his regiment. Above all, he was loyal to his country because he believed that it was the 'Land of the Gods', and would one day rule the world. The Japanese also had much more respect for authority than Western people. As children, they had to obey their fathers without question. A Japanese, it was said, had five terrors, and they were 'earthquakes, thunder, floods, fire and father'. In later life they obeyed their teachers, their employers, their officers, but, most of all, their Emperor. He was, they believed, no ordinary ruler, but was descended from the sun god Amaterasu, and more than that, was a deity in is own right.

Patriotism, then, was more than loyalty to Queen and country as we understand it. Instead, it was a religion, and many Japanese were fanatics.

118

Chapter Seventeen

Japan Becomes a Military Dictatorship 1919–40

AFTER the First World War it looked for a time as if Japan was developing into a democracy. However, she had serious economic, social and political problems which meant that, in the end, the senior officers in the army and navy seized power. These men behaved in the Far East as Hitler and Mussolini behaved in Europe. They crushed all traces of freedom at home, and tried to build an Empire abroad.

Economic and Social Problems

There were difficulties in both town and countryside.

The development of industry had meant that most Japanese workers earned higher wages and enjoyed a better standard of living. However, it was not all gain. The towns had grown too rapidly, so that many of the houses were slums: the small workshops were dirty, dangerous and crowded: hours were long: wages, though higher than they had been, were still not good enough. Added to all that, there was an earthquake in 1923, which destroyed much of Tokyo and Yokohama. Then, in the early 1930s, Japan had the same depression as the other trading countries of the world, and that meant a lot of unemployment. The town workers were discontented, so they formed trade unions and, from time to time, these organized strikes.

Out in the countryside the farmers had problems because of a fall in the prices of rice and silk. Japan was now importing rice from Formosa, and it was extremely cheap. Japanese farmers had to lower their own prices in order to compete. The problem with silk was that during the Depression the Americans stopped buying it. As a result of both these things, the incomes of most farmers were cut by a half in the early 1930s. At the same time, they had more mouths to feed, because their unemployed relations fled from the towns, and came to live with them.

Political Problems

The political question was who was to govern Japan. The two possibilities were certain political parties who wanted the country to be a democracy, and the Nationalists who wanted a military dictatorship.

Among the political parties there were Socialists and Communists, and they had been formed by discontented town workers. The government disliked them, so in 1925, the Diet passed a Peace Preservation Law which made it illegal to plan a revolution, or to try and abolish private property. Both of these are important Communist aims. The police enforced this law with much enthusiasm, even torturing prisoners, and the Communist Party ceased to exist. The less extreme left-wing groups formed the Socialist Mass Party, which managed to survive until the outbreak of war in 1940.

The other parties were not unlike the Liberals and Conservatives in Europe. The two most important were the Society of Political Friends (Seyukai) and the Democratic Party (Minseito). One or the other was in power until 1936. In 1925 the Minseito took Japan some way towards being a democracy when it gave every man the vote. However, these parties failed in the end as the majority of the people did not support them. Politicians lost respect because of bribery and corruption and there were often disorders and even fighting in the Diet. More important, the Japanese were not interested in democracy, which stood for the rights of the individual. It was a Western idea and, as such, had to be resisted, along with the other bad things that had come out of the West, like trade unions, strikes and dance-halls.

The most important Nationalist groups were two factions in the army. Both disliked foreigners, and the other political parties, and both wanted war. None the less, there were important differences between them.

First, there was the Imperial Way, or Kodo faction. Its members were, for the most part, young officers who came from peasant families, and who were angry at the distress in the countryside. They were radicals, so they were against the ruling oligarchy, and the Zaibatsu. From time to time they assassinated members of both. Abroad, they thought Japan should protect herself against Russia, so halting the spread of Communism.

Secondly, there was the Control or Tosei faction. Most of its members were senior officers who were conservative, and quite ready to work with the oligarchy and the Zaibatsu. Abroad, they were more agressive that the Kodo faction, for they wanted Japan to conquer China.

The Army Seizes Power

During the early 1930s the Nationalists became very angry. In the first place, because of the Depression, there were strikes and riots by left-wing groups in the towns. Secondly, again because of the Depression, the peasants were suffering and these were the families of the junior officers. Thirdly, the Minseito government signed the London Naval Treaty, agreeing to limit the size of the Japanese fleet.

In 1931, the Nationalists decided to take action, and the Kwantung army seized the whole of Manchuria. It moved without orders, knowing perfectly well that this action was against the wishes of the government. An officer sent to call off the attack was deliberately slow in delivering the letter, so that it arrived too late. The excuse for the attack was that Chiang Kai-shek was gaining power in China, so it was to important to take Manchuria

Japanese politicians fighting in the Diet

before he did. The real reason was that the army wanted to make itself popular, and it succeeded.

Next, several politicians who were against the occupation of Manchuria were assassinated, including the Prime Minister, Inukai. The remainder were thoroughly frightened, and few had the courage to speak against the Nationalists.

For some time, everyone in the government was uncertain and uneasy, until, in 1936, the Kodo faction tried to seize power. They assassinated several members of the cabinet, and the Prime Minister, Okada, only escaped because they killed his brother-in-law by mistake. Also, the First Division occupied the centre of Tokyo. The rebels claimed they were acting in the name of the Emperor, but he ordered that they should be crushed. The Tosei faction was only too pleased to obey, and, calling on sailors from the fleet and the Imperial Guards, they forced the First Division to surrender. That left the government completely under the control of the senior officers of the army and navy. They refused to allow anyone who might disagree with them to become a minister. Also, it was no longer the full cabinet that made important decisions, but a small group consisting of the Prime Minister, the Foreign Minister, the War and Navy Ministers, and the Chiefs of Staff of the Army and Navy.

Japan under Military Rule

Having seized power, Japan's new rulers were determined to keep it.

In 1937 Japan attacked China, which brought two advantages. The first was to unite the country against a common enemy. The second was to give the junior officers plenty to do, so that they were less likely to make trouble.

At home, the political parties were persecuted until, in 1940, they joined together to form the Imperial Rule Association, which was pledged to support the army. Japan had become a one-party State, a sure sign that democracy was dead.

Schools had to play their part by teaching that service to the State was a citizen's most important duty. There were two new subjects on the time-table. One was 'Ethics' with a textbook called *The Principles of National Policy*, and the other was military training. There was an army officer in every school who made sure the teachers ran it as the government wished.

The military rulers had a great advantage in that the country's economy recovered from the slump, but this prosperity came from a new source. Though textiles were important, it was heavy industry that took the lead — coal, iron and steel, shipbuilding, and the manufacture of motor vehicles, aircraft and armaments. Before long heavy industry accounted for three-quarters of the national output. In addition, Manchuria was now under the control of the Japanese. They developed her economy as vigorously as they did their own, so she added greatly to their wealth. Also, the government took more power. It had always given a lot of encouragement and some direction, but under the National Mobilization Law it had complete control. It could tell people where to work, fix prices and even take over entire industries and run them itself.

Since the army and navy were in charge it is not surprising that vast sums were spent on them. In 1931, the services took 500 million yen a year, which was 30 per cent of the budget, and in 1936, 4000 million yen, which was 70 per cent of the budget.

It is easy to see that, in many ways, nationalism in Japan was very like the nationalist movements in Europe, such as Fascism in Italy and Spain or Nazism in Germany. However, there were two important differences. The first was that there was no outstanding leader in Japan, like Mussolini, Franco or Hitler. Instead a group of high-ranking officers held power. The other difference is that whereas extreme nationalism was new in Europe, in Japan it was not. The average Japanese had always put his country before himself, so when he turned against democracy, it was not in any way a new movement. It was old Japan turning against the West.

Chapter Eighteen

Japan since 1945

BROADCASTING on 15 August 1945, Emperor Hirohito announced, 'The war situation has developed not necessarily to Japan's advantage.' His people knew he meant that they had been thoroughly defeated. The news was a great shock, for they had been sure that Japan would one day rule the world. Now, they saw they had been wrong, so they were ready to give up many of their old beliefs. Moreover, Japan's enemies were determined this should happen, and, as a result, there were important changes.

Emperor Hirohito

The American Occupation

When the war ended the Americans occupied Japan and their General Douglas MacArthur exercised almost total authority. He had the title 'Supreme Commander of the Allied Powers (S.C.A.P.). His policy was 'punishment and reform'.

Japan was disarmed, so she had no army, navy or air force. She lost her empire. Three million soldiers and as many civilians came home from China and the Pacific Islands. War criminals were punished. Twenty-five former leaders were tried, and seven of them hanged. Also, 700 less important men were executed, while 3000 were sent to prison. No less than 200 000 men in important positions lost their jobs. The Zaibatsu were broken up into smaller firms, since the Americans felt it was they who had found the money and materials to wage the war.

However, reform was more important than punishment, so MacArthur tried to turn Japan into a democracy. He did so in the following ways.

There was a new constitution. Wisely, the Americans did not depose the Emperor, but he had to give up all claims to being a god. He now has a position like that of the Queen in Britain. Also, real power was given to the Diet so that it became as important as our own Parliament. Women were given the vote and, indeed, the same legal rights as men.

The old political parties, the Seyukai and Minseito, reappeared and they won the most support. However, there was also a Socialist Party that was strong enough to take office for a while in 1948. What was less to the Americans' liking was the revival of the Communist Party. With the slogans 'a peaceful revolution' and 'a lovable Communist Party', it won three million votes in 1949.

There were also new measures to help the workers. A Trade Union Act allowed then to form unions, and by 1948 there were 34 000 of them with a total of seven million members. A Labour Relations Adjustment Act set up organizations to settle disputes. A Labour Standards Act regulated working conditions such as safety in factories and hours of work.

In addition, there was land reform. The Americans felt, quite rightly, that many peasants and their officer sons had become nationalists because they were discontented. To put that right, absentee landlords had to sell their land to the government, which then resold it to the peasants, allowing them a long time to pay. The proportion of farmland held by tenants fell from 40 per cent to 10 per cent.

Finally, education was reformed, for it was at school that the Japanese had learnt a lot of wrong ideas. Children no longer began their day by bowing to a portrait of the Emperor: teachers were forbidden to spread political propaganda: all the old textbooks were scrapped and new ones printed.

Education is very important to the Japanese. Before the war there were seventy universities, but now there are about four hundred. Nearly all Japanese students take their work seriously, so much so that one in twenty literally goes mad with worry.

In the late 1940s the Americans changed their policy. The Chinese

Communists beat the Nationalists under Chiang Kai-shek, so America wanted Japan to be her friend. They allowed her to rearm, and by 1960 she had an army, a navy and an air force once again. They were, however, much smaller than they had been before the war. In 1951, peace was made at San Francisco. All the powers that had fought against Japan signed the treaty, except Russia. The following year, America gave up control of Japan, though she still has bases there.

The Americans were a foreign power imposing their will on a defeated people, but much that they did suited the Japanese very well. The war shattered the old dream of a divine Emperor leading a·master race to conquer the world. Instead the Japanese have concentrated on making themselves rich.

The Japanese Economy

After the war, Japan had serious problems. Many of her factories and a quarter of her homes had been destroyed by bombing: raw materials and goods of all kinds were scarce: her merchant navy lay at the bottom of the Pacific: her empire was no more. Today, in contrast, Japan's economy is one of the strongest in the world. We must see how this came about.

There has been progress in agriculture. By 1950, the farmers were producing as much as they had done before the war, and they then increased output by one-third over the next ten years. They still grow the same amount of rice, but there are far more chickens, vegetables, fruit, pork and milk. There have been two problems. The first is that farms are still small, being about one hectare on average. The peasants have overcome this to some extent, by forming co-operatives which will, for example, sell their goods for them and buy fertilizers in bulk. The other problem is that many workers have gone to the cities. Between 1960 and 1965 alone, the number of families making a living from agriculture fell by 20 per cent. The answer to that has been mechanization. In 1955 there were 38 000 power cultivators and tractors in Japan: in 1970 there were 3.5 million. Honda helped a great deal by developing a Peasant Motor-cultivator, especially useful on small farms.

However, Japanese industry has made much more progress than agriculture. Production reached its pre-war level by 1950, and it then increased rapidly. In some years the growth rate has been as high as 20 per cent, while in Britain it has rarely been more than 5 per cent.

In the early stages of her industrial revolution Japan, like Britain, produced a great many textiles. She still does though today goods needing high technology, like chemicals and engineering, are more important. The table shows the growth of some of the more important products:

Japanese Industrial Products 1955–70

	1955	1970
Steel (millions of tonnes)	9.6	94.8
Ships (millions of tonnes)	0.5	12.9
Motor Cars (thousands)	20.0	3178.0
TV sets (thousands)	137.0	13 780.0

Japan has become the second largest producer of motor cars in the world, and she is the largest shipbuilding country. She also makes the biggest ships. The *Globtik Tokyo* is 490 000 tonnes.

Japan's imports are mainly raw materials — coal from the U.S.A., iron ore from Australia, and oil from the Middle East. She exports finished goods, such as cameras, television and radio sets, motor cycles, motor cars and ships — anything from a pocket TV to a supertanker. Mainly, these goods go to advanced countries, especially the U.S.A. and Europe, but Japan is anxious to develop trade with China. This is likely to happen because since 1978, China has opened her doors to foreign trade.

Japan is one of the most successful trading nations in the world. She had her first balance of payments surplus since the war in 1965, and it has grown enormously ever since.

Japan, then, has had what is sometimes called an 'economic miracle'. However, it is not a miracle at all, since there are obvious reasons why she has done so well. Three are outstanding — American help, investment, and few labour problems.

American help was especially important just after the war. It took three forms. There was aid, in other words, gifts of food and raw materials. Secondly, during the Korean War from 1950 to 1953, the Americans bought a great many supplies in Japan. It was this war which really started the rapid growth of the Japanese economy. Thirdly, the Americans have regularly bought large quantities of food and goods for their troops in Japan. From 1952 to 1956, for example, these purchases paid for a quarter of Japan's imports.

The Japanese have been able to invest a good deal of money in their industries because they have not spent it on other things. They do not have expensive social services and, since the Americans are there to protect them, they do not need powerful armed forces. Also taxes are low and wages are rising all the time, so people can save: many of these savings have been invested in industry.

Japan has had few labour problems. One reason why Japanese workers give little trouble is because their trade unions, though numerous, are small. In the early 1970s there were 60 000 of them, but on average they had only 200 members each. Another reason is that in the factories the Japanese show the same spirit that they did in battle during the war. They are disciplined, they are loyal and they thrive on hard work. As a result, production flows smoothly, and there are very few strikes.

Conclusion

There have been important changes in Japan since the war, yet many things are the same. Japan has copied much from the Western world, but she is still an Asiatic country in conflict with it. It is true she no longer fights wars, but she is a deadly rival in trade. Within the country there is much that is modern, but a great deal of the old Japan survives. People live in up-to-date houses with the latest gadgets, they drive cars, and they watch American films on colour television sets. None the less, many of them will

127

Modern Japan

Traditional Japan–flower arranging

study ten years for a diploma in the tea ceremony and flower arranging. Perhaps the easiest way to understand what has happened is to look at sport. The Japanese play squash and golf, but sumo wrestling still goes on, and they have taught the rest of the world judo and karate.

WORK SECTION — Japan

A general view of the Mitsui Copper Mines

Questions

1 What were firms like Mitsui called?
2 What type of industry did they own?
3 When did they first become important?
4 How did they grow in the early years?

5 How did they work with the government?
6 What happened to them after the Second World War? Why?

128

Rebellion of 1936

This is a letter from the American Ambassador, Joseph Grew, dated 1 March 1936.

The rebels were situated in the official residence of the Prime Minister and the Sanno Hotel very near us: we watched developments through glasses from our roof.

The Japanese Government quietly made all military preparations to capture or kill the rebels, meantime maintaining the most perfect discipline and order in the city, and then waited for two days until they surrendered little by little in small groups, as a result of broadcasts, leaflets dropped from aeroplanes, and a big streamer attached to a balloon, all stating that the Emperor called on the men to return to their barracks, where they would be pardoned because they had been misled, that their parents and brothers and sisters were weeping at the thought of their disobeying the Emperor, and that unless they disbanded they would be shot. This had precisely the desired effect and the whole thing was settled with very little, if any, shooting, except for the original assassinations.

The officers who had led the revolt finally surrendered after four days and the Government gave them two hours to commit hara-kiri. But they didn't commit hari-kiri because they expected civil trials as in the case of former assassins and they fully intended to use the court-room as a forum to stir up the people against the Government. It must have been a great shock to them when they were tried by court-martial and several of them sentenced to death and shot.

(Ten Years in Japan — Joseph C. Grew)

Questions

1 Which was the faction which tried to seize power in 1936?
2 What were the majority of its members?
3 Why were they discontented?
4 What were their aims?
5 What assassinations were there at the start of the rebellion? Who escaped?
6 How did the government persuade the rebels to surrender?
7 Why would the families of the rebels be especially distressed at their disobedience of the Emperor?
8 What did the government give the rebel leaders the chance to do?
9 What did the rebel leaders hope would happen?
10 What, in fact, did happen to them?
11 What does this document tell you about the way right-wing assassins had been treated in the past?
12 How had members of the left wing been treated?
13 Which faction put down the rebellion of 1936?
14 What were the majority of its members?
15 How did this faction take advantage of its success in 1936?
16 How did the rebellion help decide the government to attack China in 1937?

The American Occupation

A Japanese View — Shigera Yoshida, Prime Minister of Japan 1946–7 and 1949–55

The Occupation began its work amid chaos and confusion. Japan was bled white by a protracted war and our people were on the verge of starvation. Food was scarce, communications were disrupted, foreign trade remained at a standstill and hunger stalked the streets. Millions might have perished if it had not been for the speedy relief given by the United States Army. Similarly, our industry was completely at a stand-still for lack of materials essential for its operation. It was only with the assistance of the United States that it was revived and restored. For all these, our people will ever remain grateful.

At the same time, candour demands that we admit that there was another aspect of the Occupation which is less commendable. Quite understandably the Occupation commenced its work of reforming Japan on the erroneous assumption that we were an agressive people of ultra-militaristic traditions to be castigated thoroughly in order to be re-fashioned into a peace-loving nation. A purge was enforced which deprived our nation of a trained body of men at a crucial moment: the financial concerns were disintegrated by a complete break up of Zaibatsu, gravely retarding our economic recovery; notorious Communist leaders were released from prison, causing untold injury to our body politic; organized labour was encouraged in radical actions thus endangering law and order: education was reformed, sapping the moral fibre of our bewildered youth. Besides, our politics were so disorganized that militant unions, heavily infiltrated by Communism, ran amok in defying the authority of the Government.

Indeed, the Occupation spared no effort in drastically altering the old order, from the Imperial House to village shrines and temples.

129

Even a cursory study of our history will make it abundantly clear that our Imperial reign has, since ancient times, been characterized by an earnest solicitude for the welfare of the people. In fact our nation has been spared despotic sovereigns and rulers, despotism not being indigenous to our soil. Our record is also almost untainted by atrocities, as our people are essentially gentle, and dislike brutal strife.

(*The Yoshida Memoirs* — Shigera Yoshida)

Questions

1 Who had charge of the occupying forces? What was his official title?
2 What were the two aspects of his policy?
3 What does Yoshida say were the main problems Japan faced after the war?
4 How were these overcome?
5 What, according to Yoshida, was the wrong assumption the Americans made?
6 What mistakes does Yoshida claim the Americans made?
7 How would the Americans have justified their actions?
8 Were the results of American policy as bad as Yoshida claims?
9 What does Yoshida mean by saying there were drastic alterations to the Imperial House?
10 How would you reply to Yoshida's statements in the last three sentences of this extract?

Questions

1 Draw bar diagrams to illustrate the tables.
2 What reasons can you give for the growth of the Japanese economy since the Second World War?
3 Why did mining have the slowest growth?
4 Which of the manufacturing industries had the slowest growth?
5 At what period was it Japan's leading industry?

The Modernization of Japan 1868–1918

Questions

1 What two important events took place in Japan in the early seventeenth century?
2 What were the results of Commodore Perry's visit in 1853?
3 Who overthrew the Shogun? When? Why? What is the name of the rebellion? Who ruled Japan after the rebellion?
4 How did Japan's new masters propose to save her from the Western Powers?
5 What five classes had there been in Japan? What three classes replaced them?
6 What changes were made in the government? Why was it not democratic?
7 What were the two most important improvements in farming? How much did the yields of rice and silk increase?
8 Name three ways in which the government helped industry.
9 How did the Japanese use foreigners? What were foreigners not allowed to do?
10 How did the First World War help the Japanese economy?
11 Which industries were developed? What was the importance of (a) heavy industry, (b) light industry?
12 What did the small firms produce? What were Zaibatsu? How did they develop? How did they work with the government?
13 What progress was made by the armed forces?
14 In what ways were the Japanese unwilling to copy the West?
15 How did the Japanese view personal freedom and authority? What did they think of their country and their Emperor?

Japan's Economic Growth

	1953	1958	1965	1970
Mining	75	85	100	100
Textiles	42	59	118	180
Chemicals	24	50	128	283
Metal Goods	16	35	123	323
Electricity and Gas	35	55	120	214

1963 = 100

Give an account of the Modernization of Japan 1868–1918 under the headings: The Meiji Restoration/Society/Government Agriculture/Industry/Ideas

Japan becomes a Military Dictatorship 1919–40

Questions

1 What social problems were there in the towns? What natural disaster was there? What economic problem was there in the early 1930s? How did the town workers react?
2 What happened to the price of rice and silk? Why? How did farmers suffer as a result? What extra problems did they have?
3 What was the main political problem?
4 How did the government deal with the Communists? What happened to the other left-wing parties?
5 What were the two main political parties? Give two reasons why the mass of the people did not support them.
6 What were the two main nationalist groups? What did they have in common? How were they different — members, political attitude, foreign policy?
7 Give three reasons why the Nationalists became angry in the early 1930s.
8 What action did the Kwantung army take in 1931? What was its excuse? What was its real reason?
9 How were politicians terrorized?
10 What did the Kodo faction do in 1936? How were they crushed? What changes did the Tosei faction make in the government?
11 Why did Japan attack China in 1937?
12 What happened to the political parties?
13 What changes were made in the schools?
14 Which industries took the lead in the 1930s? How did the Japanese use Manchuria? What new powers did the government take?
15 How did military spending increase?
16 In what two ways was nationalism in Japan different from Fascism and Nazism in Europe?

Give an account of how Japan became a dictatorship under the headings: Economic and Social Problems/Political Problems/The Army Seizes Power/Japan under Military Rule

Japan since 1945

Questions

1 Who ruled Japan immediately after the war? What was his policy?
2 List five ways in which Japan was punished.
3 How was the constitution changed?
4 What political parties were there? Which were the most important?
5 Name three Acts that were passed to help the workers, and say what each of them did.
6 Why did land reform seem important? What measures were taken and with what result?
7 What changes were made in education?
8 When did America change her policy towards Japan? Why? What were the results of the change?
9 What changes did the war bring in the way the Japanese think? What have they concentrated on since the war?
10 Name four economic problems Japan faced after the war.
11 How much did farm production increase? Which foods in particular were produced in greater quantity? Name two problems the farmers faced, and say how they overcame them.
12 How much did industrial production increase between 1950 and 1970?
13 Name four of Japan's most important industrial products.
14 What does Japan import? What does she export? Where? With which country does she hope to increase her trade?
15 Name three ways in which the Americans have helped Japan.
16 Why have the Japanese been able to invest large sums in their industries?
17 Give two reasons why Japan has few labour problems.
18 In what ways is Japan still in conflict with the West?

Give an account of Japan since 1945 under the headings: The American Occupation/The Japanese Economy

131

Problems

1 Explain why Japan was able to modernize her economy so rapidly down to 1918.
2 In what ways did Japan come to resemble the Western Powers? In what ways did she remain an Asiatic power?
3 What part has been played by agriculture in the economic growth of Japan?
4 Compare and contrast nationalism in Japan with nationalism in Germany.
5 What influence did the economic depression of the early 1930s have on Japanese affairs?
6 Why did Japan become a military dictatorship?

7 Why did democracy fail in Japan before the Second World War, but succeed after it?
8 'Punishment and reform.' Show how this phrase summarizes MacArthur's policies for Japan.
9 Describe and account for Japan's 'economic miracle' since the Second World War.
10 What contributions have the United States of America made to Japan since the Second World War?
11 How far is it true that Japan is still in conflict with the West?

SECTION SIX

CHINA

Chapter Nineteen

China in 1900

CHINA is vast, being larger than the United States. Two-thirds of the land is barren, but the coastal plain and the river valleys are so fertile they can feed the largest population of any country in the world. In 1900 there were between 400 million and 500 million Chinese. Today there are 900 million.

Such a huge country is difficult to govern, but one thing that has helped is that 90 per cent of the people are of the same race, Han Chinese. Their country has been united for 2000 years, and their civilization is even older. The Chinese were the first to make many useful inventions, like the printing press, the mariner's compass, gunpowder and the wheelbarrow. During the Middle Ages they were well ahead of the Europeans. Had they kept their lead, their sailors might well have 'discovered' Europe and the history of the world would have been different. As it was, for reasons we do not understand, they stopped making progress, so it was the Europeans who discovered China.

Foreign Influence

The first explorers to arrive were the Portuguese, early in the sixteenth century, but others followed, including the British, and all were eager to trade. However, the Chinese despised both foreigners and merchants, so they would allow trade only through the port of Canton. By the nineteenth century, the Europeans were strong enough in the Far East to force the Chinese to trade. For example, in the 1840s Britain fought two 'Opium Wars'. They compelled the Chinese government to allow the British to sell their people opium and to open several ports to their ships. Other European countries were quick to demand the same rights.

Although the British took Hong Kong and the Portuguese took Macao, the Europeans did not colonize China, as they had done Africa. However, they came close to it, for they divided her into 'spheres of influence'. Any country that had a sphere of influence enjoyed a monopoly of trade in it. Britain took the most valuable region, the Yangtze valley, Russia had Manchuria, Germany had Shantung, and France, southern China. Also, there were the Treaty Ports, which the Chinese had been made to open to foreign traders. In each of these foreigners had their own settlements or 'concessions' where the Chinese government had no authority at all.

German and Japanese consulates, Shanghai

Moreover, if a foreigner left his concession, he had 'extraterritorial rights', which meant, among other things, that no Chinese court could put him on trial. The Western Powers insisted on this, since the Chinese had strange ideas of justice. One of their habits was to question suspects under torture. Because of the trade that passed through them, the Treaty Ports were the most advanced cities in China. They were the 'modern hem sewn along the edge of an ancient garment'. The most important was Shanghai, in the British sphere of influence. It had half China's modern industry, it handled half her foreign trade, and with a population of four million it was twice as large as any other city in the country.

Foreigners had a lot of control over the economy of China. They owned 40 per cent of the railways, and two-thirds of the businesses in the Treaty Ports: the British looked after the customs, collecting all the import and export duties on behalf of the government: the French ran the postal services. Many Chinese, including the government, were so heavily in debt to foreigners that a quarter of the national income went on interest and repayments.

As well as foreign business men there were missionaries. They did a little good with their schools and hospitals, but they also gave a lot of offence. Christianity seems a strange faith to the Chinese, and they heartily disliked it.

We must now mention two countries which were late in the 'scramble for China', but which were to be very important for her in the twentieth century. They were Japan and the U.S.A.

Japan took the Liaotung Peninsula after her victory in 1896 (see page 218) but France, Germany and Russia made her give it up. However, her industry was growing rapidly, she badly wanted a colonial empire, and she was waiting for the chance to win one in China. For her part the U.S.A. disliked 'colonialism' so she did not demand privileges from the Chinese. None the less she wanted to trade, and her idea was that the European countries should allow an 'open door'. They were most unwilling to agree.

Government

The rulers of China were the Manchus, who had conquered her in the seventeenth century. They did a great deal of harm. They were only interested in power and money for themselves, and as they were afraid of change, they refused to make reforms or modernize the country. At the head of the Manchu aristocracy was the Emperor, but in 1900 it was the Empress Dowager who had the real power. She was a lady of strong personality and was also tyrannical and wicked. People called her 'Old Buddha'.

For the day-to-day government there were civil servants or 'mandarins'. They were very privileged, and they won their places by passing examinations. That might seem fair, but only rich parents could give their children the long and expensive education that was needed. Also, the examinations were extraordinary. The candidates sat for days in tiny cubicles answering questions on the Chinese classics. It was a test of endurance as much as anything. Certainly, passing the examination did not prove a man was fit to rule others.

Problems

With such a government it is not surprising that China had problems. The worst was the plight of the peasants. They were rapidly becoming poorer because the population was increasing, and farms had to be divided again and again. At the same time the peasants still had to pay their taxes and their rents. Almost all of them were in debt, so they had to pay interest to moneylenders as well. Usually a peasant's landlord was also his moneylender, so he had two good reasons to hate him. From time to time there was famine and peasants died in their millions. Girls were taken into the cities in cartloads, since families, desperate for a little money, sold their daughters.

All the time there was a great hatred of foreigners and the Manchus. In 1900, there was a rebellion by people called Boxers. The British gave them this name, because they did exercises that looked like boxing. The rebels directed their anger mainly against foreigners, killing missionaries and laying siege to the legations in Peking. 'Old Buddha' sent them help in secret, but dared not do so openly for fear of war. In the end, an international force marched on Peking and saved the legations. Afterwards, in 1901, the foreign powers forced the Chinese to accept what is known as the Boxer Protocol. This included humiliating terms, like the destruction of forts and the payment of a heavy indemnity.

What was the Manchu government to do for the future? There were three possibilities, none of them pleasant. It could give way to the foreigners, but that would annoy the Chinese and lead to more rebellion. It could give way to the Chinese, but they wanted to expel the foreigners, so that would mean a war China was bound to lose. It could make the country strong by modernizing it, but that would mean losing power. No modern country would accept the rule of people like the Manchus.

Chapter Twenty

The Nationalist Revolution

As WE saw in the last section, the Manchu government had a difficult choice to make. In the end, the Empress Dowager decided, though very unwillingly, to modernize the country, so she brought in all kinds of reforms. It was too late. She died in 1908, and in 1911 there was a revolution which overthrew the Manchus. This was the work of Chinese Nationalists, and was their first important success in their struggle for power. We can most easily understand what happened by following the careers of two of their leaders, Sun Yat-sen and Chiang Kai-shek.

Sun Yat-sen

Sun trained to be a lawyer at an English school in Hong Kong, and he also studied in the U.S.A., Britain and Japan. His travels showed him how badly the Manchus were treating China, so he decided to try to overthrow them. Working from Tokyo, he formed a secret society which won over many people in China, including numbers of army officers. Sun gave his party the slogan 'Nationalism, Democracy and People's Livelihood'. These were the 'Three Principles of the People.' Nationalism meant deposing the Manchus, and driving out the foreigners. Democracy meant allowing the people to govern themselves. People's livelihood, however, was rather vague, though it did seem to mean that the Nationalists intended to share the land fairly among the peasants.

Sun organized no less than ten risings in south China, but they all failed. Then, on 10 October 1911, a day known later as the 'Double Tenth', there was a rebellion at Wuhan. A bomb went off by accident in the Russian concession, and when the police went to investigate they found a list of army officers who were plotting against the government. These officers realized they must act before they were arrested, so they at once seized the town. The rebellion then spread to other cities, and its leaders invited Sun Yat-sen to be President of the Republic of China. The government sent its best general, Yuan Shi-kai, to put down the rebels but, instead, he joined them. The Manchus saw they were beaten and decided that the infant Emperor, Henry Pu-yi, should abdicate. The rebels then made plans for the election of a National Assembly. At the same time the Nationalists formed their own political party, the Kuomintang, (K.M.T.) and, in 1912,

Sun Yat-sen

Chiang Kai-shek

they won most of the seats in the Assembly. That should have meant they were safely in power, but, in fact, their troubles were only just beginning.

When the Manchus were overthrown, Yuan Shi-kai insisted that he should be President and, since he commanded a large army, Sun Yat-sen stood down in his favour. Yuan then expelled the K.M.T. members from the Assembly and announced that he was going to take the title of Emperor. His unpopularity grew when he had to give way to Japan (see below). He was forced to abandon his grand ideas and died, perhaps of disappointment, in 1916.

China was now virtually without a government, and the military commanders in each of the provinces ruled their areas just as they pleased. These warlords, as they were called, were a mixed bunch. They included a former peasant, an ex-bandit, and a classical scholar. Fen Yu-hsiang, the so-called Christian General, boasted that he had baptized some of his heathen troops with a fire hose. Some warlords ruled well, but most of them did not. One trick was to collect taxes in advance: by 1920, the peasants of Szechwan Province had paid all they owed until 1957. Worse, there was a great deal of fighting, so crops were not gathered, and there was famine.

At the same time, Japan was causing trouble. She declared war on Germany in 1914 in return for a promise from the allies that she should have Shantung. Her troops defeated the Germans there the same year. Then, in 1915, Japan took advantage of the disorder in China to press on her what are known as the 'Twenty-one Demands'. Yuan Shi-kai was still in power at the time and he persuaded the Japanese to withdraw the worst of these demands, but he was forced to accept a number of them, much to the disgust of the Chinese.

China herself declared war on Germany in 1917, and at the Peace Conference her delegates asked that there should be an end to foreign interference in their country. The allies not only refused, but kept their promise to Japan by giving her Shantung. This was too much for the

138

Chinese, and beginning on 4 May 1919, there were violent demonstrations in Peking and other cities. This surge of national feeling is called the '4 May Movement'. Japan had gained a valuable province of China, but she had also, quite unintentionally, won the K.M.T. many supporters.

After Yuan died, Sun Yat-sen organized a Republican government that ruled the area around Canton. However, he had few troops, so he relied on the protection of the local warlord. In 1922, this man turned against him, and he fled to Shanghai, having been rescued by a young officer called Chiang Kai-shek. Sun now realized he must take any help he could find, so he turned to the newly formed Chinese Communist Party. He also looked to Russia. A number of Chinese Communists joined the K.M.T., and as for the Russians, they were only too glad to have friends, since in those days it seemed that the whole world was against them. To help the K.M.T., they sent a political agent called Borodin. He advised them to organize party cells, as the Bolsheviks had done in Russia. Each of these was a small group of agents belonging, for example, to the same factory, dockyard or regiment, and who tried to win over the people with whom they worked. This plan was a great success, for the 4 May Movement had roused many Chinese, and they gladly followed the K.M.T.

The Russians also sent the K.M.T. weapons, and showed them how to organize an army. Sun Yat-sen opened a military academy for officers at Whampoa, and put Chiang Kai-shek in charge. Chiang went to Moscow to see how the Russians trained their own officers. It was not long before Sun had a powerful force called the National Revolutionary Army, and was able to plan a Northern Expedition. The K.M.T. were to defeat the warlords one by one, and win control over the whole of China. However, Sun became seriously ill, and he died in 1925, before his army was ready to march. Chiang Kai-shek took his place as leader of the K.M.T.

Chiang Kai-shek

By 1926 the K.M.T. army was ready for the Northern Expedition so, with its allies the Communists, it advanced towards the Yangtze Valley. By March 1927 they had occupied all China south of the river. While the armies were winning battles, the peasants rose in rebellion against their landlords, and workers attacked factories. They helped the K.M.T. and the Communists a great deal, but they alarmed the Shanghai business men who were giving Chiang the money he needed for his armies. He had to choose between his Communist allies and Russian friends on the one hand, and his rich supporters on the other. He did not hesitate because, unlike Sun Yat-sen, he was to the right of his party and because he feared that when the warlords were defeated the Communists would seize power for themselves. Accordingly he ordered the Shanghai Massacres. The Communist leaders in Shanghai were murdered, and all members of the party were expelled from the K.M.T. and the National Revolutionary Army.

Later that year the K.M.T. forces advanced again. In 1928 they captured Peking and overran almost the whole of the North, except Manchuria.

China was at last under the control of the Nationalists who had won so much support from the people, and had promised them so much in return.

However, the ordinary Chinese were soon disappointed, because Chiang Kai-shek had little success with Sun Yat-sen's three aims, nationalism, democracy and people's livelihood. He did best with nationalism, because he had reunited the country. However, Manchuria was still ruled by a warlord, called the Young Marshal, who did much as he pleased. Meanwhile Japan was as big a danger as ever. There was no sign of democracy at all. Chiang was, in fact, a dictator, kept in power by the army and people such as the landlords, factory owners, merchants and financiers. With regard to people's livelihood, Chiang saw he must modernize the country, so he improved transport and communications as well as reforming the currency and the law courts. There were also changes in education, and women were given more rights. However, all this did not make much difference to the ordinary Chinese, especially the peasants. They had hoped the revolution would give them what they wanted most in the world — more land. Instead, it brought them nothing. The government was in league with the landlords and financiers, so the wretched peasants had to go on paying their taxes, their rents and their debts. They were to have their revenge, though, because later they gave the Communists the help they needed to overthrow the K.M.T.

Chapter Twenty-one

The Communist Revolution

Mao Tse-tung and the Beginnings of the Communist Revolution

IN THE late nineteenth and early twentieth centuries many educated and intelligent Chinese turned away from the beliefs their ancestors had held for centuries. The change came with the riots of 1919 — the 4 May Movement. However, it is not enough to abandon old ideas: there must be new ones to take their place. Many people became Nationalists, but a handful turned to Communism. In 1919 they founded the Chinese Communist Party, the same year that the 4 May Movement began.

The C.C.P. held its first conference at Shanghai in 1921. There were just twelve delegates, and the whole party was only fifty strong. They made up for their small numbers by being very active, and in 1922 helped organize no less than a hundred strikes among railwaymen, miners and merchant seamen.

There was an important development in 1923 when as we saw in the previous chapter, the C.C.P. formed the First United Front with the K.M.T. However, this came to an abrupt end in 1927 when Chiang Kai-shek ordered the Shanghai Massacres.

The Communists and the Nationalists were now bitter enemies, and there was fighting between them. A general called Chu-Teh led an army mutiny in central China. It failed, but Chu-Teh and his men organized the first units of the Red Army or People's Liberation Army, as it was later called. At the same time a young Communist, Mao Tse-tung, led what he called his 'autumn harvest rising' in Hunan Province. That also failed and in 1928 Mao and Chu-Teh joined forces on a remote plateau between Hunan and Kiangsi. They had only 10 000 men between them, but they decided they would make the plateau their base and hold out there for as long as they could. Other Communists also set up bases in remote parts of China.

Meanwhile, the members of the Central Committee of the Communist Party led by Li Li-san were hiding in Shanghai. These men had studied the writings of Marx and Lenin which said that only town workers would make good Communists. They knew, as well, that the Russian Revolution had been organized in the towns, so they said that the Chinese Revolution must be organized in the same way. They also took advice from Moscow which was, not surprisingly, to concentrate on the towns. Accordingly, they ordered Chu and Mao to attack two cities in their area. They failed completely, and fled back to their plateau.

Mao now made two important decisions. The first was that no matter what Marx and Lenin had written, and no matter what Li Li-san and the Russians might order, he was going to organize a revolution with the help of the peasants. After all, there were only two million town workers in China, while there were well over 400 million peasants. The second thing he decided was that the People's Liberation Army would have to be a lot stronger before it could fight the K.M.T. armies in a conventional war. Instead it would use guerrilla tactics. Mao described them:

> The enemy attacks, we retreat:
> The enemy camps, we harass:
> The enemy tires, we attack:
> The enemy retreats, we pursue.

To keep the peasants on the side of the Communists, Mao gave his soldiers *Eight Points for Attention*:

1 Speak politely
2 Pay fairly for what you buy
3 Return everything you borrow
4 Pay for anything you damage
5 Don't hit or swear at people
6 Don't damage crops
7 Don't take liberties with women
8 Don't ill-treat captives

No army had ever behaved towards the people of China as the P.L.A. did. The peasants were amazed and did all they could to help. They sent them food, cared for the wounded, laid mines, gave the Communists true information about the Nationalists and gave the Nationalists false information about the Communists. Nearly all the new recruits for the P.L.A. were peasants, most of them young, and some of them boys.

Mao and Chu had soon to test their ideas, for in 1930 Chiang Kai-shek organized an 'extermination campaign'. His men had to fight an invisible enemy that simply melted away as they advanced, but cut their communications and hit them hard when they were least expecting it. Soon, they fell back in disorder, leaving behind thousands of prisoners. Most of them joined the P.L.A. Chiang tried twice more with bigger forces, and with even more disastrous results, and meanwhile the P.L.A. grew from 10 000 men to 300 000. However, Chiang now found some German generals to advise him. They told him to stop sending his men into the jungle but, instead, to use his enormous army to surround the Communist base with a ring of blockhouses, barbed wire and motor roads: Chiang mounted a fourth and a fifth extermination campaign on these lines with great success. Mao and Chu were soon worried, for they were running out of supplies and their army had dwindled to 100 000 men. They came to a desperate decision. They must break out of Chiang's trap, though they had little idea where they would go.

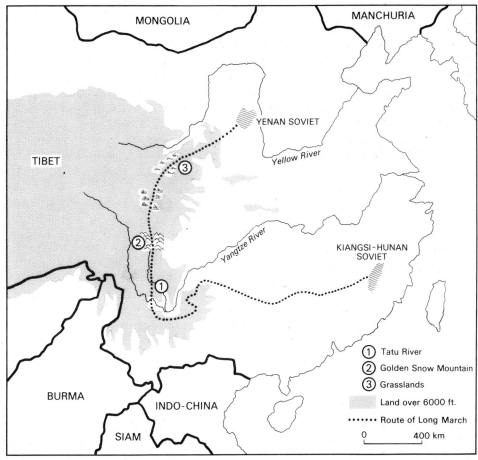

The Long March 1934–5

The Long March

In October 1936 Mao and Chu mustered their forces, 100 000 men and 34 women, and smashed their way through Chiang's lines. This was the beginning of the Long March, the most famous event in the history of the Chinese Communists. At first Mao hoped he might set up a new base, not far from the one he had left, but he soon realized the K.M.T. was too strong in southern China. He made a second desperate decision. He would go north to Shensi Province, where another Communist leader Kao Kung had a base at Yenan. As the crow flies, the distance to Yenan was about 1100 km, but to be safe Mao and his men had to go through western China, which is wild and remote. In all, they walked 10 000 km, crossing 18 mountain ranges, 24 rivers and a trackless swamp in Tibet misleadingly called the Grasslands. They also had to fight a number of battles. The survivors reached Yenan 386 days after leaving Kiangsi but only about a quarter of them were left. Most of the others had died, though a good many stayed in villages along the way to convert the people to Communism.

143

Tapestry depicting the Long March

What were the results of the Long March? Probably it saved Communism in China. There were other armies also fleeing from the K.M.T. and making their own long marches, but it was Mao and his followers at Yenan who won the final victory. Not only did the marchers save Communism, but they helped spread it, for they won converts all along their route. Their good behaviour meant the peasants were willing to listen to their ideas. Also, while the march was taking place, Mao was elected leader of the Chinese Communist Party. That meant the Chinese Revolution would go its own way, without interference from Moscow. None the less, the Long March was a retreat, and as Mao himself admitted, you do not win a war by retreating. Now he and his men were safe, he had to organize a revolt to overthrow Chiang and the K.M.T.

The Yenan Border Region

Mao's first task was to form a Communist State in the Yenan Border Region. Yenan is quite a large city, so the K.M.T. aircraft were able to find it and bomb it easily. For protection, the people burrowed into the soft rocks of the hillsides and lived in the caves they had made. The K.M.T. cut off supplies, so the Communists farmed more land, and started their own industries. There was a Communist government as well, of course, and it was efficient. The Border Region was the only part of China that was run properly.

To win over the rest of China to Communism, Mao made his people do four things. They trained cadres, they won over the peasants, they built up their army and they fought the Japanese.

The word 'cadre' has several meanings, but here it simply stands for 'Communist agent'. These men had to learn what Communism was, so

144

they studied at what was called the 'cave university of Yenan'. They had the works of Karl Marx and plenty of books on Russian Communism. However, they also had to know about the particular kind of Communism that Mao wanted in China. This was new, so there were no books about it and Mao had to write them himself. He was more than happy to do so. He finished one in nine days, working continuously without any sleep. He concentrated so hard that he was lost to everything around him. Once, someone found him with his foot in the fire and his shoe burning.

Winning over the peasants was essential, so the P.L.A. went on obeying the 'Eight Points for Attention'. In Shensi, the Communists did not drive away the landlords because they could not afford to have any enemies. However, they made them reduce their rents, which pleased the peasants. Also, they broke in virgin land, and shared it among poor people who had no farms. For their part, the peasants of Shensi helped the Communists in much the same ways as those of Hunan and Kiangsi had done.

A strong army was essential, if the Communists were to win. As Mao said, 'Political power grows out of the barrel of a gun'. The People's Liberation Army had been started by Chu-Teh in 1927, and by 1945 it was one million strong. Its morale was high and its discipline was excellent. The main problem was finding arms. The peasants made wooden cannon and primitive land-mines, but the P.L.A. captured most of its weapons from the Japanese and the Nationalists. Mao boasted, 'The K.M.T. are our ammunition bearers.'

It might seem strange that the Communists fought the Japanese as well as the K.M.T., but in fact it was a clever move. Not only had the Manchus given way to foreigners, but so had Yuan Shi-kai and Chiang Kai-shek. Mao showed the people of China that it was only the Communists that would drive out the foreigner, and this won him a lot of support. To understand what happened we must now look at the Japanese attacks on China.

The War with Japan

As Japan was a growing industrial power, she wanted to trade with China. She was especially interested in Manchuria because of its grain, coal and iron. In 1905, after defeating Russia, she leased Port Arthur and built the South Manchurian Railway. In 1915, Yuan Shi-kai agreed to several of her Twenty-one Demands, which allowed her to own mines and steel works there. Gradually, the Japanese were taking over Manchuria, and by 1930, the Young Marshal realized he must stop them before it was too late. The Japanese decided that what they could not take peacefully, they would take by force. In 1931, there was the 'Mukden Incident'. All that happened was that someone blew up a short length of railway near Mukden, but the Japanese used this as an excuse to drive the Young Marshal and his troops out of Manchuria. They did so in five weeks. It was full scale war, but the Japanese called it the 'Manchurian Incident'.

Chiang Kai-shek at once stopped his third extermination campaign against Mao Tse-tung, but soon decided he would rather fight

145

Communists than Japanese. All he did was to appeal to the League of Nations, but Japan simply left the League and the League did nothing (see page 226). Japan now renamed Manchuria 'Manchukuo', and set up a puppet government there under Henry Pu-yi, the last of the Manchu emperors. In fact, the province was part of Japan's growing empire.

In 1936 there was the 'Sian Incident'. By that time the Long March was over and Mao Tse-tung and his followers were in Shensi. The Young Marshal was also in North China, so Chiang ordered him to attack the Communists. The Young Marshal and his men said they should fight the Japanese rather than their fellow countrymen, so they refused. To try and persuade them, Chiang flew to their headquarters at Sian, and they at once kidnapped him. The Young Marshal told the Communists what he had done, and they sent one of their leaders, Chou En-lai, to negotiate. Both the Young Marshal and Chou thought that if they killed Chiang the warlords would once again seize power. Instead, they made him promise to call off his campaign against the Communists, and join forces with them against the Japanese. This was known as the 'Second United Front'. The Japanese were alarmed because the Chinese were uniting against them. Even more important, their military leaders wanted a war to enable them to win support in their own country (see page 120). They decided to attack without delay.

Yet again Japan found an excuse quite easily. One of her many rights in China was to station troops in Peking. During a night in July 1937 a small patrol of them was fired on at the Marco Polo Bridge near the city. Japan at once invaded. Two incidents in the war are worth particular mention. One was the heroic defence of Shanghai, where the Chinese held out for three months and surrendered the city only when it was completely cut off. The other was the destruction of Nanking by the Japanese. In earlier wars, they had behaved properly to their defeated enemies, but at Nanking they looted, murdered and tortured at will. They were to do the same in many more cities before their final defeat in 1945.

By 1939 the Japanese had taken all of China's ports and overrun her fertile lowlands. Chiang moved his capital to Chunking, and his armies were at least able to keep their enemies out of the mountains. The 'China Incident', as the Japanese called it, reached stalemate.

In 1941, Japan attacked the United States and Britain, so Chiang at once had allies. He even declared war on Japan himself. The Americans and the British sent him supplies, even though they had to fly them over the Himalayas after the Japanese took Burma. However, Chiang did almost nothing. He saw that, in the end, his allies would defeat the Japanese for him, and he was determined that when that day came, his armies would be intact, and able to defeat the Communists.

Clearly, the Second United Front was no more, so it was left to the P.L.A. to fight the Japanese on its own. It did well, and in its usual way, by using guerrilla tactics and working with the peasants. The Japanese answered with their 'three alls' — 'burn all, slay all, loot all'. It was no use; by 1945 the Communists had won back almost all the territory the Japanese had conquered, except the cities.

The Civil War

After the defeat of Germany, Russia declared war on Japan and occupied Manchuria. Japan surrendered soon afterwards and the Chinese Nationalists and Communists raced each other to seize the territory she had held. As we have seen, the Communists already held the countryside in the North, but even so the Nationalists reached the cities first. The reason was that the Americans lifted half a million K.M.T. troops into them, by sea and air. In Manchuria, the Russians stayed long enough to help themselves to $2000 million worth of equipment, and then withdrew. The Communists gained control of most of the province, but once again the K.M.T. took the cities. The position then was that the K.M.T. held all of south China, and the northern cities, but the P.L.A. controlled the countryside in the North.

Soon there was serious fighting which alarmed the Americans. President Truman sent General George Marshall to China, and he arranged a truce in December 1945. However, the two sides could not agree. For their part the Communists wanted a share in the government and Chiang refused this. Fighting broke out again so General Marshall went home in despair.

At first, the K.M.T. forces outnumbered the P.L.A. by three to one, and they had complete control of the air. America sent them weapons, while even Stalin favoured them. He was still clinging to his policy of 'Communism in one country'. Chiang mounted three offensives, one in Manchuria, one in Shantung and one in Shensi. Down to 1947 he seemed

K.M.T. soldier executes a P.L.A. suspect

147

to be winning, especially as his men captured Yenan. However, the P.L.A. was no longer interested in that remote border town: it was out to conquer the whole of China. It gained recruits the whole time, many of them deserters from the other side, so that by 1948, it was equal in size to the K.M.T. armies. It was able to give up guerrilla tactics and fight pitched battles in the field. First, it cut off the Manchurian towns and forced their garrisons to surrender. Then, at the end of 1948 it engaged Chiang's armies at the battle of Huai Hai, in central China. The Nationalists were routed in two months of bitter fighting and after that, offered little serious resistance. Peking and Tientsin were cut off as a result of the battle, so they surrendered early in 1949. The P.L.A. then crossed the Yangtze and, on 1 October Mao Tse-tung proclaimed the People's Republic of China. Chiang fled with the remains of his army of Taiwan.

What were the reasons for the Communists' success? First of all, there were weaknesses in the K.M.T. armies. The officers were inefficient, they ill-treated their troops, and they were corrupt. They drew pay for men they did not have, and pocketed the money themselves: they stole supplies: they even sold arms to the Communists. On the other hand, the P.L.A. was a well disciplined force, with good officers.

Secondly, there was inflation. Owing to all the fighting, food and goods were scarce and prices rose rapidly — so rapidly that they rose three hundred times between the years 1942 and 1945. Wages did not rise nearly as fast. For example, in 1943, civil servants' salaries had only one-tenth of their 1937 value. Probably, Chiang Kai-shek's government could have done little to halt this inflation, but it did not try, so even middle-class Chinese people began to favour the Communists.

However, the main reason why the Communists won their military battles was because they had already won a much more difficult political battle for the hearts and minds of the Chinese people, especially the peasants. Things might have been different if the K.M.T. had remained true to Sun Yat-sen's Three Principles of the People, but under Chiang Kai-shek, it only paid lip-service to them.

Chapter Twenty-two

Communist China

Founding the Communist State

WHEN the Communists won the civil war they saw it not as the end of their struggle, but as its beginning. They were rulers of the country with the largest population in the world, and they had to turn her into a Communist State.

Mao was desperate for help so he looked to Moscow, and in 1950 China and Russia made a Treaty of Friendship. That gave China two advantages. She had a powerful ally against her chief enemy, the United States, and Russia gave her help and advice.

Agriculture was especially important. In 1950 a law was passed to allow peasants to take land from their landlords. Cadres went to every village, and encouraged the peasants to say how they had been treated. If a landlord had been fair, he was allowed to keep a small farm for himself. If, however, he had been cruel, or had been active in the K.M.T. or had co-operated with the Japanese, then he lost all his land. More than that, he was tried before a people's court and probably executed. We do not know how many landlords died, but it is certain that more land changed owners in China during 1950 than has ever done so in any country of the world. Redistributing the land helped the Communists politically, for it won over those peasants who were not already on their side, and it destroyed their chief enemies, the landlords. However, there was no improvement in farming, for the peasants went on working in the same old ways. China needed more food, so Mao decided to make collective farms. He knew they had failed disastrously in Russia so he acted carefully, and tried to persuade his people they were a good idea.

The first stage was to encourage groups of between six and ten families to form 'mutual aid teams'. They kept their own farms, but helped each other at busy times in the year. Next came 'producers' co-operatives' of between thirty and forty families. They put all their small farms together to make a single large one. Each family still owned its land, however, and its share of the crops depended on how much it had lent to the co-operative. When the peasants had seen how efficient the co-operatives were, there came the third stage, which was the collective farm. This was likely to be a whole village of, perhaps, eighty or a hundred families. The big difference from the co-operatives, though, was that every peasant parted with his

A vegetable-growing commune, Shanghai

land, and his share of the crops depended on how much work he had done during the year. It is unlikely that the collectives were more efficient than the co-operatives, but since the peasants no longer owned the land, they were well on their way to being good Communists. No one who has property can be a Communist, any more than a man who is driving a car is a pedestrian. He must leave his vehicle and walk, if he is to make the change.

The Communists had similar plans for industry. They wanted to take it out of private hands and also make it more efficient. As with agriculture, they went forward in easy stages. Immediately after the war they just took control of foreign trade, the banks and financial institutions, like insurance companies. Later, they nationalized the few heavy industries that existed and then gradually took over the light industries. However, Mao did not want to lose the skill and experience of the former employers, so they were given jobs in their old firms, often as managers. They also had payment over and above their salaries as some small compensation for losing their businesses.

To develop industry there was a Five Year Plan which ran from 1953 to 1957. For this, the Chinese had help from the Russians. They lent 10 per cent of the capital needed, and they sent technicians and advisers who organized about a quarter of the 694 projects in the Plan. Moreover, the whole Plan followed the Russian model, for the central government controlled it closely, and it concentrated on heavy industries, like iron and steel, coal, cement, chemicals and electricity.

Mao had hoped the Plan would double industrial output, but it did far better since it increased it by 120 per cent. However, there were problems.

150

The new industries did not create many jobs, because they needed machines, rather than people. Also there were few consumer goods, like clothing and bicycles, which the ordinary Chinese were desperate to have. Centralized control did not work very well because the officials in Peking who made the decisions were too far from many of the new factories to understand their problems. Finally, the Plan only helped the towns to modernize, so the villages began to fall behind. The Chinese Communists felt this was especially unfortunate because their Revolution, unlike the one in Russia, had begun in the countryside.

As well as developing agriculture and industry, the Communists made a number of social reforms, such as improving public health, creating better working conditions in the factories and building more schools. Much was done to help women, for as Mao Tse-tung said, they 'hold up half the sky'. For example, the Marriage Law of 1950 ended arranged marriages, child betrothals and polygamy, and allowed divorce.

Finally we come to the task which Mao and his followers thought was the most important of all. This was to convert the mass of the people to Communism.

First of all they tried to destroy all the old ideas and values. They turned society upside down, so that those at the top were the workers, peasants, soldiers, and the ones at the bottom were the former landlords. The Communists attacked Confucianism, which taught blind obedience to the father of the family. They said that if a man's opinions did not agree with the teachings of Mao Tse-tung, then it was the duty of his wife and children to rebel against him. They also used the educational system to favour the children of workers and peasants. It helped them into the best jobs, and the most important positions, instead of the children from what had once been the middle-class families.

As well as attacking the old ideas, the Communists also taught their own. Cadres went into every village and factory, where they ran endless meetings to discuss the writings of Chairman Mao. Once they had won over the majority of the people, it was difficult for any individual to resist. He would be heckled and bullied until he gave way and admitted his mistakes in a painful session of 'self-criticism'. If he still refused to believe in Communism he might be sent to some remote village for a spell of very hard work. They called this 'remoulding through labour'.

The work of the cadres went on all the time, but occasionally, the government started a special campaign. One was the 'three anti' campaign of 1951, and this was directed against the cadres themselves. It seems that not all of them were a credit to the Communist Party, being guilty of the three faults of waste, corruption and bureaucracy. Next, there was the 'five anti' campaign of 1952. It was directed against the few capitalists that remained, and was really no more than an excuse to nationalize their businesses. The five faults were bribery, dodging taxes, fraud, stealing government property, and stealing State economic secrets.

However, much more remarkable than either of these was the 'hundred flowers campaign' of 1956. Mao was worried about China's five million or so intellectuals. Intellectuals are people like writers, university professors

151

and scientists who work with their brains rather than their hands. Mao badly wanted their help, but he felt he could not trust them because they were not, for the most part, convinced Communists. How could he convert them? He was sure that he and his followers could persuade anyone that Communism was right, if only they would come into the open and argue freely. Accordingly, in 1956 he made a speech in which he said, 'Let a hundred flowers bloom, let a hundred schools of thought contend'. He invited anyone to criticize the government, in any way he pleased. He thought there would be a great debate, which the Communists would be sure to win, because their ideas were the correct ones. The intellectuals would then be won over and become loyal and reliable.

At first, people could hardly believe they were being asked to speak their minds, but when they saw Mao was in earnest, some said a very great deal. So, far from the Communists winning the argument, they were overwhelmed with abuse from all quarters. Mao realized his plan had backfired, he gave orders and all criticism of his government stopped abruptly. Instead, there was a lot of self-criticism by prominent people, who confessed their faults in public, so as to save their necks. Many of them also spent some time down on the farm, being 'remoulded by labour'.

Soon after the Revolution ended in 1949, the Communist leaders began to differ. The right-wing members of the party thought it best to be cautious, and not force people to accept their beliefs too quickly. For example, they were willing to let peasants own private plots of land, and to put factory workers on bonus schemes, so that if they produced more, they had extra wages to take home. Also, they thought that if someone like a factory manager was good at his job, then his politics did not matter too much. The left wing of the party, led by Mao Tse-tung, disagreed. To them, private property was capitalism, and quite the opposite of Communism. They also believed that Communists should work for the benefit of everyone, and not to put money into their own pockets. Certainly they thought the politics of the men in charge were vitally important. They felt the same towards a manager who was not a Communist as we would towards a minister of religion was was an atheist.

Mao and the left were strong enough to cause two major upheavals, the Great Leap Forward and the Great Proletarian Cultural Revolution.

The Great Leap Forward

When the first Five Year Plan ended in 1957, the government began another. Almost at once, Mao Tse-tung brushed it aside and announced what he called the Great Leap Forward.

In the first place, China's economy was to grow rapidly, overtaking Britain in steel production, for example. Also, she was to solve the problems of the First Five Year Plan by 'walking on two legs', as Mao put it. That meant she would use traditional Chinese methods, as well as the new ones imported from Russia. There were to be projects that would create many jobs, like building dams without the aid of machines: there were to be more light industries and handicrafts: agriculture was to be encouraged:

the central government was to control only heavy industry, leaving local authorities to run everything else.

Even more important for Mao, China was to become a Communist State. Karl Marx had taught that only a highly developed industrial country could be Communist, and this was what the Russians believed. They thought of themselves as only Socialists, which is to say they were one stage short of being Communists. However China, which was still mainly agricultural, and far more backward, was proposing to become Communist in one Great Leap. Let us suppose a student who is hoping to go to a university has just entered the sixth form. How would he feel if his little brother aged 11, said he was going to a university immediately without bothering to attend a secondary school at all? Obviously, he would tell the younger boy not to talk nonsense, and this is just what the Russians told the Chinese.

Mao, however, was determined to go ahead, and was sure he could succeed if 'politics were in control'. That meant two things. In the first place, people would have to follow the ideas of the Communist Party, for example by working hard, not to make money for themselves, but to help China. Secondly, the cadres would direct operations. If there was a road to be built, the man in charge must be a dedicated Communist, rather than a trained civil engineer. Ideally, he would be both, but if there had to be a choice, it was better for him to be 'Red' than 'expert'.

How was Mao to realize all these aims? His method was to set up communes which were to be the units of the Communist State. Each was a number of collective farms grouped together, amounting to about 5000 families. The first was 'Sputnik' Commune in Hunan which started in April 1958. By the end of the year, there were no less than 23 000 covering almost the whole of China. This huge change had come about astonishingly quickly.

Each commune was almost self-sufficient, and it looked after its own affairs. Obviously, its most important work was farming, but it also developed industries. Some of these helped agriculture, for example making and mending farm equipment, manufacturing fertilizers, and refining sugar: others were handicrafts, such as mat weaving and basket making: in many communes there were even small 'backyard' blast-furnaces for smelting iron. All these industries were 'labour intensive' which meant they employed people rather than machines. There was plenty to be done, now, even during the slack season for farming. In the old days the average peasant had worked only 190 days a year, but in a commune he could work for 250.

The communes were big enough to carry out public works. They built hospitals and schools, and they made roads. For centuries, China's rivers had caused problems, sometimes running dry, and sometimes flooding. The communes tried to tame them by strengthening their banks and building dams. Millions of people, including city dwellers, turned out to help with the bigger projects. They had no earth-moving machinery, so they used such tools as they had. Many dug the earth with their bare hands, and carried it in baskets. Still, they worked with great enthusiasm and shifted countless tonnes of rock and soil. The swarms of Chinese

153

Steel mill

toiling away in cheap blue cotton clothes earned themselves the name of 'blue ants'. Even Chairman Mao became one for a time, and many important people, like university professors and scientists, followed his example. It was not an intelligent way for them to spend their time.

The commune not only found work for its members, but it looked after them as well. It took care of the elderly, and it ran schools and hospitals. As there were not enough doctors, they had medical orderlies who understood first aid and knew how to cure the more straightforward complaints. They were called 'barefoot doctors'. They did valuable work, as well as leaving the fully trained doctors free to treat those patients who were seriously ill. The doctors were good examples of people who 'walked on two legs'. They used not only modern medicine, but traditional Chinese methods as well, such as acupuncture.

Finally, each commune had its own militia, which was something like the Home Guard in Britain during the war. It kept order and it also meant that if any foreign army invaded China, it would find armed men, trained and able to resist it, all over the country.

The Great Leap Forward began in 1958, and even as soon as 1959 many people were beginning to have doubts about it. By the end of 1960, it was obvious it had failed. Why was this? Partly it was because of all the haste to begin, which meant a lack of planning and a lot of confusion. A more important reason, though, was that what the Russians had said was true — the Chinese were not ready for Communism. Very few were willing to work entirely for the communes and forget about themselves. Also, it soon became clear that enthusiasm for politics could not replace skills. There is a story of some men who had been asked to build a wall within one month. They promised they would only take a fortnight, and worked so hard that it was finished in a week. This was so splendid that the entire Provincial Party Committee came to congratulate the workers. Just as they arrived the wall fell down. Many incidents of this kind convinced people that if they wanted a job done properly, it was better to send for an 'expert' rather than a 'Red'.

In January 1961 the right wing of the Communist Party took charge. It announced that the Great Leap Forward was over, and made certain changes. The communes remained, but they were cut down to about one-third of their original size, and lost most of their duties. They became units of local government, like English counties, and only organized large projects like water-supplies and irrigation. All the day-to-day tasks in farming and rural industry were given to production brigades, which were, for the most part, the former collective farms. Each of these was a village, which was the unit the peasant understood, and for which he would work quite happily. Also, as in Russia, peasants were given plots of land for themselves and, again as in Russia, these little plots produced much more food, in proportion to their size, than the land worked by the collectives. In the factories, professional managers took over from enthusiastic, but untrained Communists, while workers were put on piece rates and bonus schemes. Slowly China's economy began to recover.

The Great Proletarian Cultural Revolution

After the Great Leap Forward had failed, the right wing of the Communist Party ruled China. There were men like Liu Shao-chi, the new Head of State, Teng Hsiao-ping, the General Secretary of the Party, and Peng Chen, the Mayor of Peking. They made changes which Mao thoroughly disliked. There was less equality, since peasants with private plots and workers on piece rates made themselves richer than their neighbours. What was worse, Communist leaders won privileges for themselves, and gave orders to the mass of the people, instead of being guided by them. Secondly, politics became less important than efficiency. Teng Hsiao-ping said, 'What does it matter if the cat is black or white, as long as it catches mice?' Mao felt the Revolution was in danger from these 'revisionists' and he was especially worried that the young people would be led astray. Accordingly, in 1966 he organized the 'Cultural Revolution'. He was helped by the left wing of the part, and by his wife Chiang Ching.

Mao chose the term 'Cultural Revolution' because he wanted to change the way people thought. Probably, he felt the Great Leap Forward had failed because too many Chinese had clung to their old beliefs. This time, though, it would be different. Everyone would be carried away with enthusiasm for Communism, and then they would all work with a will to make their country rich and powerful. So that the people understood Communism he set out his main ideas in a little book. Its title was *The Thoughts of Mao Tse-tung*, though it is more often known as *The Little Red Book of Chairman Mao*. Between 1966 and 1968, 740 million copies were printed.

Mao also hoped the Cultural Revolution would take power from the revisionists and give it back to the masses. He hoped, too, that there would be more equality between factory workers and peasants, between town and countryside, and between those who worked with their brains and those who worked with their hands.

155

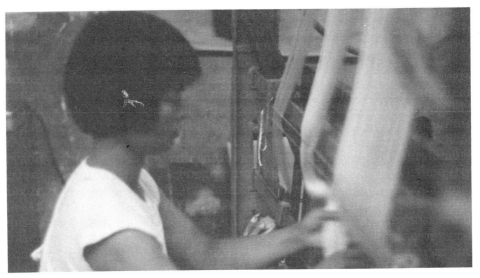

Silk weaver

In 1966, Mao first removed his more serious political rivals from power. He then swam 10 km down the Yangtze River to prove that, although he was 73 years old, he was still fit and well. Next, the schools and colleges were closed, and the young people trained to be Red Guards. Trouble began at Peking University, where the students put up 'big character posters', criticizing their teachers. Mao himself wrote one called *Bombard the Headquarters*. Soon, the movement spread to the whole of China. There were processions and demonstrations, while Red Guards searched houses looking for such things as portraits of Chiang Kai-shek and classical books. They also attacked shops that sold western-style goods, and people wearing western fashions. Millions of Red Guards were given free rail passes to travel to Peking, where they paraded in front of Chairman Mao, shouting slogans from his 'Little Red Book' and waving copies of it in the air. They certainly took Mao's advice to 'bombard the headquarters', for they criticized the right-wing Communist leaders fiercely.

Mao was like a headmaster encouraging his pupils to turn on their teachers. He did this because he felt there was no hope of reforming the party from within, so he had to use enthusiastic young Communists to attack it from outside.

In the factories, Revolutionary Committees of workers took over and gave the former managers an unhappy time. They had to make 'self-criticism' and be 'remoulded through labour' which meant sweeping the floors or minding the machines.

Mao felt that people knew too little about each other's work. Accordingly, peasants had to take factory workers' jobs for a few weeks in the year, while factory workers went on the farms. School and university courses were shortened, so that students had time for farm work. Above all, the Chinese leaders, who were said to have lost touch with the masses, had to do spells of physical labour.

156

Finally, there was a purge of the Communist Party. Many of its leaders were expelled or demoted, while all the cadres had to go to schools where they studied the works of Mao Tse-tung, and did a great deal of manual work.

Not surprisingly, there was chaos throughout China. The Cultural Revolution caused more damage than the Great Leap Forward and eventually, the People's Liberation Army felt bound to restore order. This they did in 1970, but with great loss of life. One of the least known Communist leaders, Hua Kuo-feng, announced the end of the Cultural Revolution with a quotation from Mao, 'Now it is preferable to have stability'.

For the time being, the army ruled China. For example, in place of the Revolutionary Committees in charge of factories, there were Committees of Three, representing the workers, cadres and the People's Liberation Army. Of these, the P.L.A. was the most important. This did not please Mao, for although he had said, 'Political power grows out of the barrel of a gun', he had added, 'the Party commands the gun, and the gun must never be allowed to command the Party.'

Gradually, however, the Party won back some measure of control. Quite how it did this we do not understand, but we do know that the Defence Minister, Lin Piao, died in a plane crash in 1971, apparently fleeing to Moscow. There was now an uneasy truce between the Communists of the left and right. Mao had enough power to go ahead with some of his ideas: on the other hand, Teng Hsiao-ping, who had been purged during the Cultural Revolution, came back into the government as Vice-Premier. A man who had a lot of influence at this time was the Prime Minister, Chou En-lai. An intelligent, cultured, sensible and moderate man, he did a great deal of good.

A Mao poster

Chapter Twenty-three

China since Mao Tse-tung

As MAO grew older, the problem of who should succeed him became more and more serious. Chou En-lai would have been a good choice, but he, too, was an old man, and, in fact, he died a few months before Mao. Teng Hsiao-ping also looked a likely candidate, but when Chou died in January 1976, the 'Gang of Four', led by Mao's wife, Chiang Ching, drove him from office. These people were the leaders of the left of the Communist Party. Hua Kuo-feng then became Prime Minister, and was named as Mao's successor. Although Hua was not one of the Party's outstanding leaders, the choice seemed to please Mao, who said as he was dying, 'With you in charge, I am at ease.'

Mao died on 9 September 1976, and Hua duly became Chairman of the Communist Party, as well as keeping his post as Prime Minister. Within a month, though, the Gang of Four was under arrest and Teng Hsiao-ping was Senior Vice-Premier, Vice-Chairman of the Communist Party, and Military Chief of Staff. It soon became clear that it was Teng who was really in charge. Moreover, he continually strengthened his position. For one thing, he discredited Mao, not as Khrushchev had denounced Stalin, in a single devastating speech, but a step at a time. By November 1980 he felt able to put the Gang of Four on trial, which exposed many of the evils they had done in Mao's name. By degrees, Teng also replaced Mao's former henchmen who held key positions, his greatest triumph being in 1981, when Hua Kuo-fung was sacked as Party Chairman. The man who succeeded him was Hu Yaobang. He had been attacked by Red Guards during the Cultural Revolution and, like so many of Mao's enemies made to work for years as a farm labourer. He was a close friend of Teng's.

Teng is leader of the right wing of the Chinese Communist Party, whose aim is to make China rich and strong, without bothering too much about pure Communist theories.

There have been sweeping changes in industry, education, civil rights and foreign policy.

You will remember that Mao thought the workers should have an important say in the running of their factories, and that they should think more of the good of China than of their own wages. Now, there is discipline, for the workers work, and the managers manage. Also, factories have to show profits, and their goods must be of the right quality.

Enthusiastic cadres have been dismissed and professional men have taken their places as managers with good results. For example, a group of radicals almost ruined the Anshan steel works in Manchuria, but now experts have taken charge and the works are once again efficient. In Mao's day many factories had lists at their gates, giving the names of workers who had refused pay for overtime. Today, there are bonus payments, and it is no disgrace to take them. Employees can see some point in working hard, so output is higher. On one site, it used to take 88 men 18 days to build a single storey in a block of flats: after a bonus scheme was introduced, 66 men did the work in 10 days.

In schools and colleges, as in the factories, discipline has been restored. Pupils may no longer criticize their teachers in public. Mao believed that examinations should be published in advance, and that candidates should be allowed to help each other. Today, examinations are as we know them. Under Mao, the way to win a place at a university was to be a good Communist, and anyone from the factory floor could be admitted, if his fellow workers nominated him. As a result there were many students who found higher education too difficult. Today, candidates have to pass entrance examinations. Students still have to take politics and do practical work, but they have much less of both. Moreover, the practical work must be connected with their subjects, and not just physical labour for its own sake.

The Chinese have more freedom. There are fewer restrictions on travel abroad, writers and artists may work as they please, and people may criticize the government. For a time, anyone could stick posters saying almost anything they liked on the 'democracy wall' in Peking. However, they now have to be more careful. Teng wants nothing like the 'hundred flowers' campaign, and the 'democracy wall' has been scrubbed clean.

As part of the plan to make his country richer and stronger, Teng is encouraging trade with the West. Britain, for example, has been asked to help with coal-mining, steel making and off-shore oil drilling, as well as to sell 'Harrier' vertical-take-off war planes. In 1978, Chairman Hua visited Romania and Yugoslavia, both Communist countries, but both determined to be as independent of the Soviet Union as they can. In 1979, he visited several countries in Western Europe, including Britain. He made it plain that he hoped they would be powerful, and friendly towards China. For the moment, it looks as if China is more anti-Russian than ever before.

WORK SECTION — China

Chairman Hua Kuo-feng in Britain,
October 1979

Questions

1 When did Hua come to power in China?
2 Who became the most important member of his government?
3 What new policies were introduced?
4 What was the economic importance of China's links with Britain?
5 Who is the lady in the picture?
6 What was the political importance of Hua's visit to Britain?

The Three Principles of the People

The National Government shall reconstruct the Republic of China on the basis of the revolutionary Three People's Principles.

The primary task of reconstruction is the People's livelihood. With regard to the four great needs of the people — food, clothing, shelter and transport — the Government should, in co-operation with the people, strive together to develop agriculture to feed them; to develop the textile industry to clothe them; to build many houses for them to live in; to improve and construct roads and canals to make it easier for them to travel.

Second in importance is Democracy. The government should train and direct the people so that they will gain political knowledge and be able to vote in any election or referendum.

Third comes nationalism. The government should help and guide the weak and small racial groups within its national boundaries towards self-determination and self-government. It should resist foreign aggression and, at the same time, it should revise foreign treaties so as to restore our equality and independence among nations.

Questions

1 Why did the 'Three Principles of the People' appeal strongly to the Chinese?
2 Who drew up the 'Three Principles of the People'?
3 Which political party did he found?
4 Which enemies did it defeat?
5 When, finally, did it come to power?
6 What things are included under 'People's Livelihood'? What did the peasants hope the phrase might mean?
7 How was China to become a democracy?
8 Who, in China, would nationalism favour?
9 Who was nationalism against?
10 What foreign aggression had there been against China?
11 What rights had foreigners gained in China, through treaties?
12 How far did Chiang Kai-shek carry out the 'Three Principles of the People'?

Peasants, Communists and K.M.T.

Document One

To understand the peasant support for the Communist movement it is necessary to keep in mind its economic basis. Wherever the Reds went they radically changed the situation for the tenant farmer, the poor farmer, the middle farmer, and all the 'have-not' elements. All forms of taxation were abolished in the new districts for the first year, to give the farmers a breathing space, and in the old districts only a small tax on land was collected. Secondly, they gave land to the land-hungry peasants, and began the reclamation of great areas of 'wasteland' — mostly the land of absentee or fleeing landlords. Thirdly, they took land and livestock from the wealthy classes and redistributed it among the poor.

(*Red Star over China* — Edgar Snow)

Document Two

'But how', I said, 'do you know the peasants really like the Red Army?' Several jumped up to answer.

'When we go into a new district,' one said, 'the peasants always volunteer to help our hospital service. They carry our wounded back to our hospitals, from the front.'

Another: '*On our Long March through Szechuan the peasants brought us grass shoes, made by themselves, and they brought us food and tea and hot water, along the road.*'

A Kansu peasant-soldier, 'The people help us in many ways. During battles they often disarm small parties of the enemy, cut their telephone wires and send us news about the movement of the K.M.T. troops. But they never cut our telephone lines: they help us put them up!'

Still another: 'Last April, five villages formed Soviets, where I was stationed. Afterwards we were attacked and had to retreat. The K.M.T. arrested eighteen villagers, and cut off their heads. Then we counter-attacked. The villagers led us by a secret mountain path to attack the K.M.T. We took them by surprise and disarmed three platoons.'

(*Red Star over China* — Edgar Snow)

Document Three

One day the K.M.T. soldiers came and succeeded in getting our horse and the things we had in our care. They even took our sieve. They took Father away with them.

Father came home little more than a week later. They had flogged him, he told us. They had accused him of being a Communist and of doing transport work for the Eighth Route Army. Father told the K.M.T. soldiers, 'I am a farmer from the district here. I can prove that.' They kept him locked up in a potato cellar until three old farmers guaranteed to the K.M.T. that he really was what he made himself out to be, an ordinary local farmer. After that they let him go.

One night, I dug up thirty jin of the millet we had in one of our hiding places up on the hillside. But the very next day a K.M.T. patrol came, and they took our millet. Mother began to weep and pleaded with them, 'Let us keep our millet! We are starving!' But the soldiers kicked her over and threatened her with their rifles. They said she had insulted the K.M.T. and they would stick their bayonets through her.

(Report from a Chinese Village)

Questions

Documents One and Two

1 When and why did Mao Tse-tung decide to win the support of the peasants?
2 What were the rules which he drew up for his men?

3 List the things mentioned in Document One that the Communists did for the peasants.
4 According to the soldiers in Document Two, what were the ways in which the peasants helped the Red Army?

Document Three

5 In what ways did the K.M.T. soldiers mentioned here ill-treat the peasants?

All Documents

6 Do you detect any bias in these extracts? Justify your answer.

Rival Communist Principles

Document One
Printing workers aim to increase production.

All the workers came from a printing works that turns out the weighty writings of Mao Tse-tung. Summoned to hear Premier Chou En-lai's 'state of the nation' speech to the National People's Congress, they had all studied summaries of the report and were now gathered to relate it to their own work in the coming year.

They had been greatly inspired by Premier Chou's report. Last year their unit had fulfilled its target ahead of time: this year they must do even better. There would be difficulties but these could best be overcome by careful and repeated study of the 'Works' of Chairman Mao. As one man put it, 'Chairman Mao's thinking is the moving force of everything.'

(*Reporter in Red China* — Charles Taylor)

Document Two

Kuan is puzzled. His friend Ouyang Hai has become a leader of men, a 'locomotive'.

Kuan thought: 'He must have exerted a tremendous effort in gathering the seeds at this time of year, and to exceed the work standard. Where does he get his energy from?' Kuan glanced at the knapsack, which Ouyang Hai had absent-mindedly left on the table. In it there were some well-thumbed volumes of Mao Tse-tung's writings. Kuang suddenly understood. Now he had the answer to his question. The 'locomotive' was rushing forward, just like our army and our entire country, toward new heights. The irresistible socialist build-up, the vigorous military training — all this demanded motive power and spiritual strength. And the source of unlimited strength lay right there in Mao Tse-tung's splendid ideas.

(*The Red Guard* — Hans Granquist)

Document Three
How to succeed at table-tennis

In a speech to women ping-pong players, the champion Hsu Ying-sheng warned them that technique alone was not enough, and that to play really well they must place politics in command. He urged them especially to 'exercise your minds to find out how to apply Chairman Mao's words to your table-tennis playing.' Hsu failed to explain just how Chairman Mao's rather heavy theoretical writings could be related to ping-pong, but he did have one practical hint for the girls: 'If we take the ball as Chiang Kai-shek's head and smash it with our bats, then how powerful will be our strokes!'

(*Reporter in Red China* — Charles Taylor)

Document Four
The Reaction against Mao Tse-tung

The Chinese Communist Party has endorsed the principle of 'material incentives' — bonus payments — for overtime or extra work on the grounds that they increase productivity and raise the quality of work.

The People's Daily *says the first all-round pay increases last year, plus new bonus payments, are having a tremendous effect on productivity in the drive to modernize industry and agriculture.*

Since the Cultural Revolution of the late Sixties 'material incentives' have been the dirtiest of words. But a dramatic change in attitude has taken place since the disgrace of the radical 'Gang of Four', led by Chiang Ching, the widow of Mao Tse-tung, and the second rehabilitation of Deputy Premier Teng Hsiao-ping in July 1977.

The People's Daily *outlined the results of 'material incentives' introduced in a Peking construction unit. It said that the bonuses 'for overall excellent performance and over-fulfilment of the tasks outlined in the work plan' had had a 'conspicuous effect'. For when the performance of the 2300 workers in the unit was compared with their performance during the same period of last year, it was apparent that their productivity had gone up by 53 per cent. In addition, the quality of the work had been greatly increased and so, too, had the safety record.*

A visiting businessman who knows Peking well told me that instead of the builders appearing slothful and lethargic, they seemed positively energetic. The change was dramatic.

(*Daily Telegraph* — 10 August 1978)

Questions
Documents One, Two and Three

1 Name the two movements, one in the late 1950s and one in the late 1960s, when Mao tried out his more extreme ideas.
2 How did Mao's ideas work in practice?
3 What is it which is supposed to inspire all the people mentioned in these three extracts?
4 Explain the phrase 'they must place politics in command' (Document Three).
5 What puzzles the author of Document Three? What is the only piece of practical advice the champion has?
6 What is there about these three extracts which shows that Communism is a form of religion?

Document Four

7 When did Mao Tse-tung die?
8 Which political groups struggled for power? Which was successful? Who was its leader?
9 What change of policy does this article describe?
10 How, according to this article, has the building industry been affected?
11 Whose ideas do you think are more likely to make China prosperous: those of Mao Tse-tung or Teng Hsiao-ping?

China in 1900

Questions

1 What was the population of China in 1900? What is it today?
2 What race are most Chinese? How long has China been united? Name some Chinese inventions.
3 What did the Chinese think of foreigners and merchants? Why, in the end, did the Chinese agree to trade?
4 Name the 'spheres of influence' which the various European powers had. What privileges did foreigners have in the Treaty Ports, and in the rest of China?

5 Why were the Treaty Ports the most advanced cities in China? Which was the most important?

6 Give five examples of the controls foreigners had over the economy of China.

7 What work did missionaries do? Why were they unpopular?

8 What were Japan's ambitions in China?

9 What was the policy of the U.S.A. towards China?

10 Who were the Manchus? Why was their rule harmful? Which of the Manchus held the real power about 1900?

11 How was it possible to become a civil servant? Why was it not a good system?

12 How did the increase in population harm the peasants? Why did the peasants hate their landlords? What major disaster was there from time to time?

13 What rebellion was there in 1900? When did the rebels attack? What was the attitude of the Chinese government? How did the rebellion end? What agreement did the Chinese government have to sign?

14 What three alternatives did the Manchus now have? Why were they all unpleasant for them?

Give an account of China in 1900 under the headings: Early History/Foreign Influence/Government Problems

The Nationalist Revolution

Questions

1 What was Sun Yat-sen's ambition? What was his slogan? What did it mean?

2 How did the rising of 1911 begin? What did its leaders invite Sun Yat-sen to do? When did the Manchus realize they were defeated?

3 What elections were held? What party did the Nationalists form? How successful were they in the elections?

4 Why did Yuan Shi-kai become President? Give two reasons why he became unpopular. When did he die?

5 Who ruled China after the death of Yuan Shi-kai? In what ways did China suffer?

6 What was Japan promised when she

entered the war? What action did she take against China?

7 Why were the Chinese angry at the peace treaty? How did they show their anger?

8 Why did Sun Yat-sen turn to the Communists? Why were the Russians willing to be friendly? What advice did Borodin give? Why was his plan a success?

9 What military help did the Russians send? What position did Sun Yat-sen give to Chiang Kai-shek? What plan did Sun make? Who succeeded him when he died?

10 How far had the K.M.T. and the Communists advanced by March 1927? How were they helped by the peasants and workers? What problem did this create for Chiang? How did he solve it?

11 What did the K.M.T. armies achieve in 1928?

12 How successful was Chiang Kai-shek with Sun Yat-sen's three aims? Why were the peasants especially disappointed?

Give an account of the Nationalist Revolution under the headings: Sun Yat-sen/Chiang Kai-shek

The Communist Revolution

Questions

1 When did many Chinese give up their old-fashioned ideas? When was the Chinese Communist Party founded?

2 What did the C.C.P. do in 1921 and 1922?

3 When was the First United Front formed? When and how did it end?

4 What did Chuh-Teh organize? When and where did he join forces with Mao Tse-tung?

5 How did Li Li-san think the Communist Revolution should develop? What did he order Chu and Mao to do? What happened?

6 Name two decisions that Mao made. What were his principles of guerrilla warfare?

7 Why did the peasants support the Communists? Name six ways in which they helped them.

8 Why did Chiang Kai-shek's first three 'extermination campaigns' fail?

9 What methods did he use for the fourth and fifth extermination campaigns? What did Mao and Chu decide they must do?

10 How did the Long March begin? Where did Mao decide to go? Why?

11 How many kilometres was the Long March? How many days did it take? What obstacles were met on the way? What proportion of the marchers arrived?

12 Name three results of the Long March. What did Mao plan when the march was over?

13 How was the Yenan Border Region organized?

14 What were cadres? How did they learn about Communism? Why did Mao have to write a number of books?

15 What was done to win support from the peasants?

16 What were Mao's views on having a strong army? Why was the P.L.A. a good fighting force? How did it obtain its weapons?

17 What did the Communists gain from fighting the Japanese?

18 Why was Japan interested in Manchuria? What did she gain there in 1905 and 1915? What was the 'Mukden Incident'? How did the Japanese make use of it?

19 Why did Chiang Kai-shek not fight the Japanese? What became of Manchuria?

20 Why did Chiang Kai-shek agree to the Second United Front? Give two reasons why Japan attacked China.

21 What excuse did Japan find for attacking China? Name two incidents in the war.

22 How much of China had Japan conquered in 1939? Why was there a stalemate?

23 What countries became Chiang's allies? Why did he do little to help them?

24 How did the P.L.A. fight the Japanese? How successful was it?

25 What help did the K.M.T. have when the Second World War ended? What was the position at the start of the civil war?

26 What did General George Marshall fail to do?

27 What advantages did the K.M.T. have at the beginning of the war? What offensives did Chiang mount?

28 What progress had the P.L.A. made by 1948? What battle did it win in that year?

29 What happened on 1 October 1949? When did Chiang Kai-shek flee?

30 Give three reasons for the success of the Communists.

Give an account of the Communist Revolution under the headings: Mao Tse-tung and the Beginnings of the Communist Revolution/The Long March/The Yenan Border Region/The War with Japan/The Civil War

Communist China

Questions

1 What task did the Communists face after they had won the civil war?

2 What two advantages did China gain from her Treaty of Friendship with Russia, 1950?

3 What happened to the landlords? How did redistributing their land help the Communists? Why did Mao decide to make collective farms?

4 Explain the differences between mutual aid teams, producers' co-operatives and collectives. What were the political advantages of the collectives?

5 In what stages did the Communists take over industry? What happened to the former employers?

6 How did the Russians help the Five Year Plan? In what ways was it like the Russian Five Year Plans?

7 How much did industrial production increase under the Plan? Name four weaknesses the Plan had.

8 What social reforms did the Communists make?

9 What changes did the Communists make in society? What did they say about the teachings of Confucius? What use did they make of education?

10 What work did the cadres do? What happened to people who were unwilling to accept Communism?

11 Against whom were the 'three anti' and 'five anti' campaigns directed?

12 What are 'intellectuals'? How did Mao hope to convert them to Communism?

13 What went wrong with the 'hundred flowers' campaign? What action did Mao take?

14 What were the differences between the left and right wings of the Communist Party?

15 What were the economic aims of the Great Leap Forward? How was it to be different from the Five Year Plan?

16 What was the main political aim of the the Great Leap Forward? What did the Russians feel about it?

17 What did Mao believe was the key to the success of the Great Leap Forward? What two things did this mean?

18 How long did it take to organize the communes? How large was each one, roughly?

19 What was the main work of the communes? What industries were developed? Why were plenty of jobs created?

20 What public works did the communes carry out? How was much of the work done?

21 What social work did the communes do? What medical services did they offer?

22 What was the value of the militia?

23 When did the Great Leap Forward begin? When was it clear it had failed? Give three reasons for the failure.

24 Who took charge in 1961? What changes were made in the communes? What changes were made in the factories?

25 Which changes did Mao dislike? What did he fear might happen. Who helped him organize the Cultural Revolution?

26 How did Mao hope the Cultural Revolution would change the way people thought? What book did he produce? Why?

27 What changes did Mao hope the Cultural Revolution would make?

28 How did Mao begin the Revolution? Who were the Red Guards? Describe their activities.

29 Why did Mao encourage the Red Guards?

30 What happened in the factories?

31 How did people learn more about each other?

32 What happened in the Communist Party?

33 In one word, what was the result of the Cultural Revolution? Who restored order? Who announced the end of the Cultural Revolution?

34 Who ruled China immediately after the Cultural Revolution? Why did this displease Mao?

35 What was the significance of Lin Piao's death? What happened between the left and right wings of the Communist Party during the 1970s? Which men were important in the government of China at this time?

Give an account of Communist China under the headings: Founding the Communist State/The Great Leap Forward/ The Great Proletarian Cultural Revolution

China since Mao Tse-tung

Questions

1 Who were the 'Gang of Four'? What did they do to Teng Hsiao-ping in 1976?

2 When did Mao die? Who succeeded him? What political changes were there?

3 What changes have been made in industry? With what results?

4 What changes have been made in education?

5 How much more freedom do the Chinese enjoy?

6 What contacts did the Chinese make with the West? Why?

Problems

1 What were the main problems which China faced in the early twentieth century?

2 How much influence did foreigners secure over Chinese affairs?

3 Contrast the development of China and Japan down to 1914.

4 What were the aims of the Chinese Nationalists? Account for their success and their ultimate failure.

5 What were the main differences between the Communist revolutions in Russia and China?

6 Account for the growth of the Communist Party in China down to 1945.

7 What was the importance of the Long March in the history of Chinese Communism?

8 Why was there a civil war in China after 1945? Why did the Communists win it?

9 Compare and contrast the agricultural policies of Mao Tse-tung and Stalin.

165

10 What were the main differences between the left and right of the Chinese Communist Party? How have these differences affected the history of China?

11 What were the aims behind the Great Leap Forward and the Cultural Revolution? Why were both failures?

12 What attempts have been made, at various times, to convert the Chinese people to Communism?

13 What does the Chinese Communist Party owe Mao Tse-tung?

14 What changes have there been in China since the death of Mao Tse-tung?

_____*PART TWO*_____
International Affairs since 1900

THE
FIRST WORLD
WAR

Chapter Twenty-four

The Causes of the First World War

The First World War, or the Great War as it is sometimes called, was the worst that had ever been. In four years of bitter fighting at least ten million soldiers and civilians died, a number which may have been much higher. The reasons for the war were many and complicated, though four were especially important. The first was that many of the European powers hated one another and had serious quarrels, some of them recent, some going back for hundreds of years. Secondly, they had large armies and navies with deadly modern weapons, so they were able to slaughter each other as they had never done before. Thirdly, countries made alliances with each other, which meant that if any two started a war, the rest would be bound to join in. When France and Germany fought in 1870, the war did not spread because neither country had any allies, but in 1914 things were quite different. Finally, there were a number of crises each of which brought Europe closer to boiling-point, until one comparatively small incident actually sparked off the war.

We will look at each of these causes in turn.

Differences between the European Powers

One great problem was colonies. The European countries had growing industries, and they were afraid that if there was free competition between them, they would have to pay high prices for their raw materials, and sell their finished goods cheaply. However, if a country had colonies, then it could take from them whatever it wanted, and make them buy its manu-factured goods in exchange. Moreover, it could fix its own prices, as foreigners would not be allowed to compete. For example India sent Britain raw cotton, and was also an excellent market for cotton cloth.

Britain, with the largest number of colonies, boasted that she had an empire 'on which the sun never set'. It covered one-fifth of the land surface of the globe. She had taken much of it in the seventeenth and eighteenth centuries, while in the nineteenth century she had done well in the 'scramble for Africa'.

Britain's main enemies were the powers who seemed the biggest danger to her empire. Chief among these was Russia, for her policy, like Britain's was to grab all the land that she could. They were rivals in China, since the

Russians were hoping to take the North, while the British cast greedy eyes on the valley of the Yangtze River. Further west lay Britain's prize possession, India, which Russia seemed to threaten through Afghanistan and Persia. Finally, Russia wanted to control the straits joining the Black Sea to the Mediterranean, and if she did, she would be a threat to Britain's shipping route, through the Suez Canal, to India.

After Russia, Britain thought France was her most dangerous enemy. Both shared control of Egypt, but they did not work together at all well. Also they had squabbled over the 'scramble for Africa', and as late as 1898 there was the Fashoda Crisis. General Kitchener had just conquered the Sudan, when a French explorer, Major Marchand, came out of the Sahara, ran up the French flag at Fashoda, and claimed the territory for France. The French had to give up their claim, since Kitchener had a large army, but there were bitter feelings on both sides.

France and Russia were old enemies of Britain, and then, in the early part of the twentieth century, a new rival appeared. This was Germany. In 1871 she had been united by one of her greatest statesmen, Bismarck. His policy was to avoid making enemies, so Germany did not seize colonies. She did indeed acquire a modest empire, but did so with Britain's consent. However, in 1890, the new Kaiser William II decided to be more ambitious, so he dismissed Bismarck and embarked on a *weltpolitik*, or 'world policy'. One thing he planned was a railway from Berlin to Baghdad, which would give Germany a lot of influence in the Middle East. That was bad enough for Britain, but worse was to follow. William II saw that if his country was to be a world power, she must have a fleet, so he began to build one. The British were thoroughly alarmed, and as the German navy grew, so did mutual distrust and hatred.

As well as rivalry over colonies there were even more serious problems within Europe itself.

When Germany defeated France in 1871, she took from her Alsace and Lorraine. The French never forgave the Germans for this, and were determined to win back the lost provinces, if that was ever possible. On the Place de la Concorde in Paris, the statue representing Alsace was draped in black as a reminder.

There were also troubles in the Balkans. South–eastern Europe was a complete mixture of races, but with three of them dominating the others. Two of these, the Austrians and the Hungarians, had joined together to form the Austro–Hungarian Empire. The master races occupied the middle of the Empire while there were Slavonic peoples to the north and south. Austria ruled the northern Slavs and Hungary ruled most of the southern Slavs. The third master race was the Turks, but they were in decline. Already Greece, Bulgaria and Serbia had won their freedom from Turkey, and were looking forward to the day when they would drive her out of Europe completely. Looming in the background was Russia. As we have seen, she wanted to control the entrance to the Black Sea, and it looked as if the troubles in the Balkans might give her the chance. She was particularly friendly towards Serbia, a Slavonic country like herself. Austria–Hungary was worried. She knew that the Serbs would not be content with driving

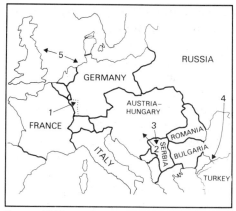

1. France hopes to recover Alsace-Lorraine from Germany
2. Serbia hopes to unite with Southern Slavs in Austria–Hungary
3. Austria–Hungary hopes to crush Serbia
4. Russia supports Serbia, hoping to gain control of the straits leading into the Mediterranean
5. Anglo–German naval rivalry

Triple Alliance. – Germany, Austria–Hungary and Italy (a sleeping partner)
Triple Entente – Russia and France (Dual Alliance), with Great Britain

Europe 1914 – main causes of tension

the Turks out of Europe, but would also ask the Russians to help them liberate the southern Slavs in their own empire. The Slavs wanted a united Slavia, or in their language, a Yugoslavia.

The Arms Race

In order to fight wars, nations need weapons. Thanks to modern science they were becoming more deadly than they had ever been, and thanks to modern industry they were produced in vast quantities.

Artillery was greatly improved, the French, for example, having an excellent 75 mm field gun. There were two new infantry weapons; the magazined rifle, which gave the soldier a much more rapid rate of fire, and, even more important, the machine-gun. It was shown very early in the war that troops armed with these weapons were all but invincible if they dug themselves trenches, and put up barbed-wire entanglements.

When it came to making weapons, the countries that led the arms race were, not surprisingly, the two leading industrial powers, Germany and Great Britain. Germany not only built up the largest and best equipped army in Europe, but also tried to challenge Britain at sea. The new German navy was largely the work of Admiral Tirpitz, who won over public opinion and persuaded the Reichstag to pass two ambitious Navy Laws, one in 1898 and the other in 1900. Tirpitz realized the German navy could not hope to match the Royal Navy for size, but the British had to keep ships all over the world to defend her empire. It was quite realistic to hope that Germany could rival Britain in the North Sea. If she controlled that, then, with her huge army, she would have Britain at her mercy.

The British were quick to see the danger. The answer of the First Sea Lord, Admiral Fisher, was a new battleship, H.M.S. *Dreadnought*, the first of many in the dreadnought class. She was launched in 1906. With her ten 300 mm (12-inch) guns and her Parsons turbines she could outgun and outrun anything afloat, and with her 280 mm (eleven inches) of armour at the waterline she was thought to be unsinkable. Fisher also introduced battle-cruisers, ships with the same weapons as *Dreadnought*, but less armour, so that they were faster.

171

However, the Germans too, could build dreadnoughts and battle-cruisers, and tried to keep up with the British. By 1914 the position was:

	Great Britain	Germany
Dreadnoughts	29	17
Battle-cruisers	9	7

Germany was left behind because she was concentrating on her army. Moreover, when the war came, the two mighty fleets did little more than fight one inconclusive battle, which was Jutland in 1916. None the less, the naval race had important results. It was fear of the German navy which, more than anything else, drove Britain to make friends with her old enemies, France and Russia.

Some attempt was made to stop the arms race. Thanks largely to the Russians there were two disarmament conferences at the Hague, one in 1899 and one in 1907. It was not that the Russians were especially peace-loving, but their industry was backward, and they were losing the arms race badly. Germany, on the other hand, was winning. She refused to co-operate, so both Hague Conferences were failures.

The Alliances

When Germany took Alsace and Lorraine in 1871, it was certain that France would always be her bitter enemy. It was equally certain that she could not fight Germany on her own, so Bismarck tried to isolate her. In 1882 he formed the Triple Alliance of Germany, Italy and Austria–Hungary. He also managed to stay friendly with Russia, even though she disliked Austria–Hungary. However, when William II dismissed Bismarck in 1890, he threw his cautious policy to the winds and, in 1893, France and Russia formed the Dual Alliance. France was glad to have an ally against Germany, and Russia to have one against Austria–Hungary. Since Russia was such a large country, and since no one knew how weak she really was, the two alliances looked nearly equal. It seemed that Britain could tip the balance by joining either.

For some time, though, Britain had not wanted allies. Her main interest was in her empire, and an ally might draw her into a European war from which she would gain nothing. She proudly described her position as one of 'splendid isolation', and made sure she was safe by keeping her fleet at the 'two power standard'. That meant it was as strong as any two other navies in the world combined. Then, in 1899, the Boer War broke out and it took Britain three years to win it. Moreover, all the European countries were disgusted at the British Empire bullying a handful of Boer farmers, and talked seriously about helping them. Britain was frightened out of 'splendid isolation', and began to look for friends.

Britain's first move was to make an alliance with Japan in 1902. Each country agreed to help the other if she went to war with more than one power in the Far East. This encouraged the Japanese to attack the Russians, which they did in 1904, winning a quick, decisive victory.

Next, Joseph Chamberlain offered Germany an alliance. Germany rejected the offer, an action she was to regret deeply later on. Other countries were not so short-sighted. After the Fashoda Crisis, Delcassé, the French Foreign Minister, saw it was useless to oppose Britain, so he tried, instead, to win her friendship. He succeeded, and in 1904 the two countries made an agreement called the 'entente cordiale'. They settled their many differences round the world in a spirit of give and take, and, most important of all, France gave up her claims to Egypt while Britain promised to support French claims to Morocco.

As for France's ally, Russia, she had already given up her ambitions in China after her defeat by Japan, so she no longer had any reason to quarrel with Britain over the Far East. Now, with French encouragement Britain and Russia made an agreement over Persia. The Russians were to have the north as their 'sphere of influence', the British were to have the south, and they were both to keep out of central Persia, which would be a buffer between them. The agreement, signed in 1907, completed what was known as the Triple Entente. It was not an alliance, but it did mean that Britain had settled her differences with two of her rivals. At the same time, her relations with Germany were growing steadily worse.

The Crises

There were five serious quarrels between the great powers. Each of the first four brought war one step nearer, and the fifth started it.

The first crisis came in 1906. Taking advantage of the 'entente cordiale', France claimed control over Morocco's police and banks. Kaiser William II at once went to Tangier, where he made a speech promising that Germany would protect Morocco. Later, he demanded an international conference to settle the problem. This met at Algeciras, in southern Spain, in 1906. It did not go well for Germany. Russia supported France, and so did Britain. The other two important powers at the conference, Spain and the United States, did the same. Moreover, France had already promised Italy she would back her claim to Libya, so the Italians took neither side, even though they were Germany's allies in the Triple Alliance. Only Austria-Hungary gave Germany any help, and that was lukewarm, because she was not interested in North Africa. France had what she wanted from the conference, but, what was more important, it showed how much the situation in Europe had changed. When Bismarck fell from power in 1890, France was isolated: by 1906, she was surrounded by friends, and it was Germany that stood alone.

The second crisis was over the Balkans. In 1881, Austria-Hungary had taken Bosnia from Turkish rule, and governed it herself, as a protectorate. However, in name at least, it still belonged to Turkey. Then, in 1908, Austria-Hungary annexed Bosnia, saying, in effect, that it was now part of her own Empire. The Bosnians were Slavs and had been hoping they might one day join with Serbia, but obviously, this was something Austria-Hungary was determined to prevent. Russia protested, but William II supported Francis Joseph, the Austrian Emperor. 'Should my august ally

173

be compelled to draw the sword', he said, 'he will find a knight in shining armour standing by his side.' Russia had to back down, so it was her turn to be humiliated.

The third crisis was over Morocco. In 1911 there was a rebellion against the Sultan, so the French sent troops to suppress it, and, indeed, to take over the country. The Kaiser at once ordered the gunboat *Panther* to Agadir, supposedly to look after German citizens in the port. Actually, he hoped to bully the French into giving Germany part of the Congo, if she, in return, gave up her claims to Morocco. This time there was a strong reaction from Britain. In a speech at the Mansion House, the Chancellor of the Exchequer, David Lloyd George, made it plain that Britain would go to war with Germany if she did not give up her demands. When the Kaiser appeared in Berlin, the crowds roared, 'Stand fast, William', but William thought better of it and contented himself with a small slice of French Equatorial Africa. Germany had received another slap in the face, and everyone knew it.

Following the crisis of 1911, Britain became alarmed at the growth of the German navy. She wanted to strengthen her home fleet quickly, so in 1912 she suggested that the French should send one of their squadrons from the English Channel into the Mediterranean, while she brought much of her Mediterranean fleet into the North Sea. France promised to look after British ships and colonies in the Mediterranean, while Britain promised to protect the north coast of France. That virtually meant that if France and Germany went to war, Britain would be honour bound to fight for France.

The fourth crisis was in the Balkans. The Turks had always ill-treated their Christian subjects, and after still more massacres in Macedonia, Bulgaria, Serbia and Greece formed the Balkan League. They then beat Turkey soundly in the First Balkan War of 1912–13. By the Treaty of London, Turkey gave up all her possessions in Europe, except Constantinople.

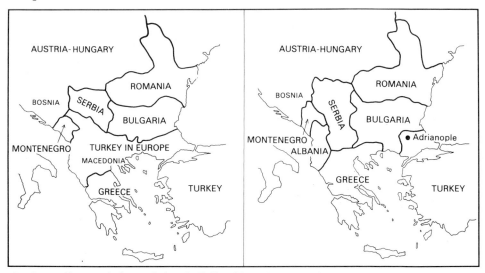

South-east Europe – before and after the Balkan Wars 1912–13 and 1913

However the victors fell out over the spoils and in 1913 there was the Second Balkan War. Serbia and Greece fought against Bulgaria, Romania attacked her as well, and Turkey took advantage of the confusion to recapture Adrianople. Bulgaria was defeated, and had to agree to the Treaty of Bucharest, which shared Macedonia between Greece and Serbia.

As a result of the Balkan Wars, Serbia doubled her area and increased her population from three million to four million. Her people were seething with excitement. They had beaten one of their oppressors, Turkey, and were now looking forward to freeing the eight million Serbo-Croats in Austria-Hungary. For her part, Austria-Hungary realized she must crush Serbia before it was too late.

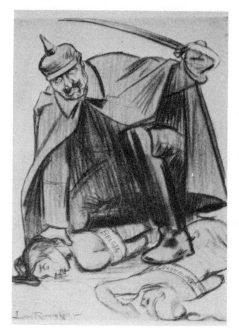

Kaiser William II crushes Belgium and Luxemburg

The final crisis soon followed. On 28 June 1914, at Sarajevo, a Bosnian Serb called Princip assassinated the heir to the Austrian throne, the Archduke Francis Ferdinand. Here was the excuse Austria-Hungary wanted. She asked Germany's opinion, and the Kaiser gave Francis Joseph a 'blank cheque'. In other words, he promised to support him, whatever he did. Austria-Hungary blamed Serbia for the assassination, and in July 1914, declared war on her. Russia began to mobilize her army, so Germany at once declared war on her, and told France to remain neutral. France refused, so Germany declared war on her as well.

What was Britain to do? She had no alliance with any European power, but ever since 1904 she had been drawing closer to France. Moreover, because of the naval agreement of 1912, she would be bound to protect the north coast of France if the Germans attacked it. Above all, Britain now saw Germany as her main rival, so she could not afford to let her become even more powerful by defeating France and Russia. All Britain needed was an excuse to join the war, and she found it in an old treaty in which she had guaranteed the neutrality of Belgium. The British asked the Germans to leave Belgium alone, but the Germans could not agree. As we shall see, their plan for the invasion of France meant sending their armies through Belgium. Britain declared war on 4 August 1914.

Chapter Twenty-five

The Western Front to 1917

GERMANY had to fight a war on two fronts, so she hoped to defeat France in six weeks, and then turn her full strength against Russia.

The Schlieffen Plan and the Battle of the Marne

As early as 1905, the German Chief of Staff, Count von Schlieffen, had made a plan for a quick victory in the west. The German army was to swing like a hammer with the end of the handle at Metz. In the left and centre there were to be holding forces, while the real strength was to be on the right — the head of the hammer. This strong right wing was to swing through Belgium, drive west of Paris, and then attack the French armies from flank and rear. Von Schlieffen died before the war began. His last words were 'Let the right wing be strong'.

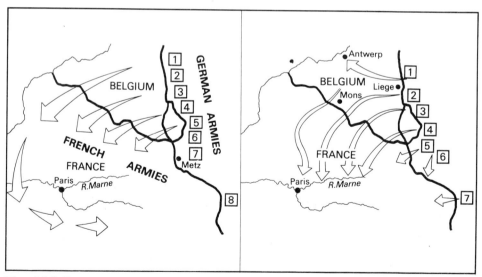

The Schlieffen Plan 1905. Von Schlieffen intended a powerful right wing to invade Belgium, sweep west of Paris and envelope the French armies.

The German Invasion 1914. When the attack came the right wing was not nearly as strong as von Schlieffen had intended. The German advance was halted at the First Battle of the Marne.

When the attack came, the French resisted bravely, but the Germans had two million men while they had only 1.3 million. Also, they wasted hundreds of thousands of their troops in useless counter-attacks. At first it looked as if the Germans were going to win, but then things began to go wrong for them. The Belgian army fought well, and held Liège for three days. It then withdrew to Antwerp, where the Germans had to blockade it with troops they badly needed elsewhere. The British Expeditionary Force also gave valuable help. It was so small that the Kaiser dismissed it as 'that contemptible little army', but all its men were highly trained professional soldiers. It checked the Germans at Mons, and, later, helped win the Battle of the Marne.

Also, the Germans made mistakes. In charge of their left wing was the Crown Prince of Bavaria, and he insisted that his army should be more than a holding force. Accordingly, the German High Command moved troops from their right wing, where they were badly needed, to their left wing, where they were not. They also sent troops to ward off a Russian invasion of East Prussia. As a result, the German right was not the mighty hammer-head that Von Schlieffen had wanted.

Trouble really began for the Germans when they reached the River Marne, thirty km from Paris. Von Kluck, commanding the First Army, and von Bulow, commanding the Second Army, suddenly realized there was a gap between them. Von Kluck moved left to close it, but that meant he could not sweep round to the west of Paris. At the same time, the French Fifth Army and the British Expeditionary Force advanced towards the gap. Moreover, General Gallieni, who was defending Paris with the French Sixth Army, saw a golden opportunity. Boldly, he decided to leave Paris,

German cavalry inspect captured trenches

and mounting his men in taxi-cabs, he rushed them into an attack on von Kluck's right flank. The German First Army had been caught off balance, its men were weary after weeks of marching, and now it was being assailed on two sides. It had no choice but to fall back to the River Aisne. The German advance was held, and the crisis was over.

Trench Warfare

Following the Battle of the Marne, both the German and the allied armies had exposed flanks, so there was a 'race to the sea' as they extended their forces northwards as fast as they could. They then prepared to ward off attacks by digging trenches, and before long these ran in an unbroken line from the English Channel to the Swiss frontier. The troops had magazined rifles and machine-guns, so their fire-power was enormous. Army leaders had expected the new weapons would be deadly in attack, but they soon found they were even more deadly in defence. If an enemy dug himself in, and protected his front with barbed-wire, it was almost impossible to defeat him.

At the beginning of the war the men wanted protection quickly so they dug shallow pits which the British described as 'lousy scratch holes'. Soon, though, they were making trenches according to a pattern, and along lines their commanders chose for them. Usually, they were on the forward slopes of hills, so that the defenders had a good field of fire. However, though they could see the enemy, the enemy could also see them, and could destroy their trenches quite easily with artillery. The answer was to site the trenches on the reverse slopes of hills, out of sight, and to have

A British gun emplacement

defence in depth, with three rows of trenches. These systems were often eight km or more from front to rear. There were still further improvements in 1917. Before then, there were many troops in the front line, and the artillery was well forward. As a result the enemy caused heavy casualties with his bombardment, and he captured many guns when he advanced. The later method was to put only a few troops in the front line, and to withdraw the guns as the enemy came forward. At the Battle of Arras in February 1917, the Germans lost two hundred guns in two days. At the Third Battle of Ypres in July they used the new tactics and lost only eight guns.

How was it possible to defeat an enemy armed with modern weapons and with such strong defences? After the war Colonel Fuller calculated that to break through a trench system 8 km deep on a front 24 km wide would need 56 divisions, or 1.2 million men. It was impossible to concentrate such a huge force and keep it supplied. None the less, both sides were determined to break through, whatever the cost.

The obvious way seemed to be to blast a gap, with artillery fire. The British began the Battle of the Somme in 1916 with an eight day bombardment, and fired two million shells. Before the Third Battle of Ypres in 1917, they delivered a nineteen-day bombardment, and fired 4½ million shells. However, no bombardment succeeded. In the first place, though the shells might fall, on an average, one to every square metre, they always missed a few of the enemy machine-gun nests. The survivors, emerging from their dug-outs when the barrage lifted, were usually able to check the enemy advance until reinforcements arrived. Secondly, the bombardment told the enemy exactly where to expect the attack, so he had plenty of time to muster his reserves for a counter-attack. Thirdly, the shells made the ground almost impassable. Attacking infantry had to pick their way round craters and through the mud, and it was very difficult to supply them with food and ammunition.

Since artillery had failed, the Germans tried poison gas. They first used it at Ypres in 1915, and it caused a panic. However, as soon as the allied troops had respirators, gas was no longer a serious threat to them.

The best hope of breaking through the trenches seemed to be with a new weapon, the tank. Colonel Ernest Swinton thought of it in 1914 when he saw an American Holt caterpillar tractor towing a gun. The Americans used these tractors in the swamplands of Louisiana, and Swinton realized that armoured vehicles, using caterpillar tracks instead of wheels, might well overwhelm the German trenches. They would be proof against machine-gun fire, and could crush barbed-wire. The generals in France were not interested, but Winston Churchill was enthusiastic. As he was First Lord of the Admiralty, it was the navy that developed the most important new land weapon of the war.

Tanks first went into action on the Somme in 1916. There was only a handful of them, and they wallowed helplessly in the mud. Then, in November 1917, the men of the Tank Corps were allowed to plan their own battle. They chose to attack near Cambrai where the Germans had their most powerful defences, the Hindenburg Line. The reason was that here there were chalk hills, so the ground was well-drained and firm. To win surprise the British made no prolonged artillery bombardment, though they did put down a creeping barrage on the day of the attack. They also blinded the German gunners with smoke shells, and sent aircraft to machine-gun the infantry. Then came the tanks. They dropped fascines (bundles of wood) to bridge the enemy's anti-tank ditches so that they could cross them, they crushed his wire, and then they turned left and right along the line of his trenches killing the men in them. They tore a gap in the defences through which the infantry advanced quite easily. The British penetrated to a depth of eight km they captured 8000 prisoners and 1000 guns, and suffered only 5000 casualties. For an assault on the Western Front, this was remarkably few. Back at home, the church bells rang to celebrate the victory, but they rang too soon. By the end of the day, most of the tanks had broken down. Also, the British High Command had refused to believe that the battle would go so well, and the only troops available to follow up the victory were cavalry. They arrived late and were, quite rightly, afraid to go further because of machine-guns. The advanced halted, the Germans mustered their reserves, and then they counter-attacked. Shortly, they regained almost all the ground they had lost.

As you can see from this description of the Battle of Cambrai, tanks failed to win the war because there were not enough of them, and because they broke down too easily.

Major Battles of the Western Front

There is no space in this book to describe all the battles that took place. The following are some of the more important.

When they failed to defeat France in 1914, the Germans stood on the defensive in the west, and concentrated on the Russians. After some remarkable victories, in which they thought they had crippled the Russian armies for ever, they again turned to the west. In 1916, their Chief of Staff, Marshal Falkenhayn, decided to attack Verdun. Defenders could always inflict heavier casualties on attackers, but only if they were prepared to give ground. Verdun meant a lot to the French, and Falkenhayn believed they would not abandon it. By refusing to retreat, they would suffer as heavily as the Germans, they would have to pour in their reserves and, as Falkenhyan put it, he would 'bleed France white'. Marshal Pétain took charge of the defence of Verdun, saying firmly, *Ils ne passeront pas* (They shall not pass). There was a terrible battle of attrition, but in the end it was the Germans who gave up.

Also in 1916, the British fought the Battle of the Somme. They suffered 60 000 casualties on the first day alone, and in the end, they hardly dented the German defences. However, it was their first major offensive of the war, and their leaders comforted themselves for their appalling losses by saying they had shown the Germans that Britain was, at last, a great military power.

In 1917 Nivelle, the arrogant French Commander-in-Chief, mounted an offensive in Champagne that he was sure would succeed. It failed, like all the rest, and the French soldiers, sickened by the war, mutinied. The British had to attack at Arras to distract the Germans. Here, the Canadians distinguished themselves by capturing Vimy Ridge.

Later in 1917 the British Commander-in-Chief, Douglas Haig, decided he would clear the Germans from their U-boat bases in the Channel ports. The result was the Third Battle of Ypres. The British undermined the German defences on Messines Hill, and blew them up with an explosion that was heard in Downing Street. Next, came the notorious Passchendaele offensive, which was a bloody slaughter in the mud. Haig ended it when his army had suffered a quarter of a million casualties. So, far from taking the Channel ports, the British had won no more than 115 square kilometres of France.

Chapter Twenty-six

The War on Other Fronts to 1917

The Eastern Front

AT FIRST Britain and France hoped for a good deal from Russia. They knew her armies were not as well equipped as those of Germany, but she had a huge population. It looked as if the Russian 'steamroller' would advance and overwhelm Germany with its sheer weight. The only problem was that the Russian communications were poor, so they were bound to take a long time to mobilize their forces. The Germans were counting on a quick victory over France, before having to meet the full force of the Russian attack.

Russia was not Germany's only problem in the east. Her ally, Austria-Hungary, was unreliable. This 'ramshackle empire' was a mixture of races, many of whom hated each other, a weakness which was reflected in the army. To give just one example, some Slav officers gave the Russians all of Austria's war plans. It was not long before the Russians realized that it was easy enough to win battles against Austria-Hungary, and time and again the Germans had to send help to their tottering ally.

When war broke out, the Russians gave the Germans an unpleasant shock by mobilizing more quickly than expected, and invading East Prussia. Britain and France waited confidently for the Russian 'steamroller' to crush Germany. However, though the Russians had plenty of men, they were short of weapons and their generals were poor. What is more, in East Prussia they met two generals who were probably the most able of the war, Paul von Hindenburg, and his Chief of Staff Erich von Ludendorff. They destroyed the Russian armies of invasion at the Battles of Tannenberg and the Masurian Lakes.

Meanwhile other Russian forces were invading Austria-Hungary, so Hindenburg struck, driving towards Warsaw. He did not take the city, but he saved Austria. All along the Eastern Front the Russians had been halted. One thing they had achieved, however, and that was to frighten the Germans into moving two army corps from France, just before the Battle of the Marne.

In 1915, the Germans realized they had lost the chance of a quick victory in the west, so they decided to defeat Russia. Falkenhayn mounted a powerful offensive and overran Poland and Lithuania. Altogether he took one million prisoners, defeating the Russians so thoroughly that it seemed

Paul von Hindenburg

German troops in Russia

they could never again be a danger. It was after these victories that Falkenhayn decided to 'bleed France white' by his attack on Verdun.

Russia, though, was not yet beaten. In 1916, one of her few able generals, Brusilov, attacked the Austro-Hungarian armies in the Carpathian Mountains. He was so successful that Romania decided to join the war on the Russian side, and Hungary was threatened from the east as well as from the north. Yet again, Hindenburg and Ludendorff came to the rescue. The Germans defeated Brusilov's men, and their armies overran most of Romania. They were glad to have her corn and oil.

The offensive of 1916 was the last serious threat from Russia, for in March 1917 there began the Revolution. The Provisional Government that overthrew the Tsar did go on with the war, and Brusilov mounted another offensive, but this one failed very quickly. Moreover, in November, the Bolsheviks overthrew the Provisional Government and at once sued for peace. The treaty was signed at Brest-Litovsk in March 1918, and the Germans were at last free to concentrate all their armies in the west.

The Balkan Front

The war begain well for the Serbians who defeated the Austro-Hungarians and invaded Bosnia. Then in 1915 Bulgaria attacked Serbia, and the Germans came to the aid of their allies. The Serbian army was defeated and took refuge in Salonica. Here, a French force joined it, and later a British one, but the Germans prevented them from moving. They called Salonica 'our largest internment camp'.

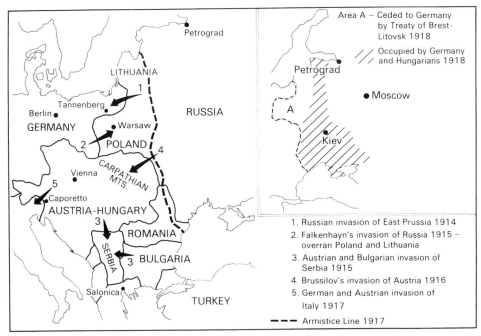

War on the Eastern, Balkan and Italian Fronts and the Treaty of Brest-Litovsk 1918

The Italian Front

At the Conference of Algeciras in 1906, Italy did not support Germany, and, as a result, became no more than a sleeping partner in the Triple Alliance. In truth, she had never been an enthusiastic member, because Austria was an old enemy. She had tried to prevent the unification of Italy and still held the Trentino and Istria, where most of the people were Italians. Italy hoped to win these two provinces and in 1915, she felt her chance had come, so she declared war. However, most of the frontier with Austria ran through the Alps, and for a time neither side made much progress. Then in October 1917, after the collapse of Russia, the Germans had some troops to spare, and they led an attack against the Italians. Many believed that Germans were invincible and none were more sure of that than the Italians. They were thoroughly defeated at the Battle of Caporetto, losing a quarter of a million prisoners. Many Italians simply threw down their arms and went home: some stood by the roadside cheering their enemies and shouting, 'Long live Austria' or 'On to Venice'. The British and French hurriedly sent some of their battle-hardened veterans, who halted the invaders on the River Piave, while the Italians returned sheepishly to the war. The rival armies faced each other across the Piave until 1918.

The War against Turkey

Turkey's defeat in the First Balkan War was a blessing in disguise for her, since it revealed how weak she really was. She eagerly accepted help from Germany, and a German, General Liman von Sanders, showed her how to reorganize her army. None the less she hesitated to join the war until, in October 1914, a German battle-cruiser, the *Goeben*, and a cruiser, the *Breslau*, sailed to Constantinople. Their arrival encouraged the Turks to declare war.

German battle-cruiser Goeben

185

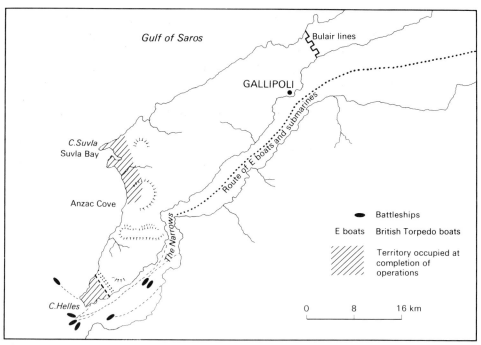

The Dardanelles operations

It was not long before Britain and France realized that Russia's great weakness was a shortage of supplies. If only they could send her enough weapons, she might be more successful. In 1915 Lloyd George and Winston Churchill thought of a plan. They would capture the Dardanelles leading into the Black Sea, send help to Russia, defeat Turkey, and then march on Austria-Hungary.

This bold, ambitious plan was mismanaged from the start. The first mistake was to send warships to fight their way through the Dardanelles on their own. They not only failed, but warned the Turks to expect an invasion. When, in April 1915, a force mainly of Anzac troops (Australian and New Zealand Army Corps) landed on the Gallipoli Peninsula, the Turks had mustered an army large enough to check it. Both sides dug trenches, so there was a stalemate, just as in France. In August, the British tried to break the deadlock by landing further down the coast at Suvla Bay. They took the enemy by surprise, but they did not press their attack, so the Turks had time to bring up their reserves and, once again, both sides dug trenches. In December 1915, the British decided to withdraw, which they did in perfect order. It was the only well organized operation of the campaign.

There was other fighting with the Turks, on their southern frontiers. In 1914, a British army from India landed on the Gulf of Persia to protect the oilfields. It advanced to Baghdad, but it was badly led, and the Turks drove it back to Kut-el-Amara. In 1916, Kut fell. The Turks took its defenders prisoner and drove them on a nightmare march through the desert, in which many died.

In 1917, the British mounted a double offensive. General Maude advanced from Basra, while General Allenby advanced from Egypt and captured Jerusalem. At the same time, Captain T. E. Lawrence (Lawrence of Arabia) led the Arabs in guerrilla warfare against their Turkish masters.

By the end of 1917, then, there was stalemate on the Western Front, in the Balkans, and in Italy. Turkey had driven the British from the Dardanelles, and was still resisting an invasion from the south. Russia, though, was out of the war so large numbers of German soldiers were free to fight elsewhere. On the other hand, France and Britain had found a new ally. Owing to the way that Germany waged war at sea, the United States declared war on her in April 1917.

Chapter Twenty-seven

The War at Sea

SINCE Germany had concentrated on her army, her fleet did not match Britain's for size. However, it was of better quality and because the British had to keep ships all over the world, the German navy was able to play an important part in the war.

Commerce Raiders

Commerce raiders were warships that attacked merchant vessels. They alarmed the British a great deal. In the Far East, Count von Spee commanded Germany's China Squadron, a force of splendid new cruisers. At Coronel in 1914 he met some old-fashioned British warships under Admiral Cradock. Cradock should not have fought, but he did, and was thoroughly defeated. Churchill was furious. It was unthinkable that the Royal Navy should lose a battle, so he sent Admiral Sturdee with two battle-cruisers to take revenge. Sturdee met von Spee at the Falkland Islands, and with his faster ships and heavier guns, he destroyed the German squadron from a safe distance.

The destruction of the cruiser *Emden* by H.M.A.S. *Sydney* was also a glorious event in British eyes, and there were other victories over commerce raiders. Generally, though, the raiders caused more excitement than trouble.

The North Sea

In the North Sea the British had assembled their best warships to form what they called their 'Grand Fleet'. Its commander was Admiral John Jellicoe. Most of it, including the dreadnoughts, was at Scapa Flow in the Orkneys, while the battle-cruisers, under Admiral Beatty, used Rosyth. The duty of the Grand Fleet was to stop the German High Seas Fleet from sailing round the north of Scotland and cutting Britain's supply routes across the Atlantic. There was an even more unpleasant possibility. If the German navy won a victory, and took command of the sea, it would be able to escort an army to invade Britain herself. Churchill said that Jellicoe 'was the only man who could lose the war in an afternoon'. Meanwhile, the British took comfort in the thought that their Grand Fleet outnumbered the German High Seas Fleet by two to one.

British dreadnought Indefatigable

From time to time the Germans sent ships to bombard British coastal towns. Twice, Beatty caught raiders and defeated them, once at Heligoland Bight and once on the Dogger Bank. These were insignificant little battles, though they gained Beatty a reputation as an admiral in the true Nelson tradition.

In 1916, the German Fleet had a new commander, Rheinhold von Scheer. He hoped to win an important victory, but knew he could do so only if he caught part of the British fleet on its own. It was a forlorn hope, but he put to sea and on 31 May came upon the British battle-cruisers near Jutland. However, instead of being lured into destruction himself, Beatty led Scheer to the Grand Fleet, which the Germans thought was far away in Scapa Flow. Two hundred and fifty warships joined battle.

The British hoped there would be a second Trafalgar, but Jutland was not like that. The day was misty, and peering through the haze, Jellicoe wondered which way to send his ships. By good fortune he made the right decision. Not only did he put himself between Scheer and his home ports, but he 'crossed his T'. Scheer at once ordered his destroyers to make a torpedo attack, and to escape them, the Grand Fleet swung away for twelve vital minutes. Meanwhile each of Scheer's vessels made a tight U-turn and escaped. In most fleets this would have led to confusion and a number of collisions, but the Germans had practised the manoeuvre so they had no problems with it. Then night fell, and in the darkness they were able to return to port.

Jutland was no triumph for the Royal Navy. Measured by tonnage it lost twice as much shipping as the German High Seas Fleet. Moreover, the Germans were the better gunners, and their ships were harder to sink. Three British battle-cruisers blew up, and Beatty said in despair, 'There is something wrong with our bloody ships today'. There had been something wrong with them since the day they were built. When an enemy shell exploded in one of their gun turrets, there was nothing to stop the flash reaching the ammunition in the magazine. The British had discovered this at the Battle of Dogger Bank, but had done nothing about it.

However, although all Germany rejoiced at the news of Jutland, the High Seas Fleet was never again a threat to Britain. The Germans looked for another kind of victory at sea.

Submarine Warfare

German U-boats were busy in the early days of the war, and in May 1915, one of them sank the liner *Lusitania*. She was a British ship, but there were Americans on board, and the United States threatened to declare war. Germany hurriedly promised not to sink neutral ships, but it was nearly impossible to distinguish these from British ships, so she decided not to sink any at all. The war on land dragged on, however, and since the soldiers had failed to bring victory, Admiral Tirpitz said the navy would. He asked that his U-boats should be allowed to sink any ships sailing to British ports. That meant that America would be sure to join the war, but she was quite unprepared, and it would be a long time before she had trained an army of any size. Tirpitz promised victory in six months, so the Kaiser's government decided to take the gamble.

The Germans began unrestricted U-boat warfare in February 1917, and very soon were sinking 600 ships a month. One merchantman in every four that left Britain failed to return. War supplies ran short, and food was rationed. The answer was to form convoys, but Jellicoe, who was now First Sea Lord, would not allow them. He said that if the merchant ships were all together, the U-boats would sink even more of them. What he could not, or would not see, was that a convoy is not just defensive. To attack it the U-boats would have to go dangerously close to the escorting warships which otherwise they had no difficulty in avoiding. Meanwhile, Tirpitz was winning. An American visitor asked Jellicoe what he could do, and he answered, 'Nothing in the present circumstances'. In the end the Prime Minister, Lloyd George, ordered the Admiralty to organize convoys. At once, losses fell from one ship in every four, to one in a hundred.

Moreover, the United States had declared war in April 1917. It would take time for her to gather her strength, but Germany's defeat was now certain.

The Blockade

By blockading Germany, the Royal Navy was doing something that was less spectacular, but much more useful than fighting the Battle of Jutland.

Unfortunately for Britain the blockade was not entirely effective, because the United States insisted that neutral countries should go on trading with Germany in everything except war materials. She changed her ideas, though, as soon as she entered the war herself. The blockade was at last complete and Germany was soon short of food and essential goods.

Chapter Twenty-Eight

The War in 1918

In 1917, the United States entered the war, and this made all the difference to Britain and France. In the first place, it helped their morale. For years their young men had been fighting and dying in the trenches, and yet the battle front had scarcely moved. After Russia's defeat, they might have lost heart if the United States had not come to their aid. Next, America provided money. Until then, it was Britain who had paid the most towards the cost of the war, but by 1917 she was almost bankrupt. The United States, though, was the richest country in the world, so she was well able to supply all the weapons and war materials that were needed. Thirdly as we have seen, America's entry into the war at last made it possible for the Royal Navy to blockade Germany effectively. Finally, the Americans sent men. There were only a few in 1917, but by 1918 they were arriving in large numbers, and at the end, there were two million American soldiers in France.

American troops parade in London, 1918

However, in 1918, it was the Germans who attacked first. Ludendorff decided on a Spring offensive in a desperate effort to win the war before it was too late. The blockade was beginning to tell, the Americans were arriving in growing numbers, and Tirpitz's U-boat campaign was failing. Moreover, with the defeat of Russia, the Germans were able to move 400 000 troops to the Western Front, which meant they had five men there to every four of their enemies. They had this superiority because allied generals like Haig and Nivelle had been sending hundreds of thousands of their soldiers to be killed in useless attacks.

The Germans began their offensive in March. There attacks were led by specially trained storm-troopers, they were determined, and their organization was efficient. Their first blow fell at the weakest point in the allied line, which was on the Somme, where the French and British armies joined. The British Fifth Army was routed. Next, the Germans attacked successfully in Flanders, and towards Paris. They caused considerable damage to the city with one of their heavy guns, Big Bertha, which had a range of 1300 kilometres.

In this crisis both the French and the British thought only of themselves. Haig began to fret about the Channel ports, fearing that the Germans would capture them and cut him off from home. Pétain, the French Commander-in-Chief, was worried about Paris. The only answer was to have a Supreme Commander in charge of both armies, who would concentrate on defeating the Germans. Haig insisted that this should be Marshal Foch. Luckily for the allies, Foch was equal to the task.

Paris was saved at a Second Battle of the Marne, and soon the German advance ground to a halt. The Germans had taken a lot of territory, but they were nowhere near winning the war, as Ludendorff had hoped. In one way, too, the German victories were a misfortune for them. Their soldiers had been told that thanks to the U-boats, the allies were short of supplies, so it would be easy to defeat them. When the Germans overran the allied trenches, and saw what had been left behind, they realized how false these tales were.

In spite of the check from Foch, Ludendorff planned another offensive. Then, to his surprise and dismay the British launched a successful attack east of Amiens. This was on 8 August, which Ludendorff called 'the black day for the German army'. It was the greatest tank battle of the war, 415 British tanks taking part in it. The real importance of the battle, though, was that for the first time German troops surrendered without fighting. They had spent the last of their courage in their attacks earlier in the year, and their morale was broken.

The whole allied front now moved forward. Partly this was because the Germans had lost heart, partly it was because of American help, but it also had a great deal to do with some new tactics which Haig and Marshal Foch had developed. They saw that most attacks succeeded in their early stages, but halted when the troops outran their supplies, and the enemy brought up his reserves. The mistake had been to press on in the hope of breaking through. Haig and Foch avoided this. As soon as one of their attacks met strong resistance, they halted it, and started another near by. Thus,

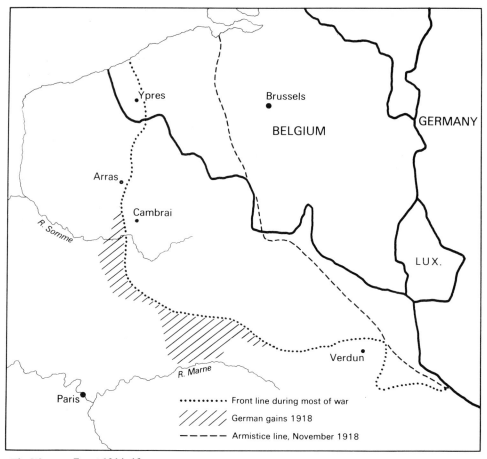

The Western Front 1914–18

instead of making a violent punch in one place, they delivered a series of rapid blows all along the front. That way, the whole German army was rolled back. Tanks were very useful, of course, because they could lead the infantry through barbed-wire and against machine-guns.

In November Hindenburg and Ludendorff decided it was time to make peace. Their armies were still in good order, but they knew they could not resist for much longer. Nor was it just the German army that was in difficulty. The Italians defeated the Austrians at the Battle of Vittorio Veneto: the allies at last broke out of Salonica and advanced through Bulgaria to the Danube: General Allenby took Damascus, and the Turks asked for an armistice. Finally, there were troubles at home in Germany, mainly because of the blockade. So many people were not properly fed that an influenza epidemic killed them in their thousands: workers went on strike and rioted: the fleet mutinied when it was ordered to make a last, desperate attempt to destroy the Royal Navy. The Kaiser abdicated on 9 November, and Hindenburg and Ludendorff withdrew into the background, leaving a civilian government to sign an armistice on 11 November 1918.

WORK SECTION — The First World War

Battlefield on the Western Front

Questions

1 In which country was this photograph taken?
2 How heavy were some of the bombardments on the Western Front?
3 Why did they fail to do what was expected of them?
4 What damage has been done to the landscape?
5 What problems are there for advancing troops?
6 What alternatives to bombardments were tried?
7 What provisions were put into the Peace Treaty because of damage like this? (See page 206)

Britain's Entry into the First World War

Statement to the House of Commons by the Foreign Secretary, Sir Edward Grey, 3 August 1914

The present crisis has originated in a dispute between Austria and Serbia. I can say this with the most absolute confidence — no Government and no country has less desire to be involved in war over a dispute with Austria and Serbia than the Government and the country of France. They are involved in it because of their obligation of honour under a definite alliance with Russia. Well, it is only fair to say to the House that that obligation of honour cannot apply in the same way to us. We are not parties to the Franco-Russian Alliance. For many years, however, we have had a longstanding friendship with France. The French fleet is now in the Mediterranean, and the Northern and Western coasts of France are absolutely undefended. My own feeling is that if a foreign fleet engaged in a war which France had not sought, and in which she had not been the aggressor, came down the English Channel and bombarded and battered the undefended coasts of France, we could not stand aside.

And there is the more serious consideration — becoming more serious every hour — there is the question of the neutrality of Belgium. When mobilization was beginning, I knew that this question must be a most important element of our policy. I telegraphed at the same time in similar terms to both Paris and Berlin to say it was essential for us to know whether the French and German governments respectively were prepared to undertake an engagement to respect the neutrality of Belgium. I got from the French Goverment this reply:

'The French Government are resolved to respect the neutrality of Belgium.'

From the German Government the reply was:

'The Secretary of State for Foreign Affairs could not possibly give an answer before consulting the Emperor and the Imperial Chancellor.'

Questions

1 Why were Austria and Serbia enemies? What caused the dispute that Grey refers to here?
2 When did France and Russia become allies? Why? Do you agree that France had no direct interest in the quarrel between Austria and Serbia?
3 When did Britain's friendship with France begin?
4 Why was the French fleet in the Mediterranean? Under what obligation did that leave Britain?
5 According to Grey, how important was the neutrality of Belgium?
6 What telegrams did Grey send to Paris and Berlin? 'What was the French reply? How would you describe the German reply?
7 Here Grey gives two reasons why Britain should declare war on Germany. What others were there? Do you think Grey chose the most important?

Document One

Extract from Memorandum by Lloyd George, 1 January 1915
(Half a million British troops will soon be available and he wonders how they could best be used.)

I cannot pretend to have any military knowledge, but the little I saw and gathered in France as to the military position convinced me that any attempt to force the carefully prepared German lines in the west would end in failure and in appalling loss of life. The French generals are convinced that even if the whole of the German Army now occupied in Poland were thrown on the Western Front, the French and British troops would still be able to hold their own. The same observation, of course, must apply to the German military position. We were told the other day that the Germans had prepared a series of trenches on their side, right up to the Rhine. After three or four months of the most tenacious fighting, involving very heavy losses, the French have not at any point gained a couple of miles. To force the line you would require at least three to one: our reinforcements would not guarantee two to one, or anything approaching such predominance. Is it not therefore better that we should recognize the impossibility of this particular task, and try to think out some way by which the distinct numerical advantage which the Allies will have attained a few months hence can be rendered effective?

Document Two

Extract from Memorandum by Winston Churchill 1 August 1916

In personnel the results of the operation on the Somme have been disastrous; in terrain they have been absolutely barren. And, although our brave troops on a portion of the front, mocking their losses and ready to make every sacrifice, are at the moment elated by the small advances made and the capture of prisoners and souvenirs, the ultimate moral effect will be disappointing. From every point of view, therefore, the British offensive has been a great failure.

Document Three

Reply of Sir Douglas Haig to an enquiry about the Battle of the Somme. 3 August 1916

(a) *Pressure on Verdun relieved. Not less than six enemy divisions besides heavy guns have been withdrawn.*

(b) *Successes achieved by Russia last month would certainly have been prevented had*

enemy been free to transfer troops from here to the Eastern Theatre.

(c) *Proof given to the world that Allies are capable of making and maintaining a vigorous offensive and of driving enemy's best troops from the strongest positions. Also impressed on the world, England's strength and determination, and the fighting power of the British race.*

(d) *We have inflicted very heavy losses on the enemy. In ONE month 30 of his divisions have been used up, as against 35 at Verdun in 5 months. In another 6 weeks the enemy should be hard put to it to find men.*

(e) *The maintenance of a steady offensive pressure will result eventually in his complete overthrow. Principle on which we should act. MAINTAIN OUR OFFENSIVE.*

Questions

Document One

1 What does Lloyd George say would be the result of an offensive in France?
2 What preparations have the Germans made there?
3 What success have the French had?
4 What superiority would the allies need to succeed? What superiority are they likely to have?
5 What does Lloyd George believe the allies should do?
6 What was the alternative to an offensive on the Western Front that Lloyd George and Churchill produced in 1916? How successful was it?

Document Two

7 What is the meaning of the first sentence of this paragraph?
8 Why are British troops pleased at the moment? How does Churchill think they will feel in the end?

Document Three

9 What was happening at Verdun in 1916? How does Haig say the offensive on the Somme has helped?
10 What successes did the Russians have in 1916? How does Haig say the offensive on the Somme has helped them?
11 What does Haig say the Somme offensive has proved to the world?
12 What losses have the Germans sustained? What difficulty does Haig think the Germans will soon have?

13 What does Haig believe should be done in the immediate future?

14 Who had the better idea about the way the battle was going — Churchill or Haig?

15 What was the result of Haig's offensives on the British army?

16 Haig believed the allies would win the war in the west: Lloyd George and Churchill thought they would win it in the east. What, in fact happened in the end?

17 Do you think Haig could have won the war by the kind of offensive he mounted on the Somme?

The War at Sea

Document One

This is a message Admiral Jellicoe sent to the sailors of the Grand Fleet, after the Battle of Jutland.

(*Iron Duke* 4 June 1916)
Memorandum

1 *I desire to express to the Flag Officers, Captains, Officers and Men of the Grand Fleet my very high appreciation of the manner in which the ships were fought during the action on 31 May 1916.*

2 *At this stage, when full information is not available, it is not possible to enter into details, but quite sufficient is already known to enable me to state definitely that the glorious traditions handed down to us by generations of gallant seamen were most worthily upheld.*

3 *Weather conditions of a highly unfavourable nature robbed the Fleet of that complete victory which I know was expected by all ranks, which is necessary for the safety of the Empire and which will yet be ours.*

4 *Our losses were heavy and we miss many most gallant comrades, but, although it is very difficult to obtain accurate information as to the enemy losses, I have no doubt that we shall find that they are certainly not less than our own. Sufficient information has already been received for me to make that statement with confidence. I hope to be able to give the Fleet fuller information on this point at an early date, but do not wish to delay the issue of this expression of my keen appreciation of the work of the Fleet, and my confidence in future complete victory.*

5 *I cannot close without stating that the wonderful spirit and fortitude of the wounded has filled me with the greatest admiration.*

I am more proud that ever to have the honour of commanding a fleet manned by such officers and men.

J. R. Jellicoe
Admiral, Commander-in-Chief

Document Two

A historian's view of Jutland.

The war could have been won on that day, but not by the men in command of the ships or the men in the Admiralty in command of them. And not in the ships which comprised England's Grand Fleet, and not with the shells which were fired by their guns. The war was not won on that day and went on for another two years, and more. Nor was there a battle won on that day. Not a battle of Trafalgar size which all England and her allies had been expecting. The Germans sank more ships and killed more men and went home to announce a victory while the British Navy held the field. Within the Admiralty none knew how to break the news of so mixed a triumph. They said a little and hesitated, and then sent for Churchill to write a suitable bulletin. He could not do it. There was no suitable way in which to proclaim that everything was wrong.

(Stanley Bonnett — *The Price of Admiralty*. Robert Hale, 1968)

Document Three

A Spartacist pamphlet issued in Germany during the war.

The inevitable has struck: hunger! hunger! In Leipzig, in Berlin, in Essen, in Brunswick, in Magdeburg, in Munich and in Kiel, and in many other places, there are riots of the starving masses in front of the food shops. In Kiel as in Brunswick, the workers of the Germania shipyard have come out on strike in protest about the food mismanagement.

Herr von Bethmann Hollweg [the German Chancellor] accuses England of the crime of having caused the hunger in Germany, and the 'war at any price' brigade and the government pimp his parrot cry. However, the German government ought to have known that this was bound to happen: war against Russia, France and England was bound to lead to a blockade of Germany.

They lied to us: German U-boats would cut off supplies to Britain, Britain would have to whine for peace and the war would end. These are fairy tales for children. The U-boat warfare is setting new enemies on Germany's throat, but there can be no thought of cutting off supplies to Britain even if Germany had ten times as many U-boats.

There is no choice. Only action counts. Arise, you men and women! Express your will, let you voice be heard:

Down with the war!

Long live the international solidarity of the proletariat!

Questions

Document One

1 What does Jellicoe say about the behaviour of his men at Jutland?
2 Why does he say the British failed to win a complete victory?
3 How far would you agree that this was correct?
4 What does Jellicoe say about the comparative losses of the British and German fleets?
5 What was the truth?
6 What does Jellicoe expect to happen in the future? Why was he to be disappointed?

Document Two

7 What does this writer say could have happened at Jutland?
8 Why does he say this did not come about?
9 Why does he describe Jutland as a 'mixed triumph'?

Document Three

10 What is hunger causing many of the German people to do?
11 Why is Germany short of food?
12 What are the results of the U-boat campaign?
13 What does the pamphlet call on the German people to do? Did they obey this call?
14 What does the last line of the pamphlet tell you about the political ideas of its authors? Read more about the Spartacists on pages 81–2.
15 What links can you see between the Battle of Jutland, this pamphlet and the defeat of Germany?

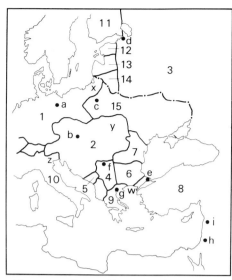

The war on Eastern Fronts 1914–18

The War on the Eastern Fronts 1914–18

Map Questions

1 Name countries 1–15 and towns a–i.
2 Name province x. What happened here in 1914? How did this influence events on the Western Front?
3 Which German general overran country 15? When? What conclusion did he draw from his victory? How did it influence events on the Western Front?
4 Name the range of mountains at y. Who invaded this region in 1916? Who defeated him?
5 On whose side did country 7 join the war? When? Why? What happened to her?
6 When did countries 11–14 gain their independence? Why was it possible for them to do so?
7 What treaty allowed the Germans to occupy the territory up to the line shown _._._.? When was it signed?
8 How did the defeat of country 3 influence events on the Western Front?
9 When did country 10 enter the war? Why?
10 Name two battles fought in region z and give their dates. Say, briefly, what happened in each.
11 On whose side did country 6 enter the war? When? Which country was defeated as a result?

12 What armies were there in town g by the end of 1915? When did they break out? How far did they advance?

13 What persuaded country 8 to enter the war? When?

14 What campaign was fought in region w? When?

15 Who took town h? When?

16 Who took town i? When? What happened as a result?

17 What happened in country 2 towards the end of 1918 which caused her to leave the war?

The Causes of the First World War

Questions

1 Why did European countries want colonies?

2 How large was the British Empire? When had the British acquired it?

3 Name three areas of the world where Britain and Russia were rivals.

4 In which continent, especially, were Britain and France rivals? What crisis was there in 1898? Describe what happened.

5 What colonial policy had Bismarck followed? What was William II's policy? What aspect of it alarmed the British considerably?

6 Why was there hatred between France and Germany?

7 Which countries were in conflict in the Balkans? How did Russia hope to take advantage of the troubles there?

8 What new infantry weapons had been developed?

9 Why did Britain and Germany lead the arms race?

10 Who was largely responsible for creating the German navy? How did he hope to challenge the British?

11 What new ships did Admiral Fisher develop?

12 Why was Germany left behind in the naval race? How did the German fleet change international relations?

13 What attempts were made to halt the arms race? Why did they fail?

14 Which countries made up the Triple Alliance? Who formed it? When? Why?

15 Which countries made up the Dual Alliance? When was it formed? Why?

16 Why did Britain follow a policy of 'splendid isolation'? When and why did she abandon it?

17 With which country did Britain make an alliance? When? What were its terms?

18 When did Britain make an agreement with France? What was it called? What were its terms?

19 When did Britain make an agreement with Russia? What was it called? What were its terms?

20 What was the significance of Britain's agreements with France and Russia?

21 What action did France take in 1906? How did the Kaiser react? What conference was called to settle the problem? Who supported France? Who supported Germany? How had the European situation changed since 1890?

22 What action did Austria–Hungary take in 1908? Why did Russia protest? Why did she back down?

23 What action did the French take in 1911? How did the Kaiser react? What did he hope to gain? Why did he back down?

24 What agreement did Britain and France make after the 1911 crisis?

25 When was the First Balkan War? Which countries fought in it? What treaty ended it? What were its terms?

26 Why did the Second Balkan War break out? What treaty ended it? What were its terms?

27 What did Serbia gain from the two Balkan Wars? What did she hope to do next? What did Austria–Hungary decide to do?

28 What happened on 28 June 1914? Why did Austria–Hungary welcome it? What encouraged her to attack Serbia?

29 Describe how Russia, Germany and France were drawn into the war.

30 Why did Britain wish to join the war on the side of the French? What excuse did she find for so doing? When did she declare war?

Describe the causes of the First World War under the headings: Differences between the European Powers/The Arms Race/The Alliances/The Crises

The Western Front to 1917

Questions

1 Describe the Schlieffen Plan.

2 Why were the French driven back at first? What help did they have from the Belgians and the British?

3 Give two reasons why the German right wing was not as strong as von Schlieffen had hoped.

4 Where did the Germans first meet serious trouble? What problem did the German First Army have? How did the allies take advantage of it? Where did it retreat?

5 Why was there a 'race to the sea'? How did the troops protect themselves? What weapons did they have?

6 Describe the four stages in the development of trench defences.

7 How many shells were fired in some of the bombardments? Give three reasons why bombardments failed.

8 When did the Germans first try poison gas. Why was it not a success?

9 Who first thought of the tank? What did he hope from it? Who developed it?

10 Where were tanks first used? Why were they not effective?

11 Where did the Tank Corps choose to attack in November 1917? Why? Describe the British attack. How successful was it?

12 Give two reasons why the British advance halted.

13 When did Falkenhayn attack Verdun? What was his plan? What happened in the end?

14 Describe the Battle of the Somme. How did the British console themselves in their defeat?

15 What happened in the French army when Nivelle's offensive failed? What action did the British have to take?

16 Why did Haig wish to take the Channel ports? Describe the battles which followed. How successful was Haig's offensive?

Describe the war on the Western Front to 1917 under the headings: The Schlieffen Plan and the Battle of the Marne/Trench Warfare/Major Battles on the Western Front

The War on Other Fronts to 1917

Questions

1 Why did Britain and France hope Russia would give them a lot of help? Why was this likely to be delayed?

How did Germany mean to use the time?

2 Why was Austria–Hungary a poor ally for Germany?

3 How did the Russians surprise the Germans at the beginning of the war? Who defeated them? Where?

4 What other failures did the Russians have in 1914? What had they achieved?

5 What successes did Falkenhayn have in 1915?

6 Describe the Russian offensive of 1916.

7 What events in Russia caused her to leave the war? What was the name of the peace treaty? When was it signed?

8 What success did Siberia have in 1914? Why was she defeated in 1915? Where did her army go? What forces joined it?

9 Why did Italy declare war on Austria–Hungary? When? At what battle were the Italians defeated? Why? Who saved Italy?

10 What action did Turkey take after the Balkan Wars? What persuaded her to join the war?

11 Who planned the Dardanelles campaign? What were their aims?

12 Why was the naval attack a mistake? Describe two landings by troops and say why both failed. When did the British leave?

13 Where did the Turks defeat the British in 1916?

14 Name two offensives mounted by the British in 1917. What did T. E. Lawrence do?

15 Summarize the position at the end of 1917.

Give an account of the war to the end of 1917 on the Eastern, Balkan and Italian Fronts, and against Turkey

The War at Sea

Questions

1 Describe the Battles of Coronel and the Falkland Islands. How dangerous were the commerce raiders?

2 What bases did the Grand Fleet use? What was its main duty? Why was it vitally important it should not be defeated?

3 Name two small victories by Admiral Beatty.

4 What was Rheinhold von Scheer's plan? What was wrong with it?

5 In what strong position did Jellicoe find himself at the Battle of Jutland? How did von Scheer escape from the trap?

6 How did British and German losses compare? In what ways was the German fleet superior? What was wrong with the British battle-cruisers?

7 What was the result of the Battle of Jutland?

8 What was the result of the sinking of the *Lusitania*? Why did the Germans decide to resume the U-boat campaign? What did Tirpitz promise?

9 When did the Germans begin unrestricted U-boat warfare? How successful were they? Why?

10 Why did Jellicoe refuse to organize convoys? Why were they organized in the end? How successful were they?

11 What did the United States do as a result of the U-boat campaign?

12 Why was the British blockade of Germany not effective, at first? When did it become so? What results did it have?

Give an account of the War at Sea under the headings: Commerce Raiders/The North Sea/Submarine Warfare/The Blockade

The War in 1918

Questions

1 Give four reasons why America's entry to the war was important.

2 Give four reasons why Ludendorff decided on a Spring offensive in 1918. Why did the Germans have superior numbers?

3 What successes did the Germans have?

4 Why did the allies need a Supreme Commander? Who was he?

5 Where were the Germans halted? In what way were their victories a misfortune to them?

6 What was 'the black day for the German army'? Why did Ludendorff give it that name?

7 What new tactics did Haig and Foch develop? How were tanks useful?

8 Why did Hindenburg and Ludendorff decide to make peace in November 1918?

9 When did the Kaiser abdicate? When was the armistice signed?

Give an account of the war in 1918 under the headings: The Importance of America's Entry into the War/Lundendorff's Offensive/The Allied Offensive/The Collapse of Germany and Her Allies

Problems

1 What were the main causes of the First World War?

2 In 1919 Germany was made to accept responsibility for starting the war. Was this fair?

3 How did colonial affairs influence the relations between the Great Powers before 1914?

4 In 1900 France and Russia were Britain's chief rivals. Explain why she entered the war on their side in 1914.

5 Why did the Gemans fail to win a quick victory in 1914?

6 Why did neither side make any important advances on the Western Front after the Battle of the Marne in 1914, until 1918?

7 Why was Russia defeated by the Central Powers?

8 What were the aims of the Dardanelles campaign? Why was it a failure for the British?

9 Explain the importance of sea power during the war.

10 Why was there no decisive battle between the surface fleets of Britain and Germany?

11 Why did the Central Powers lose the war? Why did this not happen until late in 1918?

12 What contributions to victory were made by (a) France, (b) Great Britain, (c) the United States of America?

INTERNATIONAL RELATIONS
to 1939

Chapter Twenty-nine

The Peace Treaties

The Peace Makers

IN 1919 the leaders of the countries that had won the war met at Versailles to draw up the peace treaties. The 'Big Five', America, France, Britain, Italy and Japan, were supposed to have an equal say, but Japan had done little during the war, and had little interest in Europe, so she was not often consulted. That left the 'Big Four'. However, America, France and Britain did not have much respect for Italy. Indeed, Orlando, the Italian Prime Minister, was so disgusted at the treatment he received, that he walked out of the conference for a time. As for the defeated powers, they were not allowed to join in the discussions, but had to give their views in writing.

Signing the Treaty of Versailles

Russia did not even send a delegation, for she was in the middle of a civil war. In effect, then, three men made the peace treaties, Woodrow Wilson, President of the United States, George Clemenceau, Prime Minister of France, and David Lloyd George, Prime Minister of Great Britain.

These three men faced serious problems. They had to make a peace that would last, and they had to settle new national frontiers, which was especially difficult in Eastern Europe where both the Russian and the Austro–Hungarian empires had collapsed. They made their problems much worse, however, because they could not agree among themselves.

Wilson was an idealist and, like many such people, he was so sure he was right that it was hard to reason with him. He had set out the principles he said the peace treaties should follow in 'Fourteen Points' and he clung to these with grim determination. Clemenceau said, 'God was satisfied with Ten Commandments, but Wilson had to have fourteen'.

The fourteen points contained four main ideas. The first was 'national self-determination', that is, the right of every nation to govern itself. Many nations had not had this right. They included the southern Slavs in Austria–Hungary and their discontent had helped start the war. Next, Wilson believed in freedom of the seas, and free trade. Among other things, that would stop countries like Britain seizing colonies and keeping them as trading partners for themselves alone. The United States resented this. Thirdly, Wilson said there should be general disarmament, since there could be no war without weapons. Finally, he wanted a League of Nations which could settle all disputes peacefully. He disliked the complicated web of secret treaties that had grown up before the war, and he especially disliked the underhanded diplomacy that had gone with them. He felt, too, that it was a mistake for countries to build up an alliance in the hope of becoming so strong that no one would dare attack them. That led others to do the same, and then there was an uneasy balance. So far from preventing war, the 'balance of power' had helped cause it. Now there should be 'open covenants, openly arrived at', and there would be no need to make alliances, since the League of Nations would be there to settle problems. In sum, Wilson was trying to end all the evil things which he felt had caused the war.

'Tiger' Clemenceau had quite different ideas. Three times in a hundred years the Germans had invaded his country, and since there were 70 million of them to only 40 million Frenchmen, they were likely to do so again. It was essential that Germany should be weakened permanently. Also, the war had devastated northern France, while Germany was untouched. Nor was it only the fighting that caused the damage, for when the Germans retreated in 1918 they systematically wrecked every French farm, village and town before they left it. Clemenceau wanted the Germans to pay for what they had done, and he wanted revenge.

The British public made their views plain to Lloyd George by shouting, 'Hang the Kaiser' and 'Make Germany pay!' Lloyd George duly promised to 'squeeze the lemon till the pips squeaked', but he was not as extreme as Clemenceau. He was no idealist like Wilson, and he had no tender feelings for the Germans, but he was afraid they might turn Communist if the peace terms were too severe. For example, he was against a French plan to turn the Rhineland into a separate State.

Altogether, five treaties were made, each having its own name. The most important, though, was the Treaty of Versailles with Germany, so we can group them all together under the heading 'the Versailles Settlement'.

The League of Nations

In every treaty, the Covenant of the League of Nations came first. Wilson insisted on this because he said that if it later appeared that a treaty had faults, then the League could put them right (for more on the League of Nations see Chapter 32).

Germany

Germany lost all her colonies. They went to the League of Nations, which then 'mandated' them to the countries that had won the war. America could probably have had a share, but Wilson was being high-minded about 'imperialism', so she went without.

Germany also lost territory in Europe. France took back Alsace and Lorraine, and with them the valuable deposits of iron ore in Lorraine. Belgium took the frontier towns of Eupen and Malmédy. Denmark had been neutral, but there was a plebiscite in the provinces that Bismarck had taken from her in 1864. Northern Schleswig chose to return to Denmark. In the east was the new State of Poland. She was given Upper Silesia, with its coalfields, Posen and West Prussia. She also had an outlet to the sea, the Polish Corridor. It was no use without a port, and the one that stood at the end of the Corridor was Danzig. However, its inhabitants were all Germans, so it could not be given to Poland, since that would have been

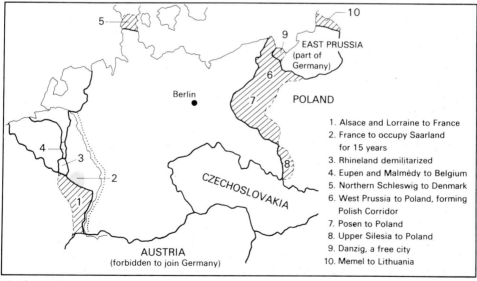

Germany's losses by the Treaty of Versailles

against Wilson's principle of 'national self-determination'. As a compromise, it became a free city under the League of Nations, and the Poles had the use of the port. East Prussia remained a province of Germany, but it was separated from the rest of the country by the Polish Corridor. Finally, Memel was given to Lithuania. In all, Germany lost four million inhabitants, three-quarters of her iron ore and much of her coal.

There were other terms as well. Germany was disarmed. She was to have no air force, only a small navy, with no submarines, and an army of 100 000 which was barely enough to keep order. Clemenceau wanted the Rhineland to be a separate State, but neither Wilson nor Lloyd George would allow that, so again a compromise was reached and it was demilitarized. Germany was forbidden to build any fortifications, or station any troops along the east bank of the Rhine, or in any of the territory to the west of it. France was to occupy the Saarland and take its coal for fifteen years, after which there was to be a plebiscite to let the inhabitants decide whether they should join France or Germany. Following the collapse of the Austro-Hungarian Empire, Austria was now a State on her own, and her inhabitants were almost all Germans. Germany and Austria were, however, forbidden to unite, because that would make Germany stronger.

Finally, Germany was ordered to pay reparations. The allies could not agree on whether she should meet the cost of the damage to civilian property, which was put at £3000 million, or the total bill for the war which was said to be £8000 million. In the end, they set up a Reparations Commission which decided on a figure of £6000 million. The section of the treaty on reparations began with a statement that Germany should be made to pay for the war, because she started it. This 'war guilt' clause made the Germans particularly angry.

South-east Europe

As the war ended, Austria–Hungary disintegrated. Austria and Hungary became separate States: the northern Slavs formed a new country, Czechoslavakia: the southern Slavs joined with Serbia and Montenegro to make Yugoslavia, so the dream which Serbia had in 1914 came true. The peace treaties recognized the new States and fixed the boundaries between them. There was a problem with Czechoslovakia because in the Sudetenland there were three million Germans. They could not stay with Austria, as she was too far away, and there was no question of them joining Germany. Accordingly they remained under Czech rule, with unhappy results in 1938.

Three other countries also gained from the fall of Austria–Hungary. Poland took Galicia, Italy took the Trentino and Istria, and Romania took Transylvania. Romania also took Bessarabia from Russia.

Bulgaria had to give Western Thrace to Greece, so losing her outlet to the Aegean.

Russia's Baltic Provinces

Lithuania, Latvia, Estonia and Finland threw off Russian rule and became independent.

Poland

Poland had been divided among her neighbours, Germany, Austria–Hungary and Russia. Now she was born again and we have already seen what territory she had from Germany and Austria. There remained her eastern frontier. According to 'national self-determination' it should have divided the Polish people from the Russians, but the two races were mixed over a wide area. To settle the problem an English stateman, Lord Curzon, suggested a frontier that seemed fair to both sides. The Poles, however, had no intention of accepting the 'Curzon Line'. They fought and won a war against the Russians, and helped themselves to so much territory that they doubled the size of their country. The Poles also took land from Lithuania, including the town of Vilna, which the Lithuanians had intended to be their capital.

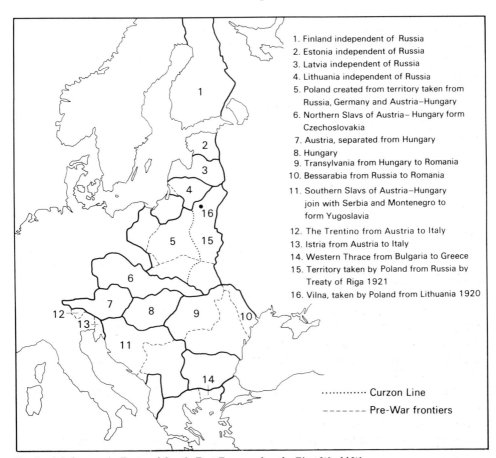

1. Finland independent of Russia
2. Estonia independent of Russia
3. Latvia independent of Russia
4. Lithuania independent of Russia
5. Poland created from territory taken from Russia, Germany and Austria–Hungary
6. Northern Slavs of Austria–Hungary form Czechoslovakia
7. Austria, separated from Hungary
8. Hungary
9. Transylvania from Hungary to Romania
10. Bessarabia from Russia to Romania
11. Southern Slavs of Austria–Hungary join with Serbia and Montenegro to form Yugoslavia
12. The Trentino from Austria to Italy
13. Istria from Austria to Italy
14. Western Thrace from Bulgaria to Greece
15. Territory taken by Poland from Russia by Treaty of Riga 1921
16. Vilna, taken by Poland from Lithuania 1920

············ Curzon Line

------- Pre-War frontiers

Territorial changes in East and South-East Europe after the First World War

Turkey

Since an allied fleet had its guns trained on Constantinople, the wretched Sultan of Turkey had to agree to humiliating peace terms. Turkey lost all her former empire. Arabia became independent, Syria, including the Lebanon, was mandated to France, while Palestine, Trans-Jordan and Iraq were all mandated to Britain. Greece was given two provinces in Turkey herself, Eastern Thrace and Ionia. Though it was on the Turkish mainland, there were some half million Greeks in Ionia, but there were plenty of Turks there as well. The Turks could not stand being ruled by people who, as they put it, had once been their slaves. Mustafa Kemal, who had made a name for himself at Gallipoli, rebelled against the Sultan, and led an army to attack the Greeks. Greece's former allies, like Britain and France, were tired of fighting, so they did not come to her aid. Mustafa Kemal overran Ionia, and then menaced Eastern Thrace. In 1923 the Treaty of Lausanne recognized both these provinces as part of Turkey.

Problems left by the Peace Treaties

The peace treaties were drawn up while people were still angry after the war, so it is not surprising that the allies were harsh to Germany. Equally, it is not surprising that the Germans claimed that the Treaty of Versailles was unfair.

In the first place, the Germans were not allowed to have any say in the peace-making, apart from submitting their views in writing. The allied statesmen drew up the treaty, and ordered the German representatives to sign. Versailles was a 'diktat', a dictated peace, and no one feels bound to keep an agreement he has made under duress. Secondly, the Germans resented the 'war guilt' clause. The truth was that Germany was only partly responsible for the war, while many of her people felt she was not responsible at all. To them, it was most unfair that she should take the entire blame and pay the entire cost. Thirdly, there was obviously one law for the victors and another for the vanquished. Wilson preached 'national self-determination' so why were there German minorities in Czechoslovakia and Poland, and why was Austria forbidden to join with Germany?

Having given the Germans plenty of reasons to be unhappy with the peace treaty, the allies did too little to stop them taking their revenge. Germany was supposed to have only a small army and navy, and no air force, but if she was allowed to rearm, she would be in a strong position. To the east, her neighbours were weak. Russia was large, but she was having a civil war: Poland was mainly agricultural: for the rest, there were only small States, many of which distrusted each other anyway. In the west, France had a population of only 40 million, against 70 million in Germany. As soon as the war ended, France made an alliance with Poland and Czechoslovakia, but that was not nearly enough on its own. What was needed was that Britain and American should give France full support, but Britain was at best lukewarm, while America decided 'to leave the Old

World of Europe to stew in its own juice'. Congress refused to ratify the peace treaties, and America did not join the League of Nations.

The soldiers in the trenches had been promised they were fighting 'a war to end wars', but the next conflict was only twenty years away.

Chapter Thirty

Europe 1920–39

BETWEEN the wars, European affairs were dominated by the two dictators, Mussolini and Hitler. However, they did not work together until 1936. Therefore we must look at Italy and Germany separately in the period before 1936, though after that their fortunes were linked, and we can consider them as one.

Italy, 1920–36

Mussolini's aim was to make Italy a powerful, important nation. We will see how he tried to achieve this in the Adriatic, in his dealings with Germany, in Africa, and in Spain.

Across the Adriatic was the little State of Albania, in which the Italians were interested. During 1923, a commission was at work, trying to settle her boundary with Greece. Among its members was an Italian general and he, with several of his staff, were killed by some Greeks. Mussolini at once occupied the Greek island of Corfu, saying he was going to keep it until the Greek government paid compensation, and gave him an apology. The quarrel went to the League of Nations though it was, in fact, settled by a Conference of Ambassadors from the Great Powers that was meeting in Paris. It decided in favour of Italy. Mussolini looked on the Corfu incident as a great triumph, for he thought he had made it plain that other countries would have to treat Italy with respect.

A much more serious problem was the possible threat from Germany. Because of this, Mussolini was willing to work with Britain and France, for a time. There were three important events. In 1925 Italy signed the Locarno Pact, by which she promised, together with Britain, to guarantee Germany's western frontier (see page 212). Secondly, in 1934 the Austrian Nazis murdered Chancellor Dolfuss, and Hitler prepared to take over the country. Mussolini did not want German soldiers on the Brenner Pass so he at once sent an army to the Austrian frontier. Hitler backed down in a hurry. Thirdly, in 1935 Hitler announced that Germany was rearming. Britain and France took fright, and Mussolini joined their representatives for a conference at Stresa. All three countries condemned Germany's action so forming what is called the Stresa Front, but it was the last time Mussolini did anything against Germany.

We come now to Mussolini's African adventure. He wanted to conquer Abyssinia, so giving his country an empire that was more worthy of her than the deserts of Libya, Eritrea and Somaliland. In 1935, there was a border incident, which gave him an excuse to start the war. An army of 400 000 invaded Abyssinia. The tribesmen fought bravely, but they could do little against the Italian armies, and nothing against their air force. In April 1936 the Abyssinian army made a desperate stand at Lake Ashangi, but the Italians defeated it soundly. Adowa was avenged. Shortly afterwards Marshal Badoglio led his troops in a triumphal parade through the streets of Addis Ababa and Emperor Haile Selassi fled abroad. The war was over. On 9 May 1936, Mussolini appeared on the balcony of the Palazzo Venezia in Rome to tell a cheering crowd that Italy at last had her empire. It was his greatest triumph, but it was also the beginning of his fall.

At the Stresa Conference Mussolini had the impression that Britain and France would approve of his invasion of Abyssinia. It was a shock to discover they were against it, and were urging the League of Nations to impose sanctions. This the League did, but it was careful to see that the sanctions were ineffective. For example, it did not place an embargo on oil which, as Mussolini admitted, would have halted his armies in a week. Britain and France, then, had the worst of both worlds. They broke the Stresa Front and made an enemy of Italy, but at the same time they did not stop her conquering Abyssinia. However, there was an unhappy result for Italy as well, since she could not afford to be without friends. She turned to Germany and this led, in the end, to her defeat in the Second World War.

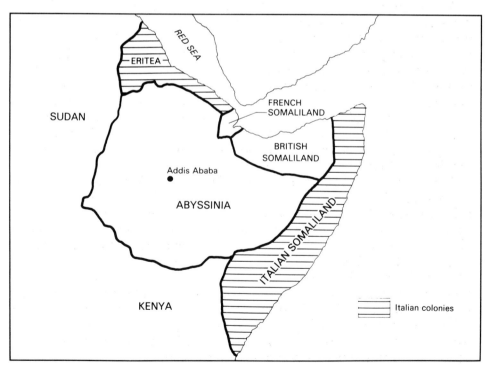

East Africa

Germany 1920–36

Immediately after the war Germany's most serious international problem was reparations. Chapter 11 describes how she fell behind on her payments and how this led to the French occupation of the Ruhr and the collapse of the mark. Gustav Stresemann then took office and, instead of resistance, adopted a 'policy of fulfilment'. This led in 1924 to the Dawes Plan for the payment of reparations and in 1925, to the two Locarno Treaties. By the first of these, Germany agreed that her western frontiers were to be permanent, and France, Great Britain, Italy and Belgium all guaranteed them. The second Locarno Treaty was about Germany's eastern frontiers. She refused to accept them as permanent, but promised she would not go to war to win back any of the territory she had lost. Only France, Poland and Czechoslavakia guaranteed this treaty. The following year, 1926, Germany joined the League of Nations. She was rather like a naughty child who has promised to be good, and is allowed to come out of her bedroom to be with the rest of the family.

Germany's co-operation with her neighbours ended when Hitler came to power. In his foreign policy he had one clear aim, which was to make Germany powerful. He intended to do this in three stages. The first was to rearm, so that he could back his demands by force. The second was to unite all German people under his rule. That meant that Austria and the lands occupied by the German minorities in Czechoslovakia and Poland would become part of Germany. The third stage was to gain *lebensraum*, or room in which to live, in Eastern Europe. Poland and much of Russia were to become German colonies, and their inhabitants, Germany's slaves.

However, when Hitler came to power in 1933, Germany had an army of only 100 000 men, so he had to be cautious. First of all, he invited the other European countries to disarm, as Germany had been made to do. They refused as he hoped and expected they would, so he started to rearm his own country, though at first, he did so in secret. Germany also left the League of Nations.

Then came a set-back. Hitler was hoping to unite Austria with Germany so he encouraged some discontented Austrians to form a Nazi party of their own. In 1934 they murdered the Chancellor, Engelbert Dolfuss, and tried to seize power. Hitler was about to announce the union of Austria and Germany, but the Austrian government acted promptly, and put down the rebellion. What was more, Mussolini at once sent troops to the Austrian frontier and made it plain he would fight rather than allow Germany to take Austria. Hitler backed down. He denied that he had anything to do with the murder of Dolfuss, and sent von Papen as ambassador to Vienna to make friends with the new Chancellor, Kurt von Schuschnigg. This was Hitler's only important failure before the outbreak of war.

In 1935 there was a stroke of good fortune. By the Treaty of Versailles the French were to hold the Saarland for fifteen years, after which its people were to decide whether to remain with France, or to rejoin Germany. When the plebiscite was held, 90 per cent of the votes were for union with

Germany. Hitler had nothing to do with the result, but that did not stop him hailing it as a great personal triumph.

Also in 1935 Hitler announced that Germany was rearming. He did this to please his people but, as we have seen, he frightened Britain, France and Italy into forming the Stresa Front. However, he made a clever move. He knew that the main reason why Britain had entered the First World War was that she had been frightened of the Kaiser's fleet. Accordingly, he suggested a treaty limiting the German surface fleet to one-third the strength of the British. The British government agreed, and the treaty was signed. Hitler hoped this might be the first step towards an alliance with Britain. That did not happen, but the naval treaty at least meant that the British were not as alarmed at German rearmament as they might have been. Moreover, France and Italy were furious with Britain, for they were naval powers too, and they were not even consulted. The Stresa Front had been weakened, even before Mussolini's invasion of Abyssinia.

In 1936, Hitler made his first real gamble. He sent troops into the Rhineland. This was not only a breach of the Treaty of Versailles, which had been forced on Germany, but also of the Treaty of Locarno, which she had signed of her own free will. The German army was still too weak to fight a war, as Hitler knew full well. He said later, 'The forty-eight hours after the march into the Rhineland were the most nerve-racking in my life.' However, the British took the view that Germany was entitled to send troops into her own territory. As for the French, they could have invaded Germany on their own with every chance of success, but apart from sending a few divisions to the frontier, they did nothing. The Rhineland crisis showed how weak Germany's enemies were. As early as 1927, Hitler had boasted, 'There is no solidarity in Europe: there is only submission'. In 1936, it certainly looked as if he was right.

Reoccupation of the Rhineland 1936

The Rome–Berlin Axis

As we have seen, Mussolini's invasion of Abyssinia cost him the support of Britain and France, so he looked instead to Germany. Hitler soon fell under Mussolini's spell. Indeed, Mussolini seems to have been the only man he truly admired, and the only one to whom he was loyal until the end. Italy and Germany became friends officially, in 1936, when they made an agreement to work together in foreign affairs. After the treaty was signed, Mussolini said, 'This Rome–Berlin line is not a diaphragm, but rather an axis, around which can revolve all those European States with a will to collaboration and peace.'

The year 1936 was also fateful, because that was when the Spanish Civil War began. The Fascist leader, General Franco, started a rebellion against the Republican government, and Mussolini saw this as a chance to increase his influence, as well as to give his armies a further taste of glory. He sent Franco arms and large number of 'volunteers'. Britain and France were annoyed because they did not want another country to turn Fascist. The French were particularly worried for they had already had Nazi Germany to the east, and if Spain was hostile as well, they would be in great danger. Relations with Italy became even worse when 'unknown' submarines sank some British and French merchant ships in the Mediterranean. Hitler, too, sent arms to Franco, but that was only to make sure the war went on. While it lasted, it was certain Italy would quarrel with her former friends.

In 1937, Italy joined the Anti-Comintern Pact, which was a treaty Germany had already made with Japan. Its aim was to stop the spread of Communism in the world. Italy also left the League of Nations to show her support for Germany.

That same year, Mussolini made his first visit to Germany. He came home most impressed and even insisted that his soldiers should learn the goose step, or Roman step, as he called it.

The Anschluss (Union) of Austria and Germany

Now that Italy and Germany were on good terms, Hitler felt safe to move against Austria. His first step was to bully the Austrian Chancellor, Schuschnigg, into lifting the ban he had imposed on the Austrian Nazi Party, and to have Nazis in his cabinet. Schuschnigg was in despair because he knew that was only the beginning. Accordingly, in 1938, he decided to hold a plebiscite, to let his people say whether or not they wanted to join with Germany. Hitler claimed that they did, and was determined that he should not be proved wrong, so he ordered his army to invade. There was no resistance and, indeed, Hitler had a hero's welcome in Vienna. Unlike 1934, Mussolini did nothing. It was all Hitler wanted of him, and he could hardly find words to show his gratitude. He said, 'I will never forget, whatever may happen. If he should ever need help or be in any danger, he can be convinced that I shall stick to him whatever may happen, even if the whole world were against him.'

Later in 1938, Hitler paid a return visit to Italy. The Duce's navy impressed him, but little else did. He particularly disliked staying with the

German troops enter Austria 1938

Hitler and Mussolini

king, for he despised monarchs, and Victor Emmanuel certainly despised him. None the less, the visit did cement his friendship with Mussolini. However, after the fall of Austria, Mussolini was a worried man, watching Hitler's progress with dismay, wondering, with good reason, where it all might end.

215

Czechoslovakia

In 1938, Hitler turned on Czechoslovakia. As success in Austria had depended on friendship with Italy, so success here depended on friendship with Poland. For one thing, Russia had a pact with Czechoslovakia, but her armies could not reach her unless the Poles let them through. The Poles had every reason to be nervous of the Germans, but Hitler had soothed their fears by signing a non-aggression treaty with them in 1934. Also, the Poles disliked the Czechs and, what is more, they hoped to gain the town of Teschen for themselves. For these reasons, then, the Poles were willing to see Germany destroy Czechoslovakia.

First of all, Hitler instructed the Sudeten Germans to make trouble. The Czech government restored order, whereupon Hitler spread stories of Czech atrocities and threatened to take revenge. The British Prime Minister, Neville Chamberlain, was desperately anxious to prevent war and believed he could do so by a policy of appeasement, which meant letting Hitler have his own way. He flew three times to Germany for talks with Hitler. He made no progress, so he asked Mussolini to arrange a conference, and Mussolini readily agreed. Hitler, Mussolini, Chamberlain and Daladier, the French Prime Minister, met at Munich, but the Czechs were not even asked to send a delegate. The result of the conference was that Britain and France agreed to tell Czechoslovakia she must give the Sudetenland to Germany. That meant she not only sacrificed territory, but also had to abandon her mountain frontier and the splendid defences she had built along it. She was now completely at Germany's mercy. At the same time, Poland took Teschen, while Hungary, determined to have her share, took Bratislava, and much of southern Slovakia.

On returning from Munich, Chamberlain stepped from his aircraft and greeted cheering crowds by waving a piece of paper. It was an agreement Hitler had signed promising 'Peace in our time'. He also said of the Sudetenland, 'this is my last territorial demand in Europe'. Chamberlain was well pleased with his policy of appeasement, but only for a short time. In fact, Hitler was angry that the Munich Conference had not given him the whole of Czechoslovakia. In March 1939, on the flimsiest of pretexts, he occupied the rest of Bohemia and Moravia, and made Slovakia a puppet State under his control. Meanwhile, Hungary took Ruthenia.

Occupation of Czechoslovakia

The destruction of Czechoslovakia 1938–9

When he occupied Czechoslovakia, Hitler did not even tell Mussolini of his plans, and all Mussolini could do was to grab Albania, as some sort of compensation. 'Why pick up four rocks?', grumbled King Victor Emmanuel. Despite these differences, though, in 1939, Italy and Germany made what Mussolini called the 'Pact of Steel'. This was a full alliance, each country promising to help the other, if she should go to war.

Poland

Poland was the next country on Hitler's list, and this time he depended on Russia. Of all the countries in Europe, Russia was the least likely to make friends with Germany. At home, Hitler persecuted Communists as vigorously as he did Jews: abroad, he had made the Anti-Comintern Pact with Japan and Italy: all the time his propaganda had been screaming abuse at Russia. As for Stalin, he knew that Nazi Germany was Russia's chief enemy. He knew as well that war must come some day, and he was busy preparing for it. None the less, in August 1939 Germany and Russia made a non-aggression pact. It is easy to understand Hitler's motive — he wanted Russia to stay neutral while he overran Poland. Stalin, too, had his reasons for avoiding war. In the first place, he was not yet ready to fight: secondly, Britain and France were suspicious of him, so they refused to make a firm alliance with Russia: thirdly, as the price of his neutrality, Hitler promised him eastern Poland.

Hitler now played the same game with Poland as he had done with Czechoslovakia. He urged the German minorities to make trouble and then complained of atrocities. He also demanded Danzig and enough land to build an autobahn through the Polish Corridor, to join Germany and East Prussia. At the same time he hoped that Britain and France would put pressure on the Poles to submit, just as they had done to the Czechs. The leaders of the two countries were quite prepared to do this, but the people of Britain particularly would not allow it. Instead, Britain and France promised Poland they would declare war if Germany attacked her.

Hitler had another disappointment also. He told Mussolini he was going to invade Poland, and because of the Pact of Steel, he fully expected him to send help. However, Mussolini knew that Italy was in no condition to fight. She was exhausted by the war in Spain and her army was poorly equipped. Mussolini had spoken of his 'forest of eight million bayonets' and he said, 'I will darken the sky with my aircraft'. He knew, though, that these were empty boasts, but how could he wriggle out of his promise to Hitler? What he did was to say he was not ready for war, and to demand impossible quantities of weapons and supplies.

Hitler realized Germany would have to fight alone, but was quite happy that she should do so. After all, he had the non-aggression treaty with Russia, and Russian neutrality was much more valuable than Italian help. He ordered the invasion of Poland on 1 September 1939. Britain and France told Hitler he must halt his armies, but he, of course, ignored them. They declared war on 3 September.

217

Chapter Thirty-one

The Far East 1894–1941

IN THE Far East, it was Japan who dominated international affairs. From 1894 until she joined the Second World War in 1941 she was trying to increase her power by conquering an empire for herself in China and the Pacific. There were a number of reasons for this.

In the first place, Japan was an industrial country, so she needed raw materials and markets where she could sell her finished goods. Secondly, Japan's population was growing, and she felt her country would become overcrowded unless many of her people emigrated. They would have been happy to go to Australia or the United States, but these countries would only admit a few at a time. If Japan had an empire of her own, then as many people as wished could go and live in it. Thirdly, many Japanese were nationalists. They believed it was Japan's mission to rule the world, and they also knew that a successful war would unite their people behind their Emperor.

Between 1894 and 1941, Japan fought five wars and then started the sixth, and largest, by attacking America.

The Sino-Japanese War 1894–5

This war was fought over Korea. China claimed Korea as a vassal State of her own, but Japan was anxious to control it. This was partly for trade, but also it was because Korea is the nearest part of the mainland to Japan, and Russia was advancing in that direction. It was important for Japan to take Korea before Russia did, so in 1894, she attacked China.

Most people expected China to win, because of her size. However, Japan's navy won the Battle of the Yellow Sea, and her armies overran Korea, invaded Manchuria and threatened Peking. China quickly asked for peace and in 1895 agreed to the humiliating terms of the Treaty of Shimoneseki. She recognized that Korea was independent which meant, in fact, leaving her at Japan's mercy. She also gave Japan the island of Formosa and, on the mainland, Port Arthur and the Liaotung Peninsula.

However, Japan was to be robbed of some of her gains. Russia, Germany and France, who also had designs on China 'advised' Japan to return Port Arthur and Liaotung. Japan had to agree, but she was bitterly angry. Worse was to follow, because in 1898, China promised to let the

218

Russians build the Trans-Siberian Railway through northern Manchuria to Vladivostock and even to make a branch line through Liaotung to Port Arthur.

The Anglo-Japanese Alliance 1902

As Britain had not objected to the Treaty of Shimoneski, Japan felt warmly towards her. At that time, Britain for her part, was impressed by the 'gallant little Jap'. Moreover, both countries were worried about Russian expansion in the Far East. Then came the Boer War, which frightened Britain out of 'splendid isolation', so in 1902 she was more than willing to make an alliance with Japan. By this treaty, each country promised to help the other if she went to war with more than one power in the Far East. Japan badly wanted revenge on Russia, but France was Russia's ally and even Germany looked dangerous, for the Kaiser was spreading alarm about the 'Yellow Peril'. Now, if either country tried to help Russia, they would have to reckon with Britain.

The Russo–Japanese War 1904–05

The quarrel between Russia and Japan was over Korea and Manchuria, both wanting these places for themselves. By 1904, Japan decided it was time to strike. She had her alliance with Britain which would keep Russia isolated: since 1896 she had doubled the number of her front-line troops, and had added 43 warships to her navy: the Trans-Siberian railway was still unfinished, so Russian reinforcements would take a long time to arrive. As it was, there were only 100 000 Russian troops in the Far East, while the Japanese army was 330 000 strong.

SWORN FRIENDS.

Russia (aside). "H'M—I DON'T LIKE THESE CONFIDENCES."

The Anglo-Japanese Alliance

"CATCH AS CATCH CAN."

Russian Bear. "HERE! I SAY, AVAST HEAVING! I WASN'T READY!"

Start of the Russo-Japanese War

On the night of 8 February 1904, without any declaration of war, Admiral Togo made a torpedo attack on the Russian Pacific Fleet as it lay in Port Arthur. The two best Russian battleships were crippled, so the Japanese had command of the sea. They poured troops on to the mainland and, in May 1904, laid siege to Port Arthur. Stossel, the Russian commander was incompetent and, on 1 January 1905, surrendered the town while he still had ample supplies and ammunition. The troops in Liaotung now joined with others that had overrun Korea, and together they advanced on Mukden. By now, there was revolution in Russia itself so the Tsar kept his best soldiers at home, and only sent second-rate troops to fight the Japanese. Also Kuropatkin, the Russian commander, was another incompetent general and he made serious mistakes. By March, the Japanese had won the battle of Mukden.

The Russians were just as unfortunate at sea. Their Pacific Fleet tried to escape from Port Arthur, but was driven back, to be destroyed by the Japanese army, when it took the town. In desperation, the Tsar's government ordered the Baltic Fleet to sail right round the world. On its way, it sank some British fishing trawlers in the North Sea, mistaking them for Japanese torpedo boats. The Russians had to make an abject apology to Britain, and pay compensation. When in May 1905, the Baltic Fleet finally arrived, Admiral Togo sank nearly all its ships in the Tsushima Straits.

By the summer of 1905, both sides wanted to end the war, Russia because she had been defeated, and Japan because she was exhausted. America offered to mediate, and the peace treaty was signed at Portsmouth, New Hampshire. Russia recognized that Korea was in Japan's 'sphere of influence' and in fact, she annexed her in 1910. Russia also handed over Port Arthur, the Liaotung Peninisula with its railway, and the southern half of the island of Sakhalin.

The Japanese people were disappointed by the Treaty of Portsmouth, but in the ten years since the war with China, their country had won the beginnings of an empire as well as equality with the Western Powers in the eyes of the world.

The First World War

Though her alliance with Britain did not require it, Japan declared war on Germany in August 1914. She was interested in Germany's possessions in the Far East. By November she had captured Kiaochow in Shantung Province and all of Germany's Pacific islands. She then did no more for her allies than help them at sea, firmly declining to send troops to fight in Europe. Instead, she took advantage of the war to press her 'Twenty-one Demands' on China. China refused the worst of them, but had to accept the remainder. She agreed that Japan should take over Germany's rights in Shantung, she gave Japan extra mining and railway rights in Manchuria, and she promised not to lease any more of her coastal territory to any power other than Japan.

In spite of Chinese protests, the Treaty of Versailles confirmed Japan's rights in Shantung, and mandated to her Germany's Pacific Islands.

When the Russian Revolution broke out, Japan sent troops into Siberia, with the excuse of helping the Czech Legion. In fact, she took advantage of her old enemy's weakness to occupy Siberia as far west as Lake Baikal, and did not withdraw until 1922.

Foreign Policy in the 1920s

During the 1920s Japan had Minseito and Seiyukai governments who were willing to settle their differences with foreign powers without fighting.

The Twenty-one Demands annoyed the Americans, who were afraid the Japanese might interfere with their trade with China. Britain was alarmed that the quarrel might lead to war and that she might be drawn into it as an ally of Japan. She had no wish at all to fight the United States. To settle the problems in the Pacific there was a conference at Washington in 1921 between the United States, Japan, Britain and France and a rather vague agreement was made to respect each other's interests. On the strength of that the British allowed their alliance with Japan to lapse in 1923.

The Washington Conference also produced a naval agreement. This fixed the proportions of battleships in the Pacific at U.S.A. (5), Britain (5) and Japan (3). In 1930, the Japanese signed the Treaty of London, accepting the same proportions for all large warships.

The Washington Conference and the Treaty of London helped good feeling between the Great Powers in the Pacific, but unfortunately, they annoyed many Japanese and were one of the reasons for the growing power of the nationalists. Japan's foreign policy changed, and she once more became aggressive.

The 'Manchurian Incident' and the 'China Incident'

In the early 1930s, Japan had serious political and economic problems. Also, Chiang Kai-shek was becoming more and more powerful in China, so there was a danger that he might invade Manchuria, which, at that time, was independent in all but name. Japan's generals felt they should forestall Chiang. The occupation of Manchuria would solve Japan's political problems by uniting the people behind the army, and it would help solve her economic problems by adding valuable territory to her empire.

Shidehara, the foreign minister of the Minseito government, was friendly towards China, so the generals decided to act alone. In September 1931 there was the 'Mukden incident', when someone blew up a short section of the South Manchurian Railway near the town. The Kwantung army used this as an excuse to attack, in defiance of orders from Tokyo, and by November had occupied the whole of Manchuria.

The next move came after the Tosei faction seized power. Its ambition was to conquer China, and after an incident on the Marco Polo Bridge near Peking in July 1937, it launched an invasion. By the end of 1938 the Japanese had occupied all the wealthier parts of China, including most of her coastline. However, the Chinese went on fighting, especially the Communists, who were particularly successful with guerrilla tactics. The

Japanese troops enter Manchuria

Japanese realized the war would not end quickly, and it was becoming a serious drain on their resources (see also page 269).

The Alliance with Germany

In the meantime Japan had other problems. When she invaded Manchuria, China complained to the League of Nations. The League condemned Japan and, in 1933, she left it. That meant an end to the uneasy friendship with America, Britain and France, so Japan was isolated. Moreover, she was frightened of Russia. Accordingly, in 1936, she made the Anti-Comintern Pact with Russia's main enemy in Europe, Germany. Both powers agreed to work together to stop the spread of Communism in the world, and there were also secret clauses whereby each promised to help the other if Russia attacked her.

In 1940, Germany, Italy and Japan signed the Tripartite Pact. This recognized Japan's right to the 'establishment of a new order in East Asia', in other words, the right to seize as much territory as she could for herself. Also, the three powers promised they would all declare war on any new power that entered the war. The country they had in mind was, of course, the United States.

Japan's conquest of Manchuria and her invasion of China had placed her firmly on the side of Italy and Germany. The Rome–Berlin Axis had become the Rome–Berlin–Tokyo triangle.

The Outbreak of War

Japan's failure to defeat China by fighting her led her to look for other means. In Europe, France had been beaten and Britain was fighting alone against Germany. Japan took advantage of this. In 1940, she made the Vichy French government give her Indo-China, and compelled the British

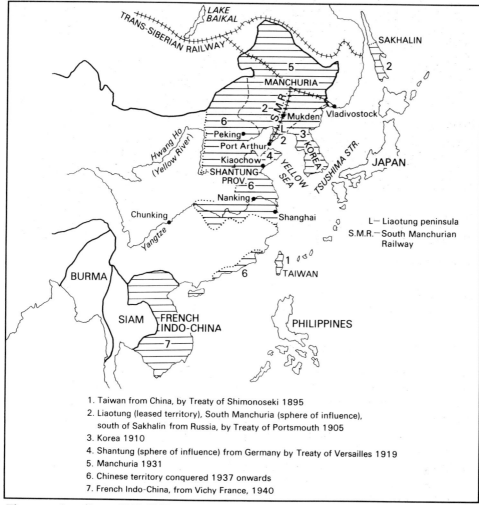

1. Taiwan from China, by Treaty of Shimonoseki 1895
2. Liaotung (leased territory), South Manchuria (sphere of influence),
   south of Sakhalin from Russia, by Treaty of Portsmouth 1905
3. Korea 1910
4. Shantung (sphere of influence) from Germany by Treaty of Versailles 1919
5. Manchuria 1931
6. Chinese territory conquered 1937 onwards
7. French Indo-China, from Vichy France, 1940

The expansion of Japan 1895–1940

to close the Burma Road, along which supplies had gone to Chiang Kai-shek. China was now cut off from the rest of the world.

However, there was one power Japan could not bully, and that was the United States. The two countries moved rapidly towards war.

The first thing that happened was that America protested at the occupation of Indo-China and ended all her trade with Japan, including a ban on oil. She persuaded Britain and Holland to do the same. Japan was now desperate, for without oil she could not continue the war in China. Next, General Tojo became Prime Minister of Japan. His nickname was 'the razor', because he believed in finding short, sharp solutions to problems. He was most unlikely to give way to the United States. Then, in November 1941 came the 'Hull Note'. This was a letter from the American Secretary of State, Cordell Hull, demanding that the Japanese should withdraw from Indo-China and China. Japan's answer came on 7 December. It was her attack on Pearl Harbor.

223

Chapter Thirty-two

The League of Nations

Origins

THE LEAGUE OF NATIONS was created at the peace settlement after the First World War. The plan was that the countries of the world should work together to prevent war. This idea was not new. For example there had been the disarmament conferences at the Hague in 1899 and 1907. Further, when the war came, it was so terrible that many people agreed that something must be done to make sure that nothing like it ever happened again. There were associations that talked about the problem in many countries, especially in America, and the idea of the League of Nations was born. Two men who were specially interested were General Smuts of South Africa, and Woodrow Wilson, the President of the United States.

During the Peace Conference there was a committee under President Wilson which drew up a document called the Covenant of the League. This contained the constitution of the League, that is the way it was to be run. Wilson insisted it should be part of all the peace treaties, so every country that signed them also agreed to the Covenant. Indeed, the word 'covenant' means 'promise'.

Organization

Broadly speaking, the League of Nations was similar to the government of a country. There was an Assembly to which all the member states sent representatives. It was like a parliament, and it held debates. Next, there was a Council which was made up of representatives of the Great Powers — Britain, France, Italy and Japan. The U.S.A. should have been there too, but for reasons we shall see later, she was not. As well as the Great Powers there were four other countries on the Council. They were elected by the Assembly and changed from time to time. The Council corresponded to the cabinet in an ordinary government. Thirdly, there was a Secretariat, or Civil Service. Its first head, or Secretary General, was an Englishman, Sir Eric Drummond. Finally, there was a Permanent Court of International Justice. The headquarters of the League was the Palace of the Nations, in Geneva, but the Court sat at the Hague.

The most important task the League had was to prevent war, by settling quarrels between countries. If two powers had a legal argument as, for example, over the meaning of a treaty, they went to the Court of International Justice. If they had any other kind of dispute, they took it to the Council and they were then bound to accept its decision. Any power that did not, and attacked its rival, was considered to be at war with all members of the League. The Council could call on them to impose sanctions on the offender, that is, to stop trading with her and, if that did not work, to send forces to fight her.

As well as keeping the peace, the League had a number of committees that tried to improve the lives of people all over the world. For example, they dealt with health, economics, drug-trafficking, slavery, and the rights of women and children. There was also the International Labour Organization (I.L.O.), which looked after workers. It drew up conventions that said what employers should do for their people, such as paying proper wages, and making their factories safe. Countries could adopt these standards if they wished, and a great many did so.

You will remember that by their peace treaties, the colonies of Germany and Turkey were mandated to countries on the winning side. The League made sure these mandated territories were properly governed.

Weaknesses

So far the League sounds impressive and so it was — on paper. However, it had a fatal weakness. It could only succeed if the Great Powers supported it, and some of them were not even members. Germany, the defeated enemy, was in disgrace and was not, at first, allowed to join. The U.S.S.R. was having a civil war, while her rulers were talking of world revolution, so there was no thought of inviting her to join. What was truly amazing though, was that the U.S.A. was not a member. During the war many Americans had been enthusiastic about the League, while President Wilson had done more than anyone to bring it into being. However, Wilson was a Democrat, and in 1918 the Republicans won control of Congress. According to the Constitution of the United States, the Upper House of Congress, the Senate, must ratify any treaty the President makes, and this it refused to do. As a result, the United States did not sign the Treaty of Versailles, and did not join the League of Nations.

Germany joined the League in 1926, but left when Hitler began rearmament in 1933. Japan also left in 1933, and Italy in 1935. The U.S.S.R. joined, at last, in 1934. However, the only Great Powers that were in the League from the beginning to the end were Britain and France. They had neither the strength nor the will to act as world policemen.

Successes and Failures

The League did have some success. The technical organizations did good work, the one on health, for example, helping to check typhus, cholera, plague and smallpox. Also, many States followed the suggestions of the

International Labour Organization. Japan was one of them, so her workers had reason to be grateful to the League.

The League also settled a number of disputes between countries. For example, when Sweden and Finland disagreed over the Aaland Islands, the League found a solution. In 1925 it probably prevented a war between Greece and Bulgaria, because there had actually been some shooting before the League stepped in.

However, Sweden, Finland, Greece and Bulgaria are only small countries. The real test would be when a Great Power decided to go against the League. This happened quite soon. In 1931 Japan invaded Manchuria, and the League appointed an International Commission under Lord Lytton to investigate. The Commission said that Japan was an aggressor, and that Manchuria should be an independent country under the protection of China. The Lytton Report was published in March 1933, but instead of leaving Manchuria, Japan left the League. In return, the League did nothing. It did not ask its members to impose sanctions on Japan, still less to fight her. After that it was clear that anyone could defy the League quite safely.

In 1935, Mussolini invaded Abyssinia, and this time the League did indeed impose sanctions, so there was an end to a certain amount of trade with Italy. However, the League was careful not to include in its sanctions an embargo on oil, which was the one thing which would have halted Mussolini's armies. Britain and France were anxious not to give Italy too much offence, because they hoped to have her support against Germany. All they did was to show once again that the League was powerless.

In 1936 Hitler sent troops into the Rhineland. This was against the Treaty of Versailles, which it was the League's duty to uphold. It did nothing. It also did nothing to stop Hitler taking Austria and Czechoslovakia. When, in 1939, he invaded Poland, the Second World War began, the League's failure was complete.

WORK SECTION — International Relations to 1939

Questions

1 When was the Abyssinian War?
2 Why was it fought?
3 What was the decisive battle?
4 How does the picture help explain the Italian victory?
5 Explain how the war affected the following:
   (a) The League of Nations.
   (b) Italy's relations with Britain and France.
   (c) Italy's relations with Germany.

Abyssinian troops

226

Italy and the Treaty of Versailles

Document One

From President Wilson's Fourteen Points:
Point Nine: A readjustment of the frontiers of Italy should be effected along clearly recognizable lines of nationality.

Document Two

The aspirations of Italy and the effort of the French and British governments to fulfil the promises they had made to get Italy's help in the war, brought about the hottest controversy of the conference. Here, President Wilson faced the acid test of his ideas on national integrity and self-determination.

Since Britain and France had made lavish promises of other people's territory to Italy, Italy expected the bargain to be kept. But the Americans considered the terms too costly. When the disagreement became acute, President Wilson appealed to the Italian people, over the heads of their representatives, to revise their extreme demands in the interest of friendly relations with their neighbours. It was a noble document, intended to reach not only the Italian public but the people of Britain and France, where the newspapers were accusing the President of unrealistic meddling.

The Morning Post *of London called his statement 'Wild West diplomacy' and the* Daily Express *spoke of it as the 'rabies of democracy'. Yet the President merely explained that the United States had not been a party of the Treaty of London; that it, too, had made sacrifices of blood and treasure for the good of all, to establish a just peace; that this peace was in jeopardy if national groups were not given the freedom to live.*

But the Italians would not scale down their demands, and Vittorio Orlando and the rest of the delegation left for Rome. At first they were given big ovations by large crowds, but in the next few weeks they were blamed for not forcing their views on the Big Four. The Cabinet of Orlando fell.

(The Forgotten Men of Versailles — Harry Hansen)

Questions

(See also the Italian Front, page 185, and the Rise of Fascism in Italy, Chapter 14).

Document One

1 What was President Wilson's aim in drawing up his Fourteen Points?

2 What were the four main ideas contained in them?

3 Which is illustrated by Point Nine?

4 What was Clemenceau's comment on the Fourteen Points?

5 Which foreign country had numbers of Italian subjects before the war? In which provinces did they live?

Document Two

6 What promises had Britain and France made to Italy? Why had they made them? In which treaty had the promises been made?

7 Why did President Wilson appeal to the Italian people directly? To which other people did he appeal? Why did he say the Italians should revise their demands?

8 How did the British press describe President Wilson's action? Do you think they were right to be critical?

9 What explanation did President Wilson give?

10 How did the Italian delegation at Versailles react?

11 What did the Italian people think of their delegation at first? Why did they change their minds?

12 What did Italy gain from the peace treaty?

13 What happened in 1919 as a result of Italian disappointment at the treaty?

14 Which political movement in Italy gained strength partly as a result of this same disappointment?

15 In Italy Wilson's principles caused trouble. In other parts of Europe there was trouble because they were ignored that is, where frontiers were *not* 'effected along clearly recognizable lines of nationality'. Where was this?

16 Do you think Wilson's principles were right?

Debate in the House of Commons on the Munich agreement — October 1938

Document One

Extracts from a speech by the Prime Minister, Mr Neville Chamberlain:
When the House met last Wednesday we were all under the shadow of a great and imminent menace. War, in a form more stark and terrible

than ever before, seemed to be staring us in the face. Before I sat down, a message had come which gave us new hope that peace might yet be saved, and today, only a few days after, we all meet in joy and thankfulness that the prayers of millions have been answered, and a cloud of anxiety has been lifted from our hearts.

After everything that has been said about the German Chancellor today and in the past, I do feel that the House ought to recognize the difficulty for a man in that position to take back such emphatic declarations as he had already made amidst the enthusiastic cheers of his supporters and to recognize that in consenting to discuss with the representatives of other Powers those things which he had declared he had already decided once for all, was a real and a substantial contribution on his part. With regard to Signor Mussolini, his contribution was notable and perhaps decisive. I think that Europe and the world have reason to be grateful to the head of the Italian Government for his work in contributing to a peaceful solution.

M. Daladier had in some respects the most difficult task of all four of us, because of the special relations uniting his country and Czechoslovakia, and I should like to say that his courage, his readiness to take responsibility, his pertinacity and his unfailing good humour were invaluable throughout the whole of our discussions.

Ever since I assumed my present office my main purpose has been to work for the pacification of Europe, for the removal of those suspicions and those animosities which have so long poisoned the air. The path which leads to appeasement is long and bristles with obstacles. The question of Czechoslovakia is the latest and perhaps the most dangerous. Now that we have got past it, I feel that it may be possible to make further progress along the road to sanity.

Document Two

Extracts from a speech by Winston Churchill:

I venture to think that in future the Czechoslovak State cannot be maintained as an independent entity. You will find that in a period of time which may be measured by years, but may be measured only by months, Czechoslovakia will be engulfed in the Nazi regime.

I do not grudge our loyal brave people the natural, spontaneous outburst of joy and relief when they learned that the hard ordeal would no longer be required of them at the moment;

but they should know the truth. They should know that there has been gross neglect and deficiency in our defences: they should know that we have sustained a defeat without a war, the consequences of which will travel far with us along our road; they should know that we have passed an awful milestone in our history, when the whole equilibrium of Europe has been deranged, and that the terrible words have, for the time being, been pronounced against the Western democracies: 'Thou art weighed in the balance and found wanting'. And do not suppose that this is the end. This is only the beginning of the reckoning. This is only the first sip, the first foretaste of a bitter cup which will be proferred to us year by year unless by a supreme recovery of moral health and martial vigour, we arise again and take our stand for freedom as in olden time.

Questions

1 How had the crisis over Czechoslovakia begun?
2 Who arranged the Munich conference?
3 Which politicians met at Munich? Which country was not invited to send a representative, even though she was deeply involved?
4 What was decided at Munich? Why was this a terrible blow to Czechoslovakia?
5 What agreement did Chamberlain bring back from Munich?
6 Why was Hitler displeased with the Munich agreement?
8 What countries, apart from Germany, took territory from Czechoslovakia in 1938?

Document One

9 Why does Chamberlain say Parliament is meeting in 'joy and thankfulness'?
10 What 'real and substantial' contribution does Chamberlain say Hitler made?
11 What is Chamberlain's opinion of Mussolini? Do you think Mussolini genuinely wanted peace?
12 Why was Daladier in an especially difficult position? What does Chamberlain say about him?
13 Do you agree with Chamberlain's opinions of Hitler, Mussolini and Daladier?
14 What does Chamberlain say has been his main aim? Which word in the last paragraph sums up his policy best?

15 What does he say will be the result of solving the Czechoslovakian crisis?

Document Two

16 What does Churchill say will happen to Czechoslovakia? How long does he think it will be?

17 What does he say about the 'joy and relief' of the British people?

18 What does he say has happened to Britain's defences?

19 How does he think the Western democracies have behaved over Czechoslovakia?

20 What does he think will be the result of the Munich agreement?

21 What does Churchill believe will be the only way for Britain to solve the problems of the future?

22 How far do you think Churchill's judgement on the Munich agreement was correct?

Japan and Liao-tung

Document One

Extract from the Treaty of Shimonoseki 1895:

China cedes to Japan to perpetuity and full sovereignty the following territories, together with all fortifications, arsenals and public property thereon:

(a) The southern portion of the province of Fengtien (The Liao-tung Peninsula)

(b) The island of Formosa, together with all islands appertaining or belonging to the said island of Formosa.

(c) The Pescadores Group of islands.

Done at Shimonoseki this 17th day of the 4th month of the 28th year of Meiji.

Document Two

Russian Note to the Japanese Government, 1895:

The Government of His Majesty, the Emperor, in examining the conditions of peace which Japan has imposed on China finds that the possession of the peninsula of Liao-tung claimed by Japan, would be a constant menace to the capital of China and at the same time it will render illusory the independence of Korea, that henceforth it would be a perpetual obstacle to the permanent peace of the Far East. Consequently, the Government of His Majesty, the Emperor, would give a new proof of his sincere

friendship for the Government of His Majesty, the Emperor of Japan, by advising it to renounce the definitive Possession of the peninsula of Liao-tung.

Document Three

Extracts from the Treaty of Portsmouth, 1905:

Article 2. The Imperial Russian Government, acknowledging that Japan possesses in Korea paramount political, military and economical interests, engages neither to obstruct nor interfere with the measures of guidance, protection and control which the Imperial Government of Japan may find it necessary to take in Korea.

Article 5. The Imperial Russian Government transfers and assigns to the Imperial Government of Japan, the lease of Port Arthur and adjacent territory and territorial waters, and all rights, privileges and concessions connected with or forming part of such lease and they also assign to the Imperial Government of Japan all public works and properties in the territory affected by the above-mentioned lease.

Questions

Document One

1 What war led to the Treaty of Shimonoseki? When was it fought?

2 Find on a map the territories which China gave to Japan.

3 How is the treaty dated? Why do you suppose the Japanese counted their years in this way?

4 What connection is there between Meiji and Japan's ability to defeat China? (See Chapter 16.)

Document Two

5 Why does the Russian government say it is concerned about Japan's occupation of Liao-tung?

6 What, in fact, were Russia's real motives?

7 How do the Russians disguise their demand?

8 Which other European countries sent similar Notes to Japan?

9 What might have happened if Japan had not complied with the Notes?

10 How did this Note encourage Japan to make an alliance with Britain? When was this alliance made?

229

Document Three

11 What war led to the Treaty of Portsmouth? How did Japan's alliance with Britain encourage her to fight this war?

12 Why was the treaty signed in the United States?

13 What does the Russian government say about Korea? What does it promise not to do there?

14 What happened to Korea in 1910?

15 Where is Port Arthur?

16 Which would have been the most important of the public works that the treaty mentions?

The League of Nations

Document One

The Covenant of the League of Nations:

Article 16: Should any member of the League resort to war in disregard of its covenants it shall ipso facto *be deemed to have committed an act of war against all other Members of the League, which hereby undertake immediately to subject it to the severance of all trade or financial relations, the prohibition of all inter-course between their nationals and the nationals of the covenant-breaking State and the prevention of all financial, commercial or personal intercourse between the nationals of the covenant-breaking State and the nationals of any other State, whether a member of the League or not.*

It shall be the duty of the Council in such case to recommend to the several Governments concerned what effective military, naval or air force the Members of the League shall severally contribute to the armed forces to be used to protect the covenants of the League.

Document Two

America and the League:

The great achievement of the Peace Conference was the League of Nations. Even though the American Congress rejected this work of an American President, it is a milestone in the history of man's slow progress towards the control and outlawry of war. For twenty years afterwards the American people deluded themselves that, because the League sat in far-off Geneva and we had no official association with it, it did not concern us. Without our political support, the League was preponderately a British bulwark, and it could not make its sanctions against Italy effective in the

Ethiopian crisis. It took a second World War, with its terrible cost, to bring the United States into the United Nations. If a nation can sit in sackcloth and ashes, the United States should do so for its selfish rejection of the League.

(*The Forgotten Men of Versailles*
— Harry Hansen)

Questions

Document One

1 What was the Covenant of the League of Nations? When was it drawn up? Of what other documents did it form a part?

2 What was the main duty of the League? How did it hope to carry out this duty, normally?

3 How did the League view a power that attacked any of its members?

4 What action were members of the League supposed to take against aggressors? (Use your own words.) What action did they take, in fact, against Japan, Italy and Germany?

Document Two

5 Who is the 'American President' the author mentions? Is it fair to say the League was his work?

6 Why did Congress reject the League?

7 Why does the author think the League was important?

8 How did the American people view the League?

9 Who, according to this author, had most influence in the League?

10 Which of the League's failures does he mention? Why were the sanctions ineffective?

11 What compelled the United States to join the United Nations?

12 What does the author think about America's rejection of the League? Why do you suppose he feels this way?

Questions

1 What policy did the U.S.A. wish European powers to adopt with regard to trade with China? (See page 135.)

2 What policy did they, in fact, follow?

3 When did Russia win concessions in Manchuria? What were they?

4 When and why did she leave Manchuria?

NOT TO BE DRAWN.

RUSSIAN OCCUPIER (*on sufferance*). "HI! YOU THERE! WE WANT THIS DRAWBRIDGE UP!"
UNCLE SAM. "SORRY, BUT I'VE JUST GOTTEN THE PROPRIETOR'S PERMISSION TO SIT ON IT."

[In face of strong opposition from Russia, the Emperor of CHINA has ratified a commercial treaty with the United States, by which certain Manchurian towns are opened to American trade.]

American trade with Manchuria, from Punch

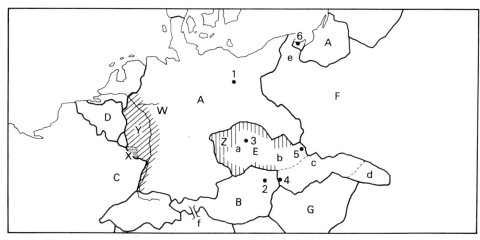

Hitler's foreign policy

Hitler's Foreign Policy

Name the following:
1 Countries A–G
   Towns 1–6
   Industrial Region W
   Regions X, Y, Z.
   Provinces a–d
   Area e
   Pass f
   Which countries occupied area W?
   When ? Why?
   With what result, in Germany?
2 What had the Treaty of Versailles for-
   bidden Germany and country B to do?
3 What happened in country B in 1934?
   What action did Mussolini take?
4 What had the Treaty of Versailles said
   about region X?
   What did the people here decide in
   1935?
5 What action did Hitler take over region
   Y in 1936?
6 Who was the Chancellor of country B
   from 1934 to 1938?
   How did he provoke Hitler in 1938?
   What did Hitler do? What action did
   Mussolini take?
7 What nationality were the people of
   region Z?
8 How did Hitler gain control of region Z
   in 1938?
9 What happened to towns 4 and 5 in
   1938?
10 What happened to provinces a, b, c
   and d in 1939?
11 What demands did Hitler make concerning town 6 and area e in 1939?
12 When did Hitler invade country F?

The Italian Empire

(See also Chapter 14 — The Rise of Fascism
in Italy).

1 Name the following:
   State 1
   Island 2
   Islands 3
   Colonies 4, 5, 6
   State 7
   Town 8
2 When did Italy acquire colonies 5 and
   6?
3 What defeat did the Italians suffer in
   State 7 in 1896?
4 What possessions did Italy acquire in
   1911? From whom did she take them?

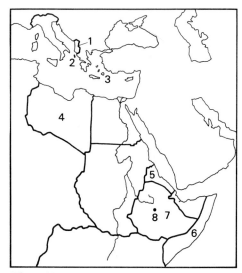

The Italian Empire

5 What happened in State 1 in 1923? What happened to island 2 as a result. How was the quarrel resolved?

6 When did Italy invade State 7? Who was its ruler? At what battle was his army defeated? When did town 8 fall?

7 How did the invasion of State 7 affect Italy's relations with Britain, France and Germany?

8 When did Italy take State 1? Why? What was Victor Emmanuel's comment?

The Peace Treaties

Questions

1 Who were the 'Big Five' and the 'Big Four'? Who, in effect, made the peace treaties?

2 What problems did they face? How did they make them worse?

3 What were the four main ideas which lay behind President Wilson's 'Fourteen Points'?

4 What did Clemenceau want from the peace treaties?

5 What did Lloyd George promise the British public? Why did he not wish to be too severe with Germany?

6 What came first in each of the peace treaties? Why did Wilson insist on this?

7 What happened to Germany's colonies?

8 List the territories which Germany lost in Europe. Say which countries took them. Be sure you can identify them on a map.

9 How many inhabitants and what mineral wealth did Germany lose?

10 What happened about Germany's armed forces?

11 What happened to the Rhineland?

12 What happened to the Saarland?

13 What were Austria and Germany forbidden to do?

14 What problem was there over reparations? How was it settled? Why was there a 'war guilt' clause in the treaty?

15 What territorial changes were there in S.E. Europe? Make sure you can identify the places on a map. Why was the Sudetenland a problem?

16 What did Poland, Italy and Romania gain?

17 What did Bulgaria lose?

18 Name Russia's Baltic provinces. What became of them?

19 What was suggested as Poland's eastern frontier? From whom did Poland win more territory?

20 What happened to the provinces of the Turkish Empire? Which Turkish provinces was Greece given? Explain how she lost them. What treaty confirmed their loss?

21 Give three reasons why Germany resented the peace treaties.

22 Why would Germany be in a strong position if she was allowed to rearm? What would have been the only way to hold her in check? What did America fail to do after the war?

Give an account of the peace treaties under the headings: The Peace Makers/ The League of Nations/Germany/Southeast Europe/Russia's Baltic Provinces/ Poland/Turkey/Problems Left by the Peace Treaties

Europe 1920–1939

Questions

1 What was Mussolini's aim?

2 How did the Corfu incident come about? How was it solved? What did Mussolini think it proved?

3 Name three things which Mussolini did to check Germany.

4 Why did Mussolini wish to conquer Abyssinia? When did the Italians invade? What were the main events of the war?

5 What action did the League of Nations take against Italy? Why was it ineffective? How did the Abyssinian war affect Italy's relations with Britain, France and Germany?

6 What was Stresemann's policy? What was agreed by the Locarno Treaties? What did Germany do in 1926?

7 What was the aim of Hitler's foreign policy? What three stages did he plan?

8 What excuse did Hitler have for rearming? When did he begin?

9 What set-back did Hitler have in 1934?

10 What happened in the Saarland in 1935?

11 Why did Britain, France and Italy form the Stresa Front? How did Hitler weaken it?

12 What actions did Hitler take in 1936? What treaties did he break? Why did the gamble succeed?

13 What agreement did Italy and Germany make in 1936?

14 How did the Spanish Civil War affect relations between Britain, France and Italy? Why did Hitler send arms to Franco?

15 What pact did Italy join in 1937? What else did she do in that year?

16 What action did Hitler take against Schuschnigg? What provoked him to invade Austria? When? Why was Hitler grateful to Mussolini?

17 When did Hitler visit Italy? What was the result of the visit?

18 Why did Hitler make friends with Poland? Why was Poland willing to be friendly with Germany?

19 What use did Hitler make of the Sudeten Germans? Why was there a conference at Munich? Who attended it? What was the result?

20 Why was Chamberlain pleased with the Munich conference? Why was Hitler displeased? What action did he take as a result?

21 Why did Mussolini take Albania for Italy? What agreement did Italy and Germany make in 1939?

22 Why did Hitler wish to be friendly with Russia? Why was such a friendship unlikely? What agreement did Germany and Russia make in August 1939? Give three reasons why Stalin accepted it.

23 What demands did Hitler make on Poland? What did he hope Britain and France would do? What was their reaction?

24 Why did Mussolini refuse to declare war in 1939? How did he escape from his obligations?

25 Why was Hitler happy for Germany to fight alone? When did Germany invade Poland? When did Britain and France declare war?

Give an account of International Relations in Europe 1920–39 under the headings: Italy 1920–36/Germany 1920–36/The Rome–Berlin Axis/The Anschluss of Austria and Germany/Czechoslovakia/Poland

The Far East 1894–1941

Questions

1 Give three reasons why Japan wanted an empire.

2 Give two reasons why Japan wished to conquer Korea.

3 What victories did Japan win in her war with China? What treaty ended it? What were its terms?

4 What set–backs did Japan have immediately after the treaty was signed?

5 Why did Japan want an alliance with Britain? Why did Britain want one with Japan? When was the alliance made? What were its terms?

6 What were the causes of the quarrel between Japan and Russia? Why did Japan feel 1904 was a good time to attack?

7 How did Japan win command of the sea? What victories did her armies win? Why were they so successful?

8 Describe the war at sea.

9 Why did both sides wish to end the war in 1905? Which country offered to mediate? Where was the peace treaty signed? What were its terms?

10 Why did Japan declare war on Germany? What was her contribution to the war? How did she take advantage of it?

11 What did Japan gain from the Treaty of Versailles?

12 What action did Japan take during the Russian Revolution?

13 What was the policy of Japanese governments in the 1920s?

14 Why did Britain allow her alliance with Japan to lapse?

15 What was decided at the Washington Conference and what were the terms of the Treaty of London?

16 How did these agreements affect Japanese politics?

17 For what reasons did Japan decide to invade Manchuria?

18 What excuse did Japan find for the invasion? When did it take place?

19 Which faction in Japan wished to invade China? What excuse did it find? When was the invasion? How much of China did the Japanese occupy? Why did the war drag on?

20 When and why did Japan leave the League of Nations? What agreement did she make with Germany in 1936? What were its terms?

21 What agreement was made in 1940? What were its terms?

22 What was the result of Japan's invasion of Manchuria and China?

23 How did Japan take advantage of the problems of France and Britain?

24 What action did the United States take against Japan? What problem did this create for Japan? What did the 'Hull Note' demand? What was Japan's reply?

Give an account of International Affairs in the Far East under the headings: Japan's Need for an Empire/The Sino-Japanese War/The Anglo-Japanese Alliance/The Russo-Japanese War/The First World War/Foreign Policy in the 1920s/The 'Manchurian Incident' and the 'China Incident'/The Alliance with Germany/The Outbreak of War

The League of Nations

Questions

1 When was the League of Nations created? How had the idea of the League been born?

2 Name two statesmen who were especially interested.

3 Who drew up the Covenant of the League? What was the Covenant? what did President Wilson insist should happen with the Covenant?

4 Name the four main organizations which made up the League and describe each one.

5 How was the League supposed to settle disputes between countries?

6 What committees did the League have?

7 What responsibility did the League have for the former colonies of Germany and Turkey?

8 Why did America not join the League? Why was this surprising?

9 Say when Germany, Italy, Japan, and Russia joined or left the League.

10 What successes did the technical organizations of the League have?

11 What disputes did the League settle between countries?

12 How did the League deal with Japan's invasion of Manchuria? What did the League do when Japan left it? What did the League's failures prove?

13 What did the League do about the Italian invasion of Abyssinia? Why was it ineffective?

14 What did the League do to check Hitler?

Give an account of the League of Nations under the headings: Organization/ Origins/Weaknesses Successes and Failures

Problems

1 What problems faced the statesmen at the Peace Conference? How far were these problems solved?

2 By what means did President Wilson seek to prevent a second World War?

3 Contrast and explain the aims of Woodrow Wilson, Clemenceau and Lloyd George at the Peace Conference.

4 How far was the Treaty of Versailles unfair to Germany?

5 How far did the peace treaties follow Wilson's principle of national self-determination?

6 'The war to end wars has ended in the peace to end peace' — Kaiser William II. What features of the Versailles settlement justified that remark?

7 What were the aims of Mussolini's foreign policy? How far did he achieve them?

8 Why was Mussolini's foreign policy a disaster for Italy?

9 Trace the steps by which Italy, from being the ally of France and Britain, became the ally of Germany.

10 What were the aims of Hitler's foreign policy? How far did he achieve them down to August 1939?

11 Why was Hitler so successful in his foreign policy down to August 1939?

12 Why did Japan follow an aggressive foreign policy?

13 What were the aims of Japan's foreign policy? How far were they achieved down to December 1941?

14 What were the reasons for the Anglo-Japanese alliance? How did it prove of value to Japan? Why was it allowed to lapse?

15 Explain why Japan was able to defeat Russia in the war of 1904–1905.

16 What were the stages by which Japan tried to control China?

17 What were the stages by which Japan, from being an ally of Great Britain, became the ally of Germany?

18 Why did Japan attack the United States in December 1941?

19 What successes did the League of Nations have?

20 Why did the League of Nations fail in its main objective of keeping peace?

235

THE SECOND WORLD WAR

Introduction

The Blitzkrieg

THE BATTLES of the Second World War were dominated by two weapons, the tank and the aeroplane. Both had been in action in the First World War, the tank being especially important towards the end. One German general complained, 'It was not the genius of General Foch which defeated us, but General Tank.' That was, however, far from true, since the allied commanders saw their infantry as their most important arm, and their tanks only as supporting weapons.

Things might have been different if the war had gone on until 1919, as there were plans not only to employ tanks in great numbers but also to send them to break through the enemy's lines, and penetrate deep into the rear, disrupting communications and chains of command. The war ended, though, before these new tactics could be tried and during peacetime commanders forgot about them and trained their armies to fight in traditional ways.

A few enthusiasts in the British army, among them Basil Liddell Hart, organized an experimental armoured force which manœuvred on Salisbury Plain, but the High Command was not interested. In Germany, too, there were some enthusiastic junior officers, including a certain Heinz Guderian, and they, too, had difficulty in convincing their superiors. However, when Hitler came to power he saw Guderian's tanks and he was at once excited. 'That's what I need,' he said, 'that's what I want to have!' As a result, when war began, Germany had six armoured, or panzer divisions, which, though not very many, were enough to make all the difference.

It was not that the Germans had more or better tanks than their enemies. The French had just as many and their quality was as good. It was the French tactics which were wrong. Their Commander-in-Chief, General Gamelin, said, 'We need tanks, of course, but you cannot hope to achieve a real breakthrough with tanks.' The diagram on the following page shows how the French expected to use their tanks — simply to support their infantry, as in the First World War.

For their part, the Germans had developed the tactics which the allies had planned to use in 1919 and had, moreover, included aircraft. They called their attack a 'blitzkrieg', or 'lightning war'. First came medium bombers which flew over the enemy rear, attacking his communications

237

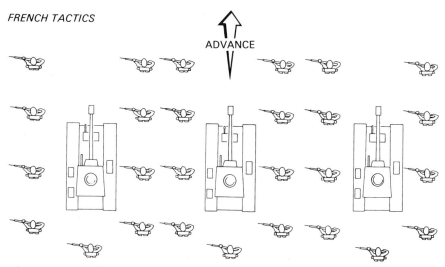

FRENCH TACTICS

ADVANCE

Infantry in open order.
Tanks dispersed among infantry to give support, e.g. destroy enemy machine-gun nests.

French tactics

and seeking out his headquarters. They did not expect to be lucky enough to kill his commanders, but, as they explained, if they scattered high explosives round them, they would hardly aid their concentration. Next came dive-bombers, which attacked the front-line troops. They might do little damage, but each was fitted with an air-operated siren. As the aircraft dived, the wind rushing through it made a hideous scream that would terrify all but the bravest men. On the ground the panzers thrust forward like spears. First there were scouting units, often motor cyclists and troops in armoured cars, who probed the enemy lines until they found a weak spot. Then came the tanks, which tore a gap in the enemy defences and pushed forward without stopping. Following them closely were motorized infantry, light artillery, anti-tank guns, and lorries bringing supplies. It will be seen that the panzer division was not just a collection of tanks, but was made up of all arms. Its general could, as a result, deal with any opposition he met. His tanks would destroy the enemy infantry, his anti-tank guns would destroy their tanks, his infantry or his artillery would destroy their anti-tank guns. Nothing was safe against his attack.

Usually the panzers would break through the enemy front at a number of points. They then closed behind it like pincer claws, cutting lines of communication. Enemy generals could not contact their troops in the field, so it was as if the nerves that run from the brain to the body had been severed. The isolated units threshed around like uncontrolled limbs, until the German infantry divisions overwhelmed them.

Such, then, was the blitzkrieg. There are several reasons why the Germans were so successful in the early years of the war, but the skill with which they used their tanks was probably the most important.

GERMAN TACTICS
(Blitzkrieg)

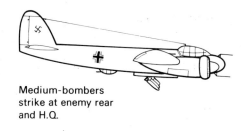

Medium-bombers
strike at enemy rear
and H.Q.

Dive-bombers strike
at enemy front line

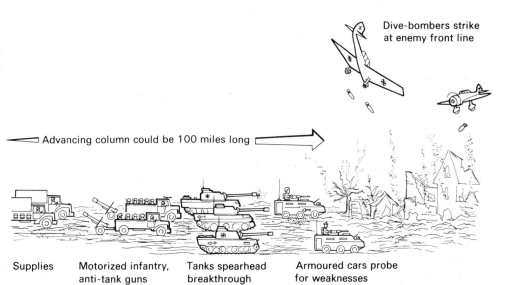

Advancing column could be 100 miles long

Supplies   Motorized infantry,   Tanks spearhead   Armoured cars probe
             anti-tank guns   breakthrough   for weaknesses

German tactics (Blitzkrieg)

Chapter Thirty-three

From the Invasion of Poland to the Battle of Britain

The Invasion of Poland

THE ATTACK on Poland began on 1 September 1939. German columns, headed by panzer divisions, broke through in the north and south, and drove eastwards. Soon, a pincer of two armies closed on Warsaw, while the remainder continued on their way. The fighting virtually ended when Warsaw surrendered on 27 September. It all happened so quickly that the Russians had to hurry in order to take the territory that Hitler had promised to leave them. Moreover, the Germans lost only 8000 dead.

The reasons for the German victory are easy to understand. The panzers did their work thoroughly, soon destroying the Polish lines of communication and their headquarters. With no one to direct it, the Polish army was completely disorganized. Also, the Poles were outnumbered. They had only 30 divisions which they spread thinly round their long frontier, while the Germans had 56 divisions which they concentrated at key points to enable them to break through. Nine of the German divisions were armoured, and all that the Poles had to fight them with was cavalry. The Germans had complete control of the air, for they destroyed most of the old-fashioned planes of the Polish air force, while they were still on the ground. Finally, the Poles had to fight alone. If the French had made a vigorous attack, they might have given them a chance, but they were scared to move. In any

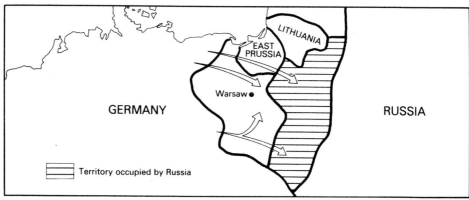

The invasion of Poland 1939

case, the Polish campaign was almost over by the time they had mobilized their army.

Hitler now offered to make peace with Britain and France, but this was only a gesture to the German people. In fact he was anxious for the war to continue, and was pleased when his offer was spurned. His main aim was still *lebensraum* in Russia, but that could wait for victory in the west.

The Invasion of Denmark and Norway, 1940

After the fall of Poland, the German generals were anxious to build up the strength of their armies before invading France. Hitler fumed and fretted, but agreed to wait. This was the time known as the 'phoney war', when nothing much happened. Britain and France began to think the Germans would not attack them and Chamberlain was foolish enough to say, 'Hitler has missed the bus'.

When in fact the next blow fell, it was not on France as Hitler had intended, but on Denmark and Norway. Germany had 80 per cent of her iron ore from Sweden, and could not fight the war without it. During winter, though, the Gulf of Bothnia freezes, so the ore had to be taken to the Norwegian port of Narvik. It went south in ships, which were safe from the Royal Navy only as long as Britain respected Norway's neutrality. Also, in 1939, Russia invaded Finland. Their attack was, at first, a miserable failure and the sight of gallant little Finland resisting mighty Russia warmed the hearts of the British and French. They resolved to send help. However, the only way they could go was through Norway and Sweden, a move that would certainly cut off Germany's iron ore.

Hitler decided he must act quickly and launched the invasion of Denmark and Norway on 9 April 1940. That same day, the Germans overran the whole of Denmark and captured every important town and airfield in Norway. The Danes did not resist, but the Norwegians recovered from the shock and began to fight. The British and French sent help and an allied force recaptured Narvik. By May, however, there was disaster in France, so the troops withdrew, leaving the Norwegians to their fate.

The only encouragement for the allies was that the Royal Navy inflicted heavy losses on the German fleet. It sank ten of Admiral Raeder's twenty destroyers, and three of his eight cruisers. Also, it badly damaged the battle-cruisers *Scharnhorst* and *Gneisenau*, and the pocket-battleship *Lutzow*. However, the Germans thought this was a small price to pay. They had saved their iron ore, and moreover, had won valuable naval bases in Norway.

Another result of the Norwegian campaign was that Chamberlain was driven from office and Churchill became Prime Minister.

The Invasion of Holland, Belgium and France, 1940

With the fighting in Norway almost finished, Hitler decided the time had come to defeat his enemies in the west. For this a comparatively junior general, von Manstein, had drawn up a daring plan, which Hitler eagerly adopted.

The attack began on 10 May 1940, when Germany invaded Holland, Belgium and Luxembourg without warning. The panzer divisions advanced swiftly, one of them commanded by a promising young general called Erwin Rommel. Holland was cut off but her armies resisted bravely until the Luftwaffe made a vicious attack on Rotterdam. The Dutch then surrendered. The French and British commanders were sure the Germans were following something like the Schlieffen Plan of the First World War, so the best divisions in the French army and the entire British Expeditionary Force raced into Belgium to meet the enemy head on.

This was just what Hitler wanted, for he had prepared a most unpleasant surprise. Further south is a region called the Ardennes. It is hilly, covered in woods and has narrow, winding roads, unsuitable for tanks and heavy vehicles. The French did not expect an attack from here and all they had opposite it was two of their poorest divisions. However, in the Ardennes there was waiting a triple line of armour and motorized infantry 160 km long. These troops were under the command of General von Runstedt, while the man who led the panzer divisions at the head of the column was General Heinz Guderian.

As soon as the French and British were well into Belgium, von Runstedt struck. This was on 14 May. The Germans crossed the Meuse and broke through the French lines at Sedan without difficulty. Guderian's panzers now raced towards the sea. Once they had left the Ardennes, they were in open, rolling country with good roads, and even plenty of garages where they could fill up with petrol. Churchill was appalled at what was happening and flew to Paris. 'Where is your strategic reserve?' he asked Gamelin, the French Supreme Commander. 'There isn't one,' said Gamelin. 'When will you counter-attack?' asked Churchill. All Gamelin could reply was 'Inferiority of numbers, inferiority of equipment, inferiority of method', and shrug his shoulders. The first of two of Gamelin's explanations were not true, but the third most certainly was.

On 20 May Guderian's men captured Amiens and Abbeville. They had reached the sea and had trapped one-third of the French army, the Belgian army, and the British Expeditionary Force. Guderian then swung north, tightening the noose. The allied troops tried to break out but failed, so it seemed they must all be captured. Then, for no apparent reason, Guderian's tanks halted for two days. It was just long enough for the British Admiralty to organize 'Operation Dynamo', the evacuation from Dunkirk. During nine days the Royal Navy and an armada of vessels of all kinds took away almost the entire B.E.F. of 200 000 men and 140 000 French troops. The Belgian army had already surrendered, while the remainder of the French army fought bitterly to cover the withdrawal. The British hailed Dunkirk as 'a miracle', though as Churchill remarked, 'Wars are not won by evacuations', and the French considered Dunkirk a betrayal.

Why, though, did the German panzers halt when they were so near complete victory? We shall never know the full reason, but it does seem

242

British soldiers under air attack on the debris-strewn beaches of Dunkirk

that Hitler and von Runstedt were afraid for their armour. They knew the countryside around Dunkirk was intersected with ditches and waterways, and they dared not allow their tanks to be bogged down in Flanders, especially as they expected heavy fighting in France.

When the Germans did turn south they met little resistance. They broke through some makeshift defences organized by General Weygand, and then took Paris without a fight. Marshall Pétain, the hero of Verdun in the First World War, now became head of the French government, and he asked for an armistice. It was signed on 21 June 1940. Hitler insisted that the ceremony should take place at the same spot, and in the same railway carriage as the armistice of 11 November 1918.

The terms of the armistice were not as harsh as they might have been. Hitler was afraid that the French colonies would go on fighting, and that the excellent French navy would join the British. He was content to occupy northern and western France while Marshall Pétain set up a government in Vichy and ruled the rest of the country. In return, the French were to remain neutral, and keep their fleet in Toulon harbour. Hitler's policy worked. Most French colonies remained loyal to Vichy and most of the French fleet stayed at Toulon. There were individuals who wanted to go on fighting and they formed the Free French Movement in Britain. However,

243

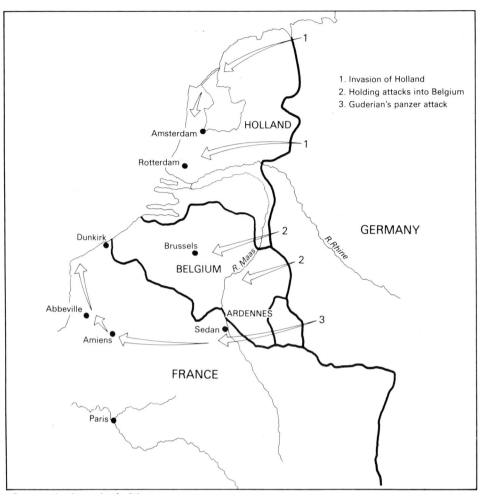

Germany's victory in the West

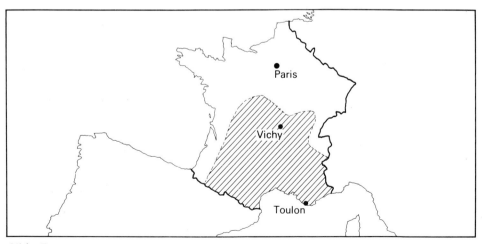

Vichy France

there was no one of any importance among them and as their leader they had a comparatively junior officer, Colonel Charles de Gaulle.

Italy Enters the War

As soon as he was sure the Germans were going to defeat the French, Mussolini decided to act quickly so that Italy should have a share of the spoils. His generals warned him that the army was in no condition to fight, but he said, 'I need only a few thousand dead to sit at the conference table as a belligerent.' He declared war on Britain and France on 10 June 1941. 'Italian people,' Mussolini shouted, 'rush to arms and show your tenacity, your courage, your valour!' The Italian people heard him in silence and dismay.

The Battle of Britain

After the fall of France, Hitler was prepared to be generous to Britain, so he offered to make peace with her. To his amazement, Churchill refused, and Hitler had to order 'Operation Sea-lion'. The German army massed on the coast of France, while fleets of barges came from the rivers of Europe to ferry them across the Channel. However, the sea swarmed with British warships and the tiny German navy, already weakened by the Norwegian campaign, could not hope to defeat them. The only way the Germans could do that was by bombing, so they had to have command of the air. Goering was confident that his Luftwaffe would not only destroy the R.A.F., but bomb the British into submission, so that the German army and navy would have little to do.

In fact, it was not at all clear how the war in the air would go. There were some experts who thought the bomber would always get through, whatever the opposition. However, bomber pilots found they had no chance against enemy fighters, so they had to have an escort of their own fighters for protection. This was indeed fortunate for the British, since, although

Fighter pilots 'scramble' to their waiting Spitfires

the Germans had far more aeroplanes in total, the fighter strengths were about equal. The R.A.F. had 820, and the Germans 1000. The aircraft were much the same in quality as well, the Messerschmitt 109 being somewhat better than the Hurricane, but barely a match for the Spitfire. The Luft-waffe scored because its pilots were more experienced, but the R.A.F. had the advantage of fighting near its own bases.

The Battle of Britain raged from early August 1940 until mid-September. It went through four stages. At first, the Germans raided coastal shipping, but this was only to test the British defences. Serious attacks began on 8 August. Goering saw that his main enemies were the Hurricanes and Spitfires of Fighter Command. He saw, too, that the way to defeat them was to destroy their airfields. The Germans pressed home their attacks and by early September were close to victory. Then the British had an extra-ordinary piece of good luck. A German bomber that had wandered off course dropped its bombs on central London and Churchill ordered a raid on Berlin as revenge. The R.A.F. bombers did little damage, but Hitler raged that though the British might scar his cities, he would raze theirs to the ground. He at once ordered the Luftwaffe to concentrate all its attacks on London. The British repaired their airfields and were more than able to resist. They beat back massive attacks on 7 September and 8 September, and then, on 15 September the Germans made their biggest effort of all. This was known later as Battle of Britain Day. It was a complete victory for the R.A.F.

The war in the air now entered its fourth, and last stage, with the Germans bombing British cities by night. The Blitz, as it was called, killed a lot of people and destroyed many buildings, but in the darkness the Germans could not discover vital targets. Even cities like Coventry, which suffered terribly, were working almost normally within a few days of being bombed. Vicious though they were, the night attacks were a confession of failure. Hitler quietly abandoned Operation Sea-lion and looked else-where.

Why did the R.A.F. win the Battle of Britain? In the first place, of course, it was because of the courage and skill of its fighter pilots, British, Commonwealth and Polish. As Churchill said of them, 'Never in the field of human conflict has so much been owed by so many to so few.' Secondly, Air Chief Marshall Sir Hugh Dowding, who directed the battle, used the right tactics. There were many, like the legless air ace Douglas Bader, who urged him to mass his fighters in 'big wings' so that they could win great battles against the Messerschmitts. Dowding, however, saw that the con-flict would be one of attrition. That meant there could be no decisive victory, but each side would wear the other down, and the winner would be the one with more aircraft at the end. Accordingly, Dowding sent his fighters into action in small groups, and ordered them to concentrate on the German bombers. Consequently, apart from driving off the big German raids in September, Fighter Command did nothing spectacular. What it did do, was to remain in being, which was far more important. Thirdly, since Dowding conserved his fighters, the Minister of Aircraft Production, Lord Beaverbrook was able to replace the ones that were lost.

There was no time to increase factory output, so Beaverbrook repaired damaged aircraft from spare parts and anything that could be salvaged from wrecks. Thanks to Dowding and Beaverbrook, the R.A.F. ended the Battle of Britain with nearly as many fighters in service as at the beginning. Unfortunately, what could not be replaced were the skilled pilots, for they took a long time to train. Fourthly, the R.A.F. had invaluable help from radar. Apart from one or two uncomfortable moments when radar stations were damaged, the British fighters always had good warning of the Luftwaffe attacks.

On the German side, it is obvious that Hitler and Goering made a big mistake when they switched their raids from the airfields to London. They, more than anyone, helped Dowding and Beaverbrook to keep Fighter Command in being. However, perhaps the main reason for the German failure was a technical one. Excellent fighter though it was, the Me. 109 had only a short range. It ran out of fuel if it stayed over England for more than half a hour.

Chapter Thirty-four

The War in the Mediterranean

EVEN though they had lost the Battle of Britain the Germans could still have done serious damage to Britain by taking control of the Mediterranean and then going on to occupy the oilfields of the Middle East and threaten India. They failed to do so. Hitler did try to win General Franco's support at a meeting at Hendaye in October 1940, but even after hours of argument he refused to enter the war on Germany's side. Afterwards, Hitler said, 'Rather than go through that again I would prefer to have three or four teeth taken out.' However, the main reason why Hitler did not make a serious effort in the Mediterranean was because he was more interested in attacking Russia. None the less the Germans did have to fight in the Balkans and North Africa, mainly to help their allies, the Italians.

The War in the Balkans and Crete

The Balkans were important to Hitler because they lay on the southern flank of the armies he was planning to send to Russia. He badly wanted peace there, so he was annoyed when, in October 1940, Mussolini told him that he had attacked Greece. All might have been well if the Italians had won a victory, but the Greeks drove them out and Hitler realized he would have to send help. He persuaded the regent of Yugoslavia, Prince Paul, to allow German troops through his country but as soon as the Yugoslavs heard what their ruler had done they overthrew him. In April 1941, the German bombers reduced the city of Belgrade to rubble and German armies overran Yugoslavia in twelve days.

It was now the turn of Greece. Churchill sent some of his best troops from North Africa, but they could not stop the Germans. Within a few weeks they withdrew, and the Greeks signed an armistice.

Hitler decided to round off his conquests in S.E. Europe by taking the island of Crete. The British had command of the sea, while the Germans had command of the air, so, from the military point of view it was an interesting exercise. The Germans dropped parachute troops who seized an airfield, and they then poured in men by aircraft and glider. The British fled from the island in six days, but the Germans had lost so many of their airborne troops that they never tried anything like the invasion of Crete again.

248

Hitler had been completely successful in S.E. Europe, but the campaign had delayed his invasion of Russia by one month and, later, he and his generals claimed that this cost them the war.

The Italian Defeats in Africa

Mussolini had grandiose plans for a 'parallel war'. While the German armies advanced in Europe, his own were to advance along the shores of the Mediterranean. It certainly looked as if he could succeed for he had 200 000 men in Libya, and 250 000 in East Africa, while Sir Archibald Wavell, the British Commander-in-Chief in the Middle East, had only 60 000.

However, nothing went well for the Italians. In November 1940 aircraft from HMS *Illustrious* put half their navy out of action as it lay in Taranto harbour. Later, the British had another naval victory at Cape Matapan.

In East Africa General Cunningham advanced from Kenya. He overran all the Italian colonies in that area, and restored Haile Selassi to the throne of Abyssinia.

In North Africa, Marshal Graziani invaded Egypt with his huge army. General O'Connor gallantly tried to check him with a force of 35 000 but, to his amazement, found he was winning a great victory. He drove the Italians out of Egypt, captured the town of Tobruk, and took 1300 guns, 400 tanks and 130 000 prisoners. O'Connor could have overrun the whole of Italian North Africa, but two things marred his victory. One was Churchill's decision to send his best troops to certain defeat in Greece. The second was the arrival in Libya of General Erwin Rommel.

Rommel's Campaigns

Three campaigns were fought in the Western Desert. This is an unpleasant place because of dust, flies, extremes of heat and cold and a complete lack of water. There are few settlements, few roads, and much of the desert is so empty and open that tanks had to find their way by navigation, like ships at sea. There was no point in defending the desert for its own sake, but there was bitter fighting there, because it was the way to Egypt, the Suez Canal, and the oilfields of the Middle East.

Rommel's force, the Afrika Korps, fought the British Eighth Army. We must compare the two sides.

As we have seen, Hitler wanted to make his main effort in Russia. For him, North Africa was just a side-show, so he gave Rommel only four divisions. To the British, however, North Africa was the only place they could hope to defeat the Germans on land. They pitted the whole might of their empire against Rommel, so they always outnumbered him.

It has sometimes been said that the German equipment was better. This is true in that German tanks were more reliable. Too many British workers were careless so that tanks often arrived with their nuts only finger-tight. Even when their crews had serviced them, they were still liable to break down, especially the 'Crusaders'. However, for the most part, the British

249

tanks were every bit as good as the Germans': their armour was as thick and their guns as powerful. The British also had a number of American 'Grants', the gun of which was larger than that of any German tank, although, being side mounted, it had a limited field of fire. As for the anti-tank guns, the German 88s were deadly weapons, but they were only converted anti-aircraft guns. The British had anti-aircraft guns which would have done just as well, but they did not adapt them.

The British, then, had superior numbers and good equipment, but they also had serious weaknesses. For one thing they did not understand armoured warfare. This is surprising for it was the British who had developed the tank in the First World War and, as we have seen, it was British soldiers, like Sir Basil Liddell Hart, who first planned the new, mobile warfare. However, it was the Germans who learnt from these experiments.

It was not that the British had failed to build tanks. They had the Royal Tank Corps, which had been formed in the First World War, while their ancient and famous cavalry regiments had, somewhat unwillingly, given up their horses in favour of tanks. However, the British organization was wrong, as were their tactics.

As we have seen, a panzer division was a mixed force containing units of all kinds. Its commander was like a carpenter, with a full set of tools, who can do any job that comes his way. In the British army, divisions were either infantry or armour. If, therefore, the commander of an infantry division met tanks, he had to contact his corps commander and ask him to send an armoured division to help him. He was like a carpenter who only carried a plane, and had to call on his mate with the saw if he wanted a piece of wood cut in two. Usually, the co-operation was not very good. The British infantry hated the armoured divisions because they said they were never there to protect them when they were needed.

As for tactics, both the Royal Tank Corps and the cavalry regiments believed in attacking the enemy armour. The cavalry in particular liked to charge 'eyeball to eyeball', as the Royal Scots Greys had done at Waterloo. This often led them into trouble.

German tactics and organization were much better. Rommel tried to avoid battles in which tanks fought with tanks on equal terms. Instead, he would lure the British armour into the murderous fire of his 88s and only when they had shot the enemy formations to pieces would he send his tanks to destroy the survivors. Rommel even used anti-tank guns in attack, which the British never did. As they moved forward the German tanks had with them light, manoeuvreable 50 mm guns. When they met the enemy, the guns fired as the tanks advanced, and then the tanks halted and fired while the guns came up. It is not surprising that British tanks suffered heavily when they came upon a mixed force like this. Indeed, the Germans were able to have close co-operation between their various arms, most of the time, because they were all combined in each panzer division.

However, Rommel did have a problem and that was his Italian allies. He could not manage without them, because he had so few German troops, but they were badly equipped and, for the most part, badly led. The British soon realized their best plan was to hit the Italians, and Rommel often had to send his Germans running hither and thither to protect them.

The war in the Western Desert swayed backwards and forwards during 1941 and 1942. The following is an outline of what happened.

Rommel attacked in March 1941, and drove the British back to Egypt, though he failed to take Tobruk. Churchill, who was determined to have a victory, poured weapons and reinforcements into North Africa. General Sir Claude Auchinleck mounted 'Operation Crusader' and, after a hard struggle, drove Rommel back to El Agheila.

Auchinleck now halted, because he had to send troops to the Far East. It was now Rommel's turn to receive reinforcements and to attack. In May 1942 he swept into Egypt, taking Tobruk on the way, and by June he was at El Alamein, about 100 km from Alexandria. Here Auchinleck stopped him.

Once again, Churchill poured in men and supplies, and demanded a victory. When Auchinleck refused to attack at once, Churchill sacked him, and appointed General Sir Harold Alexander as Commander-in-Chief, Middle East. At the same time General Bernard Montgomery took charge of the Eighth Army, in Egypt.

To Churchill's disgust Montgomery also refused to attack until he was ready. This was not until October, by which time Rommel had prepared some formidable defences. However, the British heavily outnumbered their enemies:

	British	German	Italian
Tanks	1029	220	276
Anti-tank guns	1451	550	300
Guns	908	200	300
Men	195 000	100 000 (combined)	

Two hundred and fifty of Montgomery's tanks were the new American 'Shermans', which were more powerful than any of Rommel's tanks. Also, the British had complete control of the air.

The Battle of El Alamein, which was the turning-point in the North African campaign, lasted from 23 October to 4 November 1942. There was nothing particularly clever about Montgomery's tactics. He fought a battle of attrition, which, with his superior numbers, he was almost bound to win. When, finally, Rommel retreated, Montgomery followed timidly and allowed him to escape.

'Operation Torch' — The Invasion of French North Africa

When the Americans entered the war President Roosevelt agreed to concentrate on defeating Germany before Japan. For the time being the allies were not strong enough to invade France, but it seemed a good idea to help the Eighth Army, which was then in difficulties, by attacking from the west. Accordingly, General Eisenhower led an Anglo-American force into French North Africa, though this was not until 8 November, by which time El Alamein had been fought and won.

The French decided to help the Americans and the British, mainly because the Germans occupied Vichy France. In spite of that, the invasion did not go well, which encouraged Hitler and Mussolini to pour a quarter of a million men into Tunisia. If Rommel had had a force of these numbers earlier, he could have done great things. Now it was too late. He made two counter-attacks which failed, and then he left Africa, a sick, disappointed man. The allied armies closed on Tunis, while their fleets blockaded it from the sea. The town surrendered in May 1943, and 130 000 Germans and Italians were taken prisoner.

The Invasion of Italy

Churchill and Roosevelt met at Casablanca in January 1943, to make plans. Roosevelt was keen to invade France, but Churchill persuaded him that they should attack the 'soft underbelly' of the Axis.

On 10 July 1943 the Americans and British launched 'Operation Husky', which was the invasion of Sicily. They landed more men in their first attack than were to cross the Channel on D-Day, and before long they had half a million men in Sicily. The plan was that Montgomery, with the British should push up the east coast and capture Messina to stop the enemy returning to Italy. Patton, with the Americans, was supposed to guard his left flank. What happened was that the Germans held Montgomery near Mount Etna, while Patton's men overran the rest of the island quite easily. The Americans were delighted to reach Messina before the British and greeted them with cries of 'Where've you tourists been?' However, the Americans had shepherded the Axis forces to safety. Most of them escaped to the mainland, for they kept Messina to the end.

At the height of the Sicilian campaign, on 25 July 1943, Mussolini fell from power. The Fascist Grand Council deposed him, and the king confirmed their decision, even helping in the plot to arrest the dictator. Marshal Badaglio became head of the government.

In September 1943 the allies invaded the mainland of Italy. The Italians surrendered at once, but the Germans disarmed their troops quickly and easily. The country is narrow and mountainous, so the German commander, Kesselring, was able to establish one powerful line of defence after another. The most famous of these was the Gustav Line, 100 km south of Rome. It was here that the allies destroyed the famous old monastery of Monte Cassino, believing that the Germans had fortified it. In fact, the only people in it were the abbot and a few of his monks. Hoping to turn the Gustav Line, the Americans landed some troops behind it at Anzio, but the Germans held them in a small bridgehead, and they achieved nothing. It was not until May 1944 that the allies broke through and captured Rome.

By then, 'Operation Overlord', the invasion of France, was being planned and Eisenhower and Montgomery went to Britain to lead it. Alexander was left to direct the war in Italy and his task was not so much to conquer the country, as to hold down German divisions who might otherwise have gone to France. Indeed, he had to mount 'Operation

The ruins of Monte Cassino

The war in the Mediterranean

Anvil', which was an invasion of southern France. It came too late to help 'Overlord', and weakened Alexander's forces so that he was unable to reach Austria or the Balkans ahead of the Russians. The German armies in Italy did not capitulate until April 1945.

The invasion of Italy was hardly a resounding success, for the 'soft underbelly' had proved very hard indeed. Even the more limited aim of holding down large numbers of German troops was not achieved. In Western Europe the Germans had 127 divisions, but only 22 of these were in Italy. Moreover, they were engaging an allied army of 30 divisions.

The End of Mussolini

After Mussolini was deposed, the Italians held him prisoner in a remote mountain hotel. A group of Germans carried out a daring rescue from the air, and then Mussolini ruled northern Italy for a time, as a puppet-State of Germany. In April 1945 he and his mistress, Clara Petacci, were captured by partisans who shot them and hung their bodies upside down in a square in Milan.

253

Chapter Thirty-five

The Bombing of Germany and the Battle of the Atlantic

AFTER the fall of France the only way Britain could hurt Germany was by bombing her cities: after the Battle of Britain, the Germans thought their best plan was to use their U-boats to sink the ships which brought Britain her supplies. Neither the bombers of the R.A.F., nor the U-boats of the German navy were successful.

The Bombing of Germany

When the war began, the Germans intended their bombers to support their armies, which they did most effectively. The British plan was to use their bombers to destroy their enemies' cities. They remembered the panic a few bombs on London had caused in the First World War, and they believed that massive air raids would not only destroy German industry, but the morale of her people as well. Two important men were sure of this: one was the Commander-in-Chief of Bomber Command, Sir Arthur Harris, known as 'Bomber' Harris; the other was Churchill's scientific adviser, Professor F. A. Lindemann, who later became Lord Cherwell.

As these were the British ideas, it was remarkable how little they could do at the beginning of the war. They had only 280 bombers, no reliable bombs and no proper system of navigation. By the end, however, the R.A.F. could fly 1500 aircraft at a time, they carried bombs ranging from small incendiaries to the 10 000 kg 'Grandslam', and their navigation was reasonably accurate.

Development of the Offensive

At first, the British sent their bombers on daylight raids, without fighter escorts. They lost so many aircraft that they soon switched to night bombing. The problem was that they could not find their targets. So far from being able to pin-point an oil refinery, a ball-bearing factory or a railway marshalling yard, the best they could do was to hit a town. This was making war on civilians, but the British dignified their attacks with the title of 'area bombing', and told themselves they were destroying German morale.

Lancaster bomber

The attacks grew in size. In May 1942 'Bomber' Harris ordered the first raid of 1000 aircraft. It was made on Cologne, and it killed 400 civilians. There were a few more raids of the same size, and then in 1943 and the early part of 1944, there were systematic attacks, first of all on the Rhur, then on Hamburg and finally, on Berlin. For example, between July and November, there were 33 raids on Hamburg, involving, in all, 17 000 sorties.

Meanwhile the Germans were improving their defences, their night fighters in particular becoming more and more deadly. By March 1944 the British losses were greater than one aircraft in twenty for every raid, and Harris called off the attacks. German morale had not cracked and, during 1943, Germany's output of armaments had risen by 50 per cent.

Fortunately for its own morale the R.A.F. was able to turn elsewhere almost at once. It disrupted the French railways in preparation for 'Operation Overlord'. This, the second stage of its offensive, was successful, for it stopped the Germans rushing up reinforcements to defeat the invasion. Probably, though, the French Resistance might have done as well, and saved the lives of many French civilians besides.

The third stage of the offensive was daylight bombing by the Americans. At the Casablanca Conference in January 1943, Churchill and Roosevelt had agreed that the R.A.F. was to continue its attacks by night and the U.S.A.A.F. was to mount its own by day. The Americans thought that their Flying Fortresses would be safe if they flew at a great height and kept tight defensive formations. The German fighters massacred them. Then, in December 1943, the first Mustangs came into service. Their range was 2400 km so they could fly with the bombers over Germany, and, moreover, they were better than any of the enemy fighters. Now, at last, it was

255

possible to select and destroy almost any target. The Americans had bomb sights that were so accurate that they boasted they could 'drop a bomb in a barrel from 10 000 feet'.

The fourth and final stage came after the fall of France. The allies had all the bases they needed close to Germany, and had complete control of the air. They decided the most important targets were oil refineries and communications, and had they concentrated on them, they might have shortened the war by a few months. However, Harris still insisted on terror bombing. For example, on 13 February 1945 he sent 1000 aircraft to attack Dresden, a town crowded with refugees fleeing from the Russians. The raid killed 25 000 people, but did nothing to help final victory.

Conclusion

The bombing raids of the R.A.F. did more harm to Britain than to Germany. Germany was not frightened into surrender, and there was little damage to German factories. On the other hand, Britain concentrated one-third of her war effort into her bombing offensive. Her aircraft were diverted from more important work, like protecting convoys, and her factories were unable to make enough of the more useful weapons, like tanks, landing-craft and fighter aeroplanes. There were indeed effective air raids on Germany, but they were the ones the Americans mounted, in daylight, towards the end of the war.

The Battle of the Atlantic

The Battle of the Atlantic lasted as long as the war itself. It was essential that the allies should win it, for Britain could not survive without imported food and war materials, and when America entered the war, she had to transport her men to the Mediterranean and Europe.

The German Weapons

Around Britain's coasts, the Germans laid mines. They were not a major threat, though at the beginning of the war it looked as if they might be, for the Germans had a new type, the magnetic mine. Fortunately for the British, they soon discovered the secret and learnt how to demagnetize their ships with electric cables. They called this 'degaussing'.

As in the First World War, the Germans sent out commerce raiders, but once again, they did little damage. It will be enough to look at the fate of two of them, the *Admiral Graf Spee* and the *Bismarck*.

The pocket-battleship *Admiral Graf Spee* was in the Atlantic when war broke out, and in three months managed to sink nine merchant ships. This compared with the seven that U.99 sank in a single night. Before 1939 was over, the three cruisers *Exeter*, *Ajax* and *Achilles* caught her near the mouth of the River Plate, and damaged her. She took refuge in Montevideo, a neutral port, where she was not allowed to remain. Hitler ordered her captain to scuttle her.

The *Bismarck*, a much bigger vessel, put to sea in May 1941 and caused the British great alarm by sinking the battle-cruiser *Hood*. The *Bismarck* was doomed as soon as aircraft from the *Ark Royal* found her. They crippled her with torpedoes, and then warships destroyed her with gunfire.

German aircraft were far more dangerous than surface raiders, especially the long-range Focke-Wulf Kondors. Operating from Stavanger and Bordeaux they covered much of the eastern Atlantic. They guided the U-boats to their prey and, at times, were themselves sinking more allied ships than were the submarines.

Without any doubt, though, it was the U-boats that were the chief danger to the allies. In spite of Admiral Raeder's pleading, Germany entered the war with no more than 56, and 30 of these were only 'North Sea Ducks'. During the war, however, the Germans built 1200, and towards the end they were formidable warships. For example, each one was fitted with a schnorkel and an exhaust mast, which allowed it to use its diesel engines when submerged.

Also, the man in charge of the U-boats, Admiral Dönitz, thought of new tactics for them. As soon as one of them spotted a convoy it radioed others to join it. They then formed a 'wolf pack' which often attacked at night, on the surface. Surfaced, the U-boat had two advantages. The enemy asdic (now called sonar) could not detect her, and she was faster than any of the escort vessels. Dönitz, in fact, used his submarines as torpedo boats.

Allied Counter-measures

Remembering their bitter experiences in the First World War, the British formed convoys at once. However, it was some time before they were effective. Ships had to sail with only one or two escort vessels, and even these had to turn back when they reached the limit of their range, which was only 320 km west of Ireland. Later, the British built more destroyers and special escort vessels such as frigates and the tiny corvettes of less than 1000 tonnes. Also, they set up bases in Iceland and Newfoundland so that as one escort turned back, another took over, and the convoys had protection all across the Atlantic. The Americans helped, too, even before they entered the war. In September 1940 they gave Britain 50 destroyers in return for some naval bases in the western Atlantic. They also looked after their own ships and, indeed, were soon protecting the ships of all nationalities.

To deal with the wolf packs, the British invented new equipment. This included a very powerful searchlight called the 'Leigh light'. They also had radar which would detect an enemy on the surface. To find a submerged U-boat they still used asdic which had been invented in the First World War, but there were more modern systems as well.

When they had enough warships, the British were able to use new tactics. From 1943 onwards Admiral Sir Max Horton gave each convoy a support group of frigates and destroyers. Close-escort ships remained with the convoy, but as soon as the U-boats showed themselves, the support group went after them and hunted them to destruction.

Air cover was also important, though it was limited, because the British lacked bases. They also lacked aircraft, because they were concentrating on bombing Germany. From 1941, though, there were American Catalina flying boats operating from Britain, Iceland and Canada. They covered all but 480 km of the Atlantic, a stretch of water that became known as the 'black gap'. By 1943 the Americans had their long-range Liberators which gave convoys cover all across the Atlantic. Aircraft guided warships to the submarines, and attacked them themselves with bombs and depth-charges.

The Course of the Battle against the U-boats

Comparatively little happened during the early days of the war, because the Germans had so few U-boats, and these had to make their way into the Atlantic from Germany. However, after the fall of France, they could use bases like St Nazaire, and go further into the Atlantic than the convoy escorts. From July 1941 they had what they called their 'happy time' sinking ships with little interference until first the winter came, and then the British organized escorts all across the Atlantic.

The real crisis in the Battle of the Atlantic was in the months immediately before and after the winter of 1942–3. The Germans had far more U-boats and were using them in wolf packs, concentrating on the 'black gap'. During 1942 the allies lost eight million tonnes of shipping, which was one million more than they were able to build. Then, suddenly, everything changed. Between June and August the Germans lost 79 U-boats, but sank only 60 merchant ships. Admiral Horton's support groups were in action, while American Liberators had closed the 'black gap'. Of the 79 U-boats sunk, 58 were destroyed from the air.

In the later years of the war few of the U-boats that put to sea ever returned. The allied counter-measures were almost completely effective.

The Arctic Convoys

The purpose of the Arctic convoys was to take supplies to Russia's White Sea ports. They faced not only submarines and aeroplanes, but powerful warships like the *Tirpitz*, that were lurking in the Norwegian fjords. Many vessels were sunk by U-boats and aircraft. For example, in May 1942 convoy PQ17 lost 24 of its 35 ships. Forcing through the convoys became a battle of wills, for Churchill was determined they should reach Russia, and the Germans were determined they should not. All the time, there was an overland route into Russia, through Persia, which was much easier and completely safe.

Chapter Thirty-six

The War in Russia

IN SPITE of the non-aggression pact he had made with Hitler, Stalin knew that, eventually, Germany would attack Russia. To make his country safer, he took as much territory as he could. Hitler allowed him Eastern Poland, as the price of his neutrality in 1939. Later, Stalin defeated Finland and occupied Karelia; he sent troops into Lithuania, Latvia and Estonia, and he took Bessarabia from Romania. To gain time, he curried favour with Hitler by sending him vast quantities of supplies. There were grain and oil from Russia, for example, while rubber from the Far East came along the Trans-Siberian Railway. Thanks to Stalin, the allied blockade of Germany had little effect. None the less, in 1941, Hitler decided the time had come for Germany to seize her *lebensraum* in the east.

In planning 'Operation Barbarossa' Hitler and his generals wanted to avoid fighting in the depths of Russia. They knew that if anything was going to defeat them it would be the sheer size of the country. They aimed to break through at a number of points and then trap the Russian armies with pincer movements, before they could fall back from the frontier. They expected to win decisive victories almost at once, and occupy all Russia west of the Volga before winter. Hitler was quite confident. He said to Jodl, one of his generals, 'We have only to kick in the door and the whole rotten structure will come crashing down.'

Events of 1941

The Germans attacked on 22 June 1941, taking the Russians completely by surprise. They advanced with three army groups — North, Centre and South.

Army Group North, under von Leeb, reached Leningrad, and laid siege to it. The city lost a third of its inhabitants before the war was over, but it did not fall. Moreover, the Germans were not able to link up with the Finns who were fighting on their side.

Army Group Centre under von Bock won resounding victories, and captured Smolensk. Numbers of German generals, like the brilliant tank commander Heinz Guderian, urged Hitler to attack Moscow. Hitler in fact wasted an entire month wondering what to do. Army Group South, under von Runstedt, had done remarkably well, and Hitler thought that if he

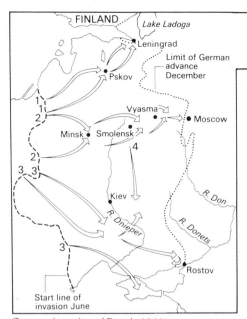

1. Army Group North – von Leeb
2. Army Group Centre – von Bock
3. Army Group South – von Runstedt
4. Guderian's attacks, cutting off Kiev

German invasion of Russia 1941   *Panzer units in Russia*

made a determined effort he could win the Ukraine with all its industry and its excellent farmland. In the end, Hitler ordered Guderian to leave Army Group Centre and sweep south behind the Russian armies defending Kiev. The move succeeded, for 600 000 Russians were surrounded and captured. Army Group South then advanced as far as Rostov, over-running almost the entire Ukraine.

Now, at last, Hitler ordered Army Group Centre to take Moscow. It won a great victory, encircling half a million Russians at Vyasma, and by December the leading troops reached the suburbs of the capital. They were too late. The autumn rains had delayed their advance and winter had begun. As the Germans ground to a halt, Marshal Zhukov launched a counter-attack and hurled the invaders back from Moscow. The Germans, who were already frightened by the thought of the coming winter, all but broke and fled. Hitler, however, acted firmly, and ordered his troops to fight where they stood. They beat off Zhukov's attacks and their panic died away.

The Germans now formed defensive 'hedgehogs', based on the towns they had captured. At first they suffered terribly because Hitler had ex-pected the war to be over before the cold weather, and they did not have proper clothing. However, supplies arrived by air, and when spring came, the German army was still intact.

Events of 1942 — Stalingrad and the Turn of the Tide

In 1942, the German army was only strong enough to attack on one front. Hitler decided this should be in the south, as he wanted the oilfields of the Caucasus.

260

Once again the Germans were successful. An army under von Kleist reached the foothills of the Caucasus and occupied some of the oilfields. However, they had a long, exposed left flank, and to defend that Hitler ordered an attack on Stalingrad. At first this was only a side-show, the main front being in the Caucasus. However it became vitally important, and for reasons that were psychological rather than military. The first assault failed, and Hitler could not tolerate failure. Also 'Stalingrad' meant 'Stalin's City', so to capture it would be a great moral victory.

The force that conducted the siege was the German Sixth Army under von Paulus. It reduced the city to rubble and took all but a narrow strip of it along the River Volga. However, the Germans were in difficulty. They were running short of planes and tanks, while their left flank was held only by unreliable allies, like Romanians and Bulgars. Zhukov sent enough men into Stalingrad to hold the Germans, but massed most of his reserves west and south of the town. On 19 November, 1942, he launched his counter-offensive, and a Russian pincer closed round von Paulus's army. Possibly it could have fought its way out, but Hitler ordered it to stand firm. It fought bravely until 31 January 1943, when it surrendered. Over 150 000 men had been killed, and the Russians captured some 92 000. Stalingrad was more than a great Russian victory: it was the turning-point of the war.

Next, the Russians pressed on to Rostov, hoping to trap von Kleist. However, thanks to the resistance of the Sixth Army, he had just enough time to escape.

Events of 1943–5

During this time the Russians first liberated their own country and then advanced into the heart of Germany. Their tactics were very like the ones used by Marshal Foch in 1918. They would attack at a certain point until resistance hardened and then switch rapidly to somewhere else. That way they rolled back the German armies. The following are the main events of each year.

In 1943 the Germans attacked a Russian salient at Kursk, in the biggest tank battle of the war. The panzer spearheads barely dented the Russian defences and they retreated. This was the last important offensive the Germans made in the east.

In 1944, the Russians reached Warsaw. Encouraged by this, the Poles rose in rebellion, hoping that Russians would come to their aid. The Russians made no move until the Germans had put down the rising, destroyed the city, killed most of the inhabitants and deported the survivors. People in the west were convinced the Russians waited deliberately, so that they would not have to deal with an independent Poland.

In 1945 the Russians reached the Elbe, captured Berlin and, on 8 May accepted the German surrender.

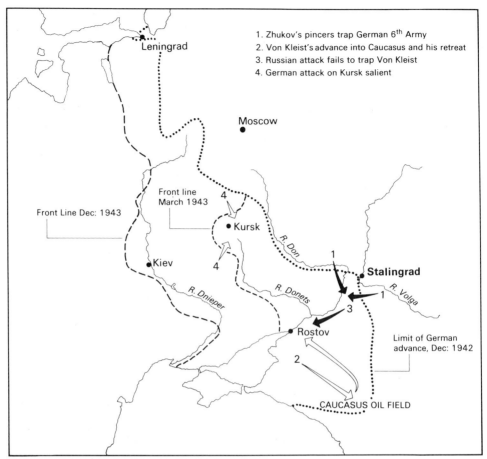

1. Zhukov's pincers trap German 6th Army
2. Von Kleist's advance into Caucasus and his retreat
3. Russian attack fails to trap Von Kleist
4. German attack on Kursk salient

The war in Russia 1942–3

Reasons for German Successes and Final Defeat

At the beginning the Germans succeeded for four main reasons. In the first place, they caught their enemies by surprise. There was no excuse for the Russians, since British intelligence had warned them, but they took no notice. Secondly, the Germans were far better at the art of war. They had perfected the blitzkrieg, and the Russians did not know how to stop it. Thirdly, the Germans were all highly trained, and many of them had already been in battle. Finally, all the German generals were able, while some, like Guderian, were brilliant. In the Russian army, most of the best officers had died in Stalin's purges. It is true that Marshal Zhukov was outstanding but too many of the others were like Marshal Budenny, who was described by his troops as 'a man with an enormous moustache, but a very small brain'. As commander of the armies in the south he had 5000 tanks, but von Rundstedt defeated him with only 600. The Russian Commander-in-Chief was Stalin, and he sent countless men to their deaths in useless frontal attacks. Later Khrushchev said he planned the war on a library globe, measuring distances with a tape-measure.

With all these advantages, why were the Germans defeated?

There was Russia itself. It is so vast that it was impossible for the Germans to overrun it as quickly as Poland or France. Moreover, there was its climate. When winter came, many Germans died of cold. More important, they had to halt their advance, which gave the Russians time to recover their strength. Another problem was that there were few metalled roads. Mostly there were only sand or dirt tracks which turned into quagmires after rain. Unexpected rain in the summer of 1941 slowed the Germans as much as the Red Army.

Next, the Russians had what seemed to the Germans unlimited men. In 1941 the Germans expected to fight 200 divisions: by the end of the year they had counted 360. They took hundreds of thousands of prisoners, yet still new armies appeared. By the end of the war, the Russians outnumbered the Germans by six to one.

Similarly, the Russians had plenty of weapons. They had far more tanks, artillery and aircraft than the Germans even in 1941, and they increased their lead as time went on. The industrial towns of the Urals were well away from the fighting and when the Russians saw they were going to lose the Ukraine they moved the machinery and workers of 500 factories to safety in Siberia. Also the Russian equipment was good. Their T34 tank was, perhaps, the best of the war and their artillery was certainly superior to the Germans'. What they did lack was lorries, but the Americans sent plenty of these, along with supplies of tinned food. As a result, the Red Army became much more mobile and able to switch its attacks rapidly from front to front when it began its advance.

For all their lack of training and poor generals, the Russian soldiers fought bravely. Also the quality of the Red Army improved as the men gained battle experience. Another thing that happened was that bright young officers won promotion and replaced Budenny and his kind.

As for the Germans, their successes in 1941 were less important than they seemed, for they badly needed complete victory before winter. This they did not achieve. Their pincers failed to close quickly enough in the early battles, so many of their enemies escaped. That meant the Germans had to do a lot of fighting deep inside Russia, something they had wanted to avoid. Also, there were delays. The Balkan campaign held up the start of the invasion for a month, and Hitler wasted the whole of August wondering whether to attack Moscow or overrun the Ukraine.

Finally, Hitler made a number of mistakes, both military and political. He took over as Commander-in-Chief of the army in December 1941, so the lance-corporal of the First World War had charge of the most powerful fighting force in the world. It was like giving a child an aeroplane to fly. Actually, he did surprisingly well. His order to stand firm at the end of 1941 probably saved the army from destruction. From then on though, it was the only instruction he would give troops that were in difficulty. 'Where the German soldier plants his foot', he said, 'he does not withdraw.' Generals lost all freedom to manœuvre, and the results were often disastrous, as at Stalingrad.

More surprising was Hitler's political failure, since he had a genius for politics. Many Russians hated Stalin and Communism, but none more than the Ukrainians. When the Germans arrived they were greeted as liberators, but Hitler was so cruel to the Russian people that they soon turned against him. In the end there were a million partisans operating behind the German lines, ambushing convoys, blowing up supply dumps and destroying communications.

Russia did far more towards victory than any other allied power, for she engaged three-quarters of Germany's forces and defeated them. America and Britain gave a lot of anxious thought to how they might win the war: in fact, Russia won it for them.

Chapter Thirty-seven

Operation Overlord —
The Invasion of France and Germany

WHEN Churchill and Roosevelt met at the Casablanca Conference in January 1943 they set up a joint Anglo-American staff to plan the invasion of France. Eisenhower was to be Supreme Allied Commander, while Montgomery was to have charge of the land forces. Eisenhower was not the greatest of generals, but he had a lot of tact, and was able to make the allied forces work as a team. Montgomery was Churchill's choice and it may have been a mistaken one. Montgomery was the kind of general who is so cautious that he never loses a battle, but equally, never wins a brilliant victory. Moreover, he had such an unfortunate manner that he upset almost everyone with whom he had dealings. In the end, his command was limited to the British force alone, though he was promoted to Field Marshal, to soothe his wounded pride.

The Invasion Plan

The River Seine divides northern France into two, so the allies had to land to the east of it, or to the west. If they chose the east, they would have a

Airborne landings in France

short crossing but would have to storm the most powerful defences in Hitler's Atlantic Wall: if they chose the west, they would have a longer crossing, but the defences were not as strong. In the end they decided to attack in the west. The idea was that the British should seize Caen and hold the Germans at bay, while the Americans overran the Cotentin Peninsula. They could then pour men and supplies into France until they were strong enough to mount an offensive.

The allies had complete control of the sea and the air, and they had far more troops than the Germans. The main problem that worried them was whether the forces that made the landings would be able to hold off the German counter-attacks until enough reinforcements arrived.

The Invasion

D-Day, the allied invasion of Europe, was 6 June 1944. At the end of it, a total of 156 000 men had landed on five beaches along 130 km of the Normandy coast. The Atlantic Wall was breached, but not everything had gone well. For example, the British had expected to take Caen in the first rush, but they dallied on the beaches, and the town did not fall for a month.

However, the Germans were also having problems. Hitler's 'intuition' had told him, rightly, that his enemies would strike west of the Seine. Now they had landed there, it told him that they had only made a feint attack, and that the real blow would come the other side of the river. Consequently, he was slow to send his reserves to meet the invaders, who thus had the time they so badly needed to bring over more troops. When, finally, the German reserves did move they were slow to arrive, for the R.A.F. had destroyed the bridges over the Seine and thoroughly damaged the French railways. Also, seven out of the ten panzer divisions that were available were hurled at the British near Caen. This was just what the allies wanted, for it gave the Americans the chance to capture Cherbourg. When

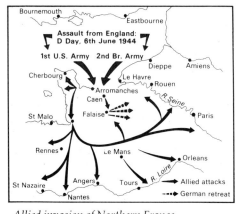

Allied invasion of Northern France

Normandy – wrecked German armour

they had done so, it was easy for them to bring in all the men and supplies they needed.

On 31 July 1944, Patton mounted his attack, and burst out of the Cotentin at Avranches. Hitler should now have withdrawn his troops, but, instead, he gave his usual instructions to stand firm. He even ordered a disastrous counter-attack, pitting 145 tanks against 2000. Patton overran Brittany, then turned back, sweeping south of the German armies. He caught many of them in the 'Falaise pocket' and, though, the trap did not close completely, he took 50 000 prisoners. The German armies had been thoroughly defeated and fled for their own frontiers.

The Liberation of France

On 15 August 'Operation Anvil' began. This was the landing of allied forces from Italy in the south of France. It was quite unnecessary since the Germans had to evacuate the region anyway, after their defeat in the north. All 'Anvil' did was to weaken Alexander's offensive in Italy.

On 25 August, Free French troops occupied Paris. By early September there were American forces in Lorraine, and others, along with the British had taken most of Belgium. One result was the capture of the bases from which the Germans had launched their V1 and V2 missiles against London. These missiles had been one of Hitler's last hopes of winning the war.

The Germans were in confusion. They had not even mined the bridges over the Rhine and they had gaps in their armies, including one of over 150 km wide in northern Belgium. If Montgomery had made a determined push into the Ruhr, nothing could have stopped him and the war would have been over in 1944. Instead, the allied armies ground to a halt. Partly that was because they had outrun their supplies, and partly it was Eisenhower's fault. He should have given such supplies as there were to Patton, because he would have pressed on. Instead he shared them with Montgomery, who was standing still.

When it was too late Montgomery decided to mount 'Operation Market Garden'. Parachute troops were to seize crossings of the waterways in southern Holland, and open the way for an advance into Germany. There were three drops altogether, and Montgomery's tanks reached the first two in time. However, at Arnhem, the Germans overwhelmed the British First Airborne Division before help could arrive. They had been expected to resist for two days, but they fought like heroes for nine, though to no avail.

It was now certain the war would drag on into 1945. This was disastrous. The allies had suffered a quarter of a million casualties since D-Day, but they were to have a half a million more in the fighting that followed. In eastern Europe the mass extermination of civilians went on unhindered, so millions died there who would otherwise have lived. Finally, the Russians were given the time to overrun much of eastern and south-eastern Europe. The Americans and the British could well have been the first to reach Berlin, Prague and Vienna.

The Battle of the Bulge

At the end of 1944 the allied commanders were confidently planning their next offensive when, on 16 December, a powerful German army burst out of the Ardennes and raced westwards. Hitler hoped it would capture Antwerp, so cutting off the British from their supplies and compelling them to withdraw in a second Dunkirk. After that the Americans could be defeated, and all Germany's forces concentrated against the Russians. These were the mad dreams of a desperate man, and there was no hope of success, but the British and the Americans had several uncomfortable days.

Amazingly, the Americans repeated the same mistake as the French in 1940. Looking at the Ardennes they felt they were defences enough in themselves, and placed only five divisions opposite them. In the hills Hitler mustered twenty divisions, seven of them armoured. There were 1000 tanks, including many of the powerful new 'Tigers'. The Germans broke through without difficulty, and as they did so a bemused General Bradley exclaimed 'Where in hell has this sonuvabitch gotten all his strength?'

Eisenhower was so desperate that he put Montgomery in charge of the American forces north of the 'bulge'. He strode into their headquarters as one of them said, 'Like Christ come to cleanse the Temple.' The battle was won by the American forces to the south. The hero was General McAuliffe. Cut off and hard pressed in Bastogne, the Germans gave him the chance to surrender. All McAuliffe said was 'Nuts', a comment the interpreter had great difficulty in translating.

The Germans were short of petrol, they had no air cover, and they were heavily outnumbered. They halted after 100 km and, on 26 December 1944 they began to retreat. It was their last effort, and they were now quite unable to defend their homeland.

The Invasion of Germany

The allies had made it plain that the Germans would have to surrender unconditionally, and that meant a fight to the finish.

In March 1945 the Americans and the British crossed the Rhine. Patton raced ahead regardless. Montgomery made elaborate plans, massed his forces in overwhelming strength and prepared his way with tremendous bombardments. The main obstacles his men met were the piles of rubble in the German cities.

On 25 April 1945 the Americans and Russians met on the River Elbe. On 30 April Hitler committed suicide. On 4 May the German army in the north-west surrendered to Montgomery. Eisenhower accepted the surrender of all the German forces on 7 May and the following day the Russians did the same.

Chapter Thirty-eight

The War Against Japan

Japan's Armed Forces

WHILE Germany's successes were due, in the main, to the skill and efficiency of her soldiers, Japan's initial advantage was the morale of her troops. In the first place Japan had already been victorious in five wars since 1894, so that her people thought she was invincible. More than that, the Japanese soldiers believed it was their duty to fight for their Emperor and their country. There was no greater glory than to die on the field of battle, and no greater disgrace than to surrender to the enemy.

Japanese troops had little need of comfort. Many of them rode on bicycles and they would live for days on nothing but rice. However, they had plenty of modern weapons, such as armoured cars, tanks and artillery. The men were highly trained, especially in amphibious operations and jungle warfare. One of their favourite tactics was to outflank an enemy's position, and then cause havoc in his rear. Even small groups were often able to cause a lot of damage in that way.

The one great disadvantage the army had was that it needed to keep four-fifths of its men in China and Manchuria. They were already fighting the Chinese and they were afraid the Russians might attack. There were only eleven divisions to spare for the war in the Pacific, which is the main reason why their offensive died away as soon as it did.

The air force was modern and powerful. The Zero fighter was especially dangerous, being better than any that the allies had in the Far East when the war began. As a result, the Japanese had control of the air, for a time.

The navy was formidable, since the Japanese had realized how the war would go at sea, just as the Germans had forecast what would happen on land. The Western allies still believed in battleships with big guns, but the Japanese, and especially Admiral Yamamoto, saw that naval battles were going to be won by aircraft-carriers. When the war broke out, the Japanese and allied fleets in the Mediterranean were fairly evenly matched, save in carriers. The British and the Dutch had none, the Americans had three, but the Japanese had ten. However, the Japanese were worried about the American Pacific Fleet, which was a modern, powerful force. It was, Admiral Yamamoto said, 'a dagger pointed at the throat of Japan'. That was why Japan's first act of war was to try and destroy it as it lay in Pearl Harbor.

Japan's Conquests

The Japanese aimed to do two things. First, they wanted to establish the 'Greater East-Asia Co-Prosperity Sphere'. That really meant they were going to take over the countries which produced the raw materials they needed, and plunder them. They particularly wanted the Dutch East Indies, with their oil, and Malaya, which produced four-fifths of the world's rubber, and two-thirds of its tin.

The second aim was to make a defensive ring, well away from Japan and strong enough to resist any attack.

War began on 7 December 1941, with the attack on Pearl Harbor. Aircraft from Yamamoto's carriers began their onslaught at 8.00 a.m., and two hours later it was all over. Of eight American battleships, four were sunk, and the remaining four badly damaged. Numerous other warships were also put out of action, as well as 349 aircraft. The Japanese lost 29 aircraft. Few victories have been more sudden or more complete. The only comfort for the Americans was that their carriers had not been in harbour at the time of attack, so they escaped. However, for the moment at least, the Japanese had control of the sea. They could concentrate their forces wherever they wanted and for six months their armies swept from victory to victory.

On the same day as Pearl Harbor the Japanese attacked Hong Kong, the Philippines and Malaya.

The British should have evacuated Hong Kong, but, instead, they sent in reinforcements. They hoped the place would resist for 100 days, but it fell in ten. The men of the garrison went into Japanese prisoner-of-war camps where they suffered horribly.

The Americans had more chance of defending the Philippines, and General Douglas MacArthur was determined to resist vigorously. However, the Japanese had control of the sea and the air, and their army of invasion drove an American and Filipino force twice its size into the Bataan Peninsula. They captured it, in spite of its powerful defences, in May 1942, and the island fortress of Corregidor soon afterwards.

In Malaya a comparatively small but excellent Japanese army faced a poorly trained force of mixed nationalities — British, Australian, Indian and Malayan. Singapore, at the tip of Malaya, was a vital naval base and to help defend it, Churchill had sent out the battleship *Prince of Wales* and the battle-cruiser *Repulse*. Japanese aircraft sank both these ships on 10 December 1941. In Malaya, the Japanese outflanked one British defensive position after another, until they reached Singapore Island. In February 1942 its garrison of 80 000 surrendered.

Soon after they began the invasion of Malaya, the Japanese struck north against Burma. They hoped to guard the rear of their troops in Malaya, complete the ring they were drawing round China, and encourage the people of India to rebel against the British. They realized the first two of these aims, and had some success with the third.

The Japanese army in Burma was only 35 000 strong, but it was so skilled in jungle warfare that by early May it had fought its way to the Indian frontier. Then the monsoon came, which stopped the campaign for the time being.

The British now had visions of the Japanese swarming over the Indian Ocean as they had done over the Pacific. Accordingly, they took Madagascar from Vichy France and sent a fleet of mainly obsolete warships to Colombo, in Ceylon. The Japanese had never dreamed of going into Madagascar and decided, reluctantly, that they did not have enough men to take Ceylon. However, the British fleet there was too tempting to ignore, so they attacked and destroyed it.

To round off their empire the Japanese needed the Dutch East Indies with their valuable oilfields. Again, they prepared the way with a naval victory, defeating a mixed force of British and Dutch ships at the Battle of the Java Sea. Soon they had occupied all the Dutch East Indies, and most of New Guinea as well. It now looked as if they might invade Australia, but they did not have enough troops for that.

In less than six months after Pearl Harbor the Japanese had realized their two main objectives. They had seized a large empire, and had thrown a strong defensive ring around their homeland. The cost had not been heavy, being 15 000 dead, 380 aircraft and four destroyers.

The Check to Japan

Having achieved all they wanted, the Japanese might have been wise to wait, on the defensive. However, they had won their victories so easily that they could not resist the temptation to go on. One plan was to capture the islands to the east of Australia, so cutting her off from America. As a first step they needed to complete the conquest of New Guinea, so they sent a fleet to attack Port Moresby. An American force fought it at the Battle of the Coral Sea. Both sides lost an aircraft-carrier, and both withdrew after the engagement, so neither side could claim a victory. It was the first major battle the Japanese had not won decisively. Also, it was the pattern for the naval battles that were to come. The two fleets had been 150 km apart and had fought with what was, in effect, a new kind of long-range artillery — aeroplanes operating from carriers. The traditional warships were out of date, including the most powerful battleships.

Another plan the Japanese had was to capture Midway Island. Admiral Yamamoto hoped that an attack there would draw the American Pacific Fleet into action so that he could destroy it. The Japanese put to sea in force, but they were over-confident. They made a number of mistakes of which the most serious was to have all their aircraft rearming on the decks of their carriers at the same time. 'Dauntless' dive-bombers caught them just before they were due to take off, and sank four Japanese carriers. The Americans lost only one carrier.

The Battle of Midway Island was the turning-point of the war in the Pacific. Pearl Harbor was avenged and the navies of the two sides were, once again, roughly equal. The Americans had time to build their new 'Essex' class carriers, and only nine months after Midway they had nineteen carriers in the Pacific, and the Japanese ten.

Curtiss Helldivers aboard a U.S. carrier

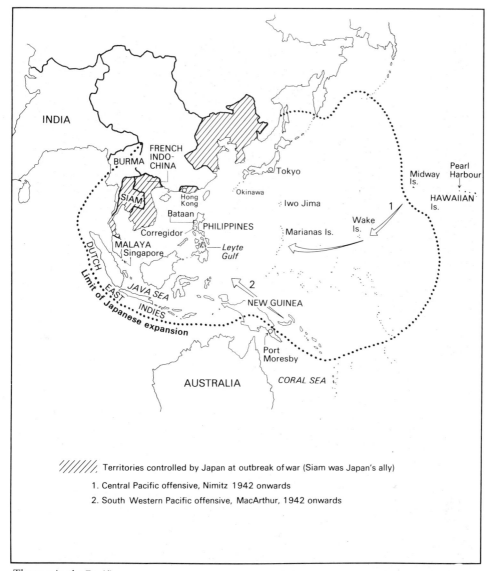

INDIA

FRENCH INDO-CHINA

BURMA

Tokyo

Pearl Harbour

Midway Is.

Okinawa

HAWAIIAN Is.

SIAM

Hong Kong

Iwo Jima

Bataan

Wake Is.

PHILIPPINES

Marianas Is.

Corregidor

MALAYA

Leyte Gulf

Singapore

1

DUTCH

JAVA SEA

2

EAST

NEW GUINEA

INDIES

Limit of Japanese expansion

Port Moresby

AUSTRALIA

CORAL SEA

////// Territories controlled by Japan at outbreak of war (Siam was Japan's ally)

1. Central Pacific offensive, Nimitz 1942 onwards

2. South Western Pacific offensive, MacArthur, 1942 onwards

The war in the Pacific

The Defeat of Japan

During the first few months of the war America was fighting with just her peacetime army and navy. Soon, though, she gathered her strength and, as her economy was sixteen times as powerful as Japan's, she was bound to win. The only thing that saved Japan for a time was that Roosevelt had agreed with Churchill on a 'Germany first' policy, so America made her main effort in Europe. Even so the allies were able to take the offensive in the Far East. They planned three attacks. The British were to drive the Japanese from Burma: in the Pacific General Douglas MacArthur was to advance from the south-east, while General Nimitz was to advance from the east, both these American forces converging on the Philippines.

First we will see what happened in Burma. There was some fighting on the Indian border in 1943 and early in 1944. Then General Slim mounted an attack with an Anglo-Indian force, and by January 1945 had reconquered the whole of Burma. This campaign was remarkable for several reasons, but two were especially interesting. In the first place, it was the only one of the war in which an advancing army was supplied entirely from the air. Burma is a land of mountains and jungles, but this did not delay the British as it might have done because American transport planes brought them all they needed. Secondly, there was the 'Long Range Penetration Corps' led by General Orde Wingate. This force was named the 'Chindits' after a mythical beast. Wingate hoped to cause confusion among the Japanese by attacking them deep inside their front line. In fact, he did very little damage to them.

In the Pacific, the Americans soon realized that if they fought systemati- cally from one island to the next the war would be long and bloody. They decided instead to go 'leapfrogging'. That meant by-passing powerful Japanese forces, so cutting them off and leaving them, as MacArthur said, to 'wither on the vine'. Using this strategy MacArthur soon cleared the south-east Pacific. For his part, Nimitz won the Battle of the Philippine Sea and took the Marianas Islands. By now, the Japanese were short of trained pilots, so the American airmen met little opposition. At what they called the 'Great Marianas Turkey Shoot', the Americans shot down 218 enemy aircraft for the loss of 29.

Both MacArthur and Nimitz were now ready to attack the Philippines, and the Japanese mustered every ship they had for the defence. If they lost the Philippines they would be cut off from the oilfields of the Dutch East Indies. Then, their fleet would either have to stay in the south and run out of ammunition or stay in the north and run out of fuel.

In October 1944 there was a four-day battle in Leyte Gulf. It was remark- able in a number of ways. It was the largest naval engagement of all time, involving 282 ships and hundreds of aircraft. At Jutland there were 250 ships and 5 seaplanes. Also, it showed yet again the importance of the aircraft-carrier. The Japanese had a brand new monster battleship of 37 000 tonnes, the *Musashi*. She was said to be unsinkable, but sink she did after nineteen hits by torpedoes and seventeen by bombs. In addition, it was at this battle that the Japanese first used kamikaze attacks. 'Kamikaze' means 'divine wind' and was the name given to a typhoon that had destroyed a Mongol fleet invading Japan in 1281. The Japanese commanders realized they would have to organize a kamikaze of their own, so they asked for pilots who would crash aircraft loaded with high-explosives on the decks of American vessels. There was no shortage of volunteers but they could not repeat the miracle of 1281.

The Battle of Leyte Gulf was a complete victory for the Americans, who destroyed the Japanese navy almost entirely.

The American army reconquered the Philippines by January 1945, after a lot of hard fighting. It then took the islands of Iwo Jima and Okinawa.

The Collapse of Japan

The American's stranglehold on Japan was now complete. Not only had they taken the Philippines, but their submarines had sunk most of Japan's merchant fleet. Moreover, the Americans had bases close to Japan, as well as complete control of the air and their Boeing B29 Superfortresses raided constantly. For example, during ten days in March 1945 they dropped a total of 10 000 tonnes of incendiary bombs on Tokyo and four other towns, devastating them all. Many of Japan's cities lay in ruins, her industry ground to a halt and her people were starving, so surrender could be only a matter of time.

By now, however, America had two atom bombs and President Truman decided to use them. On 6 August 1945 the first fell on Hiroshima. It killed 80 000 people, and many others suffered from the horrible effects of radiation. The second bomb fell on Nagasaki, three days later. Truman's excuse was that the atom bombs shortened the war, and saved lives that would otherwise have been lost in an invasion of Japan. However, Japan's collapse was certain without an invasion, as Truman knew quite well. Possibly he wanted to defeat the Japanese before the Russians arrived — they had already occupied Manchuria. Possibly he wanted to frighten the Russians with a display of American power. Certainly the Japanese did not rush to make peace, even after the bombing of Nagasaki. It was not until 2 September 1945 that General MacArthur accepted their surrender.

The Japanese surrender

WORK SECTION — The Second World War

Pearl Harbor

Questions

1. Where is Pearl Harbor?
2. What fleet was based on it?
3. Why did the Japanese wish to destroy it?
4. When did they launch their attack?
5. How successful was it?
6. What advantage did they gain from their victory?

British Defeats in North Africa

Document One

The war correspondent of the *Daily Express*, Alan Moorehead, gives his view of the fighting in 1942:

It was in the control of tanks that the Germans revealed their greatest gifts. They were tank technicians pure and simple. They were the élite of the Afrika Korps, as compact, as neat and efficient as a team of acrobats. They had been trained to the nth degree and as a group, a group that could be controlled very nearly as easily as one tank. They were self-contained. Stukas, tanks, recovery vehicles, petrol waggons, anti-tank gunners, all went forward together and their senior officers were often in the van. The co-operation between the tanks and the anti-tank gunners was their best achievement. At this moment the German tanks and the gunners are evolving a new technique in armoured warfare, for the truth is that the Germans no longer use tanks to attack equal enemy armoured forces. Let me repeat that — they do not attack with tanks. On the Alamein

Line and outside Tobruk they avoided tank action unless they greatly outnumbered us. They preferred always to send out scouts by land and air to plot the positions of our anti-tank guns. Then they used aircraft and infantry to attack those guns. They used artillery too. Then when the British guns were silenced or partially silenced, and the land-mines lifted, they used their tanks to mop up the battlefield, and break through to the unprotected British infantry.

We could not hope to marshal and drive our tanks as the Germans did. We were simply not trained to it and they had years of practice.

(*A Year of Battle* — Alan Moorehead)

Document Two

Sir Winston Churchill replies to a motion of 'No Confidence in the Central Direction of the War' in the House of Commons, 2 July 1942:

The idea of the tank was a British conception. The use of armoured forces as they are now being used was largely French, as General de Gaulle's book shows. It was left to the Germans to convert those ideas to their own use. For three or four years before the war they were busily at work with their usual thoroughness upon the design and manufacture of tanks, and also upon the study and practice of armoured warfare.

One would have thought that, even if the Secretary of State for War of those days could not get the money for large-scale manufacture, he would at any rate have had full-sized working models made and tested out exhaustively, and the factories chosen and the jigs and gauges supplied, so that he could go into mass production of tanks and anti-tank weapons when the war began.

At the beginning of the war we had some 250 armoured vehicles, very few of which carried even a 2-pounder gun. Most of these were captured or destroyed in France. For more than a year, until Hitler attacked Russia, the threat of invasion hung over us, imminent, potentially mortal. We had to concentrate upon numbers, upon quantity instead of quality. That was a major decision to which I have no doubt we were rightly guided.

We had, at the time of Dunkirk, to concentrate upon numbers. We had to make thousands of armoured vehicles with which our troops could beat the enemy off the beaches when they landed and fight them in the lanes and fields of Kent or Norfolk.

When the first new tanks came out they had grievous defects, the correction of which caused delay, and this would have been avoided if the preliminary experiments on the scale of 12 inches to the foot had been carried out at an earlier period. How do you make a tank? People design it, they argue about it, they plan it and make it, and then you take the tank and test and re-test it. When you have got it absolutely settled then, and only then, you go into production. But we have never been able to indulge in the luxury of that precise and leisurely process. We have had to take it straight off the drawing board and go into full production, and take the chance of the many errors which the construction will show coming out after hundreds and thousands of them have been made.

(*The War Speeches of Sir Winston Churchill*)

Questions

1 What were the main events in the war in North Africa down to the time that these documents were written, in July 1942?
2 What does Moorehead say about the way the Germans controlled their tanks?
3 What units does he say worked together? Find out what Stukas were.
4 What was the technique the German tanks and gunners evolved? (See page 250.)
5 How did the Germans attack the British positions?
6 Why could the British not use the same methods?
7 How does Churchill say ideas on tank warfare developed before the war?
8 How many tanks did the British have at the beginning of the war?
9 Why were there so few? What, according to Churchill, should the Secretary of State for War have done?
10 What reason does Churchill give for the poor quality of British tanks?
11 Who is Churchill trying to blame for the defeats in North Africa? Was he guilty of any mistakes himself?
12 Who do you think gives the better reasons for the British defeats, Moorehead or Churchill?
13 The motion of 'No Confidence' was heavily defeated in the House of Commons, but how do you suppose it affected Churchill's thinking about North Africa? What steps did he take later in 1942?
14 Describe the war in Egypt in the autumn of 1942.

The Bombing of Germany

Documents One, Two and Three come from a book by Hitler's Minister of Armaments, Albert Speer:

Document One

I had early recognized that the war could have been decided in 1943 if, instead of vast but pointless area bombing, the planes had concentrated on the centres of armaments production. The first attempt was made — not by us but by the British air force — to influence the course of the war by destroying a single nerve centre of the war economy. On 17 May 1943 a mere nineteen bombers of the R.A.F. tried to strike at our whole armaments industry by destroying the hydroelectric plants of the Ruhr.

The report that reached me in the early hours of the morning was most alarming. The largest of the dams, the Mohne dam had been shattered and the reservoir emptied. A torrent of water had flooded the Ruhr Valley. The electrical installations at the pumping stations were soaked and muddied so that industry was brought to a standstill and the water supply of the population imperilled. That night, employing just a few bombers, the British came close to a success which would have been greater than anything they had achieved hitherto with the commitment of thousands of bombers.

A few days after this attack 7000 men, whom I had ordered from the Atlantic Wall, were at work repairing the dams. On 23 September 1943, in the nick of time before the beginning of the rains, the breach in the Mohne dam was closed. While we were engaged in rebuilding, the British air force missed its chance. A few bombs would have produced cave-ins at the exposed building sites, and a few fire bombs could have set the wooden scaffolding blazing.

(*Inside the Third Reich* — Albert Speer)

Document Two

The Raids on Hamburg
Our Western enemies launched five major attacks on a single big city — Hamburg — within a week, from 25 July to 2 August 1943.

277

The first attacks put the water-supply pipes out of action, so that in the subsequent bombings the fire department had no way of fighting the fires. Huge conflagrations created cyclone-like firestorms: the asphalt of the streets began to blaze: people were suffocated in their cellars or burned to death in the streets. The devastation of this series of air raids could be compared only with the effects of a major earthquake.

I informed Hitler that a series of attacks of this sort, extended to six more major cities, would bring Germany's armaments production to a total halt. 'You'll straighten all that out again,' he merely said.

Fortunately for us, a series of Hamburg-type raids was not repeated on such a scale on other cities. Thus the enemy once again allowed us to adjust ourselves to his strategy.

(op. cit.)

Document Three

American Daylight Raids
Within four days in February 1944 Schweinfurt, Steyr and Cannstatt were each subjected to two successive heavy attacks. Then followed raids on Erkner, Schweinfurt, and again Steyr. After only six weeks our production of bearings had been reduced to 29 per cent of what it had been before the air raids.

At the beginning of April 1944, however, the attacks on the ball-bearing industry ceased abruptly. Thus, the Allies threw away success when it was already in their hands. As it was, not a tank, plane or other piece of weaponry failed to be produced because of lack of ball bearings, even though such production had increased by 19 per cent from July 1943 to April 1944.

(op. cit)

Document Four

The British Air Offensive. An English Scientist remembers:
The boys who flew in the Lancasters were told that the Battle of Berlin was one of the decisive battles of the war and that they were winning it. I did not know how many of them believed what they were told. I knew only that what they were told was untrue. By January 1944, the battle was lost. I had seen the bomb patterns which showed bombs scattered over a disproportionately enormous area. The bomber losses were rising sharply. There was no chance that our continuing the offensive in this style could have any decisive effect on the war. It was true that Berlin contained a great variety of important war industries, but Bomber Command was

not attempting to find and attack these objectives individually. The squadrons merely showered incendiary bombs over the city, with a small fraction of high explosive bombs to discourage the fire fighters. Against this sort of attack, the defence could afford to be selective. Important factories were protected by fire-fighting teams who could deal quickly with incendiaries falling in vital areas. Civilian housing and shops could be left to burn. So it often happened that Bomber Command 'destroyed' a city, and photographic reconnaissance a few weeks later showed factories producing as usual amid the rubble of burnt homes.

(The Flying Coffins of Bomber Command — Freeman Dyson. Observer 28 October 1979)

Document Five

Message from Sir Winston Churchill to General Devers, Commander of the United States Army Air Force in Europe — 11 October 1943:
In broad daylight the crews of your bombers have fought their way through the strongest defence which the enemy could bring against them, and have ranged over the length and breadth of Germany, striking with deadly accuracy many of the most important hostile industrial installations and ports.

I am confident that with the ever-growing power of the Eighth Air Force, striking alternate blows with the Royal Air Force Bomber Command, we shall together inexorably beat the life out of industrial Germany, and thus hasten the day of final victory.

Questions

Document One

1 What kind of bombing does Speer say would have been most effective?
2 What raid did the British make on 17 May 1943? How successful was it?
3 How, according to Speer, should the British have followed up this raid? What, in fact, did they do?

Document Two

4 When were the main attacks on Hamburg? How successful were they?
5 What was Speer afraid would happen? What, in fact, did happen?

Document Three

6 Which towns did the Americans attack? Find them on a map.

7 Why were these towns important?

8 How successful were the raids at first? What happened in the end?

9 List the three ways in which Speer thought that the allied bombing offensive might have won the war.

Document Four

10 Which bombers attacked Berlin? What were their crews told?

11 What important targets were there in Berlin? Why were few of them hit?

12 What tactics did the bombers use?

13 What tactics did the defenders use? How effective were they?

Document Five

14 What does Churchill mean by saying that the American Air Force and the R.A.F. are striking 'alternate blows'?

15 When and where was it agreed that this should be the strategy?

16 What does Churchill hope the air offensive will do?

17 Why did this not happen?

18 When and why did the bombing of Germany become effective?

The Atomic Bomb

Document One

President Truman decides to use the atomic bomb:

A month before the test explosion of the atomic bomb the Joint Chiefs of Staff had laid their detailed plans for the defeat of Japan before me for approval. In all it had been estimated that it would require until the late fall of 1946 to bring Japan to her knees. All of us fully realized that the fighting would be fierce and the losses heavy. General Marshall told me that it might cost half a million American lives to force the enemy's surrender on his home ground.

The daily tragedy of a bitter war crowded in on us. We labored to construct a weapon of such overpowering force that the enemy could be forced to yield swiftly once we could resort to it. This was the primary aim of our secret and vast effort.

I set up a committee of top men and asked them to study with great care the implications the new weapon might have for us. It was their recommendation that the bomb should be used against the enemy as soon as it could be done. They recommended further that it should be

used without specific warning and against a target that would clearly show its devastating strength. It was their conclusion that no technical demonstration, such as over a deserted island would be likely to bring the war to an end. It had to be used against an enemy target.

Let there be no mistake about it. I regarded the bomb as a military weapon and never had any doubt that it should be used. The top military advisers recommended its use, and when I talked to Churchill he unhesitatingly told me that he favored the use of the atomic bomb if it might aid to end the war.

In deciding to use this bomb I wanted to make sure that it would be used in a manner prescribed by the laws of war. That meant I wanted it dropped on a military target. Kyoto, though favoured by General Arnold as a center of military activity was eliminated when Secretary Stimson pointed out that it was a cultural and religious shrine of the Japanese.

(*Memoirs* — Harry S. Truman)

Document Two

Truman hears about the dropping of the atomic bomb:

On 6 August came the historic news that shook the world. I was eating lunch with members of the Augusta's crew when the watch officer handed me the following message:

> To the President
> From the Secretary of War
> Big bomb dropped on Hiroshima 5 August at 7.15 p.m. Washington time.
> First reports indicate complete success.

I was greatly moved. I telephoned Byrnes (the Secretary of State) aboard ship to give him the news and then said to the group of sailors around me, 'This is the greatest thing in history.'

(*Memoirs* — Harry S. Truman)

Document Three

Historians discuss the use of the atomic bomb:

G. Alperovitz — author of Atomic Diplomacy has examined in detail the military reasons for Truman's decision. He notes that '. . . before the atomic bomb was dropped each of the Joint Chiefs of Staff advised that it was highly likely that Japan could be forced to surrender unconditionally without the use of the bomb and without an invasion.' He concludes that the decision was determined by political objectives: 'Mr Byrnes did not argue that it was necessary to use the bomb against the cities of Japan in *order to win the war. Mr Byrnes's view was that our possessing and demonstrating the bomb would make Russia more manageable in Europe.' The American leaders certainly believed that it had strengthened their bargaining power. Even before the test at Alamogordo, Truman had predicted: 'If it explodes, as I think it will, I'll have a hammer on those boys!' (the Russians).*

(*The Cold War* — Hugh Higgins)

Questions

Document One

1 According to Truman, what advice did the Chiefs of Staff give him about the length of the war against Japan? How many American lives did General Marshall say might be lost?
2 What does Truman say was the main aim in making the bomb?
3 How did Truman's advisers say the bomb should be used?
4 Who else advised Truman to use the bomb? Why?
5 How does Truman say he selected the target for the bomb?
6 On which Japanese towns were atomic bombs dropped?

Document Two

7 When was the first atomic bomb dropped?
8 What was Truman's reaction?

Document Three

9 According to Alperovitz what advice did the Chiefs of Staff give on ending the war with Japan?
10 What does he quote James Byrnes as saying?
11 How did Truman feel the atomic bomb would help him?
12 How did the American use of the atomic bomb affect Stalin's foreign policy?

Map Questions — The War in Europe 1939–45

1 Name States 1–20, towns a–k, rivers v and w, regions y and z, isthmus P and province Q.
2 When did the Germans invade State 1? What happened to the area east of the line marked ._._._._.?
3 What vital raw material did Germany get from the north of State 2?

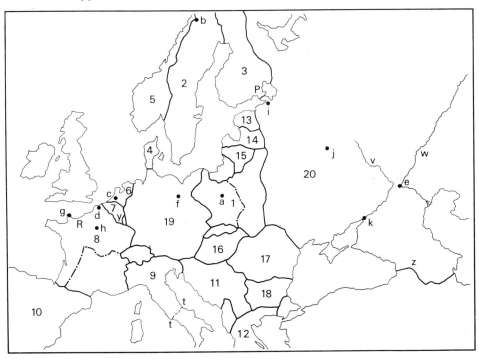

The war in Europe 1939–45

4 Which way was it transported (a) in summer, (b) in winter?

5 When and why did Russia attack State 3?

6 How did this attack help provoke the invasion of States 4 and 5?

7 Describe what happened at town b during this campaign.

8 When were States 6, 7 and 8 invaded by the Germans?

9 What happened to town C?

10 Describe region y. What attack was mounted from there in May 1940?

11 What happened near town d early in June 1940?

12 What State was created south and east of the line marked .._.._.._.?

13 When was it occupied by the Germans? Why?

14 When did State 9 enter the war?

15 What part did State 10 play in the war?

16 When and why did the Germans invade States 11 and 12?

17 Indicate the States and regions occupied by Russia before Germany attacked her.

18 Indicate, roughly, how far the Germans advanced into Russia in 1941.

19 Why did Hitler wish to take region Z? How far did his armies advance?

20 Describe what happened to town e during the winter 1942–3.

21 What happened at town a in 1944?

22 When did the Russians capture town f?

23 Which allied commander had charge of the invasion of coast R in 1944?

24 Why was it important for the allies to capture town g?

25 Which army captured town h in 1944?

26 What battle was fought as the result of a German attack from region y in December 1944?

27 When did the allies invade State 9?

28 Name the defensive line t–t.

29 When was it breached?

30 When did the war end in State 9?

From the Invasion of Poland to the Battle of Britain

Questions

1 How long did it take the Germans to defeat the Poles? How many dead did they lose?

2 Give five reasons why the Poles were defeated.

3 Why was there a 'phoney war' after the fall of Poland?

4 Why was Norway important for Germany? What did the British and French plan to do about Russia's invasion of Finland? Why did this alarm Hitler?

5 When did the Germans invade Denmark and Norway? What did they succeed in doing on the first day? What did the British and French succeed in doing? Why did they withdraw their troops?

6 What losses did the German navy have? What had the Germans gained from the capture of Norway and Denmark?

7 What political change was there in Britain?

8 Which German general drew up the plans for the invasion of Holland, Belgium and France?

9 When did the invasion begin? What happened to Holland? What plan did the British and French think the Germans were following? How did they react?

10 Why did the French not expect an attack from the Ardennes? Who commanded the German troops here?

11 Describe Guderian's attack through the Ardennes.

12 What had Guderian achieved by 20 May? What opportunity did Guderian's two-day halt give the British?

13 What may have been the reason for halting the German panzers?

14 Describe the fall of France. When and where was the armistice signed?

15 What were the terms of the armistice? Why was Hitler less harsh than he might have been? How well did his policy work? Who led the Free French Movement?

16 When did Mussolini declare war? Why?

17 Why did Hitler order 'Operation Sealion'? What preparations were made? Why did the Germans need command of the air?

18 What was the importance of the fighter aircraft? How did the fighter strength of the Luftwaffe and R.A.F. compare?

19 When was the Battle of Britain? Describe its four stages.

20 Give six reasons why the British won the Battle of Britain, four on the British side, and two on the German.

Give an account of the war until September

1941 under the headings: The Invasion of Poland/The Invasion of Denmark and Norway/The Invasion of Holland, Belgium and France/Italy Enters the War/The Battle of Britain

The War in the Mediterranean

Questions

1 How would control of the Mediterranean have helped the Germans? Why did the Germans fail to make a serious effort there? Why did they fight there at all?
2 Why did Hitler want peace in the Balkans? How did Mussolini disturb it?
3 Why did Hitler invade Yugoslavia?
4 How did Churchill try to help Greece? What happened?
5 Why was the invasion of Crete an interesting military operation? What happened? Why did the Germans never attempt another operation like it?
6 How may the campaign in the Balkans have affected the war as a whole?
7 What kind of war did Mussolini plan? Why did it seem he would succeed?
8 What naval victories did the British win?
9 What victories did the British win in East Africa?
10 Describe O'Connor's victory in North Africa? What spoiled it?
11 Describe the Western Desert. What was the point of fighting there?
12 Explain why the British forces always outnumbered those of the Axis powers in North Africa.
13 How did the British and German tanks compare? Name a particularly good German anti-tank gun.
14 Contrast the organization of British and German armies.
15 What tactics did the British army employ?
16 What tactics did Rommel use?
17 What problem did Rommel have? How did the British take advantage of it?
18 With the aid of a sketch map describe the war in the Western Desert from March 1941 until 1942.
19 How did the British and Axis forces compare at El Alamein?
20 When was the Battle of El Alamein? What kind of battle did Montgomery fight? Why did Rommel escape?

21 Why did the British and Americans decide to invade French North Africa?
22 Why did Hitler and Mussolini send heavy reinforcements to Tunisia? What happened to these troops?
23 What plan did Churchill and Roosevelt make at Casablanca?
24 What was 'Operation Husky'? What was the plan? What went wrong with it?
25 Describe Mussolini's fall from power.
26 When did the allies invade Italy? What did the Italians do at once?
27 Why did the Germans find it easy to defend Italy? What was the most famous of their defensive lines? How did the Americans try to turn it? When was it broken?
28 What became the aim of the allies in Italy? What was 'Operation Anvil'? What unfortunate result did it have?
29 How far was the allied invasion of Italy a success?
30 What did the Germans do for Mussolini after the Italians deposed him? What happened to him, in the end?

Describe the war in the Mediterranean under the headings: The War in the Balkans and Crete/The Italian Defeats in Africa/Rommel's Campaigns/'Operation Torch'/The Invasion of Italy/The End of Mussolini

The Bombing of Germany and the Battle of the Atlantic

Questions

The Bombing of Germany

1 How did the British and the Germans try to hurt each other after the Battle of Britain?
2 How did the British hope to use their bombers? Name two men who believed in this plan.
3 How was Bomber Command improved during the course of the war?
4 Why did the British switch to night bombing? What was the main problem with it? What name did the British give it?
5 When was the first 1000 bomber raid? When did the attacks reach a peak?
6 When and why were the raids called off? How had they affected Germany?

7 How did Bomber Command help 'Operation Overlord'?

8 What agreement was made at Casablanca? Why were the American daylight raids a success, in the end?

9 What was agreed should be the purpose of the bombing, after the fall of France? What, in fact, happened?

10 What were the results of the bombing offensive (a) for Germany, (b) for Britain.

The Battle of the Atlantic

1 Why was it essential for the allies to win the Battle of the Atlantic?

2 What new type of mine did the Germans develop? How did the British deal with it?

3 What happened to the *Admiral Graf Spee* and the *Bismarck*?

4 From where did German aircraft operate? Why were they dangerous?

5 How many U-boats did Germany have at the beginning of the war? How many did she have at the end? How were U-boats improved?

6 Who had charge of the U-boats? What tactics did he develop for them?

7 How much escort could the British give their convoys at first? How was this improved? How did the Americans help?

8 What new equipment did the British develop?

9 Who developed new tactics for the British? What were these tactics?

10 Why did the convoys lack air cover at first? How did the American Catalinas help? What was the 'black gap'? How was it closed?

11 Why did the U-boats do little at first? Why were they able to have a 'happy time' after July 1941? When and why did it end?

12 When was the crisis in the Battle of the Atlantic? How successful were the Germans? Why?

13 When were the U-boats defeated? Why?

14 What was the purpose of the Arctic convoys? Why were they especially dangerous? Why were they unnecessary?

Give an account of the bombing of Germany under the headings: Aims/Development of the Offensive/Conclusion

Give an account of the Battle of the Atlantic under the headings: The German Weapons/Allied Counter-measures/The Course of the Battle against the U-boats/The Arctic Convoys

The War in Russia

Questions

1 How did Stalin try to make his country safer? How did he try to gain time?

2 Why did Hitler wish to invade Russia?

3 What was the German plan of attack? What did the Germans hope to achieve before winter?

4 When did the Germans attack?

5 How far did Army Group North advance? What did it fail to do?

6 How far did Army Group Centre advance? How much time did Hitler waste? What, in the end, did he decide to do? What victory did his armies win in the south?

7 What victory did Army Group Centre win? Why did it fail to take Moscow? Which Russian general counterattacked? What saved the German armies from defeat?

8 How did the Germans spend the winter of 1941–2?

9 Where did Hitler decide to attack in 1942? How far did his armies advance? Why did he order an attack on Stalingrad? Why did the battle here become important?

10 What German army attacked Stalingrad? Who commanded it? What problems did it have?

11 Describe Zhukov's counter-attack. Why did the Germans not escape? When did they surrender?

12 What tactics did the Russians use to drive back the Germans?

13 What battle did the Russians win in 1943?

14 Why did the people of Warsaw rebel against the Germans in 1944? What did the Russians do? What conclusion did people in the West draw from that?

15 What happened in 1945?

16 Give four advantages the Germans had at first. Why were the Russians badly led?

17 Why did the Germans find it difficult to fight in Russia?

18 How superior were the Russians in numbers?
19 What weapons did the Russians have? Why were they able to go on manufacturing them? What help did the Americans send?
20 How did the quality of the Red Army improve?
21 Why did the Germans not win a quick victory in 1941?
22 What military mistake did Hitler often make?
23 What political mistake did Hitler make?
24 What proportion of Germany's land forces did the Russians defeat?

Give an account of the War in Russia under the headings: German Aims/Events of 1941/Events of 1943–45/Reasons for German Successes and Final Defeat

Operation Overlord

Questions

1 What commands were given to Eisenhower and Montgomery?
2 What alternatives did the allies have? What was their plan of invasion?
3 What three advantages did the allies have?What was their main problem?
4 When was D-Day? Where were the landings? How successful were they?
5 Name three things that went wrong on the German side.
6 What did Patton do on 31 July 1944? What mistake did Hitler make? What happened as a result?
7 What was 'Operation Anvil'? What result did it have?
8 How far had the allies advanced by early September? What good result did this have for London?
9 What opportunity did Montgomery have? Give two reasons why the allied armies halted.
10 What was 'Operation Market Garden'? Why did it fail?
11 Name three things that happened as the result of the war continuing until 1945.
12 What did Hitler hope to achieve by his attack in December 1944?
13 Explain why the Germans were so successful at first.
14 Why was the German advance halted? When?

15 Why did the Germans fight to the finish?
16 When did the British and Americans cross the Rhine? When did the war end?

Give an account of Operation Overlord under the headings: The Invasion Plan/The Invasion/The Liberation of France/The Battle of the Bulge/The Invasion of Germany

The War Against Japan

Questions

1 What were the main reasons for the high morale of the Japanese forces?
2 What equipment did the Japanese army have? What was one of their favourite tactics?
3 What disadvantage did the Japanese army have?
4 Why did the Japanese have command of the air, at first?
5 What had Admiral Yamamoto realized about the future of naval warfare? How did the strengths of the Japanese and allied navies compare? Which naval force did the Japanese fear most?
6 What were Japan's two aims at the beginning of the war?
7 When did the Japanese attack Pearl Harbor? What damage did they do? What piece of good luck did the Americans have? What advantages did the Japanese gain from the victory?
8 Describe the fall of Hong Kong.
9 Describe the fall of the Philippines.
10 Who opposed the Japanese in Malaya? What ships did the Japanese sink? When did Singapore fall?
11 Give three reasons why the Japanese invaded Burma.
12 How far had the Japanese advanced into Burma by May 1942?
13 What did the British do to stop the Japanese invading the Indian Ocean? What naval victory did the Japanese have?
14 Why did the Japanese want the Dutch East Indies? What successes did they have here?
15 What had the Japanese achieved in the first six months of their offensive?
16 What led to the Battle of the Coral Sea? Give two reasons why this battle was important.

17 Why did Yamamoto wish to capture Midway Island? Why did the Japanese lose the Battle of Midway Island?

18 Why was the Battle of Midway Island important?

19 Why was it certain the Americans would, eventually, defeat Japan? What saved her for a time? What three attacks did the allies plan?

20 Which British general reconquered Burma? When? Give two reasons why this campaign was remarkable.

21 What tactics did the Americans use in the Pacific? What successes did Mac-Arthur and Nimitz have?

22 Why did the Americans wish to take the Philippines?

23 Give three reasons why the Battle of Leyte Gulf was remarkable.

24 What was the result of the Battle of Leyte Gulf?

25 Why was Japan's position desperate by early 1945?

26 When and where did the Americans drop their atom bombs? What was Truman's excuse? What may have been his real reasons? When did Japan surrender?

Give an account of the War against Japan under the headings: Japan's Armed Forces/Japan's Conquests/The Check to Japan/The Defeat of Japan/The Collapse of Japan

Problems

1 Why did the Germans defeat the Poles and the French quickly and easily?

2 Why did the Germans invade Denmark and Norway? Why were they successful?

3 Why did the Germans lose the Battle of Britain? How did their defeat affect the future course of the war?

4 Why did the British take so long to defeat the Axis forces in North Africa?

5 How far was the allied attack on the 'soft underbelly' of the Axis a success?

6 Why did the allied air offensive against Germany fail to shorten the war significantly?

7 Why did the Germans lose the Battle of the Atlantic?

8 Why did the Germans win a number of battles in Russia in 1941? Why did they fail to secure a quick end to the war there?

9 Why were the Germans defeated in Russia, eventually?

10 Account for the allied successes in France in 1944. Why did they not end the war in that year?

11 What made Japan's leaders think she could defeat the United States of America?

12 Account for Japan's early victories and say why she was defeated in the end.

13 What was the importance of sea power in the Second World War?

14 What was the importance of air power in the Second World War?

15 What were the most serious mistakes made during the war by (a) the allies, (b) the Axis powers.

16 What part was played in the defeat of the Axis powers by (a) Britain, (b) the United States of America, (c) Russia.

17 Was the victory of the allied powers inevitable?

285

INTERNATIONAL RELATIONS
since 1945
—
THE WEST

Introduction

EVEN before the war was over, there was bad feeling between Russia and her Western allies. When it ended, and there was no longer a common enemy to fight, distrust and hatred grew. Rightly or wrongly, America and her friends thought that Communist Russia wanted to control the world, something they were determined to prevent. President Truman made this plain in a speech he gave in 1947. The statement of the 'Truman Doctrine' marked the beginning of a Cold War between Russia and the West.

In 1953 Stalin died, and by 1955 Nikita Khrushchev had come to power in the Soviet Union. Thanks largely to him, there was a thaw in the Cold War, but his efforts were spoiled by a number of crises, culminating in the Cuban missile crisis in 1962. Russia and America came close to fighting each other, and were so alarmed that they began to work for détente, that is, a better understanding. They seemed to make good progress, signing a number of agreements of which the last and the most important was the second Strategic Arms Limitation Treaty (SALT 2) of 1979. However, in December of that year, and before the American Senate could ratify this treaty, the Russians invaded Afghanistan. Progress towards détente ceased abruptly and at the time of writing, 1981, friendship between Russia and the West seems as far away as it ever did.

However, there have been hopeful changes in Western Europe. Partly for economic reasons, and partly through fear of Russia, most of the countries here are working for unity. The European Economic Community, or Common Market, has been particularly successful. There are many problems, and progress is slow, but there has been a remarkable change of attitude. For centuries the peoples of Western Europe were rivals, and fought from time to time: today, war between any of them is almost unthinkable.

Chapter Thirty-nine

The Peace Settlement

AFTER the First World War the leaders of the countries that had won met at Versailles and made a peace settlement. They argued a great deal, but they were able to reach decisions, in the end. After the Second World War Russia and her Western allies distrusted each other so much that they could not solve all the problems immediately. Some they had to postpone, and others are still with us. For example, there has never been a peace treaty with Germany.

That does not mean, though, that they did not try to agree. Churchill, Roosevelt and Stalin met at Teheran in 1943 and again at Yalta, in the Crimea, in 1945. Their chief aim was to make plans for the war, but they made others for the peace, as well. Soon afterwards Roosevelt died, and his Vice-President, Harry Truman, took his place. In Britain, the socialists won a general election, so Clement Attlee became Prime Minister, instead of Churchill. Truman and Attlee met Stalin at Potsdam, near Berlin, in 1945, just after the war ended. We must see what was decided at these three conferences.

Russia

You can see from the map how much territory Russia took. There was nothing Britain and America could do to prevent her, as the Red Army controlled it all.

Poland

Britain and France had gone to war to save Poland, and now it was over none of the Western Powers wanted her to fall into Russian hands. However, Russia had been invaded from Poland three times in the twentieth century, and Stalin was determined it should not happen again. One way was to make sure Poland had a government that was friendly to Russia, so he recognized a group of Communists called the Lublin Committee. Britain and America recognized the government Poland had had before the war, whose members were exiled in London. As a compromise, the Lublin Committee formed the government, but allowed some of the London Poles to join it. Also there were to be free elections as soon as possible. These have never been held.

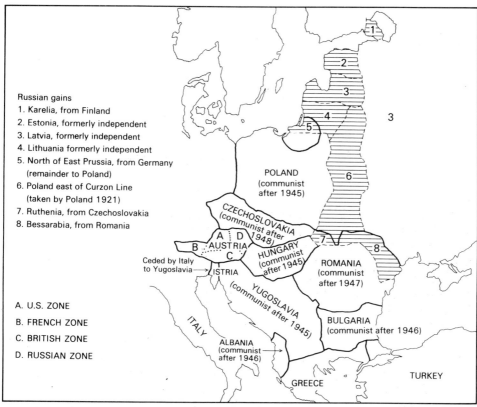

Russian gains
1. Karelia, from Finland
2. Estonia, formerly independent
3. Latvia, formerly independent
4. Lithuania formerly independent
5. North of East Prussia, from Germany
   (remainder to Poland)
6. Poland east of Curzon Line
   (taken by Poland 1921)
7. Ruthenia, from Czechoslovakia
8. Bessarabia, from Romania

A. U.S. ZONE

B. FRENCH ZONE

C. BRITISH ZONE

D. RUSSIAN ZONE

Changes in Eastern Europe after the Second World War

Poland's new frontiers 1945

289

Frontiers were a problem. Russia took everything up to the Curzon Line, so, as compensation, Poland had most of East Prussia and all German territory on her side of the River Oder and its tributary, the Neisse. Remembering how Hitler had used minorities to cause trouble, the Poles then drove out all Germans living within their frontiers. Czechoslovakia and other East European countries did the same. Sixteen million Germans were expelled, and two million of them died on their journey to the West.

Germany

The allies had insisted on unconditional surrender, so the Germans had to do exactly as they were told.

In the first place there were to be the 'Four D's' — De-Nazification, Demilitarization, Disarmament, and Democratization. As we shall see, only the first of these was successful.

Next, Germany was divided into four zones of occupation — the Russian, the American, the British and the French. Berlin, too, was divided in the same way, even though it was 160 km inside the Russian zone. Each zone had a military commander, and the four of them sat as the Allied Control Commission, which was to make any decisions needed for Germany as a whole. Also, the country was to be one economic unit, which meant its industrial goods and farm produce could be sold freely in every zone. This was especially important for the Americans and the British, since their zones had many large cities, but not enough farmland to feed all the people in them.

Germany was to pay reparations, each country taking what it wanted from its own zone. However, as Russia had suffered more than the others, the Western Powers agreed to dismantle a number of factories in their zones and send her the machinery and equipment.

Finally, war criminals were put on trial. Twenty-one leading Nazis were tried at Nuremberg. Eleven were hanged, eight were jailed and two acquitted. Many less important criminals were tried in other courts, first of all by the allies, but, in later years, by the West German government.

Germany's Allies

The Potsdam Conference set up a Council of Foreign Ministers to make peace with the countries that had fought on Germany's side during the war, namely Italy, Hungary, Bulgaria, Romania and Finland. The result was the Treaties of Paris of 1947. All these States had to outlaw their Fascist Parties, limit their armed forces and pay reparations. Romania and Finland ceded territory to Russia: Italy gave much of Istria to Yugoslavia, as well as losing all her colonial empire.

The United Nations Organizaton

This began as a wartime alliance but was kept on to replace the League of Nations. Its story is told in Chapter 49.

Zones of Occupation in Germany

German civilians leave Aachen

So much, then, was agreed at the end of the war, but there was no peace treaty with Japan, Austria or Germany. We will look at each country in turn.

Japan

Peace was eventually made with Japan by the Treaty of San Francisco in 1951. America arranged this, largely to annoy the Russians. Japan gave back all the territory she had taken since 1894. It had been reconquered anyway, so she had only to recognize that it had gone for good. In return, she became an independent country once again, instead of being ruled by the Americans. Forty-eight countries signed the treaty, but not the Russians.

Austria

When Khrushchev came to power in Russia, he was anxious to conciliate the West. Accordingly, in 1955 he agreed to the Austrian State Treaty. Austria, like Germany, had been divided into four zones, but now the occupying powers withdrew. In return, Austria promised she would always remain neutral.

Germany

Germany was the most difficult problem of all. None the less it was expected that one day Russia, America, Britain and France would withdraw, and that a reunited Germany would sign a peace treaty with them, just as had happened with Austria. However, Germany has not been reunited and is today not one country but two. Consequently, it is impossible for her to sign a peace treaty. We shall see how the problem of Germany has a great deal to do with the Cold War between Russia and the West.

Chapter Forty

The Cold War

By a 'Cold War' we mean a conflict between countries who do all they can to injure each other, without actually fighting. Before seeing how it began we must look at the aims of the Russians and the Americans. Both were idealistic and, at the same time, practical.

The Russian leaders were Communists. They believed in the teachings of Karl Marx and Lenin, in much the same way that Christians believe in the Bible. They were sure that Communism was the best hope for the human race and that one day the whole world would accept it. For many Russians, though, that lay far in the future. Stalin, especially, knew he must be realistic. He thought it best to forget about world Communism for the time being, and concentrate on making Russia herself strong. This was his policy of 'Communism in one country' which he had followed before the war. He was certainly not going to change it after the war when there was an enormous amount of damage to repair. Stalin was also concerned about security. During the war 20 million Russians had died and he thought one of the best ways to make his country safe was to keep her enemies at arm's length. That meant controlling as much of the territory around her frontiers as possible, especially in Europe.

The Americans were idealists as well, for they believed in democracy. They saw that Communism was not democratic, so they were determined to stop it spreading. Further, they imagined that Stalin's every move was a step towards world revolution, and failed to understand that most of the time he was on the defensive. However, the Americans had practical aims as well. They remembered the Depression of the 1930s and to stop any-thing like that happening again, they wanted to turn the world into one huge market for American goods. They thought democratic countries would trade with them whereas Communist ones would not. Here then, was another good reason to stop the spread of Communism.

The Beginnings of the Cold War

Even before the war ended, the allies began to disagree. You will remember that in 1944 the Russians stood by while the Germans put down the rebellion in Warsaw, and this greatly angered the Western Powers. For his part, Stalin was suspicious because the British and the Americans were

Through Hamburg come supplies for Germany

slow to invade France. He thought they were waiting until the Germans had weakened Russia so much that when the war was over they would have everything their own way. Indeed, it was only having a common enemy that held the allies together, and as soon as they had defeated Germany, they began to quarrel in earnest.

There was disagreement at the Potsdam Conference. The details need not concern us. The main reason why they were important was that they persuaded President Truman that Russia would never listen to reason but would have to be made to agree by force.

Next, the Western Powers were angry because the Russians were determined to keep control of the countries of eastern and south-eastern Europe that they had occupied at the end of the war. Here was a typical misunderstanding. The West was sure that it was all part of the plot to spread Communism in the world. Stalin was almost certainly thinking much more of putting a buffer between his enemies and his own country.

In Germany there was trouble over reparations. The Russians were supposed to send food from their zone to the big industrial towns in the West, but they said there was none to spare. The Americans and British were unwilling to starve large numbers of Germans to death, so they had to send food themselves. At the same time they were dismantling factories and despatching the machinery to Russia, as had been agreed at Potsdam.

They were quick to realize that if the Germans kept their factories they would be able to earn the money to buy food for themselves. They compared Germany to a cow, and Britain and America to two farmers who were feeding her. Meanwhile a third farmer, Russia, was milking her. The Western Powers stopped delivering machinery and the Russians were greatly annoyed.

Finally, there was fear on both sides. The Americans had dropped their atom bombs as much to frighten the Russians as to defeat the Japanese. In this they succeeded, and Stalin kept millions of men under arms. The Americans saw that if there was a war they might destroy a number of Russian cities, but they would never stop the Red Army from advancing to the Atlantic.

In little more than a year after the end of the war the Russians and their former allies were quarrelling. Churchill summed up the position in a speech he made at Fulton, Missouri. He said, 'From Stettin on the Baltic to Trieste on the Adriatic an iron curtain has descended across the Continent.' The final breach was not far away.

The Truman Doctrine, 1947

Soon after the Germans left Greece the Communists there started a rebellion. For a time, the British helped the Greek government to fight it, but by 1947 there was an economic crisis in Britain and it was not possible to keep British troops in Greece, or indeed, in Turkey, which they had also promised to help. Accordingly, they told the Americans they were going to withdraw from both countries.

Not surprisingly, President Truman was afraid that Greece and Turkey would fall under Communist control, and he was worried about the whole of Western Europe. There were strong Communist Parties in Italy and France. What if they were to seize power and call on the Red Army for help? Russia would have a vast empire stretching from the Atlantic to the Pacific and would be more than a match for the United States. Truman was determined this should not happen.

There seemed no hope of winning back those countries, like Poland, that had already fallen, but at least Communism should be prevented from spreading further. The best way to do that would be for America to help those governments who were against Communism.

In March 1947, Truman made a speech to Congress. He said, 'I believe that it must be the policy of the United States to support free peoples who are resisting subjugation by armed minorities or by outside pressures.' This became known as the Truman Doctrine. The President made no mention of Russia or of Communism, but everyone knew what he meant. The Truman Doctrine was the declaration of the Cold War.

Marshall Aid, 1948

As well as a promise of military help, the American government decided to give European countries large sums of money. This was called 'Marshall

Aid', because it was the American Secretary of State, George Marshall, who presented the plan to Congress.

The idea was to help Western Europe recover from the war. Her people were slow to start their factories working again, because they did not have the money to buy raw materials. Marshall Aid would provide that money. Once this was under way the countries would be able to export some of the goods they made, and earn the money to buy raw materials for themselves. Like a bicycle at the top of a hill they only needed a friendly push to start moving.

Churchill described Marshall Aid as 'the most unselfish act in history', but in fact, it was in America's interest that Europe should be prosperous. In the first place she would become a good trading partner: secondly, she would be strong, and stand like a shield between America and Russia: thirdly, and most important, her people would be contented, so they would not become Communists. Marshall Aid and the Truman Doctrine went together. As Truman himself said, they were 'two halves of the same walnut'.

The Americans did not give help without any strings attached. Countries who wanted Marshall Aid had to suggest worthwhile projects for the Americans to approve. They also had to match the Americans contribution with one of the same size, from their own resources. Finally they had to agree to work together, which they did through the Organization for European Economic Co-operation (O.E.E.C.).

From 1948 to 1952 America gave $13 000 million in Marshall Aid. Britain had most with $3176 million, France came next with $2705 million and West Germany third with $1389 million. To begin with, the Americans sent animal foodstuffs and fertilizers and later, machinery, fuel and raw materials. The plan was a success. The Western European countries increased their output 25 per cent in the first two years, by which time they were all producing more than had done in 1938. By 1952 they were well able to manage on their own, and did not need American help.

The Cold War Intensifies

While the Americans were making sure Western Europe stayed on their side, Stalin strengthened his hold in the East. In 1947, as an answer to the Truman Doctrine, he organized the Cominform. This was to ensure that all European Communist Parties worked together, including those in the West.

There were changes in Poland, Romania, Hungary and Bulgaria. All had coalition governments headed by Communists, but during 1947 Stalin drove the non-Communists from office. Not content with that, he also purged any Communists he thought might be disloyal to him. Some were killed, others were imprisoned while the lucky ones fled to the West.

There were changes, too, in Czechoslovakia. Here there were no Russian soldiers which meant that after the war there were free elections. The Communists were the largest party, gaining 38 per cent of the votes, so they headed a coalition government with Klement Gottwald as Prime

Minister. The country did not prosper, and the Communists saw that in the next election they were going to lose a great many votes. Accordingly, in 1948, they seized power. Gottwald formed a government entirely of Communists, President Benes resigned and, shortly afterwards, the Foreign Minister Jan Masaryk fell to his death from an upstairs window. Whether he jumped, or whether he was pushed is not known.

How far was Stalin involved? He massed Russian troops on the frontiers but apart from that, there is no evidence that he did anything. None the less, people in the West saw the loss of Czechoslovakia as yet another part of the Communist plot to control the world.

One country in Eastern Europe where Stalin did not have his way was Yugoslavia. Here there was a Communist government under Marshal Tito, although there were no Russian troops. Yugoslavia joined the Cominform, but Tito made it plain that he would not obey Stalin's orders. Accordingly, in 1948, Yugoslavia was expelled from the Cominform for 'unfriendliness'. It is significant that the Russians did not invade. Clearly, Stalin was unwilling to risk a war by sending the Red Army into lands it did not already occupy. Instead, he accepted the loss of Yugoslavia.

Germany

America and Russia had quite different plans for Germany. The Russians still feared her greatly so they wanted her united but completely under their control. They hoped that the Americans, the British and the French would withdraw so that the German Communists could seize power, and so that the Iron Curtain could move forward to the Rhine. Also, Russia was still recovering from the war, so she wanted to go on taking reparations. America, on the other hand, had no fear of Germany. She wanted West Germany to recover and become a useful ally against the Russians.

These views were so different that it was impossible to reach agreement. As a result, each side did as it pleased with the area it controlled. In East Germany the Russians put Communists in power and took reparations, while in West Germany the Americans helped with Marshall Aid.

Trouble began with the reform of the currency in the western zones in June 1948. The old Reichsmarks had fallen so much in value that people needed a great many to buy even the simplest things. The Americans, British and French decided to have a new currency in their zones, which they called the Deutschmark. One new mark was worth ten of the old, so the Germans in the western zones had less arithmetic to do. The change was not really much more important than that, but the Russians read a good deal into it. Germany now had two currencies, one in the eastern zone and another in the west. That seemed to mean that America was determined to divide Germany. Why should she wish to do that? The Russians feared that America would turn West Germany against them.

Next, America, Britain and France introduced the new currency into their own zones of Berlin. Berlin was the city the Russians wanted to be the capital of a united, Communist Germany. They were angry, so in defiance they closed the roads and railways from the west.

297

What could the Americans do now? They were determined not to abandon West Berlin, but they dared not risk a war by trying to force their way through. Instead, they and the British organized a massive airlift. The U.S.A.F. and the R.A.F. carried 2½ million tonnes of supplies to Berlin, most of it coal. Indeed, more coal went by air than would normally have gone by rail. Stalin realized the Americans would not give way, and after ten months he re-opened the roads and railways. This was in May 1949.

Almost certainly there had never been any hope of agreement over Germany, but the Berlin blockade made this plain for all to see. The only answer was to divide the country, permanently. In 1949 the three western zones became the Federal Republic of Germany. Its first Chancellor was Konrad Adenauer, a former opponent of Hitler, and a great statesman. As a Christian Democrat he was against Communism, and co-operated with the West. Perhaps his biggest achievement was to heal the breach with France. For centuries France and Germany had been enemies, but thanks to Adenauer they became firm friends.

For their part the Russians retaliated by turning their zone into the German Democratic Republic, making sure, of course, that it had a Communist government. Walter Ulbricht became Prime Minister.

Dr Konrad Adenauer

298

The North Atlantic Treaty Organization

Following the Communist coup in Czechoslovakia and the Russian blockade of Berlin, America decided to make a military alliance with her friends in the West. In 1949, the North Atlantic Treaty Organization was formed. Its members were the U.S.A., Canada, Britain, France, Belgium, Holland, Luxembourg, Italy, Iceland, Norway, Denmark and Portugal. Greece and Turkey joined in 1952. West Germany was not a member for the time being. All the states in N.A.T.O. agreed to go to war if any one of them was attacked. This was a new departure for the United States. From time to time, as in the two World Wars, she had come to the aid of countries that were already fighting, but she had never promised to do so before a war had actually begun. N.A.T.O., along with the Truman Doctrine and Marshall aid, showed that the United States realized she could not ignore the rest of the world as she had once tried to do. She would have to play a leading part in it, if she wanted to survive.

Chapter Forty-one

Co-existence and Crises 1955–62

New Men and New Policies — Khrushchev and Dulles

STALIN died in 1953, and Nikita Khrushchev became First Secretary of the Russian Communist Party in 1955. That made him, in effect, the ruler of Russia. In 1956 he caused a sensation when he denounced Stalin in a speech to the 20th Congress of the Soviet Communist Party. He not only promised changes in Russia, but also said he would follow a new foreign policy. He called this 'peaceful co-existence'. Khrushchev still believed that one day the whole world would be Communist, but he said that this could not come about through war, as Marx and Lenin had prophesied, since nuclear weapons were too dangerous to use. Instead, the Communist and capitalist countries should live together in peace until capitalism died a natural death. Khrushchev explained that in the West, it was not unusual for a vigorous young man to marry an old, wealthy woman, and for them to live together happily enough until the woman died. The young man then inherited all her money.

Khrushchev also said there could be 'different roads to socialism'. This was meant to please the satellite states. Stalin had made them do exactly as he wanted, and had made sure they were ruled by men who would obey him. Khrushchev meant to give the satellites more freedom.

The 'thaw' in the Cold War had begun even before Khrushchev made his speech, for in 1955 the Russians had agreed to the Austrian State Treaty (see page 292).

Also there were summit meetings, the first that had been held since Potsdam in 1945. Khrushchev met President Eisenhower at Geneva in 1955, Camp David near Washington in 1959, and Paris in 1960. The two leaders agreed on very little, but Khrushchev had shown he was willing to travel and talk. Stalin had hardly ever left the Kremlin, let alone Russia.

To prove he thought there could be 'different roads to socialism', Khrushchev made a friendly visit to Yugoslavia in 1956. Also, he allowed the Poles to change their government. Like the other satellite states, Poland had been ruled by Stalinists, but in 1956 there were riots and the Communist Party voted Wladislaw Gomulka into power. Gomulka had been imprisoned as a 'Titoist', so Khrushchev knew he would not obey orders from Moscow. At first the Russians threatened to invade, but the Poles said they would fight, so Khrushchev left them alone. In fact, though

Gomulka made important changes in Poland, his country remained a firm friend to Russia. 'Different roads to socialism' seemed to be the right policy.

However, Khrushchev was unlucky, for many things happened to ruin his hopes.

First of all, 1953 saw a change of government in the United States as well as in Russia. A Republican, General Eisenhower, became President, and he chose as his Secretary of State John Foster Dulles, who was bitterly anti-Communist. Where Truman had been satisfied with 'containment', or stopping the spread of Communism, Dulles wanted 'roll back'. That meant freeing countries from Communist rule. When he took office, Dulles said, 'To all those suffering under Communist slavery let us say: you can count on us.'

One thing Dulles did was to ring Russia and China with hostile alliances. N.A.T.O. had already been formed in 1949, but in 1954 there was the South East Asia Treaty Organization (S.E.A.T.O.) and in 1955, the Baghdad Pact. You can see the countries that joined them on the map on page 333. Moreover, in 1975, West Germany joined N.A.T.O. At first Russia had done nothing about N.A.T.O., but her old enemy was once again under arms, so she signed a military alliance with her satellites in Eastern Europe. This was called the Warsaw Pact.

The Hungarian Crisis

Next, there was trouble in Hungary. Here a Stalinist government was overthrown in 1956, and Imre Nagy became Prime Minister. He went much further than Gomulka had done in Poland, for he said he was going to have free elections, that there would be non-Communists in the government, and that Hungary would leave the Warsaw Pact. This was too much, even for Khrushchev. If other satellite countries did the same, Russia's

Wrecked Russian vehicles on the streets of Budapest

empire in Eastern Europe would fall to pieces, and she would lose the glacis that protected her from her enemies in the West. Red Army tanks drove into Budapest, and there was fierce fighting. The Hungarians remembered Dulles had said 'You can count on us', and made frantic appeals for help. Eisenhower and Dulles were too scared to do anything, but stood by while the Russians crushed the Hungarians with great brutality.

The crisis in Hungary made a mockery of Dulles's policy of 'roll back'. It also showed that Khrushchev's 'roads to socialism' could not be as different as some might wish.

The Suez Crisis

The Suez crisis was also happening at the same time as the Hungarian crisis. This is described in Chapter 48.

The U2 Crisis

If the summit meetings of 1955 and 1959 achieved little, the Paris meeting of 1960 was a disaster. For years American U2 spy planes had been taking photographs over Russia. They flew two and a half kilometres up and for some time this was too high for the Russians to attack them. By 1960, however, they were able to do so, and they shot down a U2 just as the summit conference was about to begin. Khrushchev could not ignore this, and said that if Eisenhower knew about the flights, then he must apologize. Eisenhower felt bound to admit he did know, but refused an apology. Khrushchev left Paris at once.

There are some unanswered questions about the U2 incident. The plane was obsolete, so why was the flight made? One theory is that the men of the 'military–industrial complex' in the United States wanted to stop Eisenhower coming to an agreement with Khrushchev. It might mean the United States government could cut down its spending on armaments. Consequently, they sent the U2 on its mission hoping it would be shot down and that this, in turn, would wreck the summit conference.

The Berlin Crisis of 1961

There was also trouble in Germany, and this time it was Khrushchev who started it. From 1958 to 1961 he tried to make America, Britain and France leave Berlin, so that the East Germans could take it. The Americans refused to give way, and Khrushchev realized the only way to compel them would be to fight a nuclear war, which he was not prepared to risk. All he could do was to allow the East Germans to act on their own, which they did by building the Berlin Wall.

Life in the German Democratic Republic was so unpleasant that between 1949 and 1958 over two million people fled to the West. The total population of East Germany was only 17.5 million, so this was a serious loss, and it was all the more so because most of the refugees were young

The Berlin Wall

and skilled. The government of East Germany closed its frontier, but it was still possible to travel to West Berlin. In the first six months of 1961, 100 000 refugees escaped that way. Clearly, the economy of East Germany was going to suffer badly if the mass flight continued so in August of 1961 its government sealed the Russian zone by building a wall. The Americans were furious but there was little they could do, except make angry noises. Neither side had won, since the Russians had failed to make the Western Powers leave Berlin, but they, in turn, had not prevented the East Germans building the Wall. However, the Berlin problem seemed comparatively unimportant compared with the Cuban crisis.

The Cuban Crisis

In 1959, Fidel Castro led a revolution which overthrew the unpleasant Cuban dictator, Batista. Once he was in power, Castro nationalized sugar plantations and sugar mills which belonged to Americans. This annoyed the American government, which threatened to stop buying Cuban sugar. Since Cuba depended entirely on her sale of sugar, Castro signed a trade agreement with Russia.

Meanwhile, Cuban exiles in the United States were plotting against Castro, and President Kennedy promised to help them. In April 1961 they invaded Cuba, landing at the Bay of Pigs. They had hoped the people would rise in rebellion, but they did not, and Castro's men soon rounded up the invaders.

303

Dr Fidel Castro   *Revolutionary Square, Havana*

Castro now declared himself a Communist, and the Russians began to send him weapons because Khrushchev was afraid the Americans would mount another invasion. Worse was to follow, though, for in 1962 photographs taken by a U2 plane showed that the Russians were building missile sites in Cuba. Russia herself was well away from America, the other side of the North Pole, and the Americans had an elaborate early-warning system stretching from Alaska to Greenland. Now, however, the Russians were able to send their rockets from Cuba, which was to the south, and only 145 km away. What was President Kennedy to do? If he did nothing, which was one possibility, it would be a sign of weakness, and would leave America in mortal danger. On the other hand, if he attacked Cuba might not the Russians start a nuclear war?

Kennedy decided he would do neither of these two things. Instead, he ordered a blockade of Cuba or, as he politely called it, a 'quarantine'. At the same time he gathered a force which could invade Cuba if necessary, he placed the American Air Force on red alert, and he had his rockets primed so that they were ready to fire. He then said he would turn back any Russian ships carrying weapons that came within 800 km of Cuba. As there were 25 ships on their way with weapons, it was now Khrushchev's turn to worry. First, he ordered the ships back home, but then he tried to bargain, offering to remove the Russian missiles in Cuba, if Kennedy would remove the American missiles in Turkey. Kennedy ignored the suggestion, and said he would invade Cuba unless he had a satisfactory answer. In the end, Khrushchev agreed to remove the Cuban missiles if the Americans promised not to carry out the invasion. Kennedy was pleased to agree. The Russians then removed the missiles, their sites were dismantled, and the land ploughed.

The Cuban crisis thoroughly frightened both the United States and Russia, for as the American Secretary of State Dean Rusk said, 'We looked into the mouth of the cannon'. A telephone link was made directly from the White House to the Kremlin, so that the two leaders could talk to each other immediately if there was another crisis. This is called the 'Hot Line'. Also, in 1963 Khrushchev and Kennedy signed a partial Nuclear Test-ban Treaty by which they agreed that nuclear tests should only be made underground. Even more important, the two countries began to work much harder to come to an understanding.

Khrushchev fell from power in 1964. He had made some progress with 'peaceful co-existence', and his successors were to go further along the road he had begun to travel.

Chapter Forty-two

Détente — 1963 onwards

A TENT is a piece of canvas, stretched to form a shelter. Détente is a French word that means the opposite of 'stretching', that is, any kind of 'slackening' or 'relaxing'. Here we use it in a special sense to mean 'the relaxation of tension between America and her allies on the one hand, and Russia and China on the other'. Détente, then, is a useful term to have because it saves a whole mouthful of words. In this chapter we must look at détente with Russia.

Origins of Détente

One reason for détente was the Cuban missile crisis, which brought the world to the brink of nuclear war. Another reason was that both Russia and America wanted to cut down the amount of money they were spending on armaments. The Soviet government in particular hoped to make life easier for its people, so that they would be happy under Communism. However, the most important reason was a quarrel between China and Russia, sometimes called the 'Sino-Soviet Split'. This has a complicated story which is outlined in Chapter 46. Here it will be enough to note that it began in 1956 with Khrushchev's speech denouncing Stalin, and ended in 1968 with the armies of the two countries fighting pitched battles over disputed border territory. Russia could not afford to be on bad terms with the two most powerful countries in the world, so having quarrelled with China, she was willing to try and settle some of her differences with the United States.

Germany and Détente

One result of détente is that much has been done to solve the problem of Germany.

Progress began in 1966 when there was a new government in West Germany. Willy Brandt was its Foreign Minister, and later became its Chancellor. He knew that if there was a nuclear war, then his country would be in the front line. He also recognized that West German hopes of regaining East Germany were idle dreams. The Russians would never allow this to happen. Much the best plan was to accept the division of Germany and to work for good relations with the countries to the east. This

Herr Willy Brandt with British Premier Harold Wilson

was Brandt's 'Ostpolitik' or 'East Policy'. It resulted in a number of treaties.

In 1970, the German Federal Republic made a non-aggression pact with Russia, and another with Poland, which also recognized the Oder–Neisse line as that country's western frontier. In 1971, there was a Four Power Agreement on Berlin, by which the United States, Britain, France and Russia recognized each other's rights and responsibilities in the city. What it amounted to was that Russia promised she would never again try to make the Western Powers leave.

All this time the East Germans were sulking. They were particularly annoyed by the agreement over Berlin, because they wanted the city for themselves. However, the Russians were becoming impatient, for they hoped for an agreement in the West, because of the trouble with China. Accordingly, they made the East German leader, Walter Ulbricht, resign, and in 1972 his successor Erich Honecker signed the 'Basic Treaty' with West Germany. By this the two countries agreed to trade, to live together as good neighbours and to exchange Permanent Missions. They did not, however, exchange ambassadors for that would have meant admitting that Germany was divided for ever. What, in effect, the West Germans were saying was, 'We hope that one day Germany will be reunited, but we realize that cannot happen for a very long time; meanwhile, we must both live in peace with each other.' Brandt put the idea neatly when he spoke of 'two states within one nation'. Twenty-seven years after the war ended, then, there was an agreement which came as close as was possible to a peace settlement for Germany.

307

Disarmament

In 1962 an American journalist calculated that since 1946 there had been 863 international disarmament meetings, involving 17 000 hours and 18 million words. This shows the difficulty the countries of the world had in agreeing about disarmament. The reason is that each is afraid it will leave the other side in a stronger position. However, since détente, the Americans and the Russians have signed the following treaties:

1 *Outer Space Treaty 1967* This banned putting nuclear weapons into outer space, or into orbit round the world.

2 *Nuclear Non-Proliferation Treaty 1968* Countries signing this promised not to share their nuclear secrets, or give any other power nuclear weapons.

3 *Sea Bed Pact 1971* This banned the placing of nuclear weapons on the sea bed beyond any country's twelve-mile limit.

4 *Biological Warfare Treaty 1972* This banned the making of biological weapons to spread disease.

5 *Strategic Arms Limitation Treaty (SALT)* Under the SALT 1 agreement of 1972, America and Russia promised not to make any more missiles until they decided exactly how many each should have. The talks took a long time and it was not until 1979 that all the details were worked out. Carter and Brezhnev then signed the SALT 2 agreement, but at the time of writing the United States Senate has still not ratified it, so it is not yet binding.

The Helsinki Conference 1973–5

This was a European Security Conference, something the Russians had wanted for a long time. At the end, it was agreed that the frontiers of Europe should be permanent, and the Russian government promised to respect human rights, in other words, to give their people more freedom.

Soviet American summit – June 15–18, 1979

Trade Agreements

Russia and the United States have made a number of trade agreements. For example, there was the Grain Treaty of 1975 by which the Americans promised to sell grain to Russia for five years. The Russians have also bought complicated equipment from the United States because they cannot, as yet, make all they need themselves. In fact, both countries have a lot to gain from trade with each other, but the Russian government does not want its people to have much contact with foreigners. It would lead to 'contamination'. That means that if the ordinary Russians realized how well-off people in the West are, they would become discontented with Communism.

Checks to Détente

How much progress has there been towards détente? Many people fear that the Russians are not in earnest. There may be proof of this in the way they treat their satellites and their own people, as well as their policy in Africa and South Asia.

It is true that some of Russia's satellites in Eastern Europe now enjoy more freedom than before. Czechoslovakia, however, was not so lucky.

In 1968, the Czech Communists overthrew Antonin Novotny and Alexander Dubcek took his place. Dubcek believed in what he called 'socialism with a human face' and under his rule the 'Prague Spring' began. That meant the Czechs had a lot more freedom and, moreover, other socialist groups were invited to join the Communists and form a new party, the Czechoslovakian National Front. This was very like what had happened in Hungary under Imre Nagy, except that Dubcek promised he would not take his country out of the Warsaw Pact. The Russians, however, felt they could not allow any of their satellites to have a government

The population demonstrate against the Russian invasion of Czechoslovakia

that was not entirely Communist. They also held that if any one country in the Communist 'family' took a step along the road to capitalism, then it was the concern of the others. In the West, this has been called the 'Brezhnev doctrine'. The Red Army invaded with other Warsaw Pact forces, and Dubcek was overthrown. The Czechs did not fight, but greeted their enemies with a sullen, bitter hatred. The Western Powers did nothing.

As well as keeping a firm hand on the satellites, the Russian government still oppresses its own people, and this in spite of its promise at Helsinki to respect human rights. Just occasionally someone who disagrees with Communism is allowed to go abroad to live. These are the 'Soviet dissidents'. Also, a few Jews have permission to emigrate from time to time. However, there are doubtless many Russians who would speak against their rulers, if they were allowed to, and there must be thousands of Jews who would like to leave.

In Africa, a number of countries have fallen to the Communists. They include the former Portuguese colonies of Mozambique and Angola, as well as Ethiopia. The pattern in Africa is for Cuban troops to help Communist rebels, while Russia remains in the background, though giving help and encouragement.

In Afghanistan in 1979, on the other hand, the Russians used their own forces, just as they had done in Czechoslovakia. There was already a Communist President, Hafizullah Amin, but they decided he was not the man they wanted. They sent thousands of troops into his country, deposed him, and put Babrak Karmal in power. Their reasons were not clear to others, but it seems that Amin was having trouble from rebellious Muslim tribesmen whom he could not control. At the same time, there was a powerful Muslim revival sweeping through the Middle East which, though strongly against the West, was also against Communism. There was a danger that the movement could spread through Afghanistan to affect the Muslim peoples in the south of Russia. Seen in this light, the Russian occupation of Afghanistan was defensive. None the less, the Russians had invaded a neutral country, and there were inevitable reactions.

The British Prime Minister, Mrs Thatcher, was swift to announce that her country would boycott the Olympic Games to be held in Moscow in 1980. In all, 64 countries did this. Most British athletes defied their Prime Minister and took part in the games.

It was the Americans who were most alarmed. They said the Russians had taken Afghanistan as a first step towards the Persian Gulf, and that their aim was to control the oilfields of the Middle East, so gaining a stranglehold on the American economy. There was, of course, no question of America ratifying the SALT 2 Treaty. Moreover, she opened military bases in any Middle East country which would have them — Egypt, Oman, Somalia, as well as Kenya and islands in the Indian Ocean. President Carter announced that his country would not sell Russia any grain, over and above the amount already promised. Ronald Reagan, who was then a candidate in the Presidential Election, tried to win the votes of the American farmers by promising that if he were elected he would lift this embargo. He did so soon after he took office.

As for the Afghans, the tribesmen resisted the Russians as best they could. They fought against helicopter gunships and tanks with inadequate weapons, many of which dated from the First World War.

Following the collapse of the SALT agreement, and finding that his country had far fewer nuclear weapons than the Russians, President Reagan threatened what he called 'the Soviets' with an 'arms race they would be bound to lose'. America was to develop the neutron bomb, which would be a good defence against the thousands of tanks the Russians had amassed. She was also to deploy medium range Pershing and Cruise missiles in Europe. There was a great outcry in the countries of Western Europe, whose people had no wish to be caught between America and Russia in a nuclear war. The result of all this was that yet another series of disarmament talks began at Geneva in December 1981. Even the most optimistic of those taking part thought it would take two years to reach agreement.

Poland

The satellite state which worries the Soviet government most is Poland. In the first place, she lies directly between Russia and her main enemies in the West. Russia had been invaded from Poland three times in less than thirty years. The Germans came in 1914, the Poles themselves in 1920 and the Germans once more in 1941. Secondly, Poland is by far the largest of the satellites, both in area and population. There are 35 million Poles and they are, moreover, a determined people. The Russians have not invaded Poland as they did Hungary and Czechoslovakia. Thirdly, the communists have not had such a firm grip on the people as in other Eastern European countries. For example, the Polish peasants have not been made to join collective farms. Also, the Roman Catholic church is strong. In 1978 the Archbishop of Cracow became Pope John Paul II and, when he revisited his native country the following year, almost the entire population greeted him with enthusiasm. There were enormous demonstrations which the government dared not prevent.

Finally, the economy of the country is weak. In 1981 foreign debts amounted to £14 billion and the government had no hope of paying even the interest which was due. Ships lay stranded in harbours around the world because they could not afford fuel and no one would give them credit. At home there were chronic shortages of essential foods such as flour and meat. People sometimes slept all night outside shops so as to be at the head of the queue in the morning. Not surprisingly, the Poles were discontented, and their country was shaken by one crisis after another, much to the alarm of the Russians. The most important events were as follows:

When the war ended Stalin seized eastern Poland and gave her much of Germany as compensation. He also made sure that she had a government

311

which was loyal to himself. It was headed by a man called Bierut. Stalin died in 1953 and in 1956, Khrushchev made his famous speech denouncing him. Also in 1956 Polish workers rioted, particularly in Poznan. As a result of both these things, the Polish communists deposed Bierut, and Wladyslaw Gomulka took his place. It was well known that Gomulka would not take orders from Moscow, so Krushchev protested. The Poles, however, made it plain they would fight rather than tolerate Russian interference, so Khrushchev withdrew his objections.

Gomulka was popular for a time, but he could not make his country prosper. In 1970, he felt obliged to increase prices whereupon there were riots in the Baltic ports. At Gdansk 56 workers were shot by the army. To pacify the people, the Communists dismissed Gomulka and Edward Gierek became party leader. With Russian help, Gierek was able to freeze prices for a time but in 1976 he had to increase them. Immediately there were strikes and riots which the government quelled by force. Gierek again increased prices in 1980, and the time the country erupted. Once more the Communists tried a change of leader and Stansislaw Kania took over from Gierek, but the people knew that a different face did not mean different policies and were determined not to be tricked again. There were strikes everywhere, the most serious being at Gdansk. Here the men at the Lenin Shipyard barricaded themselves inside the yard and formed a trade union called Solidarity. Its leader was Lech Walesa.

The workers made a number of demands, the most important being the right to have their own trade unions, free from Communist control. Reluctantly, Kania agreed, much to the anger of the Russians. The Soviet government ordered the Warsaw Pact armies to make large scale manoeuvres, but there was no invasion of Poland. Solidarity announced triumphantly, 'We are the co-masters now.'

For a short while there was an uneasy peace between Solidarity and the Polish government, but living conditions remained bad, with worse shortages and even longer queues. Lech Walesa advised patience, but he could not restrain his more extreme followers. They demanded radical changes in the system of government, including free elections. Towards the end of 1981 they announced that they were going to hold a referendum, and that was almost certan to mean the end of Communist rule.

The Russians were now in a dilemma. Either they had to fight a war or see their shield against the West damaged beyond repair. There were meetings with the Polish leaders and quite what was said we do not know. It seems, though, that the Russians told them they must restore order, or face an invasion. Be that as it may, in December 1981 the Polish army struck. Its commander-in-chief, General Jaruzelski, brushed aside the civilian Communist government and imposed martial law. He arrested all the leaders of Solidarity, including Lech Walesa, while his troops fought their way into the Gdansk shipyard, and broke strikes all over the country. The people, sullen but cowed, had no choice but to accept military rule, as well as price rises of up to 400 per cent in basic foods.

Countries in the West were quick to condemn Jaruzelski and the

Russians, but they were divided on what action to take. Europeans were anxious not to offend the Russians, knowing they would be in the front line if there was a war. As for the United States, she was in a particularly strong position because the Russians had suffered three disastrous harvests in a row. Without American wheat they would be in a desperate plight, but as with Afghanistan, President Reagan did not want to lose the votes of America's farmers by stopping the sale of grain to Russia. He contented himself by halting the export of a few industrial goods, by making swashbuckling speeches and by having a television programme beamed by satellite all over the world — a programme which few people bothered to watch. In other words, Reagan did more than enough to upset the Russians, but not nearly enough to stop them interfering in Poland.

Here, then, is yet another bar to détente. A man who ill-treats his children is unpopular with his neighbours. Similarly, the Soviet government will find it hard to reach an understanding with the West while it is forcing Communism on the Poles.

Chapter Forty-three

European Unity

Origins

THE COUNTRIES of Western Europe fought a series of wars with each other that lasted from the fall of the Roman Empire in the fifth century A.D., to the collapse of Hitler's Germany in 1945. After the Second World War, however, many people were convinced that this strife should end and that, instead, Western Europe should unite. There were good political and economic reasons for this.

The most important political reason was the wish to be free of both the Soviet Union and the United States. Russia seemed to be trying to spread Communism all over the world, and the Red Army stood on the River Elbe, in Central Europe itself. For defence, Europe depended entirely on the United States. Few people were actually hostile to the Americans, but they wanted to be independent. Clearly, the two super-powers would go on dominating Europe as long as she was disunited.

Perhaps the economic reasons for unity were stronger even that the political ones. The richest country in the world was the United States, and the explanation seemed to be that she was so large. Europeans thought that if they worked together they might, one day, be as prosperous as the Americans.

However, Western Europe is still a long way from being one country and the fault is mainly Britain's. There are three reasons for this. In the first place, Britain was the only European country that fought in the Second World War and was not invaded. All the others had the humiliation of being overrun by their enemies at one time or another. As a result Britain clung to the belief that she was still a great power. Also, she remembered that during the war it was the United States which saved her, so for help she went on looking to the Americans rather than her European neighbours. Secondly, there was the British Commonwealth. Britain traded with its members and there were strong sentimental ties. It seemed unthinkable to break with Canada, Australia and New Zealand to join with countries that had been, at best, unreliable allies, and, at worst, bitter enemies. Thirdly, the British distrusted foreigners. They despised the Germans for Hitler, and the Italians for Mussolini, while the French were simply funny. The French parliament was disorderly, and there were fifteen changes of government between 1947 and 1954. In Britain, on the other hand, the system of government was remarkably stable. It had survived the general strike of 1926, the Depression of the 1930s and both World Wars. The British could not consider allowing irresponsible foreigners to have any power over them.

Europe, therefore, had to make her way, not only without Britain, but, at times, in spite of her.

There were developments even before the war ended. In 1944, the Benelux countries, Belgium, the Netherlands and Luxembourg, agreed to form a customs union. That meant the three countries exchanged goods among themselves without collecting duties, and all charged the same duties on goods coming from outside. Soon they went further and, for economic purposes, became a united country. It was then as easy for a Belgian, for example to do business in the Netherlands or Luxembourg, as it is for an Englishman to do business in Wales or Scotland. The Benelux countries were an example for the rest of Europe.

At the same time, people were forming societies such as Jean Monnet's 'Action Committee for the Creation of the United States of Europe'.

In 1948 there was the Marshall Plan and, as you saw on page 296, the Americans insisted that the European countries should work together in administering the aid. That led to the formation of the Organization for European Economic Co-operation. It was a step towards unity, even though the members states did not surrender any of their powers to the O.E.E.C.

In 1948 the Communists seized power in Czechoslovakia, which caused a lot of alarm in the countries of Western Europe. They held a conference at the Hague where they decided to stand together against the Communist threat, and in 1949 they set up the Council of Europe. This meets in Strasbourg. It has a Committee of Ministers, a Consultative Assembly and a Secretariat. Here were the makings of a true European parliament, but the British spoilt it. They would not allow it to have any power over the member countries, and it became little more than a debating society.

After the failure of 1949 the 'Europeans', that is the people who wanted a united Europe, decided to use other methods. Instead of trying to set up a government that would control everything they began to work for co-operation in specific things like coal and steel production and defence. They thought that when there was agreement in enough of these areas, complete unity would follow.

Even here, one of the first attempts was a failure. There was a plan to create a European Defence Community. Europe would have had one army with all its men in the same uniform and under one commander. The British would have nothing to do with this, so the French rejected it as well. They were afraid that without British help, the Germans would dominate the new army.

Economic co-operation, though, has been successful. It has come about in two stages, the formation of the European Coal and Steel Community (E.C.S.C.) in 1952 and the European Economic Community (E.E.C.) or Common Market in 1958.

The European Coal and Steel Community

The E.C.S.C. was Jean Monnet's scheme, but he persuaded the French Foreign Minister Robert Schuman that it was a good one. He in turn persuaded the French government, so the project was known as the Schuman Plan. The idea was to allow the free sale of coal and steel over as wide an area as possible. For example, as things were, an inefficient works making steel expensively might stay in business because it had no competition from abroad. Under the Schuman Plan, though, cheap steel from other countries would soon come on the market, and the old-fashioned firm would either have to modernize, or go out of business. The coal and steel industries throughout the country would become more efficient and everyone would benefit.

Britain was invited to join the E.C.S.C., but she refused. However, she was unable to spoil it as she had done the Council of Europe and the European Defence Community. 'The Six', that is France, West Germany, Italy and the Benelux countries, went ahead on their own. The new community came into being in 1952 with Jean Monnet as its first President. It was a great success immediately, for steel output grew by over 40 per cent between 1953 and 1958.

The European Economic Community (Common Market)

Because the E.C.S.C. did so well, the Six were soon ready to discuss complete economic union. Their foreign ministers met at Messina in 1955 and decided to form the E.E.C. They set up a committee under Belgium's Foreign Minister, Paul-Henri Spaak, which quickly produced a plan. It was set out in the Treaty of Rome, and this was signed in 1957. The new community started life on 1 January 1958.

The aim of the E.E.C. was to do for all industries what the E.C.S.C. had done for iron and steel. There was to be a customs union, like the one the Benelux countries had made in 1944, but this time there was a common market of over 170 million people. It was expected that old-fashioned firms would go out of business, and efficient ones would thrive. What is more, manufacturers would have so many customers that it would be worth their while to use new techniques, like automation, to produce vast quantities of goods. So that they could compete, the member countries would concentrate on the things they did best. However, they might have a difficult time while some of their old industries were dying, and before their new ones were ready. To help them there was a European Investment Bank.

The E.E.C. has a well-organized government in Brussels. The most important part is the Council of Ministers for this makes all the important decisions. Each country sends its foreign, economic or agriculture minister as it thinks fit. If they do not all agree, then a 'qualified majority' can decide. No single country is able to veto a measure: it takes at least one large country and one small one to do that.

Next, there is the Common Market Commission. The Ministers have work to do at home, but the members of the Commission are in Brussels all the time. They are nominated by the government of the member countries.

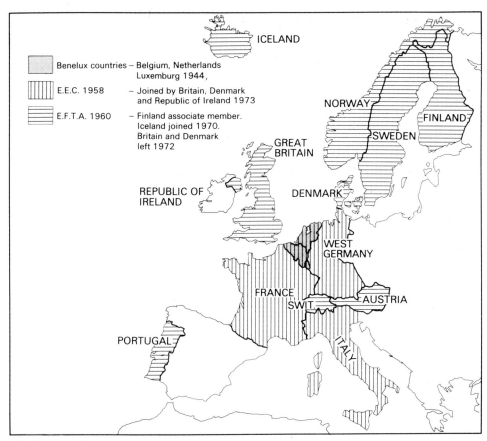

Benelux countries – Belgium, Netherlands
Luxemburg 1944,

E.E.C. 1958 – Joined by Britain, Denmark
and Republic of Ireland 1973

E.F.T.A. 1960 – Finland associate member.
Iceland joined 1970.
Britain and Denmark
left 1972

The European Economic Community

E.E.C. Building, Brussels

Their work is to propose new laws for the Community and to see that the existing ones are obeyed.

Thirdly, there is the European Parliament. It does not have anything like the authority that the British Parliament has in its own country. Broadly, its job is to give advice, for the Council of Ministers makes the decisions. However, it can dismiss the Commission if it feels it is not doing its job properly, it can reject the Community's budget, it can debate any new laws, and it can ask questions of the Council of Ministers and the Commission. At first, members of the European Parliament were nominated by the parliaments of their own countries, but in 1979 the people of Europe chose their own representatives by electing them directly. There has been no change in the law, to give the European Parliament extra power, but the Council of Ministers and the Commission will have to pay more attention to what it says now that it has the authority of the people behind it.

Finally, the E.E.C. has a Court of Justice, to settle any legal arguments.

At the same time that the E.E.C. was organized, so also was Euratom — the European Atomic Energy Commission. Its job was to develop the peaceful uses of atomic energy, not to make nuclear weapons. Euratom and the E.C.S.C. merged with the E.E.C. in 1966.

When the foreign ministers of the Six met at Messina they invited Britain to join the new Community, but she refused. Instead, in January 1960, she formed the European Free Trade Association (E.F.T.A.) with Norway, Sweden, Denmark, Switzerland, Austria and Portugal. These countries were known, with Britain, as the 'outer seven'.

Almost as soon as the E.E.C. was formed Britain realized she had made a mistake in not joining. She had stayed out partly because of the Commonwealth, but her trade with it was hardly growing at all. Her trade with her E.F.T.A. partners was increasing but at only half of the rate of her trade with the E.E.C. How long, though, could that continue when the E.E.C. customs union was complete? Britain decided she should join after all, but times had changed. While most of the Six were still ready to welcome her, France was not. Here, General de Gaulle had come to power in 1958 and he did not like the British. He pointed to their economic weakness and claimed that they were not 'ready'. Harold Macmillan's government asked to join in 1961, and Harold Wilson's in 1967. De Gaulle vetoed both applications. Then, in 1969, de Gaulle resigned and his successor, President Pompidou, said he had no objections to Britain's membership. Edward Heath's government applied, and Britain was admitted to the E.E.C. in 1973. Eire and Denmark joined at the same time.

The E.E.C. has been a success. The tariff barriers between the original Six were abolished eighteen months ahead of time: the Community had become the world's greatest trading power by 1964, importing and exporting more goods than anywhere else, including the United States: trade between members increased 600 per cent between 1957 and 1967. There is another gain which is even more important, though it cannot be measured. For centuries the countries of Western Europe fought with each other, but now that most of them belong to the same economic community, it is almost unthinkable that they should ever go to war again.

318

None the less the E.E.C. does have its problems. Countries have been unwilling to give up their sovereignty, that is, the right to manage their own affairs. For example, in the mid-1960s, de Gaulle delayed progress for a time because he objected to the rule of the 'qualified majority'. He held that no country should be made to do what she did not want to, even if all her partners voted against her. In 1979, France refused to accept shipments of Dorset lamb, even though this action was against the laws of the E.E.C. Political unity is still slow to come and it looks as if it will be a long time before there is a United States of Europe.

Secondly, the Common Agricultural Policy has had some unfortunate results. Most European farms belong to peasant families and are less than 10 hectares. They are highly inefficient, so the food they grow is expensive, but the Common Market promises to buy as much as they can produce, at high prices, and whether it is needed or not. 'Butter mountains', 'meat mountains' and 'wine lakes' accumulate. The next thing a hard-pressed housewife hears is that vast quantities of butter have been sold to the Russians at a fraction of the price she has to pay. All this may seem strange because one of the aims of the Common Market is to allow free competition so that inefficient people, producing expensive goods, go out of business. The explanation is that the governments of France, Italy and Germany need the votes of their peasants at election time, so they make sure the Community pampers them. Thirdly, there is the problem of the contributions the member States make to the Community's budget. These were worked out in such a way that Britain has to pay the largest sum, and apart from Eire and Italy, she is the poorest country in the Community. Eventually, and after a lot of argument, Mrs Thatcher had Britain's contribution reduced, though even then, she and West Germany remained the only states to pay more into the E.E.C.'s funds than they received from them. However, had Britain joined at the beginning when she had the chance, she could have made sure the rules were more in her favour.

WORK SECTION — International Relations since 1945 — The West

The Berlin airlift

Questions

1 What are the troops loading into the aircraft?
2 Why was it necessary to carry it to Berlin by air?
3 How many tonnes were carried, in the end?
4 How had this crisis over Berlin arisen? When?
5 When did it end? Why?
6 What were the results of the crisis?

The Potsdam Conference

Document One

President Truman's view of the Potsdam Conference:

I had already seen that the Russians were relentless bargainers, forever pressing for every advantage for themselves. It did not seem possible that only a few miles from the war-shattered seat of Nazi power the head of any government would not bend every effort to attain a real peace. Yet I was not altogether disillusioned to find now, that the Russians were not in earnest about peace. It was clear that the Russian foreign policy was based on the conclusion that we were heading for a major depression and they were already planning to take advantage of our setback.

Anxious as we were to have Russia in the war against Japan, the experience at Potsdam now made me determined that I would not allow the Russians any part in the control of Japan. Our experience with them in Germany and in Bulgaria, Rumania, Hungary and Poland was such that I decided to take no chances in a joint setup with the Russians.

Force is the only thing the Russians understand.

The persistent way in which Stalin blocked one of the war-preventative measures I had proposed showed how his mind worked and what he was after. I had proposed the internationalization of all the principal waterways. Stalin did not want this. What Stalin wanted was control of the Black Sea straits and the Danube. The Russians were planning world conquest.

(*Memoirs* — Harry S. Truman)

Document Two

A historian's view:

It apparently did not occur to the President that Stalin might be resisting the internationalization of the waterways in order to make it more difficult for the American commercial interests to penetrate into Eastern Europe. The notion of Stalin's playing a defensive role was for Truman unthinkable. Hitler was hardly in his grave; already Truman had substituted Stalin for Hitler as the madman who had to be stopped. The tone of the Cold War was established.

(*The Cold War* — Hugh Higgins)

Questions

Document One

1 When was the Potsdam Conference held? What statesmen attended it?
2 Why did Truman say it was difficult to negotiate with the Russians?
3 What, according to Truman, were the Russians hoping would happen in the West? When had something like it happened before?
4 Why does Truman say he will not allow Russia to share in the control of Japan? Was he successful in this?
5 What, according to Truman, is the only thing the Russians understand?
6 Why should the Americans want the Black Sea waterways internationalized? What reason does Truman give?
7 What does Truman say the Russians want to happen to them?
8 What does he say the Russians are planning?

Document Two

9 What does this writer think were Stalin's motives in refusing to internationalize the Black Sea straits and the Danube?
10 What does he say Truman thought about Stalin?

The Truman Doctrine

On Wednesday 12 March 1947 I addressed a joint session of Congress. I had asked the Senators and Representatives to meet together so that I might place before them what I believe was an extremely critical situation.

To cope with this situation I recommended immediate action by the Congress. But I also wished to state, for all the world to know, what the position of the United States was in the face of the new totalitarian challenge. This declaration of policy soon began to be referred to as the 'Truman Doctrine'. This was, I believe, the turning point in America's foreign policy which now declared that wherever aggression, direct or indirect, threatened the peace, the security of the United States was involved.

'I believe', I said to the Congress, 'that it must be the policy of the United States to support free peoples who are resisting attempted subjugation by armed minorities or by outside pressures.

320

'I believe that we must assist free peoples to work out their own destinies in their own way.

'I believe that our help should be primarily through economic and financial aid which is essential to economic stability and orderly political processes.'

After I delivered the speech, the world reaction to it proved that this approach had been the right one. All over the world, voices of approval made themselves heard, while Communists and their fellow-travellers struck out at me savagely. The line had been drawn sharply. In my address I had said that every nation was now faced with a choice between alternative ways of life.

'Our way of life,' I said, 'is based upon the will of the majority and is distinguished by free institutions, representative government, free elections, guarantees of individual liberty, freedom of speech and religion and freedom from political oppression.

'The second way of life is based upon the will of a minority, forcibly imposed upon the majority. It relies upon terror and oppression, a controlled press and radio, fixed elections and the suppression of personal freedoms.

'The seeds of totalitarian regimes,' I said in closing, 'are nurtured by misery and want. They spread and grow in the evil soil of poverty and strife. They reach their full growth when the hope of a people for a better life has died.

'We must keep that hope alive.

'The free peoples of the world look to us for support in maintaining their freedoms.

'If we falter in our leadership we may endanger the peace of the world — and we shall surely endanger the welfare of our own nation.'

When I ended my address the Congressmen rose as one man and applauded. Vito Marcantonio, the American Labour Party representative from New York was the only representative who remained seated.

(Years of Trial and Hope — Harry S. Truman)

Questions

1 What was the 'critical situation' which led President Truman to make this speech?
2 What does President Truman mean by the 'new totalitarian challenge'? What do you suppose was the old one?
3 What does America recognize in her foreign policy? How is this different from her attitude after the First World War?
4 Whom should America help?
5 What is the best way to give help?
6 What plan to help Western Europe was made in 1948?
7 What was the reaction of the rest of the world to this speech?
8 What, according to President Truman, are the marks of the western way of life?
9 What does he mean by the 'second way of life'? What are its marks?
10 What, according to President Truman, encourages it to spread?
11 What will happen if the United States does not act?
12 What was the reaction of Congress to this speech?
13 How did this speech affect relations between Russia and the Western Powers?

The Cuban Crisis — Khrushchev's View

One thought kept hammering away at my brain. 'What will happen if we lose Cuba?' I knew it would have been a terrible blow to Marxism-Leninism. It would gravely diminish our stature throughout the world, but especially in Latin America. If Cuba fell, other Latin American countries would reject us, claiming that for all our might the Soviet Union hadn't been able to do anything for Cuba except to make empty protests in the United Nations. I found myself in the difficult position of having to decide on a course of action which would answer the American threat but which would also avoid war.

Then I had the idea of installing missiles in Cuba without letting the United States find out they were there until it was too late to do anything about them. The installation of our missiles would, I thought, restrain the United States from precipitous military action against Castro's government. In addition to protecting Cuba, our missiles would have equalized what the West likes to call the 'balance of power'. The Americans had surrounded our country with military bases and threatened us with nuclear weapons, and now they would learn just what it feels like to have enemy missiles pointing at you.

(Khrushchev Remembers)

321

The Cuban Crisis — An American View

The defence of Cuba did not really require the introduction of long-range nuclear missiles. One can be sure that Khrushchev, like any other national leader, took that decision not for Cuban reasons but for Soviet reasons.

No doubt a 'total victory' faction in Moscow had long been denouncing the Government's 'no-win' policy and arguing that the Soviet Union could safely use the utmost nuclear power against the United States because the Americans were too rich or soft or liberal to fight. Now Khrushchev was prepared to give this argument its crucial test. A successful nuclearization of Cuba would make about 64 Soviet nuclear missiles effective against the United States and thereby come near to doubling Soviet striking capacity against American targets. Every country in the world, watching so audacious an action ninety miles from the United States, would wonder whether it could ever thereafter trust Washington's resolution and protection. More particularly, the change in the nuclear equilibrium would permit Khrushchev, who had been dragging out the Berlin negotiation all year, to reopen the question with half the United States lying within range of nuclear missiles poised for delivery across the small stretch of water from Florida. It was a staggering project.

(A Thousand Days — Arthur M. Schlesinger)

Questions

1 When had Castro come to power in Cuba?
2 What event in April 1961 made the Russians fear that America would attack Cuba?
3 What does Khrushchev say would happen if Cuba fell to America?
4 What problem does Khrushchev say he faced?
5 What two reasons does he give for installing missiles in Cuba?
6 With which of these two reasons does Schlesinger disagree? Whose interests does he say were uppermost in Khrushchev's mind?
7 What name is usually given to Khrushchev's 'no win' policy? Why does Schlesinger think he abandoned it at the time of the Cuban crisis?
8 How would the Cuban missiles have increased the power of the U.S.S.R.?

9 According to Schlesinger, what conclusion would the rest of the world have drawn if the United States had allowed the missiles to remain?
10 What had happened at Berlin 1961? What connection did Schlesinger see between the Cuban missiles and Berlin?
11 Using your own words, summarize the points of view given in these two extracts.

Map Questions. Russia and the Communist States of Eastern Europe

1 Name States 1–8 and cities a–g.

Stalin and Eastern Europe 1945–53.

2 Name the eight territories taken by Russia after the war. (Shaded areas i–viii.)
3 What was the main reason that Eastern Europe became Communist?
4 Why was it important for Russia that the Eastern European countries should be under her control? Which one in particular?
5 What territory was given to State 1 after the war? What rivers mark its western frontier?
6 What agreement was made about the government of State 1 in 1945?
7 In which countries were there government changes in 1947? What were these changes and why were they made?
8 What happened in State 2 in 1948?
9 Who governed State 4 after the war?
10 Why was he able to remain independent of Russia?
11 Why was he on especially bad terms with Russia after 1948?
12 Why was there a crisis over town g in 1948?
13 When was State 8 established? Why?

Khrushchev and Eastern Europe 1953–64.

14 What phrase summed up Khrushchev's policy towards the satellites?
15 What happened as a result? (a) in State 1, (b) in State 3, (c) to Russia's relations with State 4?
16 What was Khrushchev trying to do about town g from 1958 to 1961?

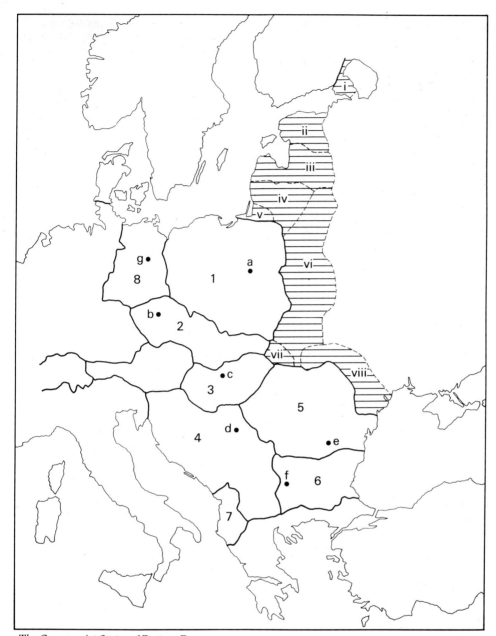

The Communist States of Eastern Europe

17 What action did the government of State 8 take in town g in 1961? Why?

Eastern Europe since Khrushchev, 1964 onwards

18 What change was there in the foreign policy of West Germany after 1966?

19 Name the treaties which were signed: (a) with Russia, (b) with State 1, (c) about town g, (d) with State 8.

20 What had to happen in State 8 before the treaty could be signed?

21 Which of the satellite States have gained a greater amount of freedom?

22 What happened in State 2 in 1968?

The Peace Settlement

Questions

1 Why was there no comprehensive peace settlement after the Second World War?
2 At what conferences were there attempts to agree on a peace settlement? Which statemen attended these conferences?
3 With the aid of a sketch map show what territories Russia took.
4 Why did Russia and the Western Powers disagree over the government of Poland? What compromise did they reach?
5 What territory did Poland lose to Russia? What was she given as compensation? What happened to the German minorities in Eastern Europe?
6 What were the 4 D's imposed on Germany?
7 How were Germany and Berlin divided? Who was to govern Germany as a whole? What plans were made for the economy of the country?
8 What arrangements were made for reparations?
9 What happened to war criminals?
10 Which countries signed the Treaties of Paris? What were the terms of the treaties?
11 What replaced the League of Nations?
12 When was peace made with Japan? Where? Why? What were the terms of the treaty? Which country did not sign it?
13 What treaty made peace with Austria? Why was it signed? When? What were its terms?
14 What was expected would happen to Germany? Why has no peace treaty been made with her?

Give an account of the Peace Settlement under the headings: Attempts to Reach Agreement/Russia Poland Germany (immediate post-war)/Germany's Allies/The United Nations/Problems of Japan/Austria and Germany

The Cold War

Questions

1 What is a 'Cold War'?
2 What ultimate aim did many Russian leaders have? What, in contrast, was Stalin's policy? How did he hope to make Russia safe?

3 What idealistic aim did the Americans have? What did they believe Stalin was doing? What practical aim did the Americans have?
4 How did the Russians and the Western Powers annoy each other during the war?
5 What conclusion did President Truman draw from the disagreements at Potsdam?
6 What problems arose over reparations? What action did the Western Powers take?
7 Why were the Americans and Russians afraid of each other?
8 What did Churchill say in his speech at Fulton, Missouri?
9 What happened in Greece after the war? What action did the British take over Greece and Turkey in 1947?
10 What did President Truman fear? What did he hope America might do?
11 When was the Truman Doctrine stated? What was its significance for the Cold War?
12 What was Marshall Aid?
13 What problem did the countries of Western Europe have after the war? How was Marshall Aid going to help them solve it?
14 Give three reasons why the Americans gave Marshall Aid.
15 Give three conditions which the Americans made.
16 How much money was given? Which country received most? How successful was Marshall Aid?
17 What was Stalin's answer to the Truman Doctrine?
18 What changes were made in Poland, Romania, Hungary and Bulgaria?
19 What government did Czechoslovakia have after the war? Why did the Communists decide to seize power? When did they do this?
20 What help did Stalin give the Czech Communists? How did the West view the Communist coup?
21 What government did Yugoslavia have after the war? Why was she expelled from the Cominform?
22 What did Russia hope would happen in Germany? What plans did the Americans have?
23 What action did the Americans and Russians take?
24 Why did the Western Powers reform

324

the currency in their zones of Germany? How did the Russians interpret this action?

25 Why did the Russians blockade Berlin?

26 What did the British and Americans do about the blockade of Berlin? When was the blockade lifted?

27 What did the Berlin blockade prove? What State was created out of the three western zones? Who was its first Chancellor? What was his policy? What was his greatest achievement?

28 What did the Russians do with their zone?

29 What events led to the formation of N.A.T.O.? What countries joined it?

30 What important change had there been in American foreign policy?

Give an account of the Cold War under the headings: Russian and American Aims/ The Beginnings of the Cold War/The Truman Doctrine/Marshall Aid/The Cold War Intensifies/Germany and the Berlin Blockade/N.A.T.O.

Co-existence and Crises 1955–62

Questions

1 What new foreign policy did Khrushchev announce in 1956?

2 How did Khrushchev try to please the satellite States?

3 What event in 1955 proved the 'thaw' had begun?

4 What summit meetings were held?

5 When did Khrushchev visit Yugoslavia? What changes did he allow in Poland?

6 To what political party did Eisenhower and Dulles belong?

7 What alliances were made against Russia? Which country joined N.A.T.O. in 1955? What was the Russian reaction?

8 Who became Prime Minister of Hungary in 1956? What three things did he say he would do? Why did Khrushchev order the invasion of Hungary?

9 What two things did the Russian invasion of Hungary prove?

10 What was the result of the loss of the American U2 in 1960?

11 Why may the U2 have been sent on its mission?

12 Why did Khrushchev allow the East Germans to build the Berlin Wall?

13 Why did the East Germans wish to build the Wall? When did they do so?

14 Why had neither the Russians nor the Americans won over Berlin?

15 When did Castro come to power in Cuba? How did he annoy the Americans?

16 What happened in Cuba in 1961?

17 Why did the Russians send missiles to Cuba? Why were the Americans alarmed?

18 Name four things President Kennedy did to cope with the crisis.

19 What bargain did Khrushchev try to make? What, in the end, did he agree to do? What did Kennedy promise in return?

20 Name two things that happened as a result of the Cuban crisis.

Give an account of relations between Russia and the Western Powers between 1953 and 1962 under the headings: Khrushchev's Policies/Dulles's Policies/ The Crises — Hungary, Suez (see Chapter 48), U2, Berlin, Cuba

Détente — 1963 onwards

Questions

1 What is the meaning of the word 'détente'?

2 Give three reasons for détente between America and Russia.

3 What was Willy Brandt's 'Ostpolitik'? Why did he introduce it?

4 What treaties did West Germany make with Russia and Poland? What agreement was made over Berlin?

5 Why did the Russians insist on a change of government in East Germany? What treaty was made between East and West Germany? What were its terms?

6 Why was it difficult to reach any agreement on disarmament? Name five treaties that have been made.

7 When was the Helsinki Conference? What was agreed there?

8 What trade has there been between America and Russia? Why are the Russians unwilling to encourage trade?

9 Who became ruler of Czechoslovakia in 1968? What changes did he make? What did he promise he would not do?

325

10 How did the Russians feel about the changes in Czechoslovakia? (Explain the 'Brezhnev Doctrine'.) What action did they take?

11 How does the Russian government treat its own people?

12 Name some African countries which have fallen to the Communists. How has this happened?

13 When did the Russians invade Afghanistan? What, probably, was their reason for doing so?

14 What did the Americans think were the aims of the Russians?

15 How did the American government react?

16 Give four reasons why the Russians are concerned about Poland.

17 What happened to Poland immediately after the war?

18 What changes were there in 1956? Why?

19 What happened under Gomulka and Gierek? Why did they both fall from power?

20 What was Solidarity? Who was its leader? How did it come into being?

21 What important concession did Solidarity win?

22 In 1981, what did Solidarity say it was going to do? Why did this alarm the Russians? What action did General Jaruzelski take?

24 What was the attitude of the powers of Western Europe? How did President Reagan handle the crisis?

Give an account of 'Détente' under the headings: Origins/Germany and Détente/Disarmament/The Helsinki Conference/Doubts about Détente/Poland.

European Unity

Questions

1 What political reasons were there for European unity after the Second World War?

2 What were the economic reasons?

3 Give three reasons why Britain hindered European unity.

4 What steps did the Benelux countries take towards unity among themselves?

5 What association did Jean Monnet form?

6 How did Marshall Aid help European unity?

7 Why was the Council of Europe set up? Why did it not become a true European parliament?

8 What did the 'Europeans' decide to do after the failure of the Council of Europe?

9 Explain the plan to create a European Defence Community. Why did it fail?

10 What was the E.C.S.C.? Who thought of it? After whom was it named? Explain how it worked.

11 What countries joined the E.C.S.C.? When did it come into being?

12 What was decided by the Treaty of Rome? When was it signed?

13 How large was the E.E.C. when it began? Explain how it increases efficiency.

14 What is the work of the Council of Ministers? How can its decisions be vetoed?

15 What is the work of the Common Market Commission?

16 What is the work of the European Parliament? What powers does it have? What changes in 1979 gave it more authority?

17 How are legal arguments settled?

18 What was Euratom? What happened to Euratom and the E.C.S.C. in 1966?

19 What did Britain do, instead of joining the E.E.C.?

20 What convinced Britain she should join the E.E.C.? Who prevented her? When, finally, did she join? Who joined with her?

21 What economic progress has the E.E.C. made? What political gain has there been?

22 Name three problems of the E.E.C.

Give an account of the growth of European Unity under the headings: Origins/E.C.S.C. and E.E.C.

Problems

1 Why was there no comprehensive peace settlement after the Second World War?

2 How have the problems of Germany complicated international relations since 1945?

3 Explain the origins of the Cold War and describe how it developed down to 1955.

4 How did Stalin attempt to counter American moves in Western Europe?

5 What events led to the division of Germany in 1949?

6 Why did Khrushchev have only limited success in bringing about a thaw in Russia's relations with the West?

7 What were the main crises that arose between Russia and the Western Powers after 1945 and how were they resolved?

8 What were the origins of détente with Russia? What progress has been made with détente? What set-backs have there been to détente?

9 Why have there been moves towards unity in Western Europe since the Second World War? What have been the main obstacles? What progress has been made?

10 What benefits have the European countries gained from economic co-operation? What problems has the E.E.C. had to face?

11 Describe the part played in European affairs since 1965 by (a) the United States of America and (b) Russia.

INTERNATIONAL RELATIONS
since 1945

—

THE FAR EAST

Introduction

SOON after the war, American hopes in the Far East had a severe blow. There was a civil war in China between the Communists under Mao Tse-tung and the Nationalists under Chiang Kai-shek. America supported the Nationalists, but in spite of the massive amount of aid she sent them, they were defeated.

As well as facing Russia in the West, America now had to face China in the East. Her policy was the same — to prevent Communism spreading any further. However, there was an important difference. Though China exploded her first atom bomb in 1964 she has never come anywhere near having as many nuclear weapons as the United States. There has been no 'balance of terror', so the United States has been much more willing to use force. As a result, there have been two major wars, one in Korea and one in Vietnam.

While America had some success in Korea, she was defeated in Vietnam. Since then she and China have been working for détente. The United States saw the need for it because of Vietnam, and China because of her quarrel with Russia.

Chapter Forty-four

The Korean War

Origins

WHEN the Second World War ended, Korea was still occupied by Japanese troops. Someone had to accept their surrender, so it was agreed that the Russians should do so in the North, and the Americans in the South. The line between them was the 38th parallel. In some ways it was the history of Germany all over again. The Russians set up a Communist government in their zone under Kim Il Sung, while in the South, the Americans set up an anti-Communist government under Dr Syngman Rhee.

The Russians departed in 1948, and the Americans soon afterwards. They left behind a divided country, with two governments, each wanting to reunite Korea under its own rule. In the end, it was the North Koreans who tried to bring this about by attacking the South. Probably it was Kim Il Sung's idea, but people in the West thought he was acting under Stalin's orders and it was all part of the Communist plot to control the world.

The Course of the War

The North Koreans attacked in June 1950. The Russians had given them tanks and aircraft, while the South Koreans had none. Within three days the North Koreans had rounded up half of the South Korean army, had captured the capital Seoul, and were sweeping south.

President Truman sent the American air force and navy into action at once, and he ordered General MacArthur, who was in Japan, to land troops as soon as he could. Truman then turned to the United Nations, and the Security Council urged all members to send help to South Korea. Russia could have prevented this by using her veto, but she was boycotting the United Nations at the time, in protest, because the United States would not allow Communist China to join. Sixteen countries answered the Security Council's call, but most of the troops came from America. Mac-Arthur, commander of the U.N. forces himself said that he dealt only with Washington, although he did accept the aim which United Nations gave him, namely to drive the North Koreans back to the 38th parallel, and no further.

American troops in Korea

The Americans arrived just in time. All the South Korean army was holding was a small area round the port of Pusan, in the south-east. Here, though, the enemy was checked. MacArthur now built up his strength and as soon as he was ready delivered a sudden, deadly blow. American marines landed at Inchon, 320 km behind the North Korean forces, and cut off their supplies. Within a week Seoul had been recaptured, the North Koreans had lost 350 000 men, and what was left of their army was fleeing north in disorder.

The thought of stopping at the 38th parallel was now more than MacArthur could bear. He wanted to overrun North Korea, and President Truman readily agreed. The United Nations Organization which should, in theory, have made the decision simply accepted the plan, even as its troops were racing northwards. The Americans captured the North Korean capital, Pyongyang, and in November 1950 MacArthur prepared a 'home for Christmas' offensive to end the war.

The Americans were not home for Christmas, however. The Chinese

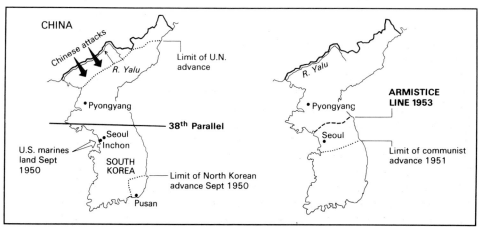

The Korean War

were alarmed by the war and with good reason. The Americans had sent help to the Kuomintang, and as soon as the Korean war had started they had ordered their Seventh Fleet to protect Taiwan. Now a powerful army, headed by a general known to hate the Chinese, was heading for their borders. It was all very well for him to say he would stop on the frontier: he had said he would stop at the 38th parallel, but had changed his mind. The Chinese gave two warnings they would come to the aid of North Korea if the Americans invaded her. The Americans ignored the warnings and when they had almost reached the Yalu River, the Chinese sent a massive force of 'volunteers' from the People's Liberation Army into North Korea. In order to round up the remains of the North Korean army, MacArthur had scattered his forces, so the Chinese were able to defeat them and drive them back, well beyond the 38th parallel.

Once again, though, the tide of war turned. The Chinese outran their supplies and they lost many men, for the fire-power of the American army was enormous. The Chinese withdrew, roughly, to the 38th parallel, and there the front remained for the winter of 1950–1.

What were the Americans to do now? MacArthur had no doubts at all. He wanted to carry the war into China, bombing Manchuria for a start. President Truman's advisers, though, thought that would be a mistake. General Omar Bradley pointed out that Russia was America's chief rival and that MacArthur's plan 'would involve us in the wrong war, at the wrong place, at the wrong time and with the wrong enemy'. President Truman decided that there would be no fighting outside Korea. General MacArthur, determined to have his own way, appealed to the American people. This was the wrong thing to do, since as a soldier, his job was to obey his President, not argue with him in public. Accordingly, in April 1951, Truman dismissed MacArthur. He came home to a hero's welcome.

Early in 1951, the Chinese mounted an offensive. They attacked in 'human waves', hoping to break though by sheer weight of numbers. The Americans mowed them down and, after they had beaten off two attacks, began to edge forwards. Knowing they had failed, and with their troops surrendering in thousands, the Chinese asked for an armistice.

It now looked as if the war was over, and talks began at Panmunjong. However, there was an unexpected problem over prisoners of war. The United Nations forces held 20 000 Chinese and 112 000 North Koreans, and of these 14 000 Chinese and 36 000 North Koreans did not want to go home. It was a great blow to their governments that so many men wished to escape from their 'Communist heaven' and it was a great propaganda victory for the West. The Chinese said that all prisoners must be made to return, the United Nations refused and the war dragged on for another two years. Neither side made important gains during this time.

The end came in 1953, after the Republican candidate, General Eisenhower, was elected President of the United States. Eisenhower had promised the American people he would end the war, so he told the Chinese they must agree to an armistice or he would use nuclear weapons. The Chinese said the prisoners of war could do as they pleased, and the armistice was signed.

Results of the Korean War

In the first place the war was a victory for neither side, since Korea remained divided, with the new frontier very close to the old. To this day there has not been a peace treaty, so technically the North and South are still at war, and the chances of their uniting under one government are remote indeed.

The United Nations Organization gained prestige. Whereas the League of Nations had always given way to aggressors, it had fought an important war, and successfully defended South Korea. On the other hand, it had failed to overrun the North.

The Chinese, too, gained prestige. Everyone knew that America was fighting the war for the United Nations and that China had, in fact, challenged the most powerful country in the world, and stopped her conquering North Korea. But at the same time, the Communists had failed to 'liberate' the South.

However, if neither side won the war, it was the Americans who won the peace. They poured aid into South Korea so that by 1971 she was three times as wealthy as the North. This was much the same as happened in Germany, where the West, which had help from America, prospered far more than the East, which was under Communist control.

A further result of the war was that Communist China and the United States became bitter enemies. There had already been plenty of hostility, because the Americans had helped Chiang Kai-shek. Now, even though the two countries had not actually declared war, their armies had fought one another. Moreover, there seemed no hope of ending the quarrel. Because of the Korean war, the Americans had decided to defend Taiwan, while, for their part, the Chinese were determined they would one day conquer it. There could be no friendly relations between China and the United States while the problem of Taiwan remained.

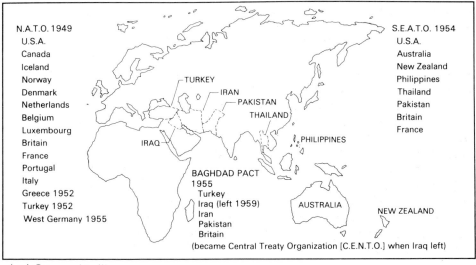

Anti-Communist alliances

Finally, the Americans decided they would have to make extra efforts if they were to stop the spread of Communism in the world. In the first place, they increased their own strength. They spent much more on weapons, increasing their military budget from $12 000 million a year to $60 000 million. They also obtained extra bases round the world, even though it sometimes meant making friends with unpleasant governments. For example, they gave aid to Franco, a notorious Fascist, so that they could have bases in Spain. Secondly, they surrounded Russia and China with an interlocking system of alliances. N.A.T.O. had been in existence since 1949, but in 1955 it was strengthened by admitting West Germany. In 1954 the Manila Pact led to the formation of the South East Asia Treaty Organization (S.E.A.T.O), the countries joining it being the United States, France, Britain, Australia, New Zealand, Pakistan, Thailand and the Philippines. Linking the two was the Baghdad Pact of 1955. The countries that signed it were Britain, Turkey, Iran, Pakistan and Iraq. This alliance was not as strong as the other two, and in 1959 Iraq left it. It was then known as the Central Treaty Organization (C.E.N.T.O.).

In short then, the United States tried to police the world much as a frontier marshal might have tried to police a cattle town. However, unlike the marshal in the traditional Wild West film, the United States was not particular about the friends she chose to help her.

Chapter Forty-five

Vietnam

The Struggle Against the French

DURING the nineteenth century the French had a colony in South East Asia called Indo-China. It was made up of Cambodia, Laos and Vietnam. They exploited it, they would not allow the people any share in the government, and as a result there was a lot of opposition to French rule, especially from the Vietnamese Communist Party, which was founded in 1930 by Ho Chi Minh. That same year the Communists organized a peasant rebellion. The French put it down but this did not discourage Ho for he saw how much a few determined men could do, as long as they had the help of friendly peasants.

In 1941, Japan occupied Indo-China, which she then ruled with the help of Vichy French officials. To fight the Japanese, Ho Chi Minh formed the Vietminh or League for Vietnamese Independence. Though men of all parties joined it, most of its members were Communists. As the war drew to a close, the Japanese began to distrust the French, so they took the government from them and almost at once they were defeated themselves. For the moment, the country had no rulers, so Ho Chi Minh thought his chance had come. In September 1945 he declared that Vietnam was an independent State.

Now the nations that had won the war took a hand. There were still Japanese troops in Vietnam, so it was agreed at the Potsdam Conference that the Chinese should go into the north of the country and accept their surrender, while the British did the same in the south. The British, however, did not want Vietnam to be independent, as it might be an example to their own colonies. Accordingly, they allowed the French to return. Almost at once there was fighting, and in 1946, a French warship bombarded Haiphong killing 6000 people. War now began in earnest.

The French thought they would win the war easily, but it dragged on. Then, in 1949 Mao Tse-tung and the Communists won the civil war in China. The Vietminh now had powerful friends over the border, so the French were alarmed. They did two things. In the first place they declared Vietnam a new State in the French Union, with a Vietnamese, Bao Dai, as its Emperor. They hoped that members of the Vietminh who were not Communists would rally to Bao Dai. Few people did, because he was so

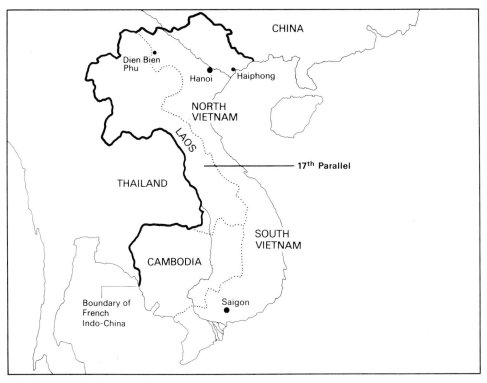

Vietnam

obviously a puppet of the French. The second move was to appeal to the Americans, and this was much more successful. They were so anxious to prevent the spread of Communism that by 1954 they were paying 80 per cent of the cost of the war.

Still the French could not defeat the Vietminh, mainly because the latter used guerrilla tactics. The French Commander-in-Chief, General Navarre, thought that if he could only make his enemies come out of the jungle and fight a pitched battle, his European troops would be sure to win.

Accordingly, in 1954, he dropped a powerful force of paratroops at Dien Bien Phu, a village which was in the heart of Vietminh territory, and lying across their communications with China. The place had an airstrip, so it should have been easy to supply, but it lay in a wide valley surrounded by hills. The Vietminh commander, General Giap, accepted the challenge. He was willing to take his time, and his men performed wonders of sheer hard work. They brought up masses of supplies on bicycles, they tunnelled through the hills so that their guns could fire directly at the enemy, and they dug trenches that zigzagged closer and closer to the French positions. Soon the Vietminh artillery had destroyed the airstrip and their anti-air-craft guns were shooting French transports out of the sky. Hardly any supplies or reinforcements arrived, so everything depended on the courage of the men on the ground. They fought well, but their strong points fell one by one, and in the end the survivors surrendered. General

Navarre had lost his pitched battle, and the French realized they had lost the war.

It so happened that at that very time, 1954, there was an international conference being held at Geneva to decide on the future of Korea and Indo-China. The fall of Dien Bien Phu meant the French were willing to let it make a settlement. By this, Laos and Cambodia were to be independent. As for Vietnam, the country was to be divided at the 17th parallel, the Vietminh withdrawing north of that line and the French Union Forces to the south. There was then to be a wait of two years so that passions would cool, after which elections were to be held to choose a government for the whole country.

North Vietnam under Ho Chi Minh

In North Vietnam Ho Chi Minh at once began creating a Communist State. He collectivized agriculture, he repaired roads and railways damaged by the war, and he developed a few nationalized industries. In all this he had some modest success, but what was more important he kept the loyal support of his people.

South Vietnam under Ngo Dinh Diem 1954–63

In South Vietnam, things were very different. Here Ngo Dinh Diem took over from Bao Dai, and became President. Diem was a Catholic, so he was against Buddhists, who were the majority of his people, and he was right-wing so he was against Communists. He knew that if there were elections he would be bound to lose, so he refused to hold them, thus breaking the Geneva agreement. He was also determined to crush any opposition. Moreover, Diem was corrupt. His brothers all had important positions which they used to make themselves rich and even his sister-in-law, Madame Nhu, became powerful. The Americans called her the 'dragon lady'. Diem's biggest mistake, though, was to support the landlords against the peasants, for that turned the mass of the people against him.

It was not long before there was a rebellion. Most of the rebels were Communists, so their enemies called them Vietcong, or Vietnamese Communists. They used guerrilla tactics, which were very effective, because the country has vast areas of mountains and jungle. Even more important, they made friends with the peasants. They damaged neither houses nor crops: they never stole: they respected the people's religion and customs: they helped with the housework and farming. The peasants already hated Diem, so when the Vietcong took every care to behave properly, they were more than willing to give them help. A man could be a guerrilla fighter one day and then, if need be, he could hide his weapons and mingle with the people. It was nearly always impossible for Diem's troops to decide who were members of the Vietcong and who were not. It was similar to the civil war in China. The guerrillas were like fish, while the peasants were the sea in which they swam.

Even though Diem was so disliked by his own people, the American government decided to help him, simply because he was fighting Communists. In 1954, President Eisenhower put forward his 'domino theory'. He said, 'You have a row of dominoes set up, you knock over the first one and what will happen to the last one is a certainty that it will go over very quickly.' The 'dominoes' were the countries of Asia, and the first one that was being pushed was South Vietnam. The Americans therefore decided to send Diem economic aid, weapons, military advisers and support troops.

When John Kennedy became President in 1961 he did even more. He saw the problem of the fish in the sea clearly enough. To catch the fish he trained a special force of American soldiers in guerrilla warfare. They were called the 'Green Berets'. To drain the sea he helped Diem's government with its 'Strategic Hamlets Programme'. Under this, Vietnamese peasants had to leave their homes and live in new villages surrounded by barbed wire. Here they could be 'protected' from the Vietcong. Possibly 40 per cent of the population was resettled. However, many Communists were swept into strategic hamlets where they went on with their work of winning people for their cause. Also the peasants were furious at having to move. They worshipped their ancestors, and the land where those ancestors were buried was sacred, so leaving it was unbearable. The Strategic Hamlets Programme meant that even more people joined the Vietcong.

While losing the war against the Vietcong, Diem also made himself enemies by persecuting the Buddhists. In 1963, as a protest, a Buddhist monk burned himself to death in the centre of Saigon. Madame Nhu sneered, calling it a 'barbecue', while Diem ordered his troops to attack Buddhist pagodas in Saigon and other cities. The Americans had already been embarrassed by their friendship with Diem, and this was the last straw. They encouraged some of his generals to overthrow him, and he was shot. In fact, none of the Presidents who came after Diem were much better than he had been.

President Johnson and the Vietnam War

Three weeks after Diem's murder, President Kennedy was himself assassinated and Lyndon Johnson became President. His ambition was to create the 'Great Society' in the United States (see pages 27–8) but he could not concentrate on that and the war at the same time. Consequently, he wanted a quick victory in Vietnam. He was sure that the Vietcong were taking orders and having help from North Vietnam, which he saw as the main enemy. He described her as a 'raggedy-ass little fourth-rate country', and was sure he could defeat her. However, he did not dare invade, because that could mean a war with China, as had happened in Korea, nor could he use nuclear weapons, because the Russians might retaliate. Johnson decided he would bomb North Vietnam with conventional weapons, until Ho Chi Minh gave up helping the Vietcong.

In 1965, the Americans launched 'Operation Rolling Thunder'. From 1965 to 1969 they dropped 4½ million tonnes of bombs, or 225 kg of high explosives for every inhabitant of Vietnam. They not only raided the

G.I.s in South Vietnam

Anti-war demonstration, New York

North, but also every place in the South where they thought the Vietcong might be. As well as loosing a torrent of high explosives the Americans dropped napalm, which burnt people to death: to destroy hiding places they sprayed many square miles of forest, killing the leaves on the trees: they ruined crops, again by spraying chemicals.

Also, Johnson poured American troops into Vietnam, until there were half a million of them there. These ground forces went on 'search and destroy missions' in which they almost gave up trying to distinguish between ordinary South Vietnamese country folk and Communists. Instead, they worked on the principle that 'if it's yellow and if it moves, shoot it'. In 1968 a patrol massacred 500 people, men, women and children, at the village of My Lai. The only explanation one of the soldiers could give was, 'I was angry, I had lost some buddies'.

The results of all this were not what President Johnson wanted. In the first place the Vietcong fought even harder, and they had extra help. The Russians and the Chinese sent more and more weapons and supplies. They went south along a route called the Ho Chi Minh trail which ran through Laos and Cambodia, both of which were neutral countries. Also, units of the North Vietnamese regular army came to fight alongside the Vietcong.

Secondly, the Americans became disgusted by the war. There were heavy casualties — 100 000 before the end — and the coffins and the wounded soldiers that came home were grim reminders of what war really meant. There was expense, for the war took $2000 million a month. There was also brutality. In most homes people saw what was happening on colour television and they were horrified that such dreadful things could be done in their name. Soon there were demonstrations with crowds chanting slogans like:

'Hey, hey, L.B.J.,
How many kids have you killed today?'

Young men who were being called up for the army burnt their draft cards in public. People sat in front of troop trains, so that they could not leave.

Then, in January 1968, the Vietcong launched what they called their Tet, or New Year offensive. They attacked every city in South Vietnam, and at Saigon they even occupied the American embassy for a time. Soon the Vietcong were driven out of the cities but they had made a remarkable show of strength. Johnson had been telling the American people that they were winning the war, but their television sets proved he was lying.

After the Tet offensive, it was not the Vietcong that cracked, but Johnson. He cut down the bombing almost to nothing, he refused to send the generals anything like the reinforcements they wanted, and he agreed to hold peace talks in Paris. Moreover, he realized that the war had destroyed any faith the American people might have had in him, and decided he would not stand again for President when his term ended in 1968.

President Nixon and the End of the War

It was the Republican candidate, Richard Nixon, who was elected in 1968. He realized his people would not let him use American troops in Vietnam, but he still hoped he might win the war, so he ordered bombing on a greater scale than ever. The cities of North Vietnam were devastated. Nixon's aeroplanes also bombed the Ho Chi Minh trail, even though it was in neutral territory, and they laid mines in Haiphong harbour, which was where the Russians and the Chinese landed war supplies.

As well as bombing, Nixon tried 'Vietnamization'. The idea was to pour arms and equipment into South Vietnam so that her own troops could wage the war on their own. All Americans came home, but President Thieu's forces were one million strong and heavily armed.

However, Nixon's bombing was no more effective than Johnson's. Vietnamization was a failure, as well, for General Giap easily routed the demoralized forces of South Vietnam. Nixon realized he was defeated, too, but he had to make it seem he had won a victory. His Secretary of State, Henry Kissinger, had the task of negotiating 'peace with honour'. The Paris talks began again, and peace was signed in 1973. There was to be a cease-fire, American prisoners of war were to be released and there were to be free elections in both North and South Vietnam.

Nixon claimed that his bombing had made the North Vietnamese 'see reason', and there were victory parades all over the United States. They were a sham. The fighting went on and the North Vietnamese won battle after battle. The war ended in 1975 with the capture of Saigon. It was renamed Ho Chi Minh City, but Ho was not there to enjoy the victory. He had died in 1968.

Reasons for the North Vietnamese Victory

'A raggedy-ass little fourth-rate country' had defeated the United States. How was this possible?

In the first place the Americans did not employ their full strength. They dared not invade North Vietnam for fear of the Chinese, and they dared not use nuclear weapons for fear of the Russians. Secondly, the Communist tactics were ideal for the jungles and mountains of Vietnam. Regular troops had little hope of finding guerrillas in such country. Thirdly, the Communists won the support of the peasants. It is certain that without that they could not have survived. Fourthly, the Vietnamese Communists had great courage. The Americans loosed as many high explosives on them as had been used by all the powers fighting in the Second World War, but it only made them all the more determined to win. Fifthly, the Communists had valuable help from Russia and China, though it did not compare with what the Americans gave the South Vietnamese. Finally, there were the rulers of South Vietnam, who were inefficient, cruel, and corrupt. They made their subjects hate them, so bringing ruin on themselves and their country. One of the many tragedies of the war is that the Americans, who believed they were fighting for freedom, none the less felt bound to support such people.

The Results of the War

The most important result of the war was the loss of life in Vietnam, for well over two million died and four million were wounded. There was wholesale destruction as well, of towns, villages, farmland and forests.

The Americans also paid in blood since they had 100 000 casualties, 56 000 of them deaths. For the country as a whole though, the cost in money had more effect. It ran into billions of dollars, causing inflation and ruining President Johnson's plans for social reform.

American prestige was badly damaged. In 1973, President Nixon said, 'Let us be proud that America did not settle for a peace that would have betrayed our allies.' In his heart, though, he knew he had lost the war and was leaving South Vietnam to her fate. It seemed to the rest of the world that it was safer to be an ally of the Communist Powers, than of the United States.

A further result was to make the United States more cautious. For example, she has done nothing to stop Communists from taking control of several African countries, including Angola and Ethiopia. The American people would not tolerate another conflict like Vietnam.

Finally, it is possible that defeat made the Americans more willing to reach an understanding with China. Had they won the war in Vietnam they might have felt confident enough to challenge the Chinese elsewhere. As it was, they lost, so it seemed better to work for détente. This is described in the next chapter.

Chapter Forty-six

Détente between the United States of America and China

WE HAVE already seen, in the last chapter, why the Americans wanted détente with China. They had lost the war in Vietnam, so they thought it better to come to terms with the Communist giant, rather than go on trying to oppose him. For their own part, the Chinese were glad to have an understanding with the United States, because they had quarrelled with the Russians.

The Sino-Soviet Split

Russia and China had been rivals before, as in the nineteenth century when Russia took Siberia. What was more remarkable was that when the Chinese Communists rebelled, before and during the Second World War, Stalin made it plain that he hoped the Nationalists would crush them. He wanted China to be strong, so that she would resist Japan and he thought, wrongly, that the Nationalists would be more likely to do this. Also he wanted 'communism in one country'. World revolution must wait until Russia was powerful enough to direct it, and in the meantime Communist Parties in other countries must not become too independent. Though he was a strong Communist at home, in his foreign policy Stalin was always a Russian nationalist. To him, Russia's interests were more important than those of Communists in other parts of the world.

Finally, in 1949, Mao Tse-tung proclaimed the 'People's Republic of China'. Stalin accepted the fact, while Mao was anxious to be on good terms with Russia. He wanted help, in case there was trouble with the United States, and he wanted economic aid. In 1950, Russia and China signed a Treaty of Friendship, and for a few years the two countries worked together, much to the alarm of the people in the West. Russia is extremely powerful, while China has a larger population than any other country. Between them, they might one day control the world.

However, in 1956 Khrushchev made his famous speech to the Twentieth Congress of the Soviet Communist Party. In this he denounced Stalin and described his own policies, saying that some of the ideas of Marx and Lenin would have to be abandoned. The Chinese were horrified. You can realize how they felt if you understand that Communism is a form of religion. It was almost as if a new Archbishop of Canterbury had said his predecessor was a wicked man, and that many of the teachings of Jesus were wrong. Inevitably, there was a lot of argument. For one thing, the Russians said that world Communism could come about by peaceful means, while the Chinese still held that there would have to be war and revolution. The Chinese accused the Russians of 'revisionism', because they had revised the theories of Marx and Lenin. The Russians accused the Chinese of 'dogmatism', because they clung rigidly to the old ideas and refused to abandon any of them in the light of modern changes, such as the hydrogen bomb. The Russians pointed out that 'dogmatism' was particularly dangerous in the nuclear age.

There was a further argument about Communist principles, beginning in 1958, when Mao announced China's 'Great Leap Forward'. This is described in pages 152–5.

There were other important disagreements, as well as those on ideas. In 1953, the Russians exploded their first hydrogen bomb. Mao was pleased, and said that the 'east wind' was blowing more strongly in the world than the 'west wind'. To the disgust of the Chinese the Russians would not try to frighten their enemies with the new weapon or, at least, not on China's behalf. For example, in 1955, the Chinese Communists bombarded Quemoy and Matsu. They are two small islands only 8 km from the mainland and were held by the Chinese Nationalists. The Americans said they would use nuclear weapons if the attack did not stop, and the Chinese hoped the Russians would threaten to retaliate. The Russians did nothing, so the Chinese felt betrayed. The same thing happened when the Chinese bombarded Quemoy again, in 1958.

Then, in 1959, the Russians broke a promise they had made to share nuclear secrets with the Chinese. Khrushchev was about to meet Eisenhower at the Camp David summit, and he wanted to make a good impression on him.

In 1960, the Russians suddenly ended economic aid to China and called home all their technical advisers who were helping to organize new industries. These men even took their blueprints with them. It was like snatching away the plates in the middle of a meal. One reason was that the Russians had no liking for the Great Leap Forward. Another was that Khrushchev hoped to show the Chinese how much they needed Russian help: he only made them determined to be independent.

Finally, there was serious fighting between Russian and Chinese armies on the borders. It happened in Sinkiang in 1962 and on the Ussuri River in Manchuria in 1968. The problem was that the frontiers had remained vague since the days of the Tsars and the Manchus, so each side thought the other was invading.

The Development of Détente

Détente began in a strange way with 'ping-pong diplomacy'. In 1971, an American table-tennis team went to China to play matches. More serious things followed in the same year. Nixon lifted the American trade ban on China, and the value of trade between the two countries grew from

President Nixon meets Chairman Mao

$5 million to $500 million in two years. Also in 1971, Communist China was admitted to the United Nations, something which, until then, the Americans had used their veto to prevent. Communist China replaced Taiwan on the Security Council, which the Americans approved, but Taiwan was even expelled from the General Assembly, which had not been part of the American plan. Then, in 1972, President Nixon accepted an invitation from Mao Tse-tung to visit China. As Nixon remarked, 'The leader of the world's most powerful nation met the leader of the world's most populous nation.' He also said there was no fundamental reason why the two countries should quarrel.

In fact, there was such a reason, and that was Taiwan. It was here that the Chinese Nationalists had fled when Mao's armies overran the mainland, and the United States not only recognized its rulers as the legal government of China, but, after the Korean war, promised to defend it against invasion. The Communists, for their part, looked on Taiwan as a province of their own country that was in enemy hands, and were determined to capture it at the first opportunity.

Then in 1976 Mao Tse-tung died. China's new leaders like Chairman Hua Kuo-feng and Senior Vice-Premier Teng Hsiao-ping were much less rigid in their Communist ideas, and more friendly towards the West. In 1979, President Carter recognized the People's Republic of China, and withdrew America's promise to defend Taiwan. The last important obstacle to friendship between the United States and China had been removed.

At the end of 1979 the Russians invaded Afghanistan, and, as a result, America and China drew even closer together. Both condemned Russia's action.

WORK SECTION — International Relations since 1945 — The Far East

French troops capture Dien Bien Phu

Questions

1 Which French general ordered the capture of Dien Bien Phu?
2 Why did he do this? When?
3 What troops are making the attack? Why was it necessary to employ them?
4 Why did the range of hills you can see in the distance become important later on?
5 Describe the recapture of Dien Bien Phu by the Communists.
6 What were the results of the battle?

The War in Vietnam

Document One

President Kennedy to President Diem December 14 1961

I have received your recent letter in which you described the dangerous condition caused by North Vietnam's efforts to take over your country. The situation in your embattled country is well known to me and to the American people. We have been deeply disturbed by the assault on your country. Our indignation has mounted as the deliberate savagery of the Communist program of assassination, kidnapping and wanton violence became clear.

Your letter underlines that the campaign of force and terror now being waged against your people and your Government is supported and directed from the outside by the authorities at Hanoi. They have thus violated the provisions of the Geneva Accords to which they bound themselves in 1954.

In response to your request, we are prepared to help the Republic of Vietnam to protect its people and to preserve its independence. We shall promptly increase our assistance to your defense effort.

(*Vietnam — History, Documents and Opinions* — ed. Marvin E. Gettleman)

Document Two

Revolutionary Warfare — Eqbal Ahmad (a Pakistani professor teaching in America): *Most compelling, but also most self-defeating, is the myth that terror is the basis of civilian support for the guerrillas. Guerrilla warfare requires a highly committed but covert civilian support which cannot be obtained at gun point. An outstanding feature of guerrilla training*

345

is the stress of scrupulously correct and just behavior towards civilians. Political work, believes General Giap, is 'the soul of the army', and a Chinese guerrilla expert explains that 'army indoctrination is primarily aimed at training the troops to gain the total support of the people'. Guerrilla use of terror, therefore, is selective. It strikes those who are popularly identified as the 'enemy of the people' — officials, landlords and the like.

The assumption that a guerrilla outfit, like a conventional army, can be controlled and commanded by a foreign government ignores the facts of revolutionary warfare. The resourceful and tough leaders and cadres who face the enemy daily, collect taxes, administer, make promises, and give hopes to the population are not easily controlled from abroad and make suspicious, exacting, and hard-to-please allies. Therefore, zone commanders are, for the most part, monarchs of what they survey.

(op. cit.)

Document Three

American Policy in Vietnam — Eqbal Ahmad.

I know how Asians feel about America's action. They call it neo-colonialism; some think it is imperialism. I know that is very wrong because Americans are naturally sympathetic to peoples' struggles for freedom and justice, and they would like to help if they could. I prefer the term 'maternalism' for American policy in Vietnam, because it reminds me of the story of an elephant who, as she strolled benignly in the jungle, stepped on a mother partridge and killed her. When she noticed the orphaned chicks, tears filled the kind elephant's eyes, 'Ah, I too have maternal instincts', she said turning to the orphans, and sat on them.

(op. cit.)

Questions

Document One

1 When did Diem become President of South Vietnam?
2 How does Kennedy say that the Communists were behaving in South Vietnam?
3 Where is Hanoi? Who was head of the government there? What part does Kennedy say this government is playing in the war?

4 What was agreed at Geneva in 1954? Why does Kennedy say the Hanoi government is breaking this agreement?
5 How did Diem himself break the Geneva agreements?
6 Why does Kennedy say he will send help to South Vietnam?
7 What help did Kennedy give? Why did he make things worse?

Document Two

8 According to this author:
  (a) How do guerrillas behave towards civilians?
  (b) How do they use terror?
  (c) How far do guerrillas obey foreign governments?
9 What are the main points over which President Kennedy and Eqbal Ahmad disagree? Which do you think is right?

Document Three

10 According to Eqbal Ahmad, how do Asians feel about America's actions in Vietnam? Why does he say those views are wrong?
11 Why does he compare America to the elephant that sat on the baby partridges? (You will first have to decide why the elephant behaved as she did.)
12 Do you think this view is correct?

China's Relations with America and Russia

Document One

Statement by President Truman 27 June 1950:

The attack upon Korea makes it plain beyond all doubt that communism has passed beyond the use of subversion to conquer independent nations and will now use subversion and war. It has defied the orders of the Security Council of the United Nations issued to preserve international peace and security. In these circumstances, the occupation of Formosa by Communist forces would be a direct threat to the security of the Pacific area and to the United States forces performing their lawful and necessary functions in that area.

Accordingly, I have ordered the Seventh Fleet to prevent any attack on Formosa.

Document Two

Khrushchev's views on Chinese Communism:

Stalin was always fairly critical of Mao Tse-tung. He used to say that Mao was a 'margarine Marxist.'

When Mao's victorious revolutionary army was approaching Shanghai, he halted their march and refused to take the city. Stalin asked Mao, 'Why don't you take Shanghai?' 'There's a population of six million there,' answered Mao. 'If we take the city, then we'll have to feed all those people. And where do we find the food to do it?'

Now, I ask you, is that a Marxist talking?

Mao Tse-tung has always relied on the peasants and not on the working class. That's why he didn't take Shanghai. He didn't want to take responsibility for the welfare of the workers. Stalin properly criticized Mao for this deviation from true Marxism. But the fact remains that Mao, relying on the peasants and ignoring the working class, achieved victory. Not that his victory was some sort of miracle, but it was certainly a new twist to Marxist philosophy since it was achieved without the proletariat. In short, Mao Tse-tung is a petty bourgeois whose interests are alien, and have been alien all along, to those of the working class.

(Khrushchev Remembers)

Document Three

An American's view of Chinese foreign policy:

In 1965 Mao made it clear enough that he did not expect the Americans to desist until they had learnt, the hard way, that they could not impose their will on revolutionary Vietnam by military violence.

The Chinese believed that the lesson of Vietnam, and no mere change of Presidents, was what made it possible for Mao in 1970 to speak differently about Nixon. 'Experience' had made Nixon relatively 'good'.

By the late autumn of 1970 inquiries reaching China had indicated that the President wished to know whether he or his representative would be received in Peking. An indirect answer was contained in an interview given to me by Chou En-lai in November, when he said that Sino-American conversations could be opened, but only if the Americans demonstrated a 'serious' desire to negotiate. To the initiated, 'serious' meant, first of all, a realistic attempt to work out a program to deal with the Taiwan

problem. As Mao and Chou saw it, that was the key to all other Asian settlements.

Very high among the reasons why Sino-American rapprochement *interested China was to improve her strategic position in dealing with Russia. With America off the Asian continent, the danger of a Soviet-American gang-up dispelled, and a seat of her own in the U.N., Peking's manœuvering power would obviously be enhanced.*

(*The Long Revolution* — Edgar Snow)

Questions

Document One

1 What order does President Truman say he has given?
2 What reasons does he give for his action?
3 How was this action to affect relations between China and America in the years to come?

Document Two

4 When were China and Russia on good terms? Why?
5 What do you suppose Stalin meant when he called Mao Tse-tung a 'margarine Marxist'?
6 Why did Mao delay the capture of Shanghai? (Obviously, he did take it in the end.)
7 What, according to Khrushchev, did this prove about Mao?
8 What does Khrushchev mean by 'the proletariat' and the 'working class'?
9 What does he say was odd about Mao's revolution?
10 What other differences of opinion were there between Russia and China?

Document Three

11 How did America's defeat in Vietnam affect her relations with China?
12 What, according to Mao Tse-tung, was the most important problem America and China would have to solve?
13 When was that problem solved?
14 What, according to this author, did China stand to gain from friendship with America?
15 Name three events in 1971 which prepared the way for President Nixon's visit to China in 1972.
16 Why was Nixon's visit only a limited success?

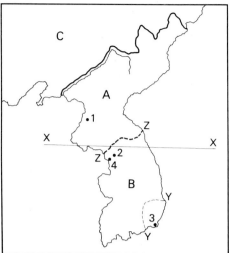

The Korean War

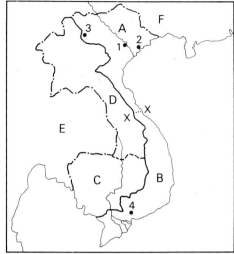

Vietnam

The Korean War

Map Questions

1 Name countries A, B, C, towns 1–4, and lines x–x, y–y and z–z.
   Name the river that follows the frontier between countries A and C.
2 When was Korea divided at line x–x? Why?
3 When did country A attack country B?
4 What force made a landing at town 4? Why was this landing important?
5 How far north did the U.N. forces advance?
6 When did country C join the war? Why? How far did its troops advance? How far were they driven back?
7 What action did General MacArthur wish to take against country C? Why was he overruled? What happened to him?
8 When did country C ask for an armistice? When was it in fact signed? Why was there such a long delay?

Vietnam

Map Questions

1 Name countries A–F, towns 1–4 and line x–x.
2 The countries within the boundary _._._._. were once one French colony. What was its name? When was it broken up?

3 What happened at town 2 in 1946? What was the result?
4 Which French general decided to fight a battle at town 3? When? Which general defeated him?
5 Who ruled country A after the French withdrew?
6 Who ruled country B after the French withdrew? What events led to his overthrow?
7 What trail led through countries D and C?
8 How did country F help country A? What other country also sent help?
9 Which American President ordered the bombing of country A? When?
10 What happened at town 4 in January 1968?
11 Which American President ordered the bombing of countries C and D? Why? When? What action did he take against town 2? Why?
12 When was town 4 captured? What was it renamed?

The Korean War

Questions

1 Why was Korea divided after the war? Where? What happened in the North? What happened in the South?
2 Why did the North Koreans attack the South?

3 Why did the North Koreans win an easy victory at first?

4 What help did President Truman send? What action did the United Nations take? Why did Russia not prevent this? Who sent most troops to Korea? What aim did the U.N. give its troops?

5 How did MacArthur defeat the North Koreans?

6 What did MacArthur decide to do after his victory? What action did the U.N. take? How far did MacArthur advance?

7 Why did the Chinese send troops to Korea? Why were they able to defeat MacArthur's forces?

8 Why was the Chinese advance checked? Where was the front during the winter of 1950–1?

9 What did MacArthur wish to do? Who disagreed with him? What was President Truman's decision? Why was MacArthur dismissed?

10 Why did the Chinese ask for an armistice? Why was it difficult to arrange one?

11 When, finally, was an armistice signed? Why?

12 Which side won the Korean war?

13 What did the U.N. gain? What had it failed to do?

14 Why did the Chinese gain prestige? What had they failed to do?

15 What happened in South Korea after the war?

11 How did the Korean war make friendship between the United States and China more unlikely than ever?

17 How did America try to increase her strength after the war?

18 What alliances were formed against Russia and China?

Give an account of the Korean War under the headings: Origins/The Course of the War/Results of the War

Vietnam

Questions

1 Which countries made up French Indo-China? Describe French rule there. Name two things Ho Chi Minh did in 1930.

2 What party did Ho Chi Minh form to fight the Japanese? What did he do in 1945?

3 Why did the Chinese and the British go into Vietnam? Why did the British re-admit the French? What resulted?

4 Why were the French alarmed in 1949? Name two things which they did.

5 Who was the French Commander-in-Chief? What kind of battle did he want? Which village did he occupy? Why? Who was the Vietminh general? Describe how he defeated the French.

6 At what conference was a settlement made for Indo-China? When was it? What were the terms of the settlement?

7 What work did Ho Chi Minh do in North Vietnam? What was his most important achievement?

8 Who became President of South Vietnam? Name two groups of people he was against. Why did he refuse to hold free elections? What shows his government was corrupt? What was his biggest mistake?

9 Who were the Vietcong? What military tactics did they use? How did they make friends with the peasants? How did the peasants help them?

10 Why did the Americans help the government of South Vietnam? What theory did President Eisenhower put forward in 1954?

11 What special force did President Kennedy send to Vietnam? What was the aim of the Strategic Hamlets Programme? How did it work? What were its results?

12 What events led to a change of government in South Vietnam in 1963?

13 Why did President Johnson want a quick victory in Vietnam? Why did he decide to bomb North Vietnam? What alternatives did he think were too dangerous?

14 Describe the American air offensive in Vietnam — quantity of bombs dropped, targets, weapons. How many troops went to South Vietnam? Describe their methods.

15 How did the Vietcong react to the American offensive? Who sent them help? How did much of it reach them?

16 How did the American people react to the war?

17 What did the Tet offensive prove to the American people?

18 What was President Johnson's reaction to the Tet offensive?

19 Why did President Nixon order even more bombing?

20 What was 'Vietnamization'?
21 Why did Nixon decide he must make peace? Who negotiated it? Where? What were the peace terms?
22 What happened in South Vietnam after the peace treaty was signed?
23 Give six reasons why the Communists won the war in Vietnam.
24 How many Vietnamese died in the war?
25 What did the war cost America in money and lives?
26 Why did America lose prestige?
27 In what two ways did the Vietnam war change American foreign policy?

Give an account of the war in Vietnam under the headings: The Struggle against the French/North Vietnam under Ho Chi Minh/South Vietnam under Ngo Dinh Diem/President Johnson and the Vietnam War/President Nixon and the End of the War/Reasons for the North Vietnamese Victory/Results of the War

Détente between the U.S.A. and China

Questions

1 Why did the Americans and Chinese want détente with each other?
2 Which side did Stalin hope would win in the Chinese civil war? Why?
3 Why did Mao want friendship with Russia? What treaty was signed? Why did it alarm the West?
4 How did the Chinese react to Khrushchev's speech denouncing Stalin? Of what did the Chinese and the Russians accuse each other?
5 When was there more argument about Communist principles?
6 What did Mao feel when the Russians exploded the hydrogen bomb? Why did the Chinese and Russians quarrel over the Quemoy incidents?

7 What promise did Khrushchev break in 1959?
8 What action did the Russians take in 1960? Give two reasons for this.
9 When was there fighting between Chinese and Russians? Where? Why?
10 How did détente begin in 1971? Name two things that also happened in 1971.
11 Which American President visited China? When?
12 What prevented a complete understanding between America and China for the time being?
13 When did Mao Tse-tung die? Who were the new rulers of China? What was their foreign policy? Name two things President Carter did in 1979.
14 What action by the Russians made the Americans and Chinese even firmer friends?

Give an account of Détente between the United States of America and China under the headings: The Sino-Soviet Split/The Development of Détente

Problems

1 What were the causes of the war in Korea? What were its results for (a) the United Nations, (b) Sino-American relations, (c) American foreign policy in the rest of the world?
2 What were the causes of the war in Vietnam? Why were the French unable to win it?
3 Why was a major battle fought at Dien Bien Phu? What were its consequences?
4 How did America become involved in the war in Vietnam? By what stages did she escalate the war?
5 Why did the Communists win the war in Vietnam?
6 Why did Sino-Soviet relations deteriorate after 1956?
7 Why have Sino-American relations improved since 1971?

INTERNATIONAL RELATIONS
since 1945
—
THE MIDDLE EAST

Introduction

THE MIDDLE EAST is important for strategic and economic reasons. It is the meeting-place of three continents, Europe, Asia and Africa, so a great power that controlled it would be able to advance into any of them. Also, it produces a great deal of oil which many countries, like those of Western Europe, must have if they are to survive.

The Arabs are the most important people in the Middle East, and it might have been better for the peace of the world if they had been strong and united. Instead, they have been weak and divided. In the 1970s there was an Islamic revival, but it has shown not only how much enthusiasm there is for this religion, but also how much disagreement there is between the different sects. For example, in September 1980, Iraq invaded the Western provinces of Iran, so starting a war that continued until the middle of 1982.

As a result, the Middle East is a 'power vacuum', and the question is, who is going to fill it? Before the First World War, Germany made a bid, by building the Berlin to Baghdad Railway. The Russians, too, had ambitions, hoping to control Persia and win an outlet to the Indian Ocean. However, until the end of the Second World War, it was Britain who had most influence in the region.

Today, Britain is no longer a world power, and the countries which might control the Middle East are America, Russia or even China.

In this book there is no space to cover all the problems of the Middle East, but we will look at the one that has caused most trouble in recent years. It is the conflict between the Arabs and the Israelis.

Chapter Forty-seven

The Origins of the State of Israel

Early History and Immigration

THE JEWS have a long history and an unhappy one. Palestine became part of the Roman Empire and, according to the Jews, it was the Romans who scattered them over the face of the earth. However that may be, the Jews were without a homeland for centuries. In 1880 there were only 24 000 Jews living in Palestine, which was under Turkish rule and inhabited mainly by Arabs.

In the late nineteenth century about half the world's Jews lived in Russia. They had been left in peace for a long time, but in the 1880s there were violent outbursts against the Jews (pogroms) and then came the Revolution and the Civil War. Millions fled, most of them going to the United States. However, the troubles in Russia also led to the Zionist movement, which hoped to make a national home for the Jews in Palestine. In 1897 some Jewish leaders founded the Zionist Organization, which raised money and bought land in Palestine for their people to settle. From 1880 to 1939 the Jewish population grew from 24 000 to nearly half a million.

Jewish Institutions

Palestine belonged to Turkey until the First World War, and afterwards it was mandated to the British. At first, the Jews had no thought of governing themselves, but simply wanted to live there. However, they organized themselves so well that they created a 'State within a State'. Israel grew in Palestine, just as a baby grows in the womb. It remains part of its mother, but develops its own organs — brain, stomach, heart and so forth.

In the first place, the Jews founded agricultural settlements. One kind was the kibbutz, in which no one had any private property, but everything was owned in common. Another kind was the moshav, which was for people who preferred to live and work in family groups. Each had its own house and farm, though the moshav sold everyone's produce and controlled important resources like water. The agricultural settlements were the work of Labour Zionists who believed that the way to rebuild the Jewish nation was by toiling in the fields, and working for the common good, rather than for their own gain.

Secondly, in 1920, the Histadrut was formed. It had a number of duties. It was a federation of trade unions, so it was a bit like the British Trades Union Congress. It was a co-operative movement, owning factories, shops, banks and public transport. It looked after education, running schools for the young, and training centres for immigrants. Finally, it looked after the sick, the elderly, widows and orphans.

Thirdly there was the Haganah, or defence organization. Bedouin Arabs often attacked Jewish settlements, so each one formed a unit of the Haganah to defend itself. There was also a field force called the Palmach, and a commando unit, neither of which was attached to settlements and would go anywhere that was necessary. At first the British disliked the Haganah, but when the Arabs rebelled in 1936, they were glad to have its help, so they legalized it.

In addition to the Haganah there were two paramilitary terrorist groups. One was the Irgun, led by Menachim Begin. The other was the Lehi, led by Abraham Stern, and known to the British as the Stern Gang.

Fourthly, the British allowed the Jews a constitution. They had an Elected Assembly, for which they all voted, and that in turn chose a National Council which was a group of ministers forming a government. The Assembly and Council even raised taxes, though individual Jews could please themselves whether they paid. Nearly all of them did.

Finally, the Jews gave themselves a common language. Those from Europe, and indeed many others, spoke Yiddish, which is a mixture of medieval Rhineland German and Hebrew, but they thought it better to have pure Hebrew instead.

Events leading to Independence

The first important step towards independence came in 1917 when a Jewish leader, Chaim Weizmann, persuaded the British government to state, 'His Majesty's Government views with favour the establishment in Palestine of a national home for the Jewish people'. This was known as the 'Balfour Declaration', after the Foreign Secretary of the time. Quite what moved the British government to do this is not at all clear, especially as they also promised the Arabs, including those in Palestine, that they would work for their freedom.

After the war, the League of Nations mandated Palestine to the British, instructing them to provide a national home for the Jews, and at the same time to look after Arab rights. The only way was to create a bi-national State, that is a State made up of the people of two nations. However, the Arabs were alarmed at the number of Jewish immigrants and the amount of land they were buying. In 1921 alone they bought 6000 hectares in the Jezreel valley. The Arabs first of all rioted, and then started a revolt which lasted from 1936 to 1939. The British put it down with help from the Haganah, so the revolt weakened the Arabs and strengthened the Jews. Also, it was clear that the two nations would never live together in peace, and it was suggested that they should divide Palestine between them. As we have seen, the Jews had already made a 'State within a State', and now they began to hope that they might have their own independent country.

During the Second World War the British were two-faced. They were glad to accept arms and food from the Jews, and to have the Jewish Brigade fighting in their army. On the other hand, they were frightened that the Arabs of the Middle East might help the Germans so they did their best to please them. A report of 1939, called the MacDonald White Paper, recommended that there should be a strict limit on the number of Jewish immigrants, that the sale of land should be controlled, and that there should be an independent State in Palestine within ten years.

After the war, the British favoured the Arabs entirely. The Middle East was of vital importance to Britain, so she tried to keep on good terms with the Arabs, who were the most powerful people there. The British tried to stop Jewish immigrants coming to Palestine, and this at a time when there were in Europe 100 000 Jewish survivors from concentration camps, and 200 000 more who were homeless. There was great indignation when the British sent the refugee ship *Exodus* back to Hamburg.

By now the world knew the full horror of Hitler's persecution, and the Jews won sympathy everywhere, especially in the United States. David Ben Gurion was determined to lead his people to freedom, and prepared the Haganah for war. The Irgun and the Lehi turned to terrorism, and in 1946, the Irgun blew up the British headquarters in the King David Hotel in Jerusalem. The British hanged or flogged any terrorists they caught, but that only made the rest more determined.

At last, in 1947, the British Foreign Secretary, Ernest Bevin, decided to dump the whole problem on the United Nations. A United Nations Special Committee on Palestine (U.N.S.C.O.P.) was set up, which recommended that there should be an end to the British mandate, and that Palestine should be divided into two countries, one for the Arabs and one for the Jews.

The British disagreed with partition, so they made things as difficult as they could. They allowed the Jordanian army into the country, and encouraged terrorists to cross the border from Syria. War had already been raging for some weeks, when on 14 May 1948, the British withdrew the last of their forces and the Israelis issued their Declaration of Independence.

Chapter Forty-eight

The Arab–Israeli Conflict

SINCE Israel became independent in 1948, she has fought four wars with her Arab neighbours. There are two fundamental reasons for this.

In the first place, the Arabs object to the very existence of Israel. It is easy to see why the Palestinian Arabs were annoyed. Let us suppose large numbers of immigrants came to Britain, bought a vast amount of land to build their own villages, organized their own trade unions, parliament and army, and then took half the country to make an independent State for themselves. This was just what the Jews did in Palestine. The Palestinian Arabs could not have done much on their own, but they have had support

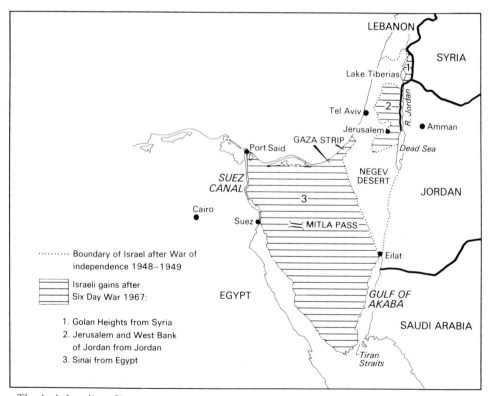

The Arab-Israeli conflict

from all the other Arab States in the Middle East, especially Egypt, Syria and Jordan.

Secondly, there are religious differences, made worse because Jerusalem is important for both sides, and whichever controls it is bound to offend the other. For Jews, Jerusalem is the very centre of their religion, as Rome is for Catholics. The Arabs are Muslims and to them, Jerusalem is the third most important city. It was from there that the Prophet Muhammad is said to have departed when he visited Heaven.

Other problems appeared as time went on, and are described in more detail later in the chapter. There was the plight of the Palestinian refugees, the activities of the Palestinian terrorists, the closing of the Tiran Straits and the Suez Canal to Israel's trade, and the use by Israel of the Jordan waters for irrigation. Also, each war had special causes of its own, on top of these. Foreign powers interfered, to make things worse. Britain and France were largely responsible for one war. Moreover, the United States and Russia were watching closely the whole time, each hoping to win some advantages for herself, and they fuelled the conflict by sending arms.

We will now look at the four wars in turn.

The War of Independence 1948–9

The Arabs were determined to prevent the Jews having a State of their own, and tried to destroy Israel as soon as she was born. The Jews, however, were ready. David Ben Gurion, their defence minister, increased the size of the Haganah from 45 000 to 60 000 and persuaded the Palmach and the Irgun to join it, so creating the Israeli Defence Force (I.D.F.). Egypt, Jordan, Syria and the Lebanon all attacked, but by the end of 1948 the Israelis had overrun most of Palestine and the Arabs admitted defeat. Armistice agreements were signed early in 1949.

The Israelis won because, in the first place, they had the larger army, and they gave it modern weapons that they had bought from Czechoslovakia. Secondly, the Israeli soldiers fought well, because they knew that if they lost the Arabs would be as merciless to their people as Hitler had been. Thirdly, the Arabs showed a poor spirit. Their troops were just hoping for plunder while their governments wanted to seize as much of Palestine as they could for themselves.

Because of the war, Israel gained one-third more territory than the United Nations had suggested. She gained population, too, for 320 000 refugees came in from Europe while the Arab governments, angry at losing the war, drove out as many again from their own countries. At the same time 700 000 Arabs fled from Israel, so the immigrants were able to take their homes and land. This is one reason why it has been very difficult to bring peace to the Middle East. The Israelis will not allow the Palestinian Arab refugees to return, and they in turn will not rest until they are given back their homes. At various times they have lived in camps in Lebanon, Syria, Jordan and the Gaza Strip, and they have often raided Israel. The Israelis described the Gaza Strip as 'a poisoned dagger pointed at our heart'.

357

The Suez Crisis 1956

In 1952 Abdel Gamel Nasser became President of Egypt. His ambition was to be leader of all the Arab peoples, so he did his best to impress them. He persuaded the Russians to give him weapons, he made the British leave their military base at Suez, and he sent help to the Algerians who were rebelling against the French. However, the most daring thing he did was to nationalize the Suez Canal, which belonged to an international company. It came about in this way.

Nasser wanted to increase the height of the dam across the Nile at Aswan, but he did not have enough money, so the Americans promised to help him. However, they withdrew their offer when Egypt recognized Communist China. In 1956 Nasser decided to nationalize the Suez Canal, and use its profits to pay for his dam. He had already annoyed the French by meddling in Algeria, and now the British feared that he might close the canal to their ships. As the Prime Minister, Anthony Eden, complained, 'Nasser has a finger on our windpipe'.

At the same time, Nasser was making difficulties for Israel. The Egyptians had always closed the Tiran Straits to the Israelis, so they could not use their port at Eilat, and had forbidden them to trade through the Suez Canal. Now Nasser organized 'fedayeen' or 'men of sacrifice' in Gaza, and encouraged them to raid Israel.

Nasser's three enemies, France, Britain and Israel, now hatched a plot. Israel was to invade Sinai, so starting a war with Egypt. Britain and France were to order both sides to stop fighting so as to save the Suez Canal from damage. Israel was to agree, but it was certain that Egypt would not, while Israeli troops remained in Sinai. That would give Britain and France the excuse to capture the Suez Canal. The only problem was Russia. However, she was putting down a rebellion in Hungary, and there was every chance that the United States would 'take care of the bear'.

At first, all went according to plan. The Israelis dropped parachute troops near the Mitla Pass and then overran the whole of Sinai in the space of a week. The British and French took their time, because they were afraid of the modern Russian weapons that Nasser had, but in the end they captured Port Said. However, it was election year in the United States, and President Eisenhower was anxious to appear as a man of peace. So far from giving support, America loudly condemned Britain and France. The United Nations did the same. As for Russia, she threatened to use nuclear weapons on them. Anthony Eden lost his nerve and agreed to stop the war. The French could not continue on their own, so they stopped fighting as well. The United States, Russia and even Britain now ordered Israel to evacuate Sinai. David Ben Gurion, now her Prime Minister, had no choice but to withdraw his troops.

As a result of the war, Israel gained no territory. However, the United Nations did send an Emergency Force into Sinai. It kept open the Straits of Tiran, so that Israel could use Eilat, and it stopped the fedayeen raids from Gaza.

Another advantage for Israel was that the United States began sending

French troops landing at Suez

her modern weapons. The American government had seen how powerful Israel was and thought she would help keep Russia out of the Middle East.

Britain and France, on the other hand, were completely humiliated. They had tried to destroy Nasser's prestige, but it stood higher than ever. They had tried to take the Suez Canal, but had been forced to withdraw almost as soon as their attack had begun. Once they had been great colonial powers who had forced their wills on countries like Egypt, but Suez proved those days had gone for ever.

The Six Day War 1967

The war began mainly because of a quarrel between Israel and Syria. The Israelis finished a carrier system to take water from the River Jordan to the Negev Desert. The Jordan has four sources, all of them in Syria, and the Syrians tried to ruin the Israeli project by diverting the headwaters of the river. The Israeli answer was to destroy their works from the air. Then, in 1967, various Arab governments began to taunt Nasser, saying he was sheltering behind the United Nations Emergency Force. Also, the Russians said, quite untruthfully, that Israel was preparing to invade Syria. These two things goaded Nasser into action. He ordered the United Nations Emergency Force out of Sinai, and, amazingly, the United Nations Secretary-General U-Thant meekly agreed. Nasser then sent his own army into Sinai to close the Tiran Straits and 'protect' Syria.

359

It was obvious war was coming, so Ben Gurion decided on a 'pre-emptive strike'. This was a polite way of saying that Israel was to hit first. On 5 June 1967, the Israeli Air Force destroyed on the ground the air forces of Egypt, Jordan, Iraq and Syria. An army under Moshe Dayan swept into Sinai, while other forces invaded Jordan and Syria. By 10 June, the Israelis had taken all the lands on the west bank of the Jordan, including the Old City of Jerusalem, the Golan Heights in Syria, and the whole of Sinai. Her frontier with Egypt was now the Suez Canal, which was closed to shipping.

This time Israel did not give up any of the territory she had conquered, so she now had reasonably secure frontiers. A surprise attack on her was much less likely to succeed. However, there were disadvantages as well. The victory had been too easy, and the Arab defeat too complete. Israel became over-confident, while, for their part, the Arabs were determined that they would one day take revenge.

The Yom Kippur War 1973

In 1970, Nasser died, and Israel lost her most determined enemy. His successor, Anwar Sadat, was a quite different man, but for the time being he kept Nasser's policies, which meant preparing for war. The Arab countries wanted to regain the lands they had lost in 1967, and they wanted revenge for their defeat. Egypt and Syria attacked Israel simultaneously on 6 October 1973. It was the holiest day in the Jewish year, being Yom Kippur, or the Day of Atonement.

The war began well for the Arabs. Wave after wave of Syrian tanks advanced into the Golan Heights. The Egyptian army crossed the Suez Canal and broke through the Israeli defences, the Bar Lev line, in three places. They then took the whole east bank of the canal. On both fronts the Israeli armies were fighting desperately, and were close to defeat.

There are several reasons why the Egyptians and Syrians fared so much better than they did in 1967. In the first place, the Israelis were taken by surprise. All their young men were trained soldiers, but they were doing their civilian jobs and it took three days to mobilize them. In the meantime only Israel's tiny professional army was in action. Secondly, the Arabs had trained their men thoroughly. The Egyptians, for example, had practised the assault on the Bar Lev Line three hundred times. Thirdly, the Arabs had vast quantities of weapons from the Russians, including missiles. These were the S.A.M. ground-to-air missile and the Saggar anti-tank missile. Both were so deadly that they nearly won the war for the Arabs.

After three days, however, the Israelis had mobilized their full strength and the tide turned. In the north, the Syrians were driven off the Golan Heights. In the south, Ariel Sharon fought his way to the Suez Canal, crossed it and then cut off the Egyptian Third Army. Just as he was about to win a decisive victory, there was a cease-fire. Other powers had intervened.

In the first place, Russia made it plain that she would not allow the destruction of Arab armies with their Russian weapons. It would mean a great loss of prestige. However, if the Russians fought for the Arabs, the Americans would have to fight for the Israelis. As the two super-powers

S.A.M. *missile base near Suez, 1973*   W*recked troop carrier on the Golan Heights*

were afraid of each other, both tried to stop the war. Secondly, the Arab States that produce oil, such as Saudi Arabia and Iraq, used the 'oil weapon'. They raised prices by 70 per cent, cut production by 5 per cent and refused to send any oil at all to the countries that were helping Israel. It was Western Europe that suffered most, and the governments there begged the United States to make Israel stop the war.

The fighting ended on 27 October. Next, Henry Kissinger, the United States Secretary of State, negotiated a truce between Israel and Egypt. Egypt was given a strip of land 10 km wide east of the Suez Canal. That meant she once again had complete control of the Canal, which was, eventually, reopened. It was harder to arrange a truce with Syria, but in May 1974 it was agreed that the Syrian and Israeli armies should go back to the positions they had held before the war. On both fronts, there was a United Nations Emergency Force to keep the peace.

Peace between Israel and Egypt

The Yom Kippur War was unlike the others in several ways but the most important difference was that when it was over almost everyone wanted peace. The United States and Russia had come close to fighting each other, so they were scared. Israel had come close to defeat, so she too was scared. As for Egypt, Anwar Sadat was able to hide how close his armies had been to disaster, and made great play of their victories at the beginning of the war. Also he had regained the Suez Canal. Honour was satisfied, and now he wanted to cut down the vast amount Egypt was spending on armaments and use the money to improve the living conditions of his impoverished subjects.

However, peace was not easy to achieve. In December 1973 America and Russia called a conference at Geneva. Syria boycotted it, while Israel refused to withdraw to her pre-1967 boundaries or to allow the Palestinian Arabs to return to their homes. The conference broke up early in 1974. For some time American statesmen, like Henry Kissinger and Cyrus Vance, worked hard to bring about an agreement, but with no result. Then, in November 1977 President Sadat did something decisive. He went to Israel to speak to the Israeli parliament, the Knesset. In December Prime Minister

361

President Anwar Sadat arrives at Ben Gurion airport

Begin accepted Sadat's invitation to make a return visit, and spoke to the Egyptian parliament. The two leaders said little that was new, but the very fact that the visits had been made was important. They showed that the two countries were determined to reach agreement.

As a result of Sadat's visit, all the other Arab States condemned him, Saudi Arabia cut off the economic aid she had been sending and Russia, to please the rest of the Arabs, ended her friendship with Egypt. Egypt now turned to the United States for arms and money, and America gave her both. The United States was now on good terms with both Egypt and Israel, so in 1978 President Carter was able to persuade President Sadat and Prime Minister Begin to meet him at Camp David. Here they agreed on a peace treaty, and this was signed in 1979. Egypt recognized the State of Israel, and Israel agreed to return Sinai to Egypt by stages, the last being in April 1982.

In October 1981 some extremist Muslim soldiers killed President Sadat while he was watching a military parade. For a while, it looked as if the peace settlement with Israel might be in danger, but the Egyptian Vice-President Hosni Mubarak took Sadat's place, and announced that he would go on with his policies.

Sadat's murder showed the risks a Muslim leader runs, if he tries to come to any agreement with Israel. A Jewish newspaper said, 'An Arab ruler cannot make peace with Israel without placing his life in a bullet's crucible.'

Also it has been impossible for Israel to make peace with her Arab neighbours, other than Egypt. They want her to give up not only Sinai, but also the lands west of the Jordan and the Golan Heights, in fact, everything she won in 1967. That would have meant giving Israel frontiers which were very difficult to defend, and she would not agree. Prime Minister Begin said that the West Bank of the Jordan was to remain part of Israel and he encouraged his people to make settlements there. Further, in December 1981, he formally annexed the Golan Heights, which was simply a way of saying Israel would never abandon them.

Unfortunately for Israel, the United States shifted its policy after Ronald Reagan became President in 1980. Mindful that his country depended on Middle East oil, he tried to force the Israelis to accept a plan put forward by Saudi Arabia. When Begin annexed the Golan Heights, Reagan suspended a Strategic Co-operation Agreement by which the United States had promised to give Israel £3000 million worth of arms. Begin's answer was to cancel the agreement entirely, demanding angrily to know whether Reagan thought Israel was a banana republic which the United States could bully at will.

The problem of the Palestinian Arab refugees remains. King Hussein of Jordan found them so unruly that he expelled them. Many went to Lebanon and from there they raided Israel so often that she occupied the south of Lebanon until yet another United Nations Emergency Force arrived. However, the Palestine Liberation Organization has a determined leader in Yasser Arafat, and it is clear it intends to go on with the struggle.

WORK SECTION

International Relations since 1945 — The Middle East

Jewish refugees arriving in Palestine

Questions

1 What problems did Jewish immigration cause before the war?
2 Why did so many Jews wish to come to Palestine after the war?
3 How many arrived in the late 1940s and early 1950s?
4 Why were there enough homes and enough land for them?
5 Why is this ship not using a harbour?

Origins of the Problems of the Middle East

Document One

Negotiations at Versailles:
Many events of the Peace Conference were dramatic and spectacular, but none exceeded in interest the appearance of a delegation of royal Arabs from the hot sands of the desert. Their arrival brought before the unsuspecting members of the Council of Four the conflicting problems of the Middle East, which bedevil the nations to this day.

Here two British factions confronted each other, one supporting the Balfour effort to create a Jewish homeland in Palestine, the other

363

backing the claims of the Sherif of Mecca, Hussein, to all the lands of the Middle East liberated from the Turks. A complicating factor was the insistence of the French that the council honour the Sykes-Picot secret agreement which divided Asia Minor into French and British zones and left the Arabs in a subordinate position. The British, who opposed this, argued that the greatest contribution to victory had been made by General Edmund Allenby's expedition which, with the help of the Arabs, threw the Turks out of the country.

The struggle of the Arabs was dramatized for me the day the Emir Feisal arrived. He was a tall Arab with sensitive features and the refined bearing of the educated man who listens attentively to the trite mumblings of others. He had come as the representative of his father, Hussein, who had proclaimed himself King of the Hedjaz with British support. On the day I first saw him the Emir was wearing a black robe with a gold cloth turban. In his belt stuck a pistol with a jewelled handle. Before the Council of Four he also wore a scimitar. He was there to get recognition for the King of the Hedjaz as head of the new Arabian federation and spoke politely but firmly of the vital help the Arabs had given the Allies and the recognition by Britain of their independent sovereignty.

But the Emir Feisal was not to be the sole spokesman for the Hedjaz. He had hardly completed his remarks when an English officer in uniform, wearing a turban like the others, came into the room. He was a man of medium height, with strong features, of which his firm chin was most prominent. Without any explanation he introduced himself as Colonel Lawrence. The prince at once yielded the floor to him.

Colonel Lawrence talked freely and with the evident determination to impress the company with the validity of the Arabian claims. He said there was no possible doubt about the rightness of the Arab position. He was so completely at ease and so persuasive that soon he had most of the company sitting on the carpet with him, as in an Arab tent.

Document Two

The Balfour Declaration:
Dear Lord Rothschild,

I have much pleasure in conveying to you, on behalf of His Majesty's Government, the following declaration of sympathy with Jewish Zionist aspirations which has been submitted to, and approved by, the Cabinet.

His Majesty's Government views with favour the establishment in Palestine of a national home for the Jewish people, and will use their best endeavours to facilitate the achievement of this object, it being clearly understood that nothing shall be done which may prejudice the civil and religious rights of existing non-Jewish communities in Palestine, or the rights and political status enjoyed by Jews in any other country.

I should be grateful if you would bring this declaration to the knowledge of the Zionist federation.

> *Yours sincerely,*
> *Arthur James Balfour*

Questions

1 Which countries in the Middle East had belonged to the Turkish Empire?
2 What did the Arabs hope would happen to all these countries?
3 Who was the leader of the Arabs? Who represented him at Versailles?
4 Which Englishman in particular supported the Arabs? What had he done during the war?
5 What agreement had the British and French made over the Middle East? What did the British say about it after the war?
6 What promise had the British made to the Jews? What were the 'Zionist aspirations' mentioned in the Balfour Declaration?
7 What is your opinion of British policy in the Middle East at this time?
8 What arrangements were made for Palestine after the First World War?
9 What happened to the other countries of the Turkish Empire?

President Sadat's Peace Initiative

This is an extract from an article in a leading British newspaper shortly after President Sadat's speech to the Israeli Parliament in November 1977.

> *Now that Sadat has Failed*
> The Sadat initiative has failed. What is going on now is not in pursuance of the initiative, but attempts to disguise and soften the failure, to save some crumbs from a venture which has commanded a good deal of admiration. All that is left is a certain amount of rhetoric to the effect that, as a result of Mr Sadat's journey to Jerusalem, things will never be the same again.

But that, in essentials, is precisely what they are.

So it is important to try to see why Mr Sadat failed. His motives cannot be sorted out, nor does this very much matter. Of his aims one can say that, very broadly speaking, he was after peace. And that is about all one can say with any precision. Peace between whom, and on what terms? Mr Sadat must have realized that he would be accused, and genuinely suspected, of aiming at a separate peace with Israel. It cannot be proved that he was not, though the narrow and ungenerous view is probably wrong. If he was aiming at something wider — peace between Israel and all the states at war with it — how far was he prepared to go in satisfying the Palestinians' claim to a separate state as part of a general Arab-Israeli settlement — or had he no hard and fast notions about this, preferring to handle it on the trot?

Mr Sadat went to Jerusalem an isolated figure. All the Arabs who matter in this context either attacked him, or failed to support him. As a pan-Arab negotiator he was therefore in an anomalous position. But the outcome would not have been much different if he had had widespread Arab blessings, because what was being sought from Israel was never going to be given. The only things the Arabs have to give Israel are intangibles like recognition, peace, guarantees. What Israel has and in the end must give is territory and considerably more than token bits of it. Egypt simply does not have the weight to compel Israel to make the sort of territorial concessions needed. Nor do all the Arabs together have this weight.

Hence the preoccupation with the role of the United States. Eisenhower once forced Ben Gurion to retreat from conquered territory. But none of Eisenhower's successors has been willing to throw that kind of weight around in the Middle East. The United States is not within a thousand miles of applying to Israel the pressures that would force her to cede territory on the scale required to create the basis for a bargain.

So the fundamental reason for Mr Sadat's failure is not any inability to see what the elements of a settlement must be. It is the absence of the forces needed to bring it about. To achieve a settlement Israel has to cede territory. She is opposed to doing so and there is nobody to compel her. We are where we have been for very many years.

(Article in the *Sunday Times* 12 February 1978)

Questions

1 Roughly how long after President Sadat's visit to Israel was this article written?
2 Do you feel the writer should have written an article like this after such a lapse of time?
3 According to the article what are people saying about the visit?
4 Does he agree with them?
5 What does he say was Sadat's aim?
6 What two things does he say are not clear about Sadat's aims?
7 What was the attitude of the other Arab States?
8 What can the Arabs give to Israel? Do you agree that these are 'intangibles'?
9 What must Israel give, if there is to be peace?
10 Why is a settlement unlikely, according to this writer?
11 After which war did Eisenhower force Ben Gurion to give up territory?
12 Does the writer think anything like that could happen again?
13 What, according to this writer, is the reason for Sadat's failure?
14 In the light of what happened after this article was written, do you agree that President Sadat failed?

The Arab-Israeli Conflict (Map)

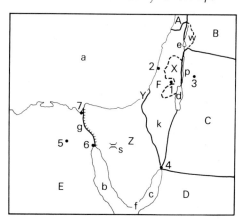

Map Questions

1 Name the following:
Countries A–F   Straits f   River p
Towns 1–7   Waterway g   Pass s
Areas of water a–e   Desert k
Regions W, X, Y, Z.

365

2 Why is town 1 important for both Jews and Arabs?

3 Why are Straits f important for Israel?

4 Which people went to live in Region Y? What terrorist group did they organize? Who encouraged them to do this?

5 Name the ruler of State E from 1954 to 1970. What action did he take with regard to waterway g in 1956? What was the result?

6 What happened at Pass s in 1956?

7 Why did Israel occupy region Z in 1956? Why was the occupation only temporary?

8 Who took town 7 in 1956? Why did they not advance further?

9 What did the U.N. send to region Z in 1956? How did it help Israel? When and why did it leave?

10 How did the Israelis plan to irrigate desert k? Who tried to stop the project? How?

11 When did Israel occupy regions W, X and Z?

12 What defences did Israel build along waterway g? When did the armies of state E break through them?

13 What happened in Region W in 1973?

14 What did Israel agree to do with Region Z in 1979?

The Origins of the State of Israel

Questions

1 How many Jews were living in Palestine in the 1880s? Who ruled Palestine? What were most of the inhabitants?

2 Why did many Jews leave Russia from the 1880s onwards? When was the Zionist movement founded? What did it do? How did the Jewish population of Palestine increase?

3 What agricultural settlements did the Jews found?

4 What were the duties of the Histadrut?

5 What was the Haganah? When and why was it legalized? What was the Palmach?

6 Name two terrorist groups.

7 Describe the government the Jews organized for themselves.

8 What common language did the Jews adopt?

9 What statement was made by the British government in 1917?

10 How did the British acquire Palestine? What kind of State did they want to create? When and why did the Arabs revolt? What were the results of the revolt?

11 What policies did the British follow during the Second World War towards the Jews and towards the Arabs? What did the MacDonald White Paper recommend?

12 Why did Britain favour the Arabs after the war? What action did she take against the Jews?

13 Who led the Jews at this time? What was his aim? What action did the Jews take against the British?

14 How did the United Nations become involved in Palestine? What did it recommend?

15 When did the British withdraw? What did they do before leaving?

Describe the Origins of the State of Israel under the headings: Early History and Immigration/Jewish Institutions/Events Leading to Independence

The Arab-Israeli Conflict

Questions

1 Give the two fundamental reasons for the conflict between Israel and her Arab neighbours.

2 What other problems appeared as time went on? Which foreign powers have interfered?

3 When was the War of Independence? Why was it fought? How did Israel prepare for it? Which countries attacked Israel?

4 Give three reasons why Israel won the war.

5 What did Israel gain from the war? How many Arabs fled from Israel? How has the existence of these refugees made it difficult to bring peace to the Middle East? To which countries did the refugees go?

6 When was the Suez Crisis?

7 What was Nasser's ambition? Why did he nationalize the Suez Canal? Why did this alarm the British? How had he already annoyed the French?

8 Name two ways in which Nasser made difficulties for Israel.

9 What plot was hatched by Britain, France and Israel? Why did they think Russia would not interfere?

10 What successes did Israel, and Britain and France have? What were the re-actions of America, the United Nations and Russia? Why did the war end? Why did Israel evacuate Sinai?

11 Name two advantages Israel had won from the war.

12 In what ways were Britain and France humiliated? What did the Suez Crisis prove about them?

13 When was the Six Day War? What action did Israel take against Syria? What goaded Nasser into action? What did he do?

14 What decision did Ben Gurion make? What territory did Israel overrrun?

15 What did Israel gain from the war? What disadvantages were there for her?

16 Who succeeded Nasser? Why did Egypt and Syria attack Israel? When did they do this?

17 What victories did the Egyptians and Syrians win? Give three reasons for their success.

18 When did the Israelis turn the tide? What victories did they win?

19 Give two reasons why there was a cease-fire.

20 What were the terms of the truces negotiated with Egypt and Syria?

21 Why did America, Russia, Israel and Egypt all want peace after the Yom Kippur War?

22 Why was the peace conference at Geneva a failure?

23 What action did President Sadat take in 1977? What did Prime Minister Begin do in return?

24 Why did Egypt turn to America for aid? What was President Carter able to do as a result?

25 What happened to President Sadat in 1981?

26 What problems remain between Israel and (a) the Palestine Liberation Organisation (b) the Arab States (c) the United States?

Give an account of the Arab-Israeli Conflict under the headings: Reasons/The War of Independence/The Suez Crisis/The Six Day War/The Yom Kippur War/Peace between Israel and Egypt

Problems

1 What were the origins and aims of the Zionist movement? How did its members try to achieve their aims?

2 How did the Jews create a 'State within a State' in Palestine?

3 Describe the stages by which the State of Israel came into being.

4 What problems did the British face in Palestine? Why were they unable to solve them?

5 Describe and account for the changes in British policy towards the Jews and the Arabs.

6 What were the fundamental causes of the conflicts between the Arabs and the Israelis? Why has it been difficult to secure a lasting peace?

7 What were the causes and results of:
   (a) The War of Independence 1948–9
   (b) The Suez Crisis 1956
   (c) The Six Day War 1967
   (d) The Yom Kippur War 1973?

8 Why has the State of Israel survived in the face of Arab hostility?

9 What was the importance of Abdul Gamel Nasser in the history of the Middle East?

10 What parts have been played by the United States of America and Russia in the Arab-Israeli conflict?

11 What steps have been taken towards a permanent peace between Egypt and Israel since 1973?

THE UNITED NATIONS

Chapter Forty-nine

The United Nations

Origins

IN AUGUST 1941, Roosevelt and Churchill drew up a document known as the 'Atlantic Charter'. It was a rather vague statement of aims, which included a 'wider and permanent system of security'. That meant the two leaders hoped that after the war there would be an organization like the League of Nations, but more effective. The words 'United Nations' were first used in January 1942 when 26 countries signed the 'Declaration by the United Nations'. They accepted the principles of the Atlantic Charter and promised to fight together against Germany, Italy and Japan. The United Nations, therefore, began as a wartime alliance.

In October 1943 America, Russia, China and Britain agreed to set up a peace-keeping organization when the war ended, and there were a number of meetings to decide what form it should take. In September 1944 there were talks at a mansion called Dumbarton Oaks, near Washington. Later, when Roosevelt, Churchill and Stalin met at Yalta in February 1945, they decided how the Security Council should vote. Finally, there was a conference at San Francisco from April to June 1945. On 26 October the representatives of fifty States met, also at San Francisco, and signed the Charter of the United Nations.

Aims

The Charter says that the United Nations is a 'centre for harmonizing the action of nations'. In other words, it is a place where all countries can work together. They hope to do two things. One is to 'save succeeding generations from the scourge of war', and the other is to solve world problems like disease and famine.

Organization

The headquarters of the United Nations is in New York. A great weakness with the League was that the United States did not join, but since the United Nations meets in her most important city, she can hardly ignore it. However, there has never been any danger of that happening.

The United Nations Building, New York

The most important part of the United Nations is the Security Council. It has permanent members which are the Big Five — the U.S.A., the U.S.S.R., China, France and Britain. There are other members as well, elected for two years by the General Assembly. Originally, there were six of these, but now there are ten. As its name suggests, the main task of the Security Council is to keep the peace, which it may do in the following ways. When two nations quarrel, it finds out why and calls on them to settle the problem without a war. If fighting starts, then it will call for a cease-fire. If the fighting stops, then it will arrange peace talks, or even send a peace-keeping force. However, if the fighting continues, it can impose sanctions on the aggressor, and call on member States to send help to the victim.

The Security Council can do any of these things only if the Big Five are unanimous. When a Great Power fell out with the League of Nations, it could only leave, as Japan did in 1933, but in the United Nations any one of the Big Five can use the veto. As a result the United Nations cannot pass a resolution against a Great Power. This recognizes the plain fact that the only way to compel an important country to obey would be by fighting a major war, and that is unthinkable. The problem is that Russia has usually been in a minority of one and has used the veto so often that she has undermined the prestige of the Security Council. However, at least she is still a member of the United Nations. Under the rules of the League she would have been forced to leave long ago.

Next, there is the General Assembly, where every member of the United Nations has one seat, and one vote, regardless of its size. It meets every year from September to December, though it can be called at other times, if there is an emergency. The Assembly debates any problem it chooses, and can pass resolutions saying what it thinks should be done. However, it cannot make any decisions: it can only pass its ideas to other organizations, especially the Security Council, and they will make up their own minds on what action to take.

For the administrative work there is a Secretariat, headed by a Secretary General. He has more powers than the Secretary General of the League had, for he may ask the Security Council or the General Assembly to debate anything he considers important. He has often played a valuable part in the peace-keeping work of the U.N. Since 1945, four men have held the post — a Norwegian, a Swede, a Burmese and an Austrian. It would be a mistake to appoint someone who was a citizen of one of the Great Powers, because it is essential for him to be fair, and to be seen to be fair.

As before the war, there is still the International Court of Justice that settles legal problems and arguments over treaties. For example, in 1979, it declared illegal Iran's arrest of the members of the United States Embassy in Teheran.

Like the League, the United Nations does valuable economic and social work, though on a bigger scale. Some of the more important organizations are the International Labour Organization (I.L.O.), the Food and Agricultural Organization (F.A.O.), the World Health Organization (W.H.O.), the United Nations, Educational, Scientific and Cultural Organization (U.N.E.S.C.O.) and the United Nations International Children's Emergency Fund (U.N.I.C.E.F.). The World Bank makes loans to poor countries to help them develop their economies, for example by building dams or starting new industries.

Weaknesses

In the first place, the United Nations is not a world government. Its members will not part with any of their sovereignty which means that they will not take orders from the U.N. There was a plan at the beginning that the United Nations should have a force of its own, but the idea was never implemented. When troops have been needed for peace-keeping, member States have so far always offered to help, but the United Nations itself has no independent force on which it can call.

Secondly, the United Nations, like the League, has been weakened because certain countries have not joined. At first, Russia and the U.S.A. kept out numbers of smaller powers, for Russia vetoed America's friends, and America vetoed Russia's. In 1955, however they came to an agreement and all these smaller powers were admitted. There remained Communist China, with one-quarter of the world's population. For a long time the United States was determined she should not join, claiming that the Nationalists in Taiwan were the legal government. Accordingly, she used her veto to keep Communist China out. Later, however, China quarrelled with Russia, so the United States was willing to be more friendly towards her. In 1971, she allowed her to join as a gesture of goodwill.

There is a third problem, which is made worse because the United Nations debates are shown on television. Strange things can happen. When a handsome South American delegate was rash enough to say he was a bachelor he had 327 proposals of marriage in his post next morning. Usually though, the results are more serious. Whenever anyone speaks at the United Nations, he knows that large numbers of his countrymen will see and hear him. As a result, he states his own case as strongly as he can, and is unwilling to give anything away to his opponents. What would you think of a goal-keeper who deliberately allowed the other team to score? However, the work of the U.N. is to reach agreements which, as a rule, can only be done when both sides are willing to make concessions. Delegates find this difficult, so the United Nations is too often a place where countries air their differences, rather than solve them.

Successes and Failures

The United Nations has done well in its economic and social work. The World Bank has made many loans to help poor countries, while the United Nations Development Programme spends $50 million a year for the same purpose. There has been disaster relief; for example, when there have been floods in India, there has been help for refugees, and much has been done to control disease. Apart from one or two remote places in East Africa, there is no longer any smallpox in the world, while many other unpleasant diseases are on the decline.

With peace-keeping, the United Nations has had less success, though it is true it has sometimes helped to stop fighting between small countries. For example, it sent peace-keeping forces to Sinai in 1956 and 1964, to the Congo in 1960, and to Cyprus in 1965. It has also sent observers to make sure countries were not breaking truces. There were some in Kashmir, between India and Pakistan, from 1948 to 1973. However, the United Nations has come nowhere near 'saving succeeding generations from the scourge of war'. For as long as it has been in existence, there has always been fighting somewhere in the world, and often in several places at once. Certainly, the United Nations has no control over the Great Powers. The only important war in which it intervened was the one in Korea, and that was possible only because the Soviet Union was boycotting the Security Council, which meant she could not use her veto. The main reason why the United States and Russia have not gone to war is because they are scared of each other's nuclear weapons. It is certainly not because they wish to obey the United Nations. Indeed, if any of the Great Powers of the world disagree, they nearly always settle the problem by talking directly to each other, and they ignore the United Nations entirely.

WORK SECTION — The United Nations

Israeli soldier hands over to U.N. soldier, Sinai 1956

Questions

1 Why was a U.N. force sent to Sinai in 1956?
2 When and where have other U.N. peace-keeping forces been sent (a) in the Middle East, (b) in other parts of the world?

The United Nations and the Korean War

(See also Chapter 44 The Korean War)

Document One

Extract from Resolution Adopted by the Security Council 25 June 1950:
The Security Council:
Noting with grave concern the armed attack upon the Republic of Korea by forces from North Korea,
Determines that this action constitutes a breach of the peace.
Calls for the immediate cessation of hostilities, and calls upon the authorities of North Korea to withdraw forthwith their armed forces to the 38th parallel.

Document Two

Resolution Adopted by the Security Council 27 June 1950
The Security Council:
Having determined that the armed attack upon the Republic of Korea by forces from North Korea constitutes a breach of the peace,
Having called for an immediate cessation of hostilities and
Having called upon the authorities of North Korea to withdraw forthwith their armed forces to the 38th parallel and
Having noted from the report of the United Nations Commission for Korea that the

373

authorities in North Korea have neither ceased hostilities nor withdrawn their armed forces to the 38th parallel and that urgent military measures are required to restore international peace and security, and
Having noted the appeal from the Republic of Korea to the United Nations for immediate and effective steps to secure peace and security,
Recommends that the Members of the United Nations furnish such assistance to the Republic of Korea as may be necessary to repel the armed attack and to restore international peace and security in the area.

Questions

1 Who ruled Korea from 1910 to 1945?
2 What happened in Korea after the war? What was the importance of the 38th parallel, mentioned in both documents?
3 When did North Korea attack South Korea?
4 What action did the Americans take?
5 Which countries are members of the Security Council? What is its main task?
6 What did the Security Council attempt to do by its Resolution of 25 June 1950? (Document One)
7 What did the Security Council recommend on 27 June 1950? (Document Two)
8 What are the reasons it gives for this recommendation?
9 How can a Great Power prevent the Security Council passing a resolution? Why did Russia not prevent the Security Council passing these two resolutions?
10 Contrast the action of the United Nations over Korea with that of the League of Nations over Manchuria 1931–3.

Problems

1 What similarities and what differences are there between the United Nations Organization and the League of Nations?
2 Why has the United Nations Organization been more successful than the League of Nations?
3 What are the main weaknesses of the United Nations Organization?
4 How far has the United Nations Organization been a success?

The United Nations

Questions

1 How did the United Nations begin?
2 Who agreed to set up a peace-keeping organization? What meetings decided the form it should take?
3 When and where was the Charter of the United Nations signed?
4 What are the two main aims of the United Nations?
5 Where is the headquarters of the United Nations? Why was this place chosen?
6 What countries are members of the Security Council? How does the Security Council try to keep the peace?
7 What did a Great Power have to do if it disagreed with the League of Nations? What can it do if it disagrees with the United Nations? What problem has this created? What advantages does it have?
8 Who has seats in the General Assembly? When does it meet? What work does it do? What powers does it have?
9 What is the work of the Secretariat? What may the Secretary General do? Why has no Secretary General been a citizen of a Great Power?
10 What is the work of the International Court of Justice?
11 Name six organizations that do economic and social work.
12 Why is the United Nations not a world government? How does it find troops for peace-keeping?
13 What important country was not a member of the United Nations for some time? When and why was she allowed to join?
14 How does television hamper the work of the United Nations?
15 Give examples of successes the United Nations has had in its economic and social work.
16 Where has the United Nations sent peace-keeping forces?
17 What is the only major war in which the United Nations has intervened? Why was this possible?

Give an account of the United Nations under the headings: Origins/Aims/Organization/Weaknesses/Successes and Failures

THE END
of the
COLONIAL
EMPIRES

CASE STUDIES

Introduction

ONE OF the driving forces of the twentieth century has been imperialism. Indeed almost all the European countries won overseas empires in earlier times, the last phase being the 'scramble for Africa' in the nineteenth century. The map of that continent came to look like a patchwork quilt, the multitude of colours showing how many different States owned colonies there. The United States came late into the race, and moreover she despised imperialism — or so she claimed. None the less she did take some colonies in the Caribbean and the Pacific, second-hand from Spain. The other latecomer, Japan, had no inhibitions at all, but seized numbers of the Pacific islands, Korea, Taiwan and Manchuria, and then tried to overrun the whole of China.

Gradually, though, imperialism weakened, and that was not only because there were so few places left to colonize. The main reason was nationalism. Foreign rule roused national feelings in the subject peoples, and especially among their educated minorities. They wanted to drive out their masters and govern their countries themselves. Eventually, almost all of them had their way. Some colonial powers withdrew more or less gracefully, as Britain did from several of her possessions: others, like the Portuguese, hung on to the bitter end. Finally, though, almost all of them had to go so that today colonies are few and far between in the world.

Unfortunately, giving up colonies, or decolonization as it is sometimes called, can cause problems. It is rather like parents leaving home for good. Everything depends on the children. If they are grown up and friendly with each other, all will be well. If they are immature and hate each other, they will fight, and the home may be ruined.

Each colony has its own story, and in this book it is not possible to tell them all. Other chapters describe what happened in Palestine and in French Indo-China. In this section we will look at two British territories that found the path to independence particularly difficult. They are India and Central Southern Africa.

Chapter Fifty

India in 1900

DISRAELI once described India as the 'brightest jewel in the British crown'. It has an area of 4.7 million square kilometres, so it is as large as Europe without Russia, and in 1900 it had a population of 300 million. From the point of view of its size, it was certainly the most important part of the Empire.

Religion and Society

There were people of many different religions in India, but two groups were especially important, the Hindus and the Muslims. The Muslims were about a quarter of the population, and the Hindus most of the remainder.

The Hindu religion affected Indian society in a number of unpleasant ways. Here we will touch on just three — the caste system, marriage customs and sacred cows.

There were four Hindu castes — Brahmans, or 'earthly gods', Kshattryas, or 'fighting men', Vaisyas, or 'cultivators', and Sudras, or 'untouchables'. The untouchables were the lowest of the low. They were made to do dirty, unpleasant jobs and, indeed, many could only live by begging. Not only was it impossible for anyone to change caste, but untouchables were forbidden to do anything that might improve their position, such as starting a business. It was their religious duty to live in misery, and it was the religious duty of the other castes to see that they did so. At any rate before the British arrived it was not a serious offence for a Brahman to kill an untouchable: it was a crime, though, if an untouchable let his shadow fall on a Brahman.

According to the Hindus, a man needs sons to look after his soul when he is dead. So as to increase their chances of having sons, girls had to marry young, possibly at the age of eight, and certainly no later than fourteen. While the birth of a son was a great event in a family, the birth of a daughter was a misfortune. At one time, girl babies were often abandoned and left to die. The British did much to stop this, but they could not make families take as much care of their daughters as they did of their sons. Another belief was that if a man died before his wife, it was the woman's fault because of some evil she had done in a previous existence. For this she had

377

to be punished. Previously there had been a practice called 'suttee' which meant that the widow was burnt together with her husband on the same funeral pyre. The British stopped suttee, but they could not prevent families treating widows with great cruelty. Many were so wretched that they burnt themselves to death of their own free will.

For the Hindus, the cow is a sacred animal. Killing one, even by accident, is a terrible sin, so the country swarmed with them, wandering about as and where they pleased. That might not have been too bad if they had yielded milk in any quantity, but most of them gave only a litre or less a day. Meanwhile, farmers grew crops for these useless animals, while people starved. Also, because the cow was sacred, everything it produced was also sacred. People collected its urine and 'purified' themselves by washing in it and drinking it. Another method of purification was to eat a mixture of everything the cow produces — milk, urine and dung.

It was the religious customs of the Hindus which, more than anything else, kept India in poverty and misery.

However, not all Hindus were ignorant and superstitious. Some had gone into trade and industry and had prospered, and they had also been to school, or even university. As a result, there was an educated middle-class which, though small, was important. Its members spoke English, they adopted English ways, but they were the people who were most opposed to British rule. In 1885 they called the first Indian National Congress, and after that it met every year. The main aim of the Congress Party was to win independence.

The Muslims had come to India as conquerers in the twelfth century A.D. and ruled much of the country until the British arrived in the eighteenth century. They won many converts, especially among the Hindu untouchables, who had no hope from their own religion. By 1900, as we have seen, they were almost a quarter of the population.

After the British conquered India, the Muslims refused to learn from them, so there were hardly any educated middle-class Muslims. There were only the leaders, who were aristocrats, owning estates, and the masses, who were poor and ignorant.

India, sacred cows

'Gai Jatra' – Hindu cow festival

By the early twentieth century the Muslims were not only in a minority, but were also some fifty years behind the Hindus. In 1906 they founded the Muslim League as their own political party. This favoured the British most of the time, for its members saw that if the British withdrew, the Hindus would seize power.

British Rule in India

The government of India was in three tiers. The highest was in London, where a member of the British cabinet was Secretary of State for India. He was assisted by the Council of India, made up of men who knew about the country. Also, the British Parliament could make laws for India, though it only dealt with important questions, like changes in the constitution.

The second tier was the central government of India which sat in the capital, Delhi. The head of the government was the Governor-General, or Viceroy, who was appointed by the British, and held office for five years. To help him, he had an executive council which was rather like the British cabinet in that each member had a department to manage, for example, communications. However, the council was nominated by the Viceroy and unlike the British cabinet was responsible to him and not to a parliament. Indeed, India had no parliament. Instead, there was a legislative council which advised the Viceroy, but it was nominated by him, and not elected by the people.

The third tier was made up of the provincial governments. There were seven provinces in British India, some of which had governors who in turn nominated executive and legislative councils.

The central government looked after things like defence which concerned the whole of India, while the provincial had governments handled local matters, like police and education.

By the early twentieth century there were a few Indians in these various councils, though, of course, they had been nominated, like all the other members. Then, in 1909, the British Parliament passed the Indian Councils Act. The changes it made are known as the Morley-Minto Reforms, because the Secretary of State for India at that time was Lord Morley, and the Viceroy was Lord Minto. What happended was that the legislative councils were enlarged to include elected Indian members. This was an important step, even though the new councillors were not chosen directly by the people, but by institutions such as universities and chambers of commerce. So that Hindus did not win all the seats, numbers were reserved for Muslims.

As well as the Governors and the Councils, there were some 5000 civil servants, all of them British. The Indian Civil Service attracted good recruits and most of its members were able and hard working. They were also very proud of what they were doing. In 1870 the Viceroy, Lord Mayo, spoke for them when he said, 'We are all British gentlemen engaged in the magnificent work of governing an inferior race'.

To defend India, and help the police keep order, there was an army of 250 000 men, about one-third of them British.

379

As well as the seven provinces ruled directly by Britain, there were about 600 States, each with its own native prince. Between them, the States covered 40 per cent of the country. Some, like Hyderabad, were large, but others were minute. It is said that one prince ruled over nothing more than a well. Britain looked after the foreign affairs, and the defence of the States, but left the princes to manage everything else.

The British did India a lot of good. In the first place, there were no more invasions or civil wars, so that the population grew rapidly. In the eighteenth century, it was perhaps 100 million: by 1900 it was 300 million: by 1940, it was almost 400 million.

The economy grew. In India, the British built one of the finest railway networks in the world: it had 40 000 km of track in 1900, and 69 000 km in 1939. Coal output was 12 million tonnes a year by 1912, which was enough to make the country self-sufficient. There was iron and steel as well, for example, the Tata Iron and Steel Company at Bihar. This was founded in 1907, and by 1938 was the biggest in the world. It was owned entirely by Indians. Cotton and jute were almost important industries. One of the most valuable exports was tea. As late as the 1820s, the British imported all their tea from China, but by 1900, Indian tea was far more popular.

Apart from the tea plantations, which were owned by Europeans, much of the native agriculture was primitive. The main crops were rice, millet and wheat, according to the area. In many parts of the country the farmers depended on the monsoon: when that failed, so did the harvest, and there was famine. In 1779, for example, nearly one half of the population of Bengal died of hunger. The British helped in two ways. In the first place, they tried to prevent famines by irrigation. They built dams and many kilometres of canals, especially in the Punjab and Sind. By 1940, 12 million hectares, or one-fifth of the cultivated land, was irrigated. Secondly, if there was a famine, the British did all they could to stay it. For example, in 1883 they introduced a Famine Code which allowed the government to make full use of the railways and steamships in order to take food to the stricken areas. Famine did not end, and there was one as late as 1943 which killed a million people. Nevertheless, far more would have died without British help.

As we have seen from the Hindu customs, India needed a lot of social reform. Until the Mutiny in 1857 the British were enthusiastic about this, and stopped such practices as infanticide and suttee. However, the Indian troops mutinied mainly because they had to do things that were against their religion. Afterwards, the British interfered only if they found something particularly nasty happening, like hanging people up with hooks driven into their backs. For the most part they left the natives to follow their old customs and concentrated on things like famine relief. The one social change they did encourage was education. It was their undoing. Progress was not remarkable, but there was enough to create an educated Hindu middle-class. Its members were the people who began the agitation against the rule of the British and, in the end, destroyed the Indian Empire.

Chapter Fifty-one

The Struggle for Independence

The Hindu Nationalists and Mahatma Gandhi

As WE SAW in the last chapter, the nationalists were members of the Hindu middle class. All of them wanted India to be free, but there were two groups, the moderates and the extremists. The moderates were prosperous men who were doing well in trade or business, and they did not want a lot of disorder. They tried to win their way by negotiating with the British. The extremists were educated Indians who were unable to find suitable jobs and were therefore frustrated. They were quite willing to use violence.

The greatest leader the nationalits had was Mohandas Gandhi. He was born in 1869, into a family of the Vaisya caste. He studied law in London, and then practised in South Africa. Here he suffered because of his colour, on one occasion being put out of a railway carriage. He found that his

Mahatma Gandhi

fellow Indians who came to South Africa as labourers suffered a great deal more, so he encouraged them in what he called 'satyagraha', or 'firmness in truth'. That meant resisting injustice, but doing so peacefully. Gandhi attracted a good deal of attention and the South African government was relieved when he returned to India in 1917.

Back in his own country, Gandhi went on working for oppressed people, but now it was the untouchables, the women, and the poor. He was so worried about the poor that he gave up every comfort in his own life, and wore nothing but a loin cloth. Churchill called him a 'half-naked fakir'. Gandhi's cure for poverty was quite impractical: it was to revive village handicrafts, especially hand spinning and weaving. With the growth of industry, textiles were made in factories. Gandhi said the work should be done once again in village homes, so that the peasants could supplement the miserable incomes they made from their farming. He set an example by doing some spinning himself, every day.

However, Gandhi was most important because he championed Hindu nationalism. Within four years of his return to India he was leader of the Congress Party. One of his conditions for accepting the post was that all its members should wear khaddar, or homespun cloth, and he even tried to make them all spin for half an hour daily.

As in South Africa, Gandhi was quite against violence, but he still believed in satyagraha. From time to time he encouraged his followers to refuse to co-operate with the British, and to disobey their laws, but never to use force. From time to time he would fast, and that always shamed his enemies into giving him what he wanted. No one dared let him die. Throughout India, millions looked on him as a saint, and he took the title 'Mahatma', which means 'great soul'.

Gandhi worked closely with two other nationalist leaders, Motilal Nehru and his son Jawaharlal. Cynical Englishmen used to call the three of them 'Father, Son and Holy Ghost'.

Agitation and Reform 1909–1939

The first step towards independence, though the British did not see it that way, was the Morley-Minto Reforms of 1909. These are described in the last chapter. Then came the First World War, and India made a handsome contribution, raising well over a million troops. They served in France, in East Africa and on the Persian Gulf, and they guarded the Suez Canal. To encourage the people of India the Secretary of State, Edwin Montagu, promised them that Britain would give them more and more say in the running of their country until, in the end, they had self-government within the Empire, just like Canada and Australia. The plan was set out in what is now called the Montagu-Chelmsford Report, published in 1918. Lord Chelmsford was Viceroy at that time.

However, all was not well between the British and the Indians. The Muslims objected to the war against Turkey, for the Sultan was the Caliph, or head of their religion. One Muslim leader urged Germany to attack India. Also, the extremist Hindu nationalists won control of the Congress

Party, and there were conspiracies against Britain. Feeling ran so high that in 1916 the Muslim League and Congress made an agreement called the Lucknow Pact, promising to work together to win self-government. This alarmed the British government, which appointed a committee under Mr Justice Rowlatt to prepare a report on ways of dealing with terrorists.

When the war ended, the government felt bound to pass Acts of Parliament to carry out both the Montagu-Chelmsford and the Rowlatt Reports.

By the Montagu-Chelmsford Reforms the British did as they had promised and granted a good deal more power to the people of India, especially in the provincial governments. However, this was not enough to please the extremists. Moreover, the Rowlatt Act gave the authorities considerable powers; for example, to arrest people and hold them without trial. Many Indians were angry and began to agitate for full self-government.

Gandhi organized a campaign of civil disobedience. His followers kept their children from school, students stayed away from college, people did not buy English goods, and they refused to pay their taxes. These tactics were new, but something even more significant was happening. Before, only the middle-classes had opposed British rule: now Gandhi was stirring the ordinary people into action.

However, Gandhi's methods were not strong enough for the Hindu extremists, so they used violence. The British retaliated, notably General Dyer. At Amritsar in 1919 he ordered his men to fire into a dense crowd and nearly four hundred people were killed. The government held an inquiry, while Gandhi did his best to keep the peace, so the Amritsar massacre did not lead to widespread disorder, as it might have done. Even so, there were riots when the Prince of Wales visited India and a number of policemen were murdered in the United Provinces.

These attempts to win self-government failed for three reasons. The first was that Gandhi objected to violence and called off his civil disobedience campaign. Secondly, a rebellion in Turkey overthrew the Sultan, so the Muslims no longer objected to Britain's anti-Turkish policy. The Muslim League once again became pro-British and the Lucknow Pact ended. Thirdly, the moderates regained control of the Congress Party, and they decided it would be best to work the new constitution that had been introduced by the Montagu-Chelmsford Reforms.

The peace did not last for long. When it had introduced the Montagu-Chelmsford Reforms, the British government had promised to revise the constitution of India after a while. It appointed a commission under Sir John Simon to do the work, and it arrived in India in 1928. This might have been a popular move, but there were no Indians on the Simon Commission, and so the leaders of Congress were furious. Their country was to have a new system of government, but they were to have no say in what form it should take. Accordingly, Congress appointed a constitutional commission of its own under Motilal Nehru. It also gave Britain one year to grant India dominion status. This ultimatum expired at the end of 1929, so in January 1930 Jawaharlal Nehru, who was then President of Congress, declared that India was an independent country. Gandhi played his part by organizing another campaign of civil disobedience, which he began in a remarkable way. Only the government had the right to make salt, and he decided he would break this law. He led a horde of pilgrims on foot to the coast at Dandi, where he evaporated some sea water to make a small quantity of salt. It was, of course, only a gesture, but the long walk to the sea caught the public eye, while the attack on the salt monopoly was something even the most uneducated Indian could understand. There were now disturbances in many places.

The Viceroy at this time was Lord Irwin, who is better known by his later title of Lord Halifax. He persuaded the British government to call a Round Table Conference in London to discuss giving India dominion status. He also came to an understanding with Gandhi, called the Gandhi-Irwin Pact, and Gandhi agreed to go to the Round Table Conference. He caused quite a stir in Britain because, as usual, he wore nothing but his loincloth. The Round Table Conference failed in the end, mainly because of differences between Congress and the Muslim League.

The British felt they had done all they could to win co-operation, so they arrested the Congress leaders and imposed a constitution they had drafted themselves. This was done by the Government of India Act of 1935. Churchill growled, 'We are there for ever', but the new Act was the last step before independence. Though the British kept some control over the central government, the provinces were to have complete freedom. Also, India was to be a federation of all its provinces and princely States, though that was not to come into being until at least half the States had agreed to join. The princes were suspicious, and the Second World War broke out before enough of them had accepted the idea.

Jinnah and Pakistan

As it became clear that the British would one day withdraw from India, the Muslims grew more and more afraid that they would be governed by Hindus. The only answer for them was to have a separate Muslim State. In 1933, Choudhril Rahmat Ali coined the name 'Pakistan'. It was made up from the names of the provinces where most of the people were Muslims — Punjab, Afghanis (North West Frontier Province), Kashmir, Sind and Baluchistan. 'Pakistan' also means 'the land of the pure'. In 1934, Muhammed Ali Jinnah became President of the Muslim League, and he was soon to lead his people to independence.

The final break between the Hindus and the Muslims came in 1937. That year there were the first elections for the new provincial legislatures set up by the Government of India Act. In most provinces Congress won large majorities but the Muslim League hoped, none the less, that some of them would be invited to join the various governments, to make coalitions. Congress, however, was unwilling to do this, which made it plain that if ever India was independent and united, the Hindus would dominate the Muslims, giving them no share in the government.

In 1940, the League passed the 'Pakistan Resolution', demanding two Muslim States, one in the east of India and one in the west. Jinnah also raised the cry 'Islam is in danger' and called on the masses to support Pakistan. To rouse the ordinary Muslims, the League spread absurd stories about what would happen if they did not have a country of their own. They said that Muslim schools would become Hindu temples, and that Muslim girls would have to take dancing lessons.

We have already seen that Gandhi appealed to the Hindu masses in the 1920s, and now Jinnah appealed to the Muslims. It was dangerous. Even though their leaders were quarrelling, ordinary Hindus and Muslims lived together peacefully enough, and respected each other's religions. For example, the Muslims ate beef, but as the cow is sacred to the Hindus, a Muslim butcher would usually wrap any beef he sold with great care, and the Muslim housewife would keep it out of sight on her way home. Hindus often held noisy processions, but during a Muslim service quiet is important at certain times, so a procession would fall silent as it went past a mosque. However, all that sort of thing now came to an end. Urged on by their leaders, both sides did all they could to give offence and soon many people were burning to take revenge for the insults they had suffered.

The Second World War

In the middle of all these troubles came the Second World War. Once again India played a vital part, sending supplies and raising an army of two million men. Indians fought well against the Germans in North Africa, and against the Japanese in Burma. The Gurkhas of Nepal were the allied troops which the Japanese feared most.

Politically, though, things were far from satisfactory. Congress refused to co-operate with the British unless they promised to give India her independence as soon as the war was over. Churchill at first refused, but when Japan entered the war he had to show the Americans he was doing all he could to win Indian support. In 1942 he sent Sir Stafford Cripps to offer independence. However, the 'Cripps offer' included a separate Pakistan, and Congress rejected it because it still hoped to keep India united. Gandhi now started more civil disobedience, hoping to make the British hand over power at once. It was called his 'quit India' campaign. He chose to mount it as the Japanese were advancing rapidly through Burma. There was also a rebellion. However, the British were firm and were able to keep control until after the war.

Independence

When the war ended, there were two quarrels taking place. One was between Britain and Congress, which was demanding independence. The other was between Congress, which wanted a united India, and the Muslim League, which wanted a separate Pakistan. The Viceroy, Lord Wavell, summoned a conference at Simla in 1945, hoping to persuade Congress and the League to agree. The conference failed and Jinnah called on his followers to take direct action to secure an independent Pakistan.

'Direct action' was just a polite term for violence, and in 1946 there was a lot of rioting, especially in Calcutta.

The British were in despair, so they announced that if Congress and the League could not reach agreement, then in June 1948 power would be given to the individual provinces and States. However, some sort of agreement was reached. In March 1947 Lord Mountbatten became Viceroy, and he drew up a plan to divide the country. Congress, very unwillingly, accepted a separate Pakistan. The League, no less unwillingly, agreed that Pakistan should be much smaller than it had hoped. The States were allowed to join India or Pakistan as their rulers wished. Since there was serious trouble in many places, Mountbatten decided to bring independence forward to August 1947, even though that meant drawing the new frontiers in a hurry. Both the Punjab and Bengal had to be divided.

Many people now realized they would have rulers of a rival religion, so they fled in terror. Five million Hindus left West Pakistan, and six or seven million Muslims moved in. There was also an exchange of population in Bengal, though here the numbers were smaller. Now was the time to pay off old scores, and as the refugees fled through hostile country, they were massacred. Many of the killings took place on trains. When they stopped at stations gangs would board them and murder anyone of a rival religion. How many died we shall never know, but it may have been 400 000 — more than were were killed from the entire British Commonwealth during the Second World War. People appealed to the British to keep order, but they were too few to do anything. 'You wanted independence', they said, 'and now you've got it'.

Pakistan became independent on 13 August 1947, and India the following day. There was great rejoicing.

Jinnah and Mountbatten at independence celebrations

India and Pakistan

Chapter Fifty-two

Central Southern Africa

CENTRAL Southern Africa is the region now occupied by Zimbabwe, Zambia and Malawi. In the nineteenth century there was a lot of fighting there with the strong tribes preying on the weaker ones. To the east of the region there were people like the Bemba and the Yao who sold other blacks to Arab slave-traders. In the west of what is now Zimbabwe there were the Matabele, who terrorized their neighbours to the east, the Mashona. Even today there is rivalry between these two.

The first Europeans to arrive were missionaries, for example Dr Livingstone, who organized his Zambesi expedition in 1858, but sooner or later others were bound to come as colonists. It could have been the Boers, who were just across the Limpopo, or it could have been the Portuguese, who owned neighbouring Mozambique and Angola. In fact it was the British.

Cecil Rhodes and the British South Africa Company

The man who forestalled both the Boers and the Portuguese was an English emigrant to South Africa, Cecil Rhodes. He made himself a millionaire mining for diamonds, but being rich did not satisfy him. He once said, 'My ruling purpose is the extension of the British Empire.' Part of his dream was to see a string of British colonies running the length of Africa, and joined by a railway from Cape Town to Cairo. For that, it was essential to take Central Southern Africa, or the way would be barred.

In 1888 Rhodes sent Charles Rudd to Bulawayo, the capital of Matabeleland, where he met King Lobenguela. In return for a small pension, 1000 rifles and a gunboat, Lobenguela gave the British mining rights in Mashonaland. The following year Rhodes persuaded the British Prime Minister, Lord Salisbury, to grant a Royal Charter to his new British South Africa Company. The Charter gave the Company the right to make settlements, open mines and organize a police force and an army. In 1890 a column of pioneers moved north in their covered wagons, guided by a famous hunter called F. C. Selous. In Mashonaland they built a fort which they named 'Fort Salisbury' in honour of the Prime Minister, and they called their new country 'Rhodesia'.

It was not long before the settlers had trouble with the natives. That

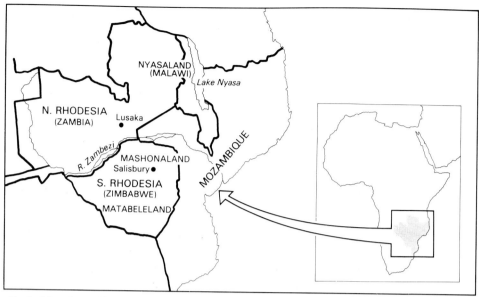

Central Southern Africa

ended in 1896 when the white men not only put down a rebellion by the Mashona, but also defeated the Matabele, and occupied their land as well.

In the 1890s, the British South Africa Company sent settlers north of the Zambesi and made another colony called Northern Rhodesia. This is now Zambia. Moreover, in 1891 Britain took Nyasaland, which is modern Malawi. That completed her empire in Central Southern Africa.

There was good land in Southern Rhodesia, especially on the High Veld, and numbers of people came from Britain to farm it. Northern Rhodesia and Nyasaland however had little to recommend them, so few settlers arrived and the two countries made slow progress for the time being.

Colony and Protectorates

The Charter of the British South Africa Company expired in 1923, and Southern Rhodesia became a self-governing colony. Its economy grew rapidly enough. There was mining for gold, asbestos, chromium, iron and coal. The country had steel-works and factories making textiles, clothing, shoes and iron goods. However, agriculture was more important than industry, the most important crop being tobacco. It was Southern Rhodesia's tobacco exports that paid for the goods she needed from abroad. Of these, oil became more and more important as time went on.

Even though she was prospering, Southern Rhodesia had race problems. A great many immigrants came from Britain so that by 1951 the white population was 138 000. There were two million Africans, but the whites were an important group. They ruled the country and they discriminated against the Africans in many ways.

One of the main problems was land. A Land Apportionment Act set aside areas for whites and areas for blacks. A white man could not own land in a black area and a black man could not own land in a white area. That might seem fair, but the white settlers, who were less than one-tenth of the population, had half the land, and that was the best there was. The natives had only a quarter of the country and the remainder either belonged to the Crown, or was barren waste. The Land Apportionment Act was not meant to be fair to both races, but was intended to separate them, by preventing blacks from coming into white areas, except as labourers.

In industry, only whites could train for skilled jobs. In 1958 the average wage for whites was £1000 a year and for blacks £80.

Partly because of labour problems, all blacks had to carry passes, which prevented them moving quickly from one job to another. Needless to say, they resented this.

There were plenty of other things that humiliated the blacks. In the towns the better restaurants and hotels were for whites only. All white children had an education whereas most black children did not. If a black committed a crime he would be more severely punished than a white who was guilty of the same offence. Very few blacks had the right to vote. The law said nothing about colour, but all electors had to be able to read and write, and to have a certain income. Since most blacks were poor and illiterate they did not qualify. In 1951 there were 53 000 electors, but only 450 were Africans.

In 1924, Northern Rhodesia became a British Protectorate. It had not made much progress under the British South Africa Company, but in the late 1920s copper-mining began in the north of the country. Exports were worth £3 million in 1933 and £89 million in 1957. The copper belt is still Zambia's main source of wealth.

Since Northern Rhodesia was ruled from Britain the Africans were much less at the mercy of the whites than those in Southern Rhodesia. Also, because there was little good land there were hardly any white settlers. However there were problems on the copper belt. In 1951 the average wage for a black was £60 a year, whereas a skilled white could earn £1400 or more.

During this period Nyasaland remained a British Protectorate, which it had been since 1891. There is little good farmland and no minerals in any quantity, so there were few white settlers and the country remained backward. However, there was a large native population, rather more than in either of the two Rhodesias. To make a little money men would go for a time to the farms and factories of Southern Rhodesia, or to the copper belt in Northern Rhodesia. When they came home they brought stories of how badly Africans were treated in these two countries.

Federation 1953–63

In 1953 the two Rhodesias and Nyasaland formed a federation. Each kept its own government for local affairs, but there was a federal government as well which looked after such things as finance, industry and trade. There were three main reasons for the change.

In the first place the whites in Northern Rhodesia felt they would be safer if they joined hands with the much larger number of whites in Southern Rhodesia. The white leader in Northern Rhodesia was Roy Welensky, a forceful man who, in his younger days, had been an engine-driver and a heavyweight boxing champion. Godfrey Huggins, the Prime Minister of Southern Rhodesia, also wanted federation.

Secondly, there were good economic reasons. Southern Rhodesia had her agriculture and Northern Rhodesia her copper-mines, while Nyasa-land sent workers to both. Obviously the three countries would be more likely to prosper if they joined together.

Thirdly, there was British imperialism. After the war the Empire crumbled. For example India became independent and the Boers won control of South Africa. The white settlers of Central Southern Africa, though, were still loyal and it was possible that if they were given the chance they would form a new dominion which would remain true to Britain, like Canada, Australia and New Zealand.

From the start, the blacks were against federation. They knew it would give the whites of Southern Rhodesia control over the blacks in all three countries. Welensky was foolish enough to describe the federation as a 'rider and a horse'. The Africans had no doubt who would be the horse.

In spite of black opposition, the Federation of Rhodesia and Nyasaland was formed in 1953. Godfrey Huggins became its first Prime Minister. Roy Welensky was knighted for his work in helping to create the federation and later he succeeded Huggins as its Prime Minister.

As was expected, federation brought a lot of benefits. There were new roads and railways, but what was most impressive was the Kariba Dam, across the Zambesi River. It holds back the largest man-made lake in the world, being 280 kilometres long. Generators at the dam made electricity for Rhodesia's industries, and for the copper belt.

However, black opposition destroyed the federation. National feeling grew rapidly, and African National Congress Parties were organized in all three countries. Their leaders were Kenneth Kaunda in Northern Rhodesia, Joshua Nkomo in Southern Rhodesia, and Dr Hastings Banda in Nyasa-land. From the late 1950s there were riots, and the British government appointed a Royal Commission under Lord Monckton to look at the problem. It reported that there was no hope of peace unless the Africans had more say in the running of these countries, and that their hatred of the federation was deep. Accordingly, Britain decided to end the federation. In 1964 Nyasaland became independent, and took the name of Malawi. Northern Rhodesia also became independent and was known as Zambia. In both these countries there were elections with every man, black or white, having a vote. Banda became President of Malawi, and Kaunda, President of Zambia.

However, in Southern Rhodesia, the whites were strong enough to reject the idea of 'one man one vote'. They did so because it would have meant a black government. The British saw it as their duty to look after the Africans so they said that Southern Rhodesia could not have her freedom until steps had been taken towards black majority rule. The term some people used was NIBMAR, or No Independence Before Majority Rule. The white Rhodesians would have none of this, and they decided to rebel. On 11 November 1965 their Prime Minister, Ian Smith, made a Unilateral Declaration of Independence — U.D.I.

The Smith Regime

Since many people thought Mr Smith acted against the law they did not talk about his government, but his regime. The regime had two main problems, sanctions and guerrilla warfare.

Since U.D.I. was rebellion, the British might have tried to put it down by force. However they decided instead to use economic sanctions which meant they refused to trade with Rhodesia. They won support from the United Nations, which also imposed sanctions, making them more and more severe until in 1963 it forbade any of its members to carry on any trade at all with Rhodesia. That should have brought the country to its knees at once. She made her living by exporting tobacco, and had to import oil if she was to survive. However, the farmers switched to other crops and managed to sell any tobacco they did grow, in secret. As for oil, most of that came through South Africa.

Guerrillas were a more serious problem. They all belonged to the Patriotic Front, but this was made up of two groups. One, headed by Joshua Nkomo of the Matabele tribe, operated from Zambia: the other, headed by Robert Mugabe, and recruiting most of its members from the Mashona, operated from Mozambique. They quarrelled with each other, but hatred of Smith held them together on the whole. They attacked farms, exploded bombs in Salisbury, shot down aircraft with Russian missiles and kidnapped schoolchildren. One of their worst atrocities was the cold-blooded murder of seven Roman Catholic missionaries at Musami in 1977.

The government had security forces to fight the guerrillas. Most of the men were Africans, though they had white officers. One of the best units was the Selous Scouts, who were experts at tracking. They were named after the hunter who led the first pioneers to Rhodesia. From time to time the army raided Zambia and Mozambique to destroy guerrilla camps.

The war was a disaster for Rhodesia. By 1979, 18 000 people had died, half of them Africans. Farming in the Tribal Trust lands nearly collapsed. For example, the guerrillas stopped cattle dipping, which the government had once made compulsory, and, as a result, close on a million beasts died from diseases carried by ticks. The health of humans suffered too. Many country clinics and hospitals closed, and the guerrillas disrupted tse-tse fly control schemes, so sleeping sickness became common.

From time to time there were negotiations. Ian Smith met the British Prime Minister, Harold Wilson, on H.M.S *Tiger* in 1966 and on H.M.S. *Fearless* in 1968. Wilson kept to the NIBMAR policy, so the talks made no progress. Then in 1977 the Americans intervened, because the Patriotic Front was looking to the Russians for help. The United States Ambassador to the United Nations, Andrew Young, and the British Foreign Secretary, Dr David Owen, toured the African States most concerned. In the same

Terrorist attack on a Red Cross team, Rhodesia 1978

year the United States Secretary of State, Cyrus Vance, met James Callaghan and David Owen in London, and between them they drew up a peace plan.

Ian Smith rejected the plan, because it would have left the Rhodesian whites at the mercy of the Patriotic Front guerrillas. However, he was moved to start negotiations with the African moderates. In 1978 he agreed to a new constitution and to elections on the basis of 'one man one vote', which was bound to mean black majority rule. Bishop Abel Muzorewa became Prime Minister and Ian Smith had a post in his government. The country took the name of Zimbabwe Rhodesia.

That, however, was not the end of the troubles. The war went on because the Patriotic Front had not played any part in the negotiations and boycotted the elections. It could also point to things in the new constitution which still discriminated against blacks. For example, there were a number of seats in Parliament reserved for whites, and the white members could veto any law, even though they were in a minority. Also, whites still controlled the armed forces and the police.

Britain, for her part, did not recognize the Muzorewa government so sanctions were not lifted. Most African States supported the Patriotic Front, and Britain dared not offend them, because she had made important investments in them. The Nigerian government gave a warning of what could happen when it nationalized everything in its country owned by British Petroleum.

Then, in 1979, Mrs Thatcher called a constitutional conference in London. Ian Smith, Abel Muzorewa, Joshua Nkomo and Robert Mugabe attended. After weeks of hard bargaining and after the Foreign Secretary, Lord Carrington, had lost his temper with the Patriotic Front leaders several times, a new constitution was agreed. The guerrillas were to come out of the bush, and there were to be fresh elections in which everyone would take part. A Commonwealth force, mainly of British soldiers, was to supervise. In the meantime, Bishop Muzorewa stepped down and Lord Soames became governor. For a brief period, Rhodesia was once again a British colony.

Probably the most important negotiations did not take place in London. It seems likely that the 'front line' African States, that is the ones that border on Zimbabwe, were tired of the war and told the Patriotic Front leaders that they must accept a fair settlement.

Zimbabwe since Independence

The new elections were held in February 1980, the three main rivals being Bishop Muzorewas's United African National Council, Joshua Nkomo's Zimbabwe African People's Union, and Robert Mugabe's Zimbabwe African National Union. ZAPU represented the Matabele tribe and ZANU, the Mashona. Rhodesia's 200 000 whites and many Western countries waited nervously for the result. The man they dreaded was Mugabe who was not only a former guerrilla leader, but a Marxist. The fear was that if he came to power he would invite in the Russians, that those whites who were not massacred would flee, and that the economy of the country would be ruined.

Mugabe's ZANU party did win the election, with a handsome majority and, on 18 April 1980 Zimbabwe became independent. Prince Charles represented the Queen at a ceremony in which Britain handed over her last colony in Africa.

Mugabe, though, had no intention of ruining his country and handing it to the Russians. He urged all the tribes and races 'to forgive each other and forget and to join hands in a new amity'. He invited his chief African rival, Joshua Nkomo, to join his government as Home Minister. To the whites, Mugabe made it plain that he wanted them to stay, for Zimbabwe needed their skills. At the time of writing, early 1982, they were leaving at the rate of between one and two thousand a month, but that is nothing like the mad rush which was expected. Salisbury's white business men still have their handsome bungalows in the suburbs, and white farmers have kept their land—even Ian Smith is farming at Selukwe, as well as drawing his Prime Minister's pension. Today, Zimbabwe is one of the most prosperous countries in Africa.

WORK SECTION — The End of the Colonial Empires — Case Studies

Caste in India

Document One

British Rule in India — A British View:
In writing this Report we have made no allusion to the events of the last few months in India. We have not altered a line of our Report on that account, for it is necessary to look beyond particular incidents and to take a longer view.

No one of either race ought to be so foolish as to deny the greatness of the contribution which Britain had made to Indian progress. It is not racial prejudice, nor imperialistic ambition, nor commercial interest which makes us say so plainly. It is a tremendous achievement to have brought to the Indian sub-continent and to have applied in practice the conceptions of impartial justice of the rule of law, of respect for equal civic rights without reference to class or creed, and of a disinterested and incorruptible civil service. In his heart, even the bitterest critic of British India knows that India has owed these things mainly to Britain.

(*The Simon Report 1930*)

Document Two

The Caste System in 1926:
Regarded as if sub-human, the tasks held basest are reserved for them: dishonour is associated with their name. Some are permitted to serve only as scavengers and removers of night soil. They may neither possess nor read the Hindu scriptures and, except in rarest instances, they may not enter a Hindu temple to worship or pray. Their children may not go to school. They may not draw water from the public wells. They may not enter a court of justice: they may not enter a dispensary to get help for their sick: they may stop at no inn. In some provinces they may not even use the public roads. Some, if not all, pollute beyond caste men's use, any food upon which their shadow falls. Food, after such defilement, can only be destroyed.

(*Mother India* — Katherine Mayo)

Document Three

The Caste System in 1980:
India's Harijan untouchables were taught a grim lesson last week when upper caste Hindus laid siege to Bihar village. They reduced to cinders all 30 huts in the Chamar (the lowest born Harijan community of leather workers) enclave. The inmates were gunned down as they fled. Among the victims were four women, three boys (including a two-year old) and two teenage girls.

New Delhi's smug claim that the number of complaints lodged under the 1976 Protection of Civil Rights Act (which punished Harijan-baiting with imprisonment) fell from 5108 to 3425 between 1976 and 1977 proves nothing. No one is ever jailed for violating the Act. Few sufferers dare to voice complaints. Even when they do, prosecution usually peters out. At least twenty per cent of the cases registered in Madras collapse because witnesses are frightened or bribed into silence.

(*Observer* 2 March 1980)

Questions

Document One

1 Why was the Simon Commission appointed?
2 Why was it unpopular in India?
3 How did the Indians show their discontent?
4 What conference was held in London to settle the disagreement? What famous Indian leader attended it? Why did it fail?
5 What Act of Parliament followed the publication of the Simon Report? What did it say?
6 What do you suppose the 'events of the last few months' were? (First line of Document)
7 What benefits does the Report say British rule has brought to India? Would the authors of Documents Two and Three agree?

Document Two

8 What are the four Hindu castes?
9 What work may members of the lowest caste do?
10 What things may they not do?
11 What harm may their shadows do?

Document Three

12 Which people were responsible for the attack on the village?
13 Which people were the victims?

14 What Act was passed in 1976?
15 Why has it been ineffective?
16 Document Two was written in 1926 and Document Three in 1980. How much change would there seem to have been in the attitude of the Hindus to the caste system in those 54 years?

The Kariba Dam

Questions

1 On what river is this dam?
2 How large is the lake behind it?
3 What use is made of the electricity generated here?
4 What government was responsible for building the dam?
5 When was this government set up? Why?
6 When was it ended? Why?

Black Majority Rule in Zimbabwe (Southern Rhodesia)

This is a newspaper account of the agreement Mr Ian Smith made with certain African leaders in March 1978:

Rhodesia's multi-racial transitional government, established by yesterday's epoch-making agreement between Mr Ian Smith and three Black leaders is expected to be functioning within a month. Mr Smith, Bishop Muzorewa, the Rev. Ndabaningi Sithole and Chief Chirau will form the executive council, the supreme decision-making body which is charged with leading Rhodesia to independence under Black rule on 31 December.

Rhodesians, Black and White, reacted with a mixture of caution and scepticism to the signing of an agreement which will terminate White rule in Rhodesia by the end of the year. 'We have had agreements before, but what we need is a settlement,' a White business-man commented, summing up the general weariness

after nearly two decades of constitutional wrangling. Most White Rhodesians appear to accept that Mr Ian Smith had reached the best possible agreement under enormous pressures. Business and mining leaders welcomed the agreement, but had reservations about a full settlement and international recognition.

Black Rhodesians in general welcomed the pact, especially the commitment to 31 December as a firm date for independence under Black rule, which appeared to have removed some of the Africans' deep and widespread distrust of Mr Smith. Supporters of the three Black movements whose leaders reached the accord with Mr Smith were jubilant and confident that it would produce an accepted settlement. But the uncommitted man-in-the-street in Highfields, Salisbury's largest Black township was more cautious, expressing fears about the danger of civil war unless the 'boys in the bush' — the guerrillas — were included in the deal. Mr Josiah Chinamano, acting president of the African National Council, Mr Joshua Nkomo's internal organization, called the agreement 'a prescription for further bloodshed in our country'.

'The war cannot be ended by talking to those who are not involved in it,' Mr Chinamano said, 'Settlement is not possible when Mr Smith talks only to his friends. No peace is possible without involving in the talks the fighters and their leaders, the Patriotic Front.'

(*Daily Telegraph* 4 March 1978)

Questions

1 What provoked Mr Smith into agreeing to black majority rule?
2 With which Africans was he willing to make an agreement?
3 What did the agreement say?
4 The newspaper talks about 'leading Rhodesia to independence'. From whom was the country to be independent?
5 The newspaper also talks about 'nearly two decades of constitutional wrangling'. Who had been wrangling, and what were they discussing?
6 How do the following feel about the agreement:
   (a) White Rhodesians.
   (b) Black supporters of the three leaders who signed the agreement.
   (c) The ordinary blacks.
   (d) The leaders of the Patriotic Front.
7 Which was proved right?

India in 1900

Questions

1 Why was India the most important part of the British Empire?

2 How many Hindu castes are there? Which was the lowest? How did its members suffer?

3 What unfortunate marriage customs did the Hindus have?

4 What problems are caused by the sacred cows?

5 How had an educated Hindu middle-class been created? What party did it form? What was its aim?

6 When did the Muslims come to India? Why did they win many converts? What proportion of the population were they?

7 What were the two Muslim social groups?

8 What political party did the Muslims found? What was its policy? Why?

9 What was the highest tier of the government of India?

10 Who chose the Governor-General? Name two councils which assisted him? How were they chosen?

11 How many provinces were there in British India? How were they governed?

12 What was the work of the central government and the provincial governments?

13 What changes were made by the Morley-Minto Reforms?

14 Who staffed the Indian Civil Service? What were its standards?

15 Describe the Indian army.

16 How many States were there? Who ruled them? How much of India did they cover? Which of their affairs did Britain look after?

17 How did the population of India grow? What was the reason?

18 Name five ways in which the economy of India grew under British rule.

19 Why did the harvest sometimes fail? What happened as a result? Name two things the British did to help.

20 When and why did the British give up serious attempts at social reform? What was the one social change they encouraged? What was its result?

Give an account of India in 1900 under the headings: Religion and Society/British Rule in India — Government, the Economy, Social Reform

The Struggle for Independence

Questions

1 What differences were there between the moderate and extremist nationalists?

2 When was Gandhi born? Where did he first practise law? Why did he encourage his fellow Indians in Satyagraha? What did this mean?

3 What people did Gandhi work for when he returned to India? What was his cure for poverty? How did he set an example?

4 What political position did Gandhi accept? What was his condition for so doing?

5 What methods did Gandhi use? What title did he take?

6 Name two other leaders with whom Gandhi worked.

7 What was the first step India took towards independence? What did India contribute to the First World War? What were her people promised as a result? What report was issued?

8 Why did the Muslims and the Congress Party turn against the British? What agreement did they make? How did the British react?

9 Describe two Acts of Parliament passed after the war.

10 Describe Gandhi's campaign of civil disobedience. What was especially significant about it?

11 Where was there a massacre? When? What happened as a result?

12 Give three reasons why the attempt to win self-government failed.

13 Why was the Simon Commission appointed? When? Why did the Congress leaders object? What action was taken by the two Nehrus and by Gandhi?

14 Who suggested the Round Table Conference? What did it discuss? Why did it fail?

15 When did Parliament pass the Government of India Act? Why? What did the Act say?

16 Why did the Muslims want a separate State? How was the name 'Pakistan' coined? What position did Jinnah take?

17 When was the final break between the Hindus and the Muslims? Why did it happen?

18 What resolution did the Muslim League pass in 1940? How did Jinnah rouse the Muslim masses?

19 How had ordinary Hindus and Muslims behaved towards each other in the past? How did they behave after 1940?

20 How did India contribute to the Second World War?

21 What did Congress demand in return for its co-operation? What was the 'Cripps offer'? Why did Congress refuse it? What action did Gandhi take?

22 What two quarrels were taking place when the war ended? Who was Viceroy? How did he try to solve them? When he failed, what did Jinnah do?

23 What ultimatum did the British give? Who became Viceroy? What agreement did he persuade the League and Congress to accept?

24 Where were there large exchanges of population? Why? What happened to many of the refugees?

25 When did India and Pakistan become independent?

Give an account of the Struggle for Independence under the headings: The Hindu nationalists and Mahatma Gandhi/Agitation and Reform 1909–1939/Jinnah and Pakistan/The Second World War/Independence

Central Southern Africa

Questions

1 Which modern States make up Central Southern Africa? Why was there a lot of fighting there in the nineteenth century?

2 Why was Cecil Rhodes anxious to control Central Southern Africa?

3 Explain how Rhodesia was founded.

4 What tribes did the settlers defeat?

5 Name two other colonies which were founded in the 1890s. Which of the three colonies attracted most white settlers? Why?

6 What happened to Southern Rhodesia in 1923? How did her economy develop?

7 What was the white population of Southern Rhodesia by 1951? How many blacks were there?

8 What did the Land Apportionment Act say?

9 What advantages did the whites have in industry?

10 Why did the blacks have to have passes?

11 Name four other ways in which the blacks were humiliated.

12 What happened to Northern Rhodesia in 1924? How did its economy develop?

13 Why were there fewer race problems in Northern Rhodesia? Where did they exist?

14 Why were there few white settlers in Nyasaland? How did its people learn to dislike the whites?

15 When was the Federation of Rhodesia and Nyasaland formed?

16 Give three reasons why it was formed.

17 Why did the blacks dislike federation?

18 Name two Prime Ministers of the federation.

19 What benefits did federation bring?

20 What political parties did the blacks organize? Who were their leaders?

21 When and why did Britain end the federation? What happened to Nyasaland and Northern Rhodesia?

22 Why did Britain refuse Southern Rhodesia her independence? How did the white Rhodesians react?

23 What action did Britain and the United Nations take against Southern Rhodesia? Why was it ineffective?

24 What guerrilla groups were there? How did the Rhodesian government try to deal with them?

25 How did the war affect Rhodesia?

26 Which Prime Minister had talks with Ian Smith? Where? Why did they fail?

27 Why did the Americans intervene? Who drew up a peace plan?

28 Why did Ian Smith reject the peace plan? What action did he take?

29 What happened as a result?

30 Why did the war continue?

31 Why did Britain refuse to recognize the new government?

32 What conference was held in London in 1979? Who attended it? What agreement was reached?

33 Which party won the elections of 1980? Who was its leader?

34 What had been feared would happen if he came to power? What, in fact, were his policies?

Give an account of Central Southern Africa under the headings: Cecil Rhodes and the British South Africa Company Colony and Protectorates/Federation 1953–1963/The Smith Regime/Zimbabwe since Independence

397

Problems

India

1 How has religion influenced Indian society and politics?

2 By what means did the British control India in the early twentieth century?

3 What benefits did British rule bring India?

4 What problems did the British encounter in India and what attempts did they make to solve them?

5 What was the importance to India of the career of Mahatma Gandhi?

6 By what steps did the British grant independence to India and Pakistan? Why did Britain remain unpopular in India?

7 Why did Pakistan become a separate State from India?

8 Why did the granting of independence to India and Pakistan cause so much bloodshed?

Central Southern Africa

9 What benefits did British rule bring to Central Southern Africa?

10 Why was there conflict between blacks and whites in Central Southern Africa?

11 Why was the Federation of Rhodesia and Nyasaland created in 1953? What benefits did it bring? Why was it a failure?

12 Why did Ian Smith make a Unilateral Declaration of Independence in 1969?

13 What problems did Rhodesia face after U.D.I.? What attempts were made to solve them?

14 Why did Ian Smith agree to black majority rule in 1978? Why did agreement fail to end the troubles in Rhodesia?

15 By what stages did Zimbabwe (Southern Rhodesia) secure her independence?

INDEX